Chr

New ENGLISH FILE

Intermediate Teacher's Book

Paul Seligson and Clive Oxenden are the original co-authors of *English File 1* (pub. 1996) and *English File 2* (pub. 1997).

OXFORD
UNIVERSITY PRESS

OXFORD
UNIVERSITY PRESS

Great Clarendon Street, Oxford OX2 6DP

Oxford University Press is a department of the University of Oxford. It furthers the University's objective of excellence in research, scholarship, and education by publishing worldwide in

Oxford New York

Auckland Cape Town Dar es Salaam Hong Kong Karachi Kuala Lumpur Madrid Melbourne Mexico City Nairobi New Delhi Shanghai Taipei Toronto

With offices in

Argentina Austria Brazil Chile Czech Republic France Greece Guatemala Hungary Italy Japan Poland Portugal Singapore South Korea Switzerland Thailand Turkey Ukraine Vietnam

OXFORD and OXFORD ENGLISH are registered trade marks of Oxford University Press in the UK and in certain other countries

First published 2006
2010 2009 2008 2007 2006
10 9 8 7 6 5 4 3 2 1

ISBN-13: 978 0 19 451803 1
ISBN-10: 0 19 451803 5

Printed and bound by Grafiasa S. A. in Portugal

ACKNOWLEDGEMENTS

The authors would like to thank all the teachers and students round the world whose feedback has helped us to shape *New English File*.

Special thanks to Beatriz Martin for her help with the Communicative photocopiable activities.

Finally, very special thanks from Clive to Maria Angeles, Lucia, and Eric, and from Christina to Cristina, for all their help and encouragement. Christina would also like to thank her children Joaquin, Marco, and Krysia for their constant inspiration.

The Publisher and Authors would like to thank the following for their invaluable feedback on the materials: p.207 *We Are Family* words and music by Nile Rodgers and Bernard Edwards © 1979 Bernard's Other Music and Sony Songs Inc. All rights on behalf of Bernard's Other Music administered by Warner /Chappell Music Ltd. Reproduced by permission, p.208 *You Can Get It If You Really Want* words and music by Jimmy Cliff © 1970 Island Music Limited, Universal/ Island Music Limited. Used by permission of Music Sales Limited. All Rights Reserved. International Copyright Secured, p.209 *Our House* words and music by Cathal Smyth and Christopher Foreman © 1982 EMI Music Publishing Ltd. Reproduced by permission of International Music Publications Ltd. All Rights Reserved, p.210 *Sk8er Boi* words and music by Lauren Christy, Scott Spock, Graham Edwards and Avril Lavigne © 2002 Warner/Chappell Music, Mr Spock Music, Holly Lodge Music, WB Music Corp, Rainbow Fish Publishing and Almo Music Corporation, p.211 *Holding Out For A Hero* from the Paramount Motion Picture 'Footloose' words by Dean Pitchford, music by Jim Steinman. © 1984 by Ensign Music Corporation. International Copyright Secured. All Rights Reserved, p.212 *Ironic* words and music by Alanis Morissette & Glen Ballard © 1995 Music Corporation Of America Incorporated/Vanhurst. PlaceMusic/MCA Music Publishing/Aerostation Corporation, USA. Universal/MCA Music Limited. Used by permission of Music Sales Limited. All Rights Reserved. International Copyright Secured.

The publisher would like to thank the following for their kind permission to reproduce photographs and other copyright material: Allstar pp.158 (Warner Brothers/The Color Purple, United Artists/Some Like it Hot); Alamy pp.159 (Direct Photo/ Eiffel Tower); Corbis Images pp.156 (Benelux/men), 174 (Bettmann/Rosie Ruiz), 208 (Janni Chavakiszefa/weight lifter, Gary Salterzefa/ballet dancer); Empics p.174 (PA Photos/DPA/Ben Johnson); Getty Images pp.141 (Larry Dale Gordon), 153 (Ian Sanderson/young couple), 155, 156 Martin Riedl/women), 157 (Zia Soleil), 159 (Time Life Pictures/Kenneth Branagh), 224 (Hulton Archive); The Kobal Collection pp.158 (20th Century Fox/Cleopatra, Gandhi/ Columbia/Goldcrest, Jan Chapman Productions/CIBY 2000/ The Piano; NHPA p.159 (Yves Lanceau/cat), Cheetah; Oxford University Press pp.153 (Medio Images/middleaged couple) 176 (Image Source/skeleton); Rex Features pp.176 snail

Illustrations by: Phil Disley pp.143, 147, 152, 154, 187; Martina Farrow pp.207, 210; Gavin Reece p.180; Colin Shelbourn pp.140, 145, 148, 161, 177, 178, 183, 186, 193; Duncan Storr p.226; Kath Walker pp.141, 144, 146, 149, 150, 160, 162, 179, 181; Annabel Wright p.212

Picture research by: Cathy Blackie

Contents

Syllabus checklist

Pronunciation	Speaking	Listening	Reading
/ʊ/ and /uː/, understanding phonetics	talking about eating habits	an interview with an English chef	Food: fuel or pleasure?
/ɔː/ and /ɜː/	telling an anecdote talking about sport	an interview with a football referee	When you hear the final whistle
word stress, adjective prefixes and suffixes	families	psychologist talking about position in family Song: *We are family*	We are family
saying numbers	money questionnaire	song: Ka-*ching* understanding a news bulletin	My life without money
sentence stress, strong adjectives	How long…?	an interview with Karen	It was just a holiday but it changed my life
stress in compound nouns	talking about road safety	a journey from London to the south of France; road safety	Race to the sun
sentence stress	talking about mobile phones talking about manners	an interview about politeness and the English	Culture shock
-eigh, -aigh, -igh	matching people with their jobs	radio interview	Do I really look like this?
sentence stress	talking about abilities	psychologist talking about learning new skills; song: *You can get it if you really want*	Never give up
/ʌ/ or /juː/?	talking about education	radio interview about a TV programme	So school today is easy? Think again
sentence stress	describing your dream house	people's dream houses song: *Our house*	Houses you'll never forget
/s/ or /z/?	talking about a close friend and friendship; things you used to do, have, etc.	interview about *Friends Reunited* people talking about friendship	Do you need to 'edit your friends'?

Pronunciation	Speaking	Listening	Reading
-ough and *-augh*	planning a new city	an expert talks about how to slow down in life	Slow food and slow cities
sentence stress, *the*, /θ/ and /ð/	topics men and women talk about men v women	two journalists talk about a spa song: *Sk8er Boi*	A gossip with the girls?
word stress	talking about work imagining doing other jobs	an interview with Jessica, the librarian	From librarian to political reporter … in a month!
consonant sounds: /g/, /dʒ/, /k/, /ʃ/, /tʃ/	shopping questionnaire talking about complaining	understanding a radio programme	Making a complaint – is it worth it?
sentence stress	cinema questionnaire	an interview about working with Steven Spielberg	Famous films that moved us (literally!)
word stress	talking about a person you admire	a radio competition about heroes and icons; song: *Holding out for a hero*	Heroes and icons of our time
sentence stress	How lucky are you?	the conclusions of stories about bad luck and good luck song: *Ironic*	Bad luck? Good luck? Can we make our own luck?
intonation in question tags	a police interview roleplay	interview with a detective	Jack the Ripper – case closed?
revision of sounds, linking	talking about TV habits	four people talk about objects they couldn't live without	Couple switch on after 37 years without power

What do Intermediate students need?

The intermediate level is often a milestone for students: at this point, many students really begin to 'take off' in terms of their ability to communicate. Some students, however, may see the intermediate level as a 'plateau' and feel that they are no longer making the progress they were before. Students at this level need fresh challenges to help them to realize how much they know and to make their passive knowledge active, together with a steady input of new language.

Grammar, Vocabulary, and Pronunciation

At any level, the basic tools students need to speak English with confidence are Grammar, Vocabulary, and Pronunciation (G, V, P). In *New English File Intermediate* all three elements are given equal importance.

Each lesson has clearly stated grammar, vocabulary, and pronunciation aims. This keeps lessons focused and gives students concrete learning objectives and a sense of progress.

Grammar

Intermediate students need

- to revise and extend their knowledge of the main grammatical structures.
- to practise using different tenses together.
- student-friendly reference material.

At this level there is as much emphasis on consolidating and putting into practice known grammar as learning new structures. We have tried to revise known grammar in fresh and stimulating contexts and new structures are presented clearly and memorably. The **Grammar Banks** give students a single, easy-to-access grammar reference section, with clear rules and example sentences. There are then two practice exercises.

➲ Student's Book *p.130.*

The oral grammar practice exercise in the Student's Book encourage students to use grammatical structures in controlled and freer contexts.

The photocopiable Grammar activities in the Teacher's Book can be used for practice in class or for self-study.

➲ Teacher's Book *p.142.*

Vocabulary

Intermediate students need

- systematic expansion of topic-based lexical areas.
- to 'build' new words by adding prefixes and suffixes.
- practice in pronouncing new lexis correctly.
- to put new vocabulary into practice.

Every lesson in *New English File Intermediate* has a clear lexical aim. Many lessons are linked to the **Vocabulary Banks** which help present and practise high-frequency, topic-based vocabulary in class and provide a clear reference bank designed to aid memorization. The stress in multi-syllable words is clearly marked and phonemic script is provided where necessary.

➲ Student's Book *p.144.*

Students can practise using the vocabulary from all the **Vocabulary Banks** in context with the **MultiROM** and the *New English File* Student's website. There is also a photocopiable activity to revise the vocabulary from each File.

➲ Teacher's Book *p.197*

Pronunciation

Intermediate students need

- practice in pronouncing sounds and words clearly.
- to be aware of rules and patterns.
- to be able to use phonetic symbols in their dictionary.
- an awareness of word and sentence stress.

Clear *intelligible* pronunciation (not perfection) should be the goal of students at this level. Research shows that correct pronunciation of individual sounds and syllable stress plays a key role in effective oral communication. Pronunciation is given a great deal of importance in *New English File Intermediate* and every lesson has a pronunciation focus which often prepares students for a speaking activity.

➲ Student's Book *p.10.*

New English File has a unique system of sound pictures, which give clear example words to help students to identify and produce the sounds. If your students have not used *New English File* before, the Teacher's Book provides clear guidance on how to introduce the sound pictures system.

➲ Teacher's Book *p.14.*

The pronunciation focus is linked to the **Sound Bank**, a reference section where students can see and practise common sound–spelling patterns.

➲ Student's Book *p.157.*

Throughout the book there is also a regular focus on word and sentence stress where students are encouraged to **copy the rhythm** of English. This will help students to pronounce new language with greater confidence.

Speaking

Intermediate students need

- topics that will motivate them to speak.
- the key words and phrases necessary to discuss a topic.
- to feel their pronunciation is clear and intelligible.
- practice in more extended speaking.
- time to organize their thoughts before speaking.

The ultimate aim of most students is to be able to *speak* English. Every lesson in *New English File Intermediate* has a speaking activity where students get the chance to put into practice grammar, vocabulary, and pronunciation that has been worked on earlier in the lesson. Many of these activities have a planning stage and students are also encouraged to use some key phrases provided in **Useful language**.

➲ Student's Book *p.71.*

Photocopiable Communicative activities can be found in the Teacher's Book. These include pairwork activities, mingles, and speaking games.

➲ Teacher's Book *p.171.*

Listening

Intermediate students need

- interesting, integrated listening material.
- confidence-building, achievable tasks.
- practice in 'getting the gist' and listening for detail.
- practice in dealing with authentic spoken language.

Listening is still a problem for many students at intermediate level and *New English File Intermediate* addresses this with motivating and integrated listening texts and tasks which are challenging in terms of speed, length, and language difficulty, but which are always achievable. Longer listenings are broken into separate parts with different tasks, to avoid memory overload. The Teacher's Book often suggests alternative ways of dealing with a listening, such as pausing and listening in sections. Students are exposed to a wide variety of accents, including some non-native speakers of English.

➲ Student's Book *p.91.*

New English File Intermediate also contains seven songs which we hope students will find enjoyable and motivating. For copyright reasons, five of these are cover versions.

Reading

Intermediate students need

- engaging topics and stimulating texts.
- exposure to a wide variety of authentic text types.
- challenging tasks which help them read better.

Many students need to read in English for their work or studies or will want to read for pleasure about their interests. Reading is also vital in helping to extend students' vocabulary and to consolidate grammar. The key to encouraging students to read **outside** class is to give them motivating material and tasks **in** class which help them develop their reading skills. In *New English File Intermediate* reading texts have been adapted from a variety of real sources (newspapers, magazines, the Internet) and have been chosen for their intrinsic interest, which we hope will stimulate students to react and respond.

➲ Student's Book *p.73.*

The **Revise & Check** sections include a more challenging text which helps students to measure their progress.

➲ Student's Book *p.51.*

Writing

Intermediate students need

- clear models.
- an awareness of register, structure, and fixed phrases.
- a focus on 'micro' writing skills.

Worldwide, people are writing in English more than ever, largely because of the importance of email and the Internet. *New English File Intermediate* has one Writing lesson per File, where students study a model before doing a guided writing task themselves. These writing tasks focus on both electronic and 'traditional' text types, and provide consolidation of grammar and lexis taught in the File.

There is also always a focus on a writing 'micro skill', for example, punctuation, spelling, or connecting expressions.

➲ Student's Book *p.97.*

Practical English

Intermediate students need

- to consolidate and extend their knowledge of functional language.
- to know what to say in typical social situations.
- to get used to listening to faster, more colloquial speech.

Students will need to use English if they travel to an English-speaking country or if they are using English as a *lingua franca.* The seven *Practical English* lessons revise and extend common situations (for example, introducing yourself and others, or making polite requests) and go on to introduce and practise the language for new situations (for example, expressing opinions or apologizing). These lessons also highlight other useful 'Social English' phrases such as *It's a pity there isn't a…, I'm allergic to…*To help these everyday situations come alive there is a story line involving two main characters, Mark (American) and Allie (British) which continues from *New English File Pre-intermediate.* Don't worry if you or your students haven't used the previous level – there is a summary of the story so far in the first episode.

➲ Student's Book *p.16.*

The Practical English lessons are also on the *New English File Intermediate* ***Video*** which teachers can use instead of the class audio. Using the video will make the lessons more enjoyable and will help students to roleplay the situations.

Extracts from the video (the first dialogue from each lesson) are also on the MultiROM.

Revision

Intermediate students need

- regular revision.
- motivating reference and practice material.
- a sense of progress.

Intermediate students need to feel that they are increasing their knowledge and improving their skills. At the end of each File there is a Revise & Check section. **What do you remember**? revises the grammar, vocabulary and pronunciation of each File. **What can you do?** provides a series of skills-based challenges and helps students to measure their progress in terms of competence. These pages are designed to be used flexibly according to the needs of your students.

➲ Student's Book *p.18.*

The photocopiable Communicative, Grammar, and Vocabulary activities also provide many opportunities for recycling.

➲ Teacher's Book *pp.140, 171, 197.*

Study Link

The Study Link feature in *New English File Intermediate* is designed to help you and your students use the course more effectively. It shows **what** resources are available, **where** they can be found, and **when** to use them.

The Student's Book has these Study Link references:

- from the Practical English lessons ➲ MultiROM and website.
- from the Grammar Bank ➲ MultiROM and website.
- from the Vocabulary Bank ➲ MultiROM and website.
- from the Sound Bank ➲ MultiROM and website.

These references lead students to extra activities and exercises that link with what they have just studied.

The Workbook has these Study Link references:

➲ the Student's Book Grammar and Vocabulary Banks.

➲ the MultiROM.

➲ the student's website.

The Teacher's Book has Study Link references to remind you where there is extra material available to your students.

Student's Book organization

The Student's Book has seven Files. Each File is organized like this:

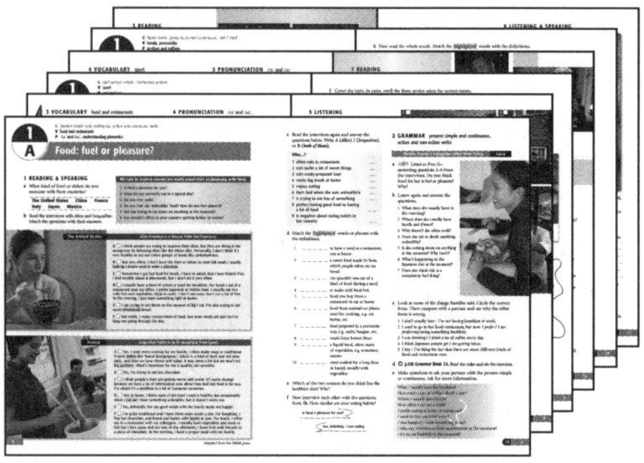

A, B, and C lessons Three four-page lessons which form the core material of the book. Each lesson presents and practises **Grammar** and **Vocabulary** and has a **Pronunciation** focus. There is a balance of reading and listening activities, and lots of opportunities for spoken practice. These lessons have clear references ➔ to the Grammar Bank, Vocabulary Bank, and Sound Bank at the back of the book.

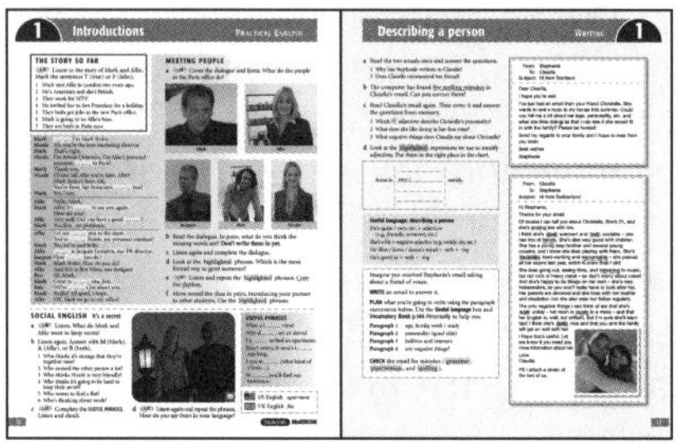

Practical English One-page lessons which teach functional language (making suggestions, apologizing) and also social English (useful phrases like *Just a minute, It's a pity*). The lessons link with the *New English File Intermediate Video*.

Writing One-page focuses on different text types and writing 'micro' skills like punctuation and spelling.

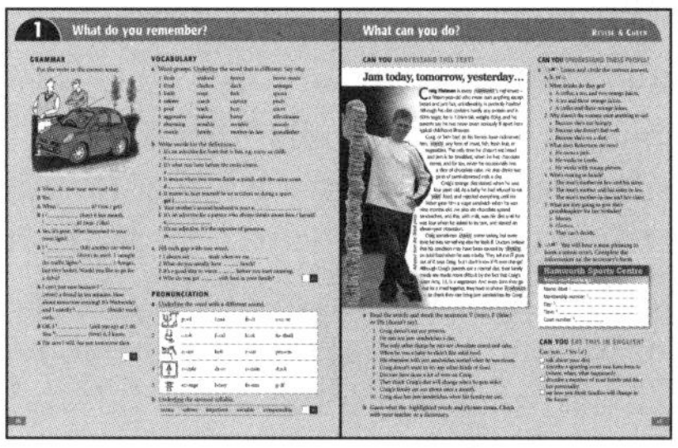

Revise & Check A two-page section – the left- and right-hand pages have different functions. The **What do you remember?** page revises the **Grammar**, **Vocabulary**, and **Pronunciation** of each File. The **What can you do?** page provides **Reading**, **Listening**, and **Speaking** 'Can you…?' challenges to show students what they can achieve.

The back of the book

In the back of the Student's Book you'll find these three Banks of material:

Grammar Bank (*pp.130–143*)
Two pages for each File, divided into A–C to reflect the three main lessons. The left-hand page has the grammar rules and the right-hand page has two practice exercises for each lesson. Students are referred ➔ to the Grammar Bank when they do the grammar in each main A, B, and C lesson.

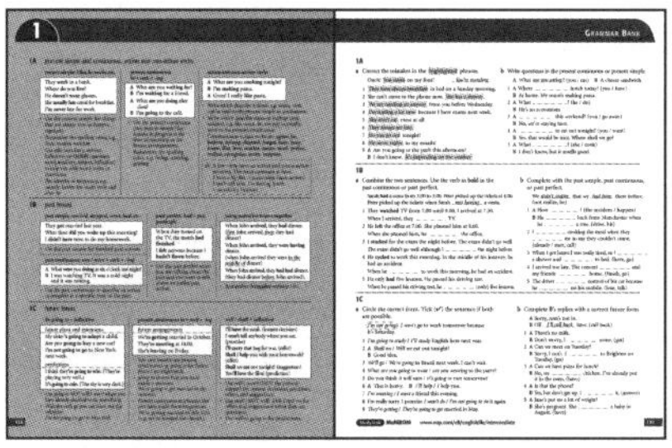

Vocabulary Bank (*pp.144–155*)
An active vocabulary resource to help students learn, practise, and revise key words. Students are referred ➔ to the Vocabulary Bank from the main lessons.

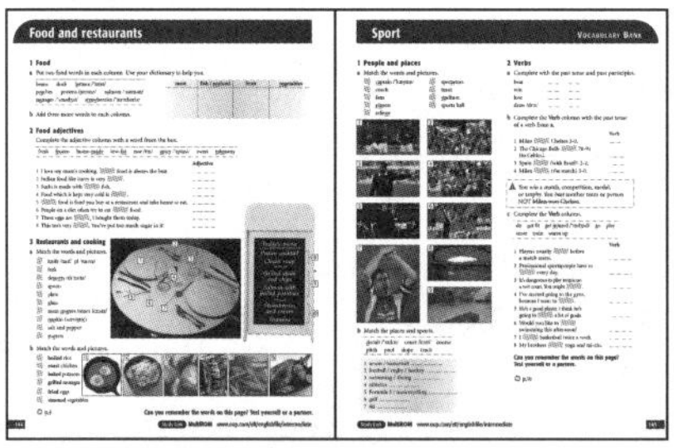

Sound Bank (*pp.157–159*) A three-page section with the *English File* sounds chart and typical spellings for all sounds. Students are referred ➔ to the Sound Bank from the main lessons.

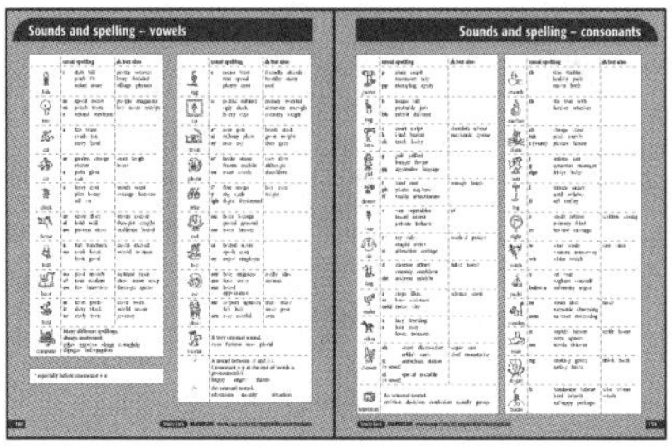

You'll also find:

- **Communication activities** (*pp.116–121*) Information gap activities and role plays.
- **Listening scripts** (*pp.122–129*) Scripts of key listenings.
- **Irregular verbs** (*pp.156*)

More for students

Workbook Each A–C lesson in the Student's Book has a three-page section in the Workbook. This provides all the practice and revision students need. Each section ends with:

- **More Words to Learn**, which reminds students of new vocabulary from the lesson which is not in the Vocabulary Bank.
- **Listening**, which gives students extra listening practice based on the theme of the lesson. The material is on the audio section of the MultiROM.

Each Practical English lesson has a one-page section in the Workbook, and includes 'Practical English reading'.

There is also a Key booklet.

MultiROM

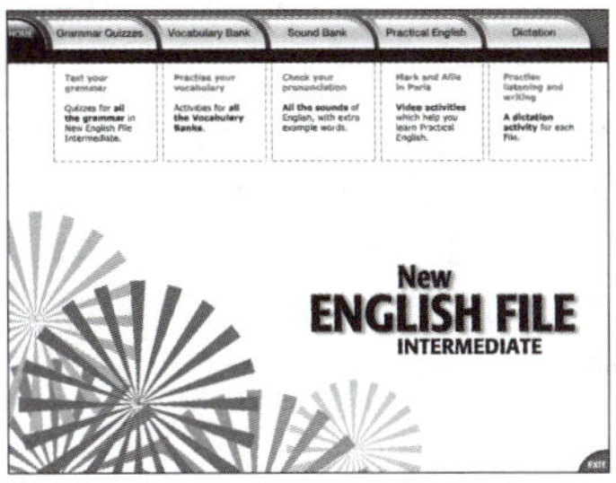

The MultiROM has two functions:

- It's a CD-ROM, containing revision of **Grammar**, **Vocabulary**, **Pronunciation**, **Practical English** (with extracts from the Video), and **Dictation** activities.
- It's an audio CD for students to use in a CD player. It has the audio material for the Workbook listening activities.

Student's website

www.oup.com/elt/englishfile/intermediate

Extra learning resources including

- grammar activities
- vocabulary puzzles
- pronunciation games
- Practical English activities
- learning records
- weblinks
- interactive games
- quicktests

More for teachers

Teacher's Book The Teacher's Book has detailed lesson plans for all the lessons. These include:

- an optional 'books-closed' lead-in for every lesson.
- **Extra idea** suggestions for optional extra activities.
- **Extra challenge** suggestions for ways of exploiting the Student's Book material in a more challenging way if you have a stronger class.
- **Extra support** suggestions for ways of adapting activities or exercises to make them more accessible for weaker students.

All lesson plans include keys and complete tapescripts. Extra activities are colour coded in green so you can see where you are at a glance when you're planning and teaching your classes.

You'll also find over 80 pages of photocopiable materials in the Teacher's Book:

Photocopiable Grammar activities *see pp.140–163*

There is a photocopiable Grammar activity for each A, B, and C lesson.

Photocopiable Communicative activities *see pp.171–194*

There is a photocopiable Communicative activity for each A, B, and C lesson.

Photocopiable Vocabulary activities *see pp.197–204*

There is a photocopiable Vocabulary activity for each File.

Photocopiable Song activities *see pp.207–212*

Photocopiable Quicktests and **End-of-course test** *see pp.216–224*

All the photocopiable material is accompanied by clear instructions and keys.

Video This is a unique 'teaching video' that links with the Practical English lessons in the Student's Book. The video has a story line which features Allie (British) and Mark (American). Each video section can be used with the tasks in the Student's Book Practical English lessons as an alternative to using the Class cassette / audio CD. It shows students language in clear contexts and will help them to role play each scene. Extracts of the video also appear on the MultiROM.

The *New English File Intermediate* package also includes:

- **Three class cassettes / audio CDs**
  These contain all the listening materials for the Student's Book.
- **Test booklet**
  This contains full-length tests for each File of *New English File Intermediate.*
- **Teacher's website**
  www.oup.com/elt/teacher/englishfile/intermediate
  This gives you extra teaching resources, including
  – a guide to *New English File* and the Common European Framework
  – wordlists
  – ideas for end-of-lesson coolers
  – mini web-projects
  – customizable cloze tests
  – student learning records
  – flash cards
- **Teacher Link emails**
  You can subscribe to this free email service at www.oup.com/elt/teacherlink. Every two weeks you'll receive lesson ideas. These will build up into a resource of ideas for every lesson and every level of New English File. You'll also receive updates and information about the course.

The Common European Framework of Reference

CEF mapping documents and Portfolios are available for download on the English File Teacher's site, www.oup.com/ elt/teacher/englishfile.

What is the CEF? What are its aims?

The CEF, developed by the Council of Europe, encourages us to learn languages and develop our ability to communicate with people from other countries and cultures. It consists of a carefully developed descriptive framework. It has educational and social aims – these are very often closely linked, and include the following:

- to encourage the development of language skills, so that we can work together more effectively.
- to encourage the development of inter-cultural awareness and 'plurilingualism'.
- to examine and define *what we can do* with a language.
- to help us compare the language levels of individuals in an accurate and impartial way, across different countries, education systems, ages, and cultures.
- to encourage learner autonomy and lifelong learning.
- to promote a coherent approach to language teaching – not by imposing a system, but by encouraging the sharing of ideas.

What are the CEF levels?

There are six global levels in the CEF. Behind these levels are a very large number of competences which make up a person's language ability – these are defined by 'descriptors'. The levels are intended to be common reference points. It's important to remember that they are *purely descriptive* – they don't necessarily correspond to a year of study, or to 100 hours of study. Everyone has different aims and learns at different speeds, in different environments, and in different ways. The CEF is careful to point out that the levels are not 'linear' – that is, the time needed to move from A1 to A2 may not be the same as that needed to move from B1 to B2 or C1 to C2, and progress from level to level slows down as we move up the levels.

A real strength of the CEF for students is that it focuses on the positive – on what students can do, not on what they can't do. All levels of performance from A1 upwards are valued, and students should feel positive about the growing list of things that they know they can do.

proficient	**C2**		This level doesn't equal 'native speaker' mastery – though a student at this level would be a very successful learner who can use a language with real precision and fluency.
	C1		At this level students command a wide range of language.
independent	**B2**		This level is where language use begins to become more 'abstract', for example giving opinions, summarizing a short story or plot, or giving detailed instructions.
	B1	***New English File Intermediate***	At this level students can maintain a conversation and express ideas. They can also begin to deal with problems and situations where they meet unpredictable language.
basic	**A2**		This level has lots of descriptors for social functions, for example greeting people, asking about work and free time, and making invitations.
	A1		This is the lowest level of 'generative language use' – students can interact in a simple way and ask and answer simple questions.

The CEF recognizes a level of ability below **A1**, which includes descriptors like *'can say yes, no, please, thank you'*, 'can use some basic greetings', 'can fill in uncomplicated forms'.	For a breakdown of the six global levels above, see chapter 3 of the CEF.
The CEF also recognizes that there can be levels between these six global levels, like **A1+**, **A2+**, **B1+** and **B2+**.	For detailed scales for each area of competence, see chapter 4 of the CEF.

What is a Portfolio?

The European Language Portfolio is a document for learners. It has three parts:

- the Passport
- the Biography
- the Dossier

The main aim of the Portfolio is to facilitate mobility in Europe by presenting an individual's language qualifications in a clear and comparable way. It allows all language and language-learning experiences (whether in the classroom or not) to be recorded, and it should be regularly updated. In a teaching situation where a coursebook is used over a year of study, we'd recommend updating the Portfolio several times a year, perhaps at the end of each term.

The Passport

This is a summary of language-learning experience, including time spent abroad; courses attended; books used; an assessment grid for each language skill area (graded from **A1–C2**); and any certificates or diplomas. It also outlines future plans for language learning.

The Passport shows at a glance the user's current level of language proficiency in different languages.

The Biography

This summarizes the learner's language-learning history, including languages they've grown up with, their language-learning experience at school and university, and how they use their languages now. It helps learners plan their learning by asking them to reflect on how and where they learn languages, and how they can develop autonomous learning.

The Biography also contains the CEF checklists for self-assessment.

The Dossier

This is a collection of pieces of personal work of different kinds which illustrate what the learner has achieved in different languages. This work could include written work from a course (for example from the Writing lessons of *New English File Intermediate*), self-assessment sheets, and audio and video recordings – anything that can 'prove' the learner's language history and level.

Is New English File CEF-compatible?

Yes, definitely. The CEF focuses on using language for a communicative purpose, and so does *New English File*. The CEF encourages the development of the ability to 'do things' in a foreign language, not just to 'know about' that language – though you also need to 'know about' a language in order to function successfully in that language. As the CEF says, '…a language learner has to acquire both form and meaning'. For example, a B1 descriptor might be 'I can ask for and follow detailed directions' – in order to do this, students need to know lexical items (*left, right, straight on, first, second, third*), grammatical elements like imperatives (*take the…, turn…*), fixed phrases (*You can't miss it*), and probably be able to ask for repetition and clarification. *New English File* teaches the language and skills that students will need in order to develop their range of communicative competences.

Here are some examples of how *New English File* fits with the aims of the CEF:

- The **Study Link** feature, which helps students see where they can find extra help and extra practice. The CEF states that learners need to take responsibility for planning and carrying out their own learning, and that they need to 'learn to learn' and to be made aware of the ways they can do this. One of the main obstacles to autonomous learning is that students don't know what to do, and **Study Link** helps to make it clear. There are regular **Study Link** references to the Grammar Bank, the Vocabulary Bank, the MultiROM, and the student's website.
- A **Grammar**, **Vocabulary**, and **Pronunciation** syllabus that gives students the linguistic competences they need to be able to communicate successfully.
- Regular **receptive and productive work** in the four skills – every lesson has speaking activities, and every File has listening, reading, and writing – the emphasis is on what students *do* with English.
- Clear **lesson aims** for each lesson, so learners know what the lesson objectives are.
- The **Practical English** lessons, which are based on situations in which learners may find themselves – these all focus on language use for real, concrete purposes, and they help to develop both the receptive and productive competences of learners.
- The **'What can you do?'** pages at the end of every File, which ask students to see what they can achieve with the language they've studied.
- The ***English File* pronunciation pictures** – these help students to work on pronunciation autonomously, and to use dictionaries more effectively.
- A **Workbook**, **MultiROM**, and **student's website** which all give students extra practice and learning resources.
- A **Teacher's Book** which gives you all the support you need, including extra photocopiable material and ideas so you can respond to your students' needs.

Remember – you can find full CEF mapping and Portfolio documents at www.oup.com/elt/teacher/englishfile.

1 A

G present simple and continuous; action and non-action verbs
V food and restaurants
P /ʊ/ and /uː/, understanding phonetics

Food: fuel or pleasure?

File 1 overview

This first File (**1A–1C**) focuses on the present, the past, and the future. The first lesson, **1A**, revises the present simple and present continuous, and introduces the concept of action and non-action verbs. The second lesson, **1B**, brings together the three past (narrative) tenses, which were taught separately in the previous level of *New English File*. Finally, the third lesson, **1C**, contrasts the three future forms, *going to*, *will*, and the present continuous (for future).

Lesson plan

In this first lesson SS revise the present simple and continuous. SS also learn to distinguish between action and non-action verbs (sometimes called stative and dynamic verbs). This distinction will help them later to use other continuous forms correctly. The topic of the lesson is food, firstly looking at different attitudes to food round the world, and then at a British chef's experience of opening an English restaurant in Chile. Pronunciation focuses on the difference between the /ʊ/ and /uː/ sounds, and emphasizes the usefulness of knowing phonetics, by showing SS how they can use their dictionary to find or check the pronunciation of 'irregular' words.

If you would like to begin the first lesson without the book, there is a photocopiable 'getting to know you' activity on *p.171* and *p.172* (instructions *p.164*), and two photocopiable revision grammar activities on *pp.140–141*. (key *p.139*).

Optional lead-in (books closed)

- Write **FOREIGN RESTAURANTS** on the board. Then elicit from SS the different kinds of foreign restaurants in their town, e.g. *Chinese, Italian, Vietnamese, Thai,* etc. Write them on the board (eliciting the spelling from SS if you want to revise the alphabet), and ask SS which they think are the most popular and why.
- Then ask them if they think food from their country is popular abroad, and if yes, which dishes in particular.

1 READING & SPEAKING

a • Books open. Focus on the question and give SS a few moments in pairs to think of some food and dishes. Make sure SS are clear about the difference between *food* (meat, fish, pasta, etc.) and *dishes* (fish and chips, pizza, curry, etc.).

• Get feedback from different pairs and write their ideas on the board. Accept all appropriate suggestions. You could also include drinks.

Some possible suggestions
The US: burger, apple pie; **China:** fried rice, noodles; **France:** cheese (e.g. Roquefort), pâté; **Italy:** pasta, pizza; **Japan:** sushi, seaweed; **Mexico:** fajita, chilli con carne.

b • Focus on the title of the file and elicit / explain the meaning of *fuel* in this context (= sth that gives you energy) and *pleasure* (= sth that makes you happy). Explain that they are going to read part of an article where women from different countries were interviewed about their attitudes to food and diet.

• Now focus on the photos and ask SS to tell you what food they can see.

• Focus on questions 1–6, and make sure SS understand them, especially questions 5 and 6. Point out that *cut down* = eat less of something, and that *diet* in this context = the food people eat regularly. SS may already know the other meaning of *diet* = to eat less food in order to lose weight.

• Tell SS to read all Alice's answers once before trying to match them to questions 1–6 (by writing the numbers in the boxes). Then they do the same for Jacqueline. Remind SS of the importance of guessing the meaning of new / unknown words from context. Get SS to compare their answers with a partner's and then check answers.

Alice Freeman	A 6	B 3	C 4	D 2	E 5	F 1
Jacqueline Fabre	A 3	B 5	C 6	D 4	E 1	F 2

c • Focus on the task. Get SS to read the article again and answer questions 1–9 with the correct initial. Check answers. You could encourage SS to justify their answers by referring to the article.

1 Both	**6** Alice
2 Jacqueline	**7** Both
3 Alice	**8** Jacqueline
4 Jacqueline	**9** Both
5 Jacqueline	

d • Focus on the highlighted words and phrases, and the definitions 1–10. Give SS a few minutes to match them, individually or in pairs, and check answers. Model and drill pronunciation.

1 eat out	**6** fat
2 honey /ˈhʌni/	**7** dishes
3 portions	**8** wholemeal /ˈhəʊlmiːl/
4 heat up	**9** soup /suːp/
5 takeaway	**10** stew /stjuː/

Extra support

You could go through the whole article with the class (with the paragraphs in order) clarifying the meaning of other new words and expressions.

Extra challenge

Put SS in pairs, **A** and **B**. Write questions 1–6 on the board and get SS to close books.

- **A** then tells **B** from memory how Alice answered the questions, and **B** does the same for Jacqueline. Tell SS to answer in the third person. Monitor to make sure that SS remember to add *-s* to present simple verbs and to use *doesn't* for negatives.

e • Now ask the whole class whose diet they think is healthier, and why. Accept all opinions but ask SS to justify them.

> This is a matter of opinion. Both have reasonably healthy diets, but Jacqueline's is more varied and she enjoys food more. On the other hand, Alice eats less fat and sugar.

f • Focus on the speech bubbles. SS now use questions 1–6 from **1b** to interview each other in pairs. Encourage them to ask for / give more information, e.g. if they don't cook, they should say why they don't, etc.

Extra idea

You could get SS to interview you first. Show them by your answers how much detail you want them to give.

- Get feedback from the whole class to see if they agree about question 6. In a multilingual class, compare what is happening in their countries.

2 GRAMMAR present simple and continuous; action and non-action verbs

a • 1.1 Focus on the photo of sushi (a Japanese dish of small cakes of cold rice often wrapped in seaweed and sometimes with raw fish) and elicit from SS what it is. Ask them if they have ever tried it, etc.

- Explain that SS will hear Rumiko, a Japanese woman, answering questions 2–6 from the article.
- Tell SS that when they listen the first time they should not write anything but just try to get a general understanding of what Rumiko says and to decide if food is 'fuel or pleasure' for her.
- Play the tape / CD once. When the recording is finished, ask the whole class *Do you think food for her is fuel or pleasure?* Ask SS to justify their opinions.

> Probably more pleasure, as she likes cooking, enjoys eating out, and likes the variety of food and restaurants.

b • Now focus on the questions. Play the tape / CD again, pausing between questions to give SS time to make a note of the answers (or alternatively, to answer them orally with a partner.) Play the tape / CD one more time if necessary and then check answers.

> 1 Just a cup of coffee in the office. She doesn't get up early enough to have breakfast.
> 2 In sushi restaurants and ones that serve organic food.
> 3 She works late, her kitchen is too small, and her boyfriend is a better cook than she is.
> 4 She drinks a lot of coffee.
> 5 No, she doesn't need to because she has a healthy diet and does regular exercise.
> 6 It's getting worse, more westernized. As a result, people are getting fatter.
> 7 No, she doesn't. She likes the fact that there are more different kinds of restaurants and food / more variety when you eat out.

1.1 CD1 Track 2

(tapescript in Student's Book on *p.122*)

I = Interviewer, R = Rumiko

I Rumiko, what do you eat in a typical day?

R I don't usually have breakfast because I can't get up early enough to eat! I normally just buy a coffee and drink it in the office.
I usually have lunch in a restaurant near the office with people from work. When I was younger, I used to go to fast food restaurants and have pizza, or fried chicken and chips, but now I prefer eating something healthier, so I go to sushi restaurants or restaurants which serve organic food. And for dinner I eat out a lot too.

I Do you ever cook?

R Well, I like cooking, but I work very late every day and also my kitchen's too small. My boyfriend's a better cook anyway.

I Do you ever eat unhealthy food?

R Well, I don't eat a lot of sweet things but I drink a lot of coffee every day. I think I'm addicted to caffeine.

I Are you trying to cut down on anything at the moment?

R No. I eat healthily and I do exercise regularly, so I don't think I need to cut down on food.

I Are people's diets in your country getting better or worse?

R Oh, probably worse. I think the diet in Japan today is much more westernized than before and that's why some people are getting fatter. But personally, I like the fact that there are more different kinds of food and restaurants now. I enjoy the variety, it makes eating out much more fun.

Extra support

If there's time, you could get SS to listen again with the tapescript on *p.122* so they can see exactly what they understood / didn't understand. Translate / explain any new words or phrases.

c • Focus on the instructions. Give SS a minute in pairs to choose the correct form. Check answers, getting them to explain why (in their L1 if necessary). For 2 and 5, they may simply 'feel' that *prefer* and *like* are right without being able to explain why. This would be a good moment to explain about action / non-action verbs (see **Grammar notes** on *p.16*).

> 1 I don't usually have (It's a habitual action)
> 2 I prefer (non-action verb, not normally used in the continuous)
> 3 I drink (It's a habitual action)
> 4 are getting (It's an action in progress at the moment)
> 5 I like (non-action verb, not normally used in the continuous)

d • Tell SS to go to **Grammar Bank 1A** on *p.130*. If your SS have not used the *New English File* series, explain that all the grammar rules and exercises are in this part of the book.

- Go through the examples and read the rules with the class.

Grammar notes

Present simple

- At this level SS should be clear about the form and use of the present simple.
- Remind SS of the difference in pronunciation of the third person *-s*, i.e. /s/ (verbs ending in an unvoiced consonant, e.g. *cooks, eats*), /z/ (verbs ending in a vowel sound or voiced consonant, e.g. *plays, has*), and /ɪz/ (verbs where you add *-es*, e.g. *watches, finishes*).
- Remind them too of the irregular pronunciation of (he / she / it) *says* /sez/ and *does* /dʌz/.

⚠ The present simple is also occasionally used to refer to the future, e.g. *The next train leaves at 7.30.* This use is not dealt with here.

Present continuous

- SS who don't have a continuous form in their language may need reminding that this is the form they must use when they are talking about actions in progress now.
- Remind SS of the other use of the present continuous for future arrangements. This will be revised fully together with the other future forms in **1C**.

Action / Non-action verbs

- These are often called Dynamic / Stative or Progressive / Non-progressive verbs. We have called them Action / Non-action as we think this helps to make the difference clearer for SS. There are several verbs, apart from *have*, which can be both action and non-action, e.g. *think* (**action** = mental activity; **non-action** = have an opinion) and also *see, look, feel.* At this level it may be best to use *have* as one clear example.

- Focus on the exercises for **1A** on *p.131*. SS do the exercises individually or in pairs. Check answers either after each exercise or after they have done both. Where relevant, get SS to tell you why the wrong sentences are wrong.

a 1 They always have breakfast
2 She's having a shower.
3 We need an answer
4 I'm studying a lot now
5 She doesn't eat
6 They are always late.
7 Are you going out
8 He never replies
9 It depends on the weather.

b 1 are you having
2 does he do
3 Are you going away
4 Do you want
5 is she cooking

- Tell SS to go back to the main lesson on *p.5*.

e • Focus on the question prompts. Elicit the questions from the class to make sure they use the right form and drill pronunciation getting SS to copy the rhythm by stressing the 'information' words.

What do you usually have for breakfast?
How many cups of coffee do you drink a day?
Where do you usually have lunch?
How often do you eat out a week?
Do you prefer eating at home or eating out?
Do you need to buy any food today?
Are you hungry? Do you want something to eat?
Are you taking any vitamins or food supplements at the moment?
Are you trying to eat healthily at the moment?

Extra support

You could write the full questions on the board and underline the stressed words to help SS get the rhythm right.

- Monitor as SS work in pairs making sure they are using the present simple and continuous correctly. The focus here should be on accurate practice of the grammar rather than on fluency.

3 VOCABULARY food and restaurants

a • Focus on the quiz. Quickly go through the questions, and then set a time limit of about five minutes for SS to answer in pairs.

Extra idea

You could divide the class into teams and make this a competition.

- Check answers and write them on the board, getting SS to spell some of the words.

Possible answers

1 **red** - apple / strawberry / cherry, **yellow** - banana / lemon / grapefruit, **green** - apple / pear / grapes
2 meat, fish, eggs, etc.
3 cheese, cream, yoghurt, etc.
4 toast, bread, cereal, eggs, croissant, etc.
5 biscuits, sweets, fruit, crisps, nuts, chocolate, etc.
6 lettuce, tomatoes, carrots, onions, beans, potatoes, etc.
7 plate, spoon, knife, fork, salt, pepper, tablecloth, oil, vinegar, glass, etc.

b • Tell SS to go to **Vocabulary Bank *Food and restaurants*** on *p.144*.

- Focus on section **1a Food**, and get SS to do it in pairs. Check answers and model and drill pronunciation. Draw SS' attention to the fact that the phonetic transcription is given for words where the spelling / pronunciation relationship is unusual.

meat	fish / seafood	fruit	vegetables
duck	prawns	peaches	beans
sausages	salmon	strawberries	lettuce

- Now do **1b**. Give SS time to add words. Then write the column headings on the board, and elicit words from SS. Drill pronunciation.

Extra idea

When you check answers to **1a**, copy the chart on the board. Then elicit SS' extra words (**b**) and write them on the board in the chart for other SS to copy down any new words.

- Now get SS to do section **2 Food adjectives.** Correct answers.

1 Home-made	5 Takeaway
2 spicy	6 low-fat
3 raw	7 fresh
4 frozen	8 sweet

- You may want to teach the two opposites of *sweet* (sour and bitter).
- Finally, get SS to do section **3 Restaurants and cooking**, and check answers.

a **1** plate **2** fork **3** glass **4** salt and pepper **5** napkin **6** knife **7** spoon **8** starters **9** main courses **10** desserts
b **11** fried **12** boiled **13** baked **14** grilled **15** steamed **16** roast

- SS may ask what the difference is between *baked* and *roast*, as both mean cooked in the oven. *Roast* always means cooked with fat, and is used especially for meat and potatoes. *Baked* is used for bread, cakes and most sweet things, and also fruit or vegetables.
- Finally, focus on the instruction 'Can you remember the words on this page? Test yourself or a partner'.

Testing yourself

- For **Food** SS can cover the columns and try to remember the words in each category. For **Food adjectives** they can try to remember the adjectives by covering the **Adjective** column and reading the sentences. They can uncover, one by one, to check. For **Restaurants and cooking** they can cover the words and look at the pictures and try to remember the words.

Testing a partner

- Alternatively, SS can take it in turns to test each other. **B** closes the book and **A** defines or explains a word for **B** to try and remember, e.g. **A** *What do you call food which you buy at a restaurant and take home to eat?* **B** *Takeaway food.* After a few minutes, SS can change roles.
- In a monolingual class, SS could also test each other by saying the word in their L1 for their partner to say in English.

Study Link SS can find more practice of these words and phrases on the MultiROM and on the *New English File Intermediate* website.

- Tell SS to go back to the main lesson on *p.6*.

c • Here the words and phrases from the **Vocabulary Bank** are put into practice.

- Put SS into pairs, preferably face to face. Focus on the questions. Check SS understand *feeling a bit down* (= a bit depressed) in 3b. SS take turns to ask and answer the questions. The student who is asked a question should return it using *What / How about you?*
- Monitor and help with any new food words SS may want to use.
- If there's time, get some quick feedback from the class.

Extra idea

You could get SS to ask you the questions in **3c** first before asking each other.

4 PRONUNCIATION /ʊ/ and /uː/, understanding phonetics

Pronunciation notes

There are two focuses here. First, SS work on distinguishing between two similar sounds (one long and one short) and they look at the typical spellings for these sounds. Then there are exercises to show them how useful it is for them to be able to understand the phonetic transcription of words given in dictionaries.

a • Focus on the sound pictures. If your SS are not familiar with them, explain that the sound pictures give a clear example of a word with the target sound and they help them remember the pronunciation of the phonetic symbol (there is one for each of the 44 sounds of English).

- Elicit the two words (*bull* and *boot*) and point out that *bull* is a short sound and *boot* is a long sound (the two dots in the phonetic symbol tell you this).

b • Now focus on the words and give SS a few moments in pairs to put them in the right column. You could suggest that the best way is to practise saying each word with a long sound and then with a short sound and see which sounds correct. Tell SS to be careful with double *o* words as this combination of letters is sometimes pronounced /ʊ/ and sometimes /uː/.

Extra support

You could play the tape / CD first for SS to hear the words before they try to put them in the right column. You could also tell SS how many words go in each column.

c • 1.2 Play the tape / CD once for SS to check their answers. Then play it again pausing after each word for SS to repeat.

1.2 — CD1 Track 3

bull /ʊ/	boot /uː/
butcher	food
cook	fruit
good	juice
sugar	mousse
	soup
	spoon

d • Now tell SS to go to the **Sound Bank** on *p.157*. Explain that here they can find all the sounds and their symbols and also the typical spellings for these sounds plus some more irregular ones.

- Focus on *bull* and *boot*, and the different words and spellings. Point out again that SS have to be careful with words with double *o*, as some are pronounced /ʊ/ and others are pronounced /uː/.

Study Link SS can find more practice of English sounds on the MultiROM and also on the *New English File Intermediate* website.

- Tell SS to go back to the main lesson on *p.6*.

e • Now focus on the information box and read it with SS. Emphasize that understanding phonetic symbols means that they can check the pronunciation of new words in a dictionary, as well as their meaning.

f • 1.3 Focus on the task. Tell SS to look at the phonetics, individually or in pairs, and to try and work out the exact pronunciation of each word. They can look at the **Sound Bank** on *p.157* to check the pronunciation of individual symbols.

• Before you play the tape / CD, elicit from the class how they think each word is pronounced. Play the tape / CD word by word, and get SS to listen and repeat after the tape / CD.

1.3 CD1 Track 4

1 knife biscuit salmon
2 sausages lettuce sugar
3 yoghurt menu diet

Extra idea

Get SS to cover the words and just look at the phonetics and practise saying the words.

g • 1.4 Give SS a moment to read the six sentences. Then play the tape / CD once the whole way through for SS to hear them. Then play it again pausing after each sentence for SS to repeat. Finally, get SS to practise saying the sentences themselves (quietly) before asking individual SS to say them.

1.4 CD1 Track 5

1 The first course on the menu is lettuce soup.
2 What vegetables would you like with your steak?
3 Do you want yoghurt or chocolate mousse for dessert?
4 I take two spoonfuls of sugar in my coffee.
5 Sausages and biscuits aren't very good for you.
6 Would you like a fruit juice?

5 LISTENING

a • Do this as an open class question and see what SS think. Give your opinion too!

b • 1.5 Focus on the instructions and the photos. Tell SS that when they listen the first time, they should just try to get a general understanding of what Kevin says and to try to number the photos in the order that they are mentioned. When they listen the second time SS will be questioned more on details.

Extra support

Before you play the recording you could pre-teach a few key words or phrases which you think your SS might not know.

• Play the tape / CD once for SS to number the photos 1–5. Check answers getting SS to tell you what each photo shows.

1 A Frederick's, Kevin's restaurant
2 E a trifle (typical English dessert, made with fruit, cake and cream)
3 B a gastropub (a pub with a restaurant)
4 D a restaurant kitchen (with only men working there)
5 C Stilton (an English cheese)

c • Focus on the questions and quickly go through them. Play the tape / CD again. You could pause after each question is answered and give SS time to answer each question. When the recording is finished, get SS to compare with a partner. You may need to play the recording (or part of it) again before checking answers.

1 Because he liked the country, and Chileans are pro-European and open to new things.
2 Frederick is his father's name.
3 Because they don't expect the English to be good cooks.
4 English breakfasts and desserts, e.g. trifle, English teas with cakes and sandwiches. They are all very popular.
5 In gastropubs (pubs which are also restaurants) because they serve food which is good but not too expensive.
6 One. Many reasons – women don't like the unsocial hours, and they don't like the atmosphere – there's a lot of shouting and it's very hot.
7 English cheese, especially Stilton.

Extra support

After checking answers, you could get SS to have a final listen with the tapescript on *p.122* so they can see exactly what they understood / didn't understand. Translate / explain any new words or phrases.

1.5 CD1 Track 6

(tapescript in Student's Book on *p.122*)

I = Interviewer, K = Kevin

I Kevin, why did you decide to open a restaurant in Chile?
K I'd always wanted to have my own restaurant and it would have been very expensive to do that in England. I'd visited Chile as a tourist and loved it, and I thought it would be a good place because Chileans are very pro-European, and are quite open to new things, new ideas. So I opened *Frederick's*.
I Right. Why did you call the restaurant *Frederick's*?
K Because Frederick's my father's name. It's my second name too.
I What kind of food do you serve?
K Mainly international dishes like pasta, steak and fries, risotto – but we also do several English dishes as well.
I Were Chilean people surprised when they heard that an English chef was going to open a restaurant here?
K Yes, they were – very! I think people don't usually expect the English to be good cooks.
I Is your chef English?
K No, he's Chilean – but I've taught him to make some English dishes.
I What kind of English dishes do you have on your menu?
K Well, we're open in the morning, and we serve traditional English breakfasts, and then we have a lot of English desserts at lunchtime, for example trifle – that's a typical English dessert made with fruit and cake and cream. And we do proper English teas in the afternoon – tea with cakes or sandwiches.
I Are the English dishes popular?
K Yes, especially the desserts and cakes. I think people here in Chile have a very sweet tooth.
I People who visit England always say that the food isn't very good, or that you have to spend a lot of money to eat well. Do you agree?

K I think eating good food's never cheap. But I think that today, the best place for a tourist to eat in England is in a pub, especially the ones called gastropubs – pubs which are also restaurants. These pubs are beginning to serve really good food that's not too expensive.
I I see. You said earlier that your chef was a man. Do you have any women working in your kitchen?
K Yes, one, but the rest are all men. In fact, I think that's typical all over the world – there are far more men than women in restaurant kitchens.
I Why do you think that is?
K I think there are a lot of reasons. The most important reason is probably the unsocial hours. Most women don't want a job where you have to work until late at night. Then there's the atmosphere. Women don't like being shouted at, and there's a lot of shouting in restaurant kitchens. It's also usually incredibly hot and I think women don't like that either.
I And finally is there any English food that you really miss here?
K The thing I miss most living in Chile is English cheese. I really miss Stilton – which is a wonderful English blue cheese. It's not as famous as some of the French cheeses like Roquefort but I think it should be. You should try it!
I I will! Kevin, thank you very much.
K Thank you.

d • Get SS to answer the questions with a partner and then get feedback or you could simply ask the whole class. You could also tell them about food you miss or would miss.

6 SPEAKING

a • Tell SS that they are going to give their opinion about various topics related to food. Focus on the phrases in **Useful language**. Elicit / explain what they mean and drill the pronunciation.
• Focus on the instructions, and divide SS into groups of three if possible. Give them enough time to think of reasons and examples.

b • Monitor while SS are debating, and encourage them to use the phrases for agreeing and disagreeing. Don't over-correct, but make a note of any errors that you may want to focus on when they finish speaking.

Extra support

Start by saying what you think about sentence 1, giving examples if you can, and then get SS to agree or disagree with you and say why.

Extra photocopiable activities

Grammar
present simple and continuous *p.142*
Communicative
A time for everything *p.173* (instructions *p.164*)

HOMEWORK

Study Link **Workbook** *pp.4–6*

1B If you really want to win, cheat

G past tenses: simple, continuous, perfect
V sport
P /ɔː/ and /ɜː/

Lesson plan

In this lesson SS revise past tenses. In *New English File Pre-intermediate* they learnt the past continuous and the past perfect in separate lessons, so this is the first time they are brought together. The topic is sport, and the two angles are cheating in sport, and what happens to sportspeople when they retire. The vocabulary focus is on words and phrases connected with sport and the pronunciation focuses on two more sounds which SS often have problems with, /ɔː/ and /ɜː/.

Optional lead-in (books closed)

Ask SS what *to cheat* means, and elicit a translation / explanation (= to act in a dishonest way to get an advantage for yourself). Then elicit typical ways in which people cheat, e.g. in an exam or in a card game.

1 GRAMMAR past tenses: simple, continuous, perfect

a • Books open. If you didn't do the lead-in, make sure SS understand the meaning of *cheating*. Then do this as an open class question and elicit sports and different ways of cheating, e.g. taking drugs.

b • Focus on the photos and ask SS what they can see. Elicit / teach the word *sword* /sɔːd/ (in picture 3).

• Focus on the task, get SS to read the article, and then ask the class to say how the three people cheated.

> Diego Maradona used his hand to score the winning goal.
> Fred Lorz went in a friend's car for part of the marathon.
> Boris Onischenko changed part of his sword; it turned on the 'hit' light without him hitting his opponent.

• Elicit or explain / translate any vocabulary that is causing problems, and tell SS that they will be doing sports vocabulary later in the lesson.

c • Focus on the highlighted verbs in the first text. Elicit that *were playing* is past continuous, *protested* is past simple and *had scored* is past perfect.

• Then get SS to underline an example of each tense in the other two texts. Check answers.

> 2 past simple: won, finished, was, took, started, didn't win
> past continuous: was waiting, were cheering, was shouting
> past perfect: had travelled
> 3 past simple: protested, said, examined, made, could, went, called
> past continuous: was competing, was winning, was showing, was scoring
> past perfect: had changed, hadn't hit

d • Give SS time in pairs to match the tenses to the rules. Check answers.

> 1 past simple 2 past continuous 3 past perfect

e • Tell SS to go to **Grammar Bank 1B** on *p.130*. Go through the examples and read the rules with the class.

Grammar notes

Past simple

• SS should be clear about the use of the past simple for completed past actions. However, they will probably need to revise the irregular verbs, which are on *p.156*. Encourage SS to highlight the ones they find difficult to remember and to test themselves periodically.

• Remind SS of the different pronunciations of the *-ed* ending (regular verbs): /t/ (verbs ending in an unvoiced consonant, e.g. *looked, finished*), /d/ (verbs ending in a vowel sound or voiced consonant, e.g. *played, phoned*) and /ɪd/ (verbs ending in /t/ or /d/ + *-ed*, e.g. *protested, started, ended*).

Past continuous

• Remind SS that this is the past equivalent of the present continuous. It is used for actions in progress in the past which are often 'interrupted by a short completed action' (past simple.), e.g. *I **saw** an accident when I **was driving** here this morning.*
*Sorry, we **were watching** a film when you **called** and we **didn't hear** the phone.*

Past perfect

• This tense was previewed in *New English File Pre-intermediate* but may be new for some of your SS. If so, you will need to make the form and use clear. We use the past perfect when we are talking in the past and we want to refer to an action which happened earlier, e.g. *When I **got** home I **saw** that somebody **had broken** the window* (i.e. the window was broken before I came home). Refer SS to the irregular past participles on *p.156* as this tense requires the participle form.

⚠ It is important to point out to SS that in some cases the past simple or past perfect are both possible.

Using past tenses together

• Tell SS that these three tenses are often used together when we tell a story or anecdote in the past. Most verbs tend to be in the past simple (First, … then …, etc.), but we often use the past simple in conjunction with either or both the past continuous and past perfect, e.g. *I **got** home late and my wife **had** already **finished** her lunch and **was watching** the news on TV.*

• Focus on the exercises in **1B** on *p.131*. SS do the exercises individually or in pairs. Check answers either after each exercise or after they have done both.

a 1 were watching
2 had left
3 had studied
4 was cycling
5 had only had
b 1 did the accident happen?, was driving, hit
2 had already started, called
3 had, went
4 had finished, had gone
5 lost, was talking

- Tell SS to go back to the main lesson on *p.9*.

f
- Focus on the instructions. If necessary, let SS quickly read the texts again.
- Put SS in pairs and make sure they cover the texts. Give them a few minutes to remember and retell the stories between them using the three narrative tenses and then get feedback from three different pairs.

Text 1: were playing, scored, protested, gave, showed, had scored
Text 2: won, was waiting, were cheering, started, had travelled
Text 3: was competing, won, protested, examined, discovered, had changed

2 SPEAKING

a
- Focus on the instructions and make sure SS understand what an anecdote is (an informal true story about something that happened to you).
- Give SS time to choose which anecdote they are going to tell, and to plan the story. Encourage them to think about the vocabulary they are going to need, especially verbs.
- Monitor and help SS with their planning and with any specific vocabulary.

Extra idea

Model the activity first by telling them an anecdote of your own. Pause from time to time and encourage SS to ask you questions.

b
- Put SS in pairs (or threes). Monitor while they are telling their anecdotes but don't correct too much as the aim here is to encourage fluency, and SS are unlikely to use all the tenses perfectly.
- If SS are enjoying the activity (and you have time), you could get them to change partners and tell their story again, or to tell one of the other anecdotes.

3 LISTENING

a
- Either do this in pairs or as an open class question, eliciting disadvantages on the board. You could also ask SS if they can think of any advantages.

Possible disadvantages
Players and fans often insult them; people focus on the mistakes they make, not on the right decisions; they have to travel a lot, etc.

b
- 1.6 Focus on the photo and the instructions. Give SS a few minutes to read the questions first. Then play the tape / CD once. Get SS to compare with a partner. Then check answers.

1 b 2 c 3 b 4 a 5 a 6 b 7 a

c
- Play the tape / CD again. Pause after each of the referee's answers, and tell SS in pairs to try to remember the question and as much detail as they can of his answer. Give them time to discuss this. Then elicit the interviewer's question and the referee's answer in as much detail as possible.
- Ask the last question to the whole class. Encourage SS to give reasons to justify what they say.

Extra support

If there's time, you could get SS to listen to the tape / CD with the tapescript on *p.122* so they can see exactly what they understood / didn't understand. Translate / explain any new words or phrases.

1.6 CD1 Track 7

(tapescript in Student's Book on *p.122*)
I = Interviewer, JA = Juan Antonio

I What was the most exciting match you refereed?
JA It's difficult to choose *one* match as the most exciting. I remember some of the Real Madrid–Barcelona matches, for example the first one I ever refereed. The atmosphere was incredible in the stadium. But really it's impossible to pick just one – there have been so many.
I Who was the best player you ever saw?
JA During my career there have been many great players, like Johan Cruyff and Diego Maradona. It's very difficult to say who was the best but there's one player who stands out for me, not just for being a great footballer but also for being a great human being and that was the Brazilian international Mauro Silva, who used to play in here in Spain, for Deportivo La Coruña.
I What was the worst experience you ever had as a referee?
JA The worst? Well, that was something that happened very early in my career. I was only 16 and I was refereeing a match in a town in Spain and the home team lost. After the match, I was attacked and injured by the players of the home team and by the spectators. After all these years I can still remember a mother, who had a little baby in her arms, who was trying to hit me. She was so angry with me that she nearly dropped her baby. That was my worst moment, and it nearly made me stop being a referee.
I Do you think that there's more cheating in football than in the past?
JA Yes, I think so.
I Why?
JA I think it's because there's so much money in football today that it has become much more important to win. Also football is much faster than it used to be so it's more difficult for referees to detect cheating.
I How do footballers cheat?
JA Oh, there are many ways, but for me the worst thing in football today is what we call 'simulation'. Simulation is when players pretend to have been fouled when they haven't been. For example, sometimes a player falls over in the penalty area when, in fact, nobody has touched him and this can result in the referee giving a penalty when it wasn't a penalty. In my opinion, when a player does this he's

cheating not only the referee, not only the players of the other team, but also the spectators, because spectators pay money to see a fair contest.
I What's the most difficult thing about being a referee?
JA Ah, the most difficult thing is to make the right decisions during a match. It's difficult because you have to make decisions when everything's happening so quickly – football today is *very* fast. Also important decisions often depend on the referee's *interpretation* of the rules. Things aren't black and white. And of course making decisions would be much easier if players didn't cheat.
I So, in your opinion fair play doesn't exist any more.
JA Not at all. I think fair play does exist – the players who cheat are still the exceptions.

4 VOCABULARY sport

a • Focus on the quiz, and get SS to do it in pairs or small groups. Set a time limit, e.g. two minutes. Check answers, making sure SS can say the numbers correctly.

1 90 minutes (+ added time for stoppages).
2 Two.
3 Six.
4 Every two years.
5 42.195 kilometres.
6 Eighteen.
7 400 metres.

b • Tell SS to go to **Vocabulary Bank** ***Sport*** on *p.145*. Get SS to do section **1 People and places** individually or in pairs. Check answers, and model and drill the pronunciation.

a 1 players 2 fans 3 referee 4 spectators 5 coach 6 team 7 captain 8 stadium 9 sports hall
b 1 court 2 pitch 3 pool 4 track 5 circuit 6 course 7 slope

• In **1a** point out that the *coach* is the non-playing person in charge of a sports team. He / She is in charge of training, tactics, and team selection.

⚠ In British English the coach of a football team is often referred to as a manager.

In **1b** point out that you usually use both words to describe the place where you do a sport, e.g. *tennis court, football pitch.*

• Then do the same for section **2 Verbs**.

⚠ Point out that in **b** and **c** SS should write the verbs in the Verb column **not** in the shaded gaps in the sentence. By doing this they can later use the sentences to test their memory.

a beat, beat, beaten lose, lost, lost
win, won, won draw, drew, drawn
b 1 beat 2 lost 3 drew 4 won
c 1 warm up 2 train 3 get injured 4 get fit 5 score 6 go 7 play 8 do

• Finally, focus on the instruction 'Can you remember the words on this page? Test yourself or a partner'.

Testing yourself

For **People and places a)** SS can cover the words, then look at the photos to try and remember the words. In **b)** they can cover the words in the list and look at the sports to remember the places. In **Verbs** they can cover the past tense / past participle forms and the **Verb** columns and try to remember the verbs.

Testing a partner

See **Testing a partner** *p.17*.

Study Link SS can find more practice of these words on the MultiROM and on the *New English File Intermediate* website.

• Tell SS to go back to the main lesson on *p.10*.

c • In this activity, words from the **Vocabulary Bank** are put into practice. Focus on the instructions. Give SS a few minutes to answer the questions in pairs. Get feedback from as many pairs as possible. Encourage SS to give you their information in sentences, e.g. *The team is Flamingo. They're a football team in the first division. They play in a stadium called...*

5 PRONUNCIATION /ɔː/ and /ɜː/

Pronunciation notes

The focus is on two long sounds which are often mispronounced because of the sometimes irregular relationship between sound and spelling. The biggest problem is *-or* which is sometimes /ɔː/ and sometimes /ɜː/, and the *-ought* / *-aught* endings which are usually /ɔː/.

a • Focus on the sound pictures and elicit the words and sounds: *horse* /ɔː/ and *bird* /ɜː/.

• Give SS a few minutes to put the words in the right column. Warn them to be careful with the *-or* words which may go in one or other columns.

b • 1.7 Play the tape / CD once for SS to check their answers. (See tapescript below)

1.7 CD1 Track 8

horse /ɔː/	bird /ɜː/
ball	hurt
caught	serve
court	shirt
draw	world
fought	worse
score	
sport	
warm up	

⚠ Point out that *caught* and *court* are pronounced exactly the same although they have a different spelling and that *fought* and *caught* share the same vowel sound.

c • Tell SS to go to the **Sound Bank** on *p.157*. Go through the different spellings. Emphasize that *-or* is usually pronounced /ɔː/ but that there are a few very common words where it is pronounced /ɜː/, e.g. *world, work, word*, and *worse / worst.*

Study Link SS can find more practice of English sounds on the MultiROM and also on the *New English File Intermediate* website.

- Tell SS to go back to the main lesson on *p.10*.

d • 1.8 Focus on the sentences and give SS time to practise saying them individually or with their partner.
- Then elicit the first sentence from a student or SS and then play the same sentence on the tape / CD to see if they said it correctly. Do the same for the rest of the sentences. Then, if necessary, use the recording for SS to listen and repeat.

> 1.8 CD1 Track 9
> 1 I got hurt when I caught the ball.
> 2 Her serve's worse than the other girl's.
> 3 It was a draw – the score was four all.
> 4 It's the worst sport in the world.
> 5 We warmed up on the court.
> 6 They wore red shirts and white shorts.

6 SPEAKING

- This topic-based speaking activity takes into account that not all SS are interested in sport! Focus on the instructions and the chart, and point out the two alternative 'routes'.

Extra support

Get SS to interview you with the first few questions from whichever group you belong to. Elicit extra questions to show possible follow-up questions.

- Monitor while SS interview each other. Correct any pronunciation errors with the vocabulary they have just learnt, and help them with any new vocabulary they need. Make a note of any common mistakes, and if necessary, have a correction spot at the end of the activity.
- Get some feedback from a few individual SS.

7 READING

a • Focus on the photos and captions, and elicit that they were all top sportspeople who have now retired.
- Focus on the questions, and explain *reach their 'peak'* (= be at their best). Get SS to ask and answer in pairs.
- Get feedback and give SS the answers about what these people do now.

> At time of going to press, **Michael Jordan** is in advertising and owns several businesses including his own clothing line and fragrance; **Muhammad Ali** has Parkinson's disease, which doctors believe was caused by punches he received to the head. He still makes celebrity appearances.
> **Franz Beckenbauer** is at present working on the committee which organizes the World Cup.
> **John McEnroe** won seven 'Grand Slam' titles. Since retiring from professional tennis in 1992 he has combined TV commentating with playing in 'veteran' tournaments. In 2006 he made a comeback on the ATP doubles professional tour (and won the first tournament he played in).

b • Focus on the article and the instructions. Make sure SS understand the word *retire* (stop doing a job / sport because you are 65 / too old to do the sport).
- Give SS a few minutes to read the article once all the way through (without worrying about the meaning of individual words), and elicit that most sportspeople find it difficult to retire.

c • Go through sentences A–F to make sure SS understand them. Explain that *career* is the time a person spends doing his / her job or field of work.
- Now explain that these are the first sentences from paragraphs 1–6. They tell you what each paragraph is about, and are known as 'topic sentences.' Tell SS that in order to match the 'topic sentences' to their paragraphs, they must read each paragraph carefully to understand what it is about.
- Set a time limit for SS to read the text again and match the topic sentences to the right paragraphs.
- Get SS to compare with a partner and then check answers.

> 1 F 2 E 3 C 4 B 5 A 6 D

- Finally, go through each paragraph with the class and elicit / translate / explain the meaning of any new vocabulary, e.g. *jockey*, etc.

d • Focus on the instructions. Tell SS to try to remember, or to guess, all the nouns, and then tell them to check their answers in the article. Elicit the answers onto the board and get SS to underline the stressed syllable in the multi-syllable words. Then model and drill the pronunciation.

> 2 <u>glam</u>our
> 3 loss
> 4 recog<u>ni</u>tion
> 5 <u>fail</u>ure
> 6 re<u>tire</u>ment

- Finally, quickly test SS by getting them to cover the new words and then asking them, e.g. *What's the noun from depressed?*

e • If your class know a lot about sport, get them to do this in pairs. If not, do it as an open class question.

Extra photocopiable activities

Grammar
past tenses *p.143*
Communicative
What a cheat! *p.174* (instructions *p.164*)

HOMEWORK

Study Link **Workbook** *pp.7–9*

1 C

G future forms: *going to*, present continuous, *will* / *shall*
V family, personality
P prefixes and suffixes

We are family

Lesson plan

In this lesson the three most common future forms are contrasted. SS will have studied them all separately, but may not have had to discriminate between them. The lesson emphasizes that the future form you use normally depends on what the speaker wants to say, e.g. whether he / she wants to express a plan or pre-arranged event, or make an 'instant' decision at that moment. The initial lesson context is the changing 'shape' of the family and SS revise and extend family vocabulary. From there they move to adjectives of personality and the lesson ends with a listening, where a psychologist talks about how our personality is defined by our position in the family.

Optional lead-in (books closed)

- Revise family words by doing this quiz with the class either orally or on the board.
  What do you call...
  1 your mother's brother? (my uncle)
  2 your father's sister? (my aunt)
  3 your aunt and uncle's children? (my cousins)
  4 your sister's son? (my nephew)
  5 your brother's daughter? (my niece)
  6 your wife's brother? (my brother-in-law)
  7 your husband's mother? (my mother-in-law)
  8 the person who was your wife? (my ex-wife)
- Make sure SS can pronounce and spell the words correctly.

1 VOCABULARY & SPEAKING family

a • Books open. Focus on the pictures and the question. Elicit answers and reasons from the whole class, but don't tell them if they are right yet. Then give them a minute to read the first paragraph of the article to check.

> The typical family of the future, according to the article, is the picture on the left. It is 'long and thin' because families will have only one child, and people will live longer, so there will be more generations but fewer people in each.

b • SS now read the whole article and focus on the meaning of the highlighted words. When they have matched the words and definitions, get them to compare with a partner. Then check answers, and model and drill the pronunciation.

1 great-grandparents	6 extended family
2 an only child	7 great-great-grandparents
3 single-parent families	8 half-brothers
4 cousins	9 stepmother
5 in-laws	10 couples

You may also want to teach *stepbrother* / *sister* (= the children of your stepmother / stepfather, but who don't have the same mother or father as you and are not blood relatives).

c • Put SS in pairs or groups of three. Now go through the seven predictions again, making sure SS are clear exactly what they mean. Then focus on questions 1–3 and explain that SS have to discuss each prediction using these questions.

• Before SS start, focus on the phrases in **Useful language** and drill pronunciation getting SS to underline the stressed words and syllables, e.g. I think so / I don't think so and maybe / perhaps.

• Discuss the first prediction with the whole class, and find out if it is true now with younger SS, and if the class think it will be true in the future.

• Now give SS time to discuss the other six predictions in pairs or small groups. Monitor and help where necessary and encourage SS to give reasons for their opinions.

• Get feedback from some pairs / groups.

Some of these predictions may refer to issues which are culturally sensitive for your SS, e.g. single-parent families or divorce.

2 GRAMMAR future forms

a • 1.9 Focus on the instructions. Play the tape / CD once and get feedback from the class. You could pause after each dialogue.

> 1 grandson / grandmother; they are talking about what he's going to do next year.
> 2 father / daughter; they are talking about what time she's going to come back.
> 3 mother / son; he is asking her if he can borrow her car.

b • Go through the sentences and check SS understand *crash* (= when a vehicle hits something, e.g. another vehicle). Make it clear that SS don't have to number sentences in order but simply have to match two to each conversation.

Extra challenge

Get SS in pairs to decide before they listen again which sentences are from which dialogue.

Play the tape / CD again. Check answers.

> A 1 B 3 C 1 D 2 E 3 F 2

1.9 CD1 Track 10

(tapescript in Student's Book on *p.122*)

1 **A** So what are you going to do next year, dear? Are you going to go to university?
B No, Gran. I've already told you three times. I'm not going to university. I'm going to look for a job. I want to earn some money.
A Oh, all right, dear, you don't need to shout. I'm not deaf. What's the time now?
B Ten past five. Shall I make you a cup of tea?
A Oh yes, dear, that'd be lovely.

2 **A** See you tomorrow, then.
B Hold on a minute – where are you going?
A Out. It's Friday night, remember?
B What time are you coming back?
A I'm not coming back. I'm staying at Mum's tonight.
B I think you need a coat. It's going to be cold tonight.
A Dad – nobody wears coats any more! Bye!

3 **A** Can I use your car tonight?
B No.
A Why not?
B You'll crash it again.
A I won't. I'll be really careful. I'll drive slowly. I promise.
B OK. Here you are. But be careful.
A Thanks. See you later.

c • Focus on the instructions. Make sure SS understand the words, especially *arrangement* (= something that will happen in the future where all the details, e.g. place / time, have been agreed). Check answers.

plan / intention: C
arrangement: D
prediction: B, F
promise: E
offer: A

• From this, elicit from SS that generally speaking we use *going to* for plans and predictions, *will / won't* for predictions, offers and promises, and the present continuous for arrangements.

d • Tell SS to go to **Grammar Bank 1C** on *p.130*. Go through the examples and read the rules with the class.

Grammar notes

going to

- SS should be familiar with the form and meaning of this. The important thing to emphasize is that we use *going to* for things **we have already decided to do**, i.e. it is our plan or intention.
- *Going to* can also be used to express a prediction, e.g. *I think it's going to rain.*

Present continuous

- Emphasize that:
  – whenever we use the present continuous (for future arrangements especially when a time / place has been agreed), *going to* is also possible. However, with the verbs *go, come, leave, meet, have* (dinner, etc.) we tend to use the present continuous.

will / shall

Point out:
  – the use of *will / won't* for instant decisions at the moment of speaking, offers, and promises.
- A typical mistake here is to use the present simple for offers, e.g. ~~*I carry your bag for you*~~.
  – the use of *will / won't* for predictions, e.g. *I think it will rain. She won't come.*
  – *Shall I...?* is used for offers too, e.g. *Shall I help you?*
  – *Shall we..?* is used to make a suggestion, e.g. *Shall we see a film?*
- Apart from these two important uses *shall / shan't* is only used (with *I / we*) in very formal written English.
- Remind SS that in spoken English *will* is almost always contracted to *'ll*.

⚠ For predictions, emphasize that *will / won't* and *going to* can both be used. However, when you can see that something is about to happen it is more common to use *going to*, e.g. *He's **going to** crash* (I can see him going towards a tree).

• Focus on the exercises for **1C** on *p.131*. SS do the exercises individually or in pairs. Check answers either after each exercise or after they have done both.

a 1 I'm going to study
2 Shall we
3 We're going
4 ✓
5 ✓
6 I'll help
7 I'm meeting
8 I won't do
9 ✓

b 1 I'll get
2 I'm going (to go)
3 we're having / we're going to have
4 I'll answer
5 She's having / She's going to have

Extra idea

Get SS to read the dialogues in **b** aloud to practise the rhythm.

• Tell SS to go back to the main lesson on *p.13*.

e • Focus on the instructions and go through the sentences. Elicit from SS the questions they need to ask (the first four are present continuous and the last four are *going to*), e.g. *Are you seeing a relative this weekend? / Are you having dinner with your family tonight? / Are you going to leave home in the near future? / Are you going to go on holiday with your family this year?*

⚠ Make sure SS realize that they ask a positive question not a negative one for the second and last sentences.

• Now tell SS to stand up and move around the classroom asking their questions until they find someone who answers *yes* for each one, in which case they must ask for more details.

• Stop the activity and ask SS to sit down when one student has a name for all the questions, or when you think SS have had enough. Get feedback.

Extra support

Drill the questions for SS to practise the rhythm. Elicit a few 'extra information' questions for each one, e.g. (for the first one) *Who are you seeing? Where? Why?*, etc.

3 READING

a • Ask the question to the whole class and elicit opinions.

b • Focus on the photos and the article, and stress that Wendy is the younger sister and Carnie is the older sister (you could write this on the board to remind SS).

• Now focus on the instructions. Then do the first one with the whole class. Ask them which of the two sisters they think had a more eccentric hairstyle, the older (Carnie) or the younger (Wendy). If SS don't seem to have any ideas, ask them which child do they think is normally more of a rebel, the older or the younger one.

• SS continue predicting in pairs. Get feedback from a few pairs, but don't tell them if they're right or wrong.

Extra support

If SS find it hard to predict or don't have many ideas, do this as a whole class activity before they read.

c • Now set a time limit for SS to read the article carefully to check and correct their answers. Tell them to underline the part of the text which gave them the answer.

1 C 'she had bright red spiky hair'
2 W 'I always thought Carnie was really cool'
3 C 'I used to follow them, but she hated that'
4 W 'I desperately wanted to be with her'
5 W 'I sometimes think poor Wendy has spent all her life competing with me'
6 C 'I wasn't interested in studying'
7 W 'Wendy used to tell my parents'
8 C 'I used to pinch her and bite her'
9 C 'I was very jealous of Wendy'
10 W 'She always defended me'

• Now ask SS if their predictions were right. Ask what things they think are typical in their relationship (e.g. Wendy always followed Carnie and friends but Carnie didn't want her around) and what things they thought were surprising (e.g. Wendy always defended Carnie).

d • Focus on the instructions. Tell SS that they must try and guess the correct meaning by looking at the context. Do number 1 with the whole class. By reading the whole paragraph '*I desperately wanted to be with her and her friends...*', it is clear that *cool* must be a positive adjective.

• Give SS a few minutes in pairs to choose the meaning of each word or phrase and then compare with their partner. Encourage them to give reasons for their choice.

• Check answers, and point out the pronunciation of *criticize* /krɪtɪsaɪz/ and *close* /kləʊs/.

1 b **2** a **3** a **4** a **5** b **6** a **7** a **8** b

Extra support

You could go through the whole text with the class eliciting / explaining / translating any other new vocabulary.

e • Focus on the question. Then give SS a few minutes to discuss it in pairs, or you could discuss it with the whole class.

HOW WORDS WORK...

• This regular feature focuses on small grammar or vocabulary points that come out of a reading or listening. Go through the examples and then the rules.

• Emphasize that reflexive pronouns are made by adding *self* (or *selves* in the plural) to the possessive adjective (*my*, *your*, etc.). The exception is *himself*, where *self* is added to the object pronoun.

⚠ You may want to teach SS the expression *by* + reflexive pronoun = alone, e.g. *I cooked it by myself.*

• Now focus on the exercise and give SS a minute or two to do it individually or in pairs. Check answers.

1 each other	**4** each other
2 itself	**5** each other
3 ourselves	**6** myself

4 VOCABULARY personality

a • Focus on the instructions. If SS can't remember the adjectives, tell them to find them in the article about Wendy and Carnie. Check answers, and the pronunciation of the adjectives.

1 talkative	**3** shy
2 quiet /kwaɪət/	**4** jealous /dʒeləs/

• You could ask SS if they can remember which sister the adjectives go with (Wendy was quiet and shy, Carnie was jealous and talkative).

b • Tell SS to go to **Vocabulary Bank *Personality*** on *p.146*. Focus on section **1 What are they like?** and elicit / teach that the question *What's he / she like?* = What kind of personality does he / she have?

• Now give SS, in pairs, enough time to complete the sentences with the adjectives.

Extra support

Let SS use their dictionaries to help them with this section.

Check answers and model and drill pronunciation.

2 Competitive	**10** Independent
3 Selfish	**11** Bossy
4 Aggressive	**12** Affectionate
5 Charming	**13** Reliable
6 Sensible	**14** Sensitive
7 Sociable	**15** Ambitious
8 Manipulative	**16** Jealous
9 Moody	

⚠ Point out the difference between *sensible* and *sensitive* (these are false friends in some languages).

• Now go through the adjectives again with the class. For each one ask SS if they think it's a positive, negative, or neutral characteristic (You may not always agree, e.g. some people see ambitious as negative and some as positive.).

• Now focus on sections **2 Opposite adjectives** and **3 Negative prefixes**. Explain that with some adjectives of personality, the opposite is a completely different word, but for others you simply add a negative prefix. Then give SS time to do the exercises. Either correct answers after each section or after they have done both.

2 clever – stupid
generous – mean
insecure – self-confident
lazy – hard-working
quiet – talkative
shy – extrovert
3 unfriendly, unimaginative, unkind, unreliable, unselfish, unsociable, untidy
dishonest, disorganized
impatient, irresponsible, insensitive

- Elicit that *un-* is by far the most common negative prefix. Explain also that *im-* is used before adjectives beginning with *p* or *m*, e.g. *impossible*, *immature*, and *ir-* before adjectives beginning with *r*, e.g. *irregular*.
- Finally, focus on the instruction 'Can you remember the words on this page? Test yourself or a partner'.

Testing yourself
For **What are they like?** SS can cover the list of adjectives 1–16 and read the definitions and try to remember the words. They uncover, one by one, to check. For **Opposite adjectives** SS can cover the words in the list and remember the opposite adjectives and for **Negative prefixes** they can cover the chart and look at the adjectives in the list to remember the prefixes.

Testing a partner
See **Testing a partner** *p.17*.

Study Link SS can find more practice of these words on the MultiROM and on the *New English File Intermediate* website.

- Tell SS to go back to the main lesson on *p.15*.

c • Tell SS to close their eyes and try to remember adjectives of personality they have just learnt. Then tell them to open their eyes and write down the first three that come to mind.
- Now tell SS that in fact this is a personality test! This is what the adjectives they have chosen mean: the first adjective they wrote is how they see themselves, the second is how other people see them, and the third is what they are really like (This activity is based on a real personality test.).

5 PRONUNCIATION prefixes and suffixes

a • Focus on the adjectives, and elicit / explain that 1–4 are grouped according to their endings, and that 5 is adjectives with negative prefixes. Get SS individually or in pairs to practise saying the adjectives, and to underline the stressed syllable. Do not check answers yet.

b • 1.10 Play the tape / CD once for SS to check and check answers. Drill the pronunciation.

1 jealous ambitious generous
2 sociable reliable
3 responsible sensible
4 competitive talkative aggressive sensitive
5 unfriendly insecure impatient

1.10 CD1 Track 11
1 jealous ambitious generous
2 sociable reliable
3 responsible sensible
4 competitive talkative aggressive sensitive
5 unfriendly insecure impatient

- Now play the tape / CD again pausing after each group for SS to repeat. Elicit that neither the endings (or suffixes) *-ous*, *-able*, etc. nor the prefixes (*un-*, *im-*, etc.) are stressed. You could also point out the schwa sound in the endings *-ous* = /əs/, *-able* and *-ible* = /əbl/.

c • Now give SS time to practise saying the adjectives correctly.

6 LISTENING & SPEAKING

a • Focus on the question, and get a show of hands for each position in the family to create class statistics to see how many oldest children, etc. there are.

b • 1.11 Focus on the instructions and the chart. Point out that they should listen for four more adjectives for each column, and that they will hear the recording at least twice.
- Play the tape / CD once the whole way through, pausing between sections if necessary.

c • Get SS to compare with a partner. Then play the tape / CD again, pausing after each kind of child for SS to add to / check their answers and to listen for more details.
- Check answers, and ask SS for extra examples / information.

Oldest children	Middle children	Youngest children	Only children
self-confident	independent	charming	spoilt
ambitious	competitive	affectionate	selfish
responsible	sociable	relaxed	organized
bossy	jealous	lazy	responsible
aggressive	moody	manipulative	

1.11 CD1 Track 12

(tapescript in Student's Book on *p.122*)
C = Continuity announcer, P = Presenter, N = Norah
C It's eight o'clock and time for *Breakfast Time*.
P Good morning, everyone. Our guest this morning is the American writer Norah Levy. Norah's here in Britain this week promoting her new book *'We are family'*, which is all about how our position in the family affects our personality. Welcome Norah.
N Thank you.
P Now is this really true, Norah? That our position in the family affects our personality?
N Sure. OK, other factors can influence your personality too, but your position in the family is definitely one of the strongest.
P So tell us a bit about the oldest children in a family – the first born.
N Well, the oldest children get maximum attention from their parents and the result is that they're usually quite self-confident people. They make good leaders. The famous Prime Minister, Winston Churchill, was a first born child. They're often

imaginative, ambitious and they're more likely to go to university than their brothers or sisters. They often get the top jobs too. Oldest children are also responsible people, because they often have to look after their younger brothers or sisters. The downside of this is that sometimes this means that when they're older they worry a lot about things. They can also be quite bossy, and even aggressive, especially when they don't get what they want.

P What about the middle child?
N Well, middle children are usually independent and competitive.
P Competitive?
N Yes, because they have to fight with their brothers and sisters for their parents' attention. And they're usually sociable, they like being with people, probably because they have always had other children to play with. However, on the negative side middle children are often jealous of their brothers and sisters and they can be moody.
P And youngest children?
N If you're the youngest in a family, you'll probably be very charming, very affectionate, and probably quite a relaxed person. This is because parents are usually more relaxed when they have their last child. On the other hand, youngest children are often quite lazy. This is because they always have their older brothers and sisters to help them. And they can be quite manipulative – they use their charm to get what they want.
P OK, that's all very interesting. Now, I'm an only child. People often have the idea that only children like me are spoilt. Is that true?
N Well, of course it's true! Only children are the only ones – they don't have to share with anyone – so they're often spoilt by their parents and their grandparents. As a result they can be quite selfish. They think of themselves more than of other people.
P OK. Well, that sounds like a good description of me! Is there any good news?
N Yes, there is. On the positive side, only children are usually very organized and responsible, and they can be very imaginative too.
P Well, thank you, Norah, and good luck with the book. And now it's time for the news headlines…

Extra support

If there's time, you could get SS to listen again with the tapescript on *p.122* so they can see exactly what they understood / didn't understand. Translate / explain any new words or phrases.

d • Focus on the instructions. Demonstrate the activity by telling SS about yourself and someone in your family, and saying if the information is true for you or not.

• Then put SS in pairs and get them to do the same. Monitor and help with vocabulary if necessary. Don't over-correct but encourage SS to communicate.

• Get feedback from a few pairs asking if they agree with what the psychologist said.

7 1.12 ♫ SONG *We are family*

This song was originally made famous in 1979 by the group Sister Sledge. If you want to do this song in class, use the photocopiable activity on *p.207*.

Study Link SS can find a dictation and a Grammar quiz on all the grammar from File 1 on the MultiROM and more grammar activities on the *New English File Intermediate* website.

1.12 CD1 Track 13

We are family

Everyone can see we're together
As we walk on by
And we flock just like birds of a feather
I won't tell no lie
All of the people around us they say
'Can they be that close?'
Just let me state for the record
We're giving love in a family dose

We are family
I got all my sisters with me
We are family
Get up everybody, sing
We are family
I got all my sisters with me
We are family
Get up everybody, sing

Living life is fun and we've just begun
To get our share of this world's delights
High hope we have for the future
And our goal's in sight
No we don't get depressed
Here's what we call our golden rule
Have faith in you and the things you do
You won't go wrong, oh no
This is our family jewel

We are family…, etc.

Extra photocopiable activities

Grammar
future forms *p.144*
Communicative
Future questions *p.175* (instructions *p.165*)
Vocabulary
Describing game *p.197* (instructions *p.195*)
Song
We are family p.207 (instructions *p.205*)

HOMEWORK

Study Link **Workbook** *pp.10–12*

1 PRACTICAL ENGLISH

Function Introducing people, meeting people again
Language *Let me introduce you to…, It's great to see you again,* etc.

Lesson plan

This is the first in a series of seven **Practical English** lessons where SS learn and practise functional language. There is a story line, which is a continuation of the story in the **Practical English** lessons in *New English File Elementary* and *Pre-intermediate*. However, the story is completely self-standing, so it is not a problem if your SS have not used these books previously. These lessons feature two main characters, Mark Ryder, an American, and Allie Gray, who is English. They both work for a music company, MTC.

In the first part of the lesson SS meet Allie, who gives a quick summary of how she met Mark and what happened between them. She explains that they are now going to be working together in the Paris office of MTC, where she will be Mark's boss. Mark is about to arrive for his first day in the office.

Study Link These lessons are on the *New English File Intermediate* Video / DVD, which can be used instead of the Class Cassette / CD (see introduction *p.9*). The main functional section of each episode (normally the first section, but in **File 1** the second section) is also on the MultiROM with additional activities.

Optional lead-in (books closed)

Introduce the lesson by giving SS the information in the first paragraph above. If all or some of your SS used *New English File Pre-intermediate*, ask them if they remember Mark and Allie and elicit as much information about them as you can.

THE STORY SO FAR

1.13

- SS listen to Allie introducing herself and talking about how she and Mark met and what happened previously. Focus on the photos of Allie and Mark, and then on sentences 1–7.
- Play the tape / CD once the whole way through, and tell SS not to write anything, just to listen. Then play it again, pausing if necessary for SS to mark the sentences T or F. Get them to compare answers with a partner before you check answers, and elicit why the F sentences are false.

1 F (a year ago)
2 T
3 F (They work for MTC.)
4 F (for a conference)
5 T
6 F (Allie is going to be Mark's boss.)
7 T

1.13 CD1 Track 14
(tapescript in Student's Book on *p.123*)
ALLIE
My name's Allie Gray and I'm from Cambridge in England. I met Mark about a year ago. He's from San Francisco. We both work for MTC, a music company. I was working in the London office and he came there on business. We got on really well and we really liked each other.
Anyway, at the end of his trip, he invited me to go to a conference in San Francisco. We had a great time again. And then something amazing happened. When I was in San Francisco, I was offered a job in our new office in Paris.
When I told Mark, he told me that he was going to work in the Paris office too!
There's just one little thing. His job is marketing director – but mine is managing director – so I'm going to be his boss. I've been in Paris for three weeks now, and I love it. Mark arrived from San Francisco yesterday. He's coming into the office this morning.

Extra support

Let SS listen again with the tapescript on *p.123* so they can see exactly what they understood / didn't understand. Elicit / explain / translate any new words or phrases.

MEETING PEOPLE

a • 1.14 Tell SS to cover the dialogue with their hand or a piece of paper. Focus on the photos and tell them that the people all work in the Paris office. The SS are going to listen to them being introduced to Mark and they have to listen to find out what their jobs are.

Extra support

Before you play the tape / CD, you could elicit / give possible jobs in a (music) company and write them on the board, making sure you include the jobs mentioned: Managing Director, Sales Director / Head of Sales, PR (public relations) director, Marketing Manager, Personnel Manager, secretary, designer, receptionist, personal assistant (PA)

- Play the tape / CD once the whole way through. Then play it again, pausing after each person is introduced to give SS time to write their jobs in. Check answers.

Allie is the managing director.
Mark is the marketing director.
Nicole is Allie's personal assistant.
Jacques is the PR director and Ben is the designer.

- Elicit also that Jacques and Nicole are French, and Ben is English.

b • Now get SS to uncover and look at the dialogue. In pairs, they should read it and see if they can remember or guess the missing words. Stress that they shouldn't write the words in the dialogue. Ideally, they should write in pencil alongside.

c • Play the tape / CD again for them to check. Then go through the dialogue line by line and check answers. Find out how many SS had guessed the words correctly. Where they had not guessed correctly, see if their alternative also fits.

1.14 CD1 Track 15

M = Mark, N = Nicole, A = Allie, J = Jacques, B = Ben

M **Hi**. I'm Mark Ryder.
N Ah, you're the new marketing director.
M That's right.
N I'm Nicole Delacroix. I'm Allie's personal assistant. **Welcome** to Paris!
M Thank you.
N I'll just tell Allie you're here. Allie? Mark Ryder's here. OK. You're from San Francisco, **aren't** you?
M Yes, I am.
A Hello, Mark.
M Allie. It's **good** to see you again. How are you?
A Very well. Did you have a good **journey**?
M Yes, fine, no problems.
A Let me **introduce** you to the team. You've **met** Nicole, my personal assistant?
M Yes, we've said hello.
A **This** is Jacques Lemaître, our PR director.
J How **do** you do?
M Mark Ryder. How do you do?
A And this is Ben Watts, our designer.
B Hi, Mark.
M Great to **meet** you, Ben.
B We've heard a lot about you.
M Really? All good, I hope.
A OK. Shall we go to my office?

d • Now focus on the key phrases (highlighted in the dialogue) and the task. Elicit / explain that *How do you do?* is the most formal way to greet someone when you shake hands with them at a first meeting. It is not a real question (it really means *nice to meet you*), and the normal response is to 'echo' the question *How do you do?* (= nice to meet you too) or use another expression like *Pleased to meet you. How do you do?* is nowadays mostly used in formal (e.g. business) contexts. *Pleased / Nice / Good / Great to meet you* are very common ways of greeting people you have just met in a more informal context.

e • **1.15** Play the tape / CD pausing after the 'beep' for SS to repeat the highlighted phrases. Encourage them to copy the rhythm and intonation.

1.15 CD1 Track 16

M = Mark, N = Nicole, A = Allie, B = Ben

M Hi. I'm Mark Ryder.
N Welcome to Paris!
N You're from San Francisco, aren't you?
M It's good to see you again.
A Did you have a good journey?
A Let me introduce you to the team.
A You've met Nicole, my personal assistant?
A This is Jacques Lemaître, our PR director.
M How do you do?
M Great to meet you, Ben.
B We've heard a lot about you.

Extra support

You could get SS to read the dialogue in pairs to practise rhythm and intonation.

f • Get SS to stand up in pairs. Tell them they are going to move around introducing each other to other pairs. When they introduce their partner they should say what his / her name is, what he / she does and where he / she is from (make sure they know all this information about each other). A typical exchange (where Student A is Suzanne and Student B is Alain) would be:

Student **A** *Hello. This is Alain. / Let me introduce Alain. He's from Lyons and he's at university, studying biology.*
Students **C** and **D** *Nice to meet you.*
Student **B** *And this is Suzanne…*

Extra support

You could elicit this exchange and write it on the board so SS remember what they have to say.

• Encourage SS to use different phrases, e.g. *Great to meet you / We've heard a lot about you*, etc. and let the activity go on until each student has introduced his / her partner at least twice.

SOCIAL ENGLISH It's a secret

a • **1.16** Focus on the photo and ask *Where do you think they are?* (Walking in Paris, by the Seine). Then focus on the question and elicit ideas. Play the tape / CD once the whole way through and check the answer. Ask SS why they think Allie and Mark want to do this.

They want to keep their relationship a secret.

b • Focus on the instructions. Go through the questions and then play the tape / CD again. Get SS to compare answers, and then play it one more time if necessary. Check answers, and elicit / explain the meaning of any words or expressions SS didn't understand, e.g. *weird* (= strange).

1 A 2 B 3 M 4 B 5 M 6 M

1.16 CD1 Track 17

(tapescript in Student's Book on *p.123*)

M = Mark, A = Allie

A What a lovely view! The river's beautiful, isn't it?
M Paris is so romantic. I can't believe we're here together at last.
A Yes, it's weird.
M Weird? It's wonderful. I really missed you.
A Me too.
M Why don't we sit down?
A So did you like the office?
M Yes, it's great. How do you get on with everyone?
A OK. But we'll see. I've only been here three weeks. What did you think of them?
M I thought Jacques was very nice, and Nicole…
A What about Nicole?
M She was very friendly.
A You know we have to keep things a secret.
M What things?
A You know, us. Our relationship. I don't want the people in the office to know we're together.

M No, of course not. But it isn't going to be easy.
A No, it isn't. How's the hotel?
M It's OK, I guess, but it's not like having my own place. I have to find an apartment.
A Don't worry. It won't take you long. What are you thinking?
M Do you really want to know? I was wondering what kind of a boss you'll be.
A Well, you'll find out tomorrow.

Extra support

Let SS listen one more time with the tapescript on *p.123* so that they can see exactly what they understood / didn't understand. Help them with any new vocabulary or expressions.

c • 1.17 Now focus on the **USEFUL PHRASES**. Give SS a moment to try to complete them, and then play the tape / CD to check.

1.17 CD1 Track 18

M = Mark, A = Allie
A What a **lovely** view!
M Why **don't** we sit down?
M I **have** to find an apartment.
A Don't worry. It won't **take** you long.
M I was **wondering** what kind of a boss you'll be.
A **Well**, you'll find out tomorrow.

Extra idea

Ask SS if they can remember who said each phrase (and in what context), e.g. Allie says *What a lovely view!* (about the river).

d • Play the tape / CD again, pausing for SS to repeat. In a monolingual class, elicit the equivalent expressions in SS' L1.

HOMEWORK

Study Link **Workbook** *p.13*

1 WRITING DESCRIBING A PERSON

Lesson plan

This is the first of seven Writing lessons; there is one at the end of each File. In today's world of email communication, being able to write in English is an important skill for many SS. We suggest that you go through the exercises in class, but set the actual writing (the last activity) for homework, although SS may also want to do the planning in class.

In this lesson SS consolidate the language they have learnt in **File 1** by writing an informal email describing a friend.

a • Focus on the two emails and the instructions. Set a time limit for SS to read them and answer the questions. Check answers.

1 Because a friend of Claudia's, Christelle, wants to stay in her house in Scotland. Stephanie wants to know a bit more about Christelle, and if Claudia thinks she would get on with Stephanie's family.
2 Yes, Claudia recommends Christelle.

b • Now focus on the five underlined spelling mistakes and get SS to correct them in pairs. Check answers by getting SS to spell the words correctly. Write them on the board.

studying friends responsible listening usually

c • Focus on the instructions. Give SS a few minutes to re-read Claudia's email and answer the questions. SS can do this orally or in writing. Check answers.

1 extrovert, sociable, hard-working, responsible, independent
2 going out, seeing films, listening to music
3 She's a bit untidy, her English isn't very good

Extra idea

You could ask SS a few more comprehension question about Christelle, e.g. *How old is she? What does she do? What do you know about her family?*, etc.

d • Focus on the chart and the highlighted expressions. Get SS to fill it in, while you copy it on the board. Then check answers and write them in the right place.

Anna is	incredibly very / really quite a bit	untidy.

• Finally, focus on the **Useful language** box and go through the expressions.

WRITE an email

Go through the instructions. Then either get SS to plan and write the email in class (set a time limit of 20 minutes) or get them just to plan in class, or set both the planning and writing for homework.

If SS do the writing in class, get them to swap their emails with another student to read and check for mistakes before you collect them all in.

Extra idea

If you decide to get SS to do their planning in class, you could also get them to tell a partner about the friend they are going to write about, using the paragraph ideas 1–4 to help them.

1 REVISE & CHECK

The File finishes with two pages of revision. The first page, **What do you remember?**, revises the grammar, vocabulary, and pronunciation. These exercises can be done individually or in pairs, in class or at home, depending on the needs of your SS and the class time available. If SS do them in class, check which SS are still having problems, or any areas which need further revision. The second page, **What can you do?**, presents SS with a series of skills-based challenges. First, there is a reading text (which is of a slightly higher level than those in the File) and two listening exercises. Finally, there is a speaking activity which measures SS' ability to use the language of the File orally. We suggest that you use some or all of these activities according to the needs of your class.

GRAMMAR

1 did you get	**6** had changed
2 bought	**7** 'm meeting / 'm going to meet
3 Do you like	**8** finish
4 hit	**9** 'll pick you up
5 was driving	**10** 'll love / 're going to love

VOCABULARY

a **1** seafood (not an adjective)
2 fried (not a kind of meat)
3 roast (a way of cooking – the others are cutlery)
4 pitch (not a person but a place)
5 beat (verb, not a place)
6 affectionate (the others are adjectives with a negative meaning)
7 moody (the others are adjectives with a positive meaning)
8 family (it's a 'group' – the others are individual members)
b **1** spicy **2** starter **3** draw **4** injured **5** stepfather **6** selfish **7** mean
c **1** for, out **2** for **3** up **4** on

PRONUNCIATION

a **1** course (It's /ɔː/)
2 food (It's /uː/)
3 roast (It's /əʊ/)
4 draw (It's /ɔː/)
5 frozen (It's /əʊ/)
b menu, referee, impatient, sociable, irresponsible

CAN YOU UNDERSTAND THIS TEXT?

a **1** F **2** DS **3** T **4** T **5** F **6** F **7** DS **8** T **9** DS **10** T
b **nutritionist** = an expert on diet
rejects = doesn't want
solid = the opposite of liquid
craves = wants very much
choking = not being able to breathe because you have something in your throat
in advance = before you do something

CAN YOU UNDERSTAND THESE PEOPLE?

a **1** c **2** b **3** c **4** a **5** c
b **1** Mark Reid **2** 040155 **3** Sunday **4** 6–7 **5** 5

1.18 CD1 Track 19

1 **A** I'm going to have a coffee. What do you want?
B I'll have an orange juice.
A What about Sally and Tim?
B Get them orange juice too. They said they were thirsty.
A Are you sure? I thought Sally wanted tea.
B No, she wanted something cold.
A OK, then.
2 **A** Shall we stop and have something to eat?
B I don't want anything to eat. But let's stop – I'd like some water and I need to go to the toilet.
A Aren't you hungry? It's lunchtime – I'm starving.
B No, I really don't want anything.
A You're not on a diet, are you?
B No, but I'm not feeling 100 percent. It must be something I ate last night.
3 **A** It's a pity Robertson isn't still playing for us. He was much better than the players we've got now.
B Yeah, he was amazing.
A What happened to him, do you know?
B He retired. I think he opened a pub.
A No, that was Gallagher. He opened a pub in Leeds.
B Oh yes, that's right. I remember now. Robertson's working as a coach at Liverpool. With the junior team, the 16-year-olds.
A Oh really? Well, I think he'd be a good coach.
4 **A** Where are you going?
B Just for a run. I won't be long.
A Well, don't be late for lunch. Remember my mum's coming.
B Oh right. Anyone else or just your mum?
A Your sister's coming – don't you remember?
B Oh yeah, that's right. I'm glad Ann's coming. I think she'll get on well with your mum. Do you need any help with the lunch?
A I'm OK for the moment but I will later. So don't be too long.
B Right, I'll be about 20 minutes.
5 **A** We must get Olivia a present. It's her birthday next week.
B Why don't we just give her some money?
A Oh come on – that's so impersonal. It's her 21st birthday and she's our only granddaughter.
B Well, you choose something for her then.
A That's so typical. I have all the work of going and finding something.
B Well, then give her money like I said before. We're not her generation. We don't know what kind of things she likes.
A Speak for yourself. I think I'll get her a sweater.
B She never wears sweaters.
A Oh, you're so helpful!

1.19 CD1 Track 20

A Sports centre. Good afternoon.
B Hello. I'd like to book a tennis court for Sunday, please.
A Are you a member?
B Yes, the name's Reid – R-E-I-D. Mark Reid.
A What's your membership number, please?
B It's 040155.
A Right, thanks. Here we are. A court for Sunday. Let's see. What time did you want it for?
B From eight to nine in the evening.
A I'm afraid they're all full then. We've got one from five to six or six to seven.
B Six to seven, then.
A OK, Mr Reid, that's court number 5 booked for you then.

Extra photocopiable activities

Quicktest 1 *p.216*

G present perfect and past simple
V money
P saying numbers

2A Ka-ching!

File 2 overview

Lesson **2A** looks at money and numbers and revises the most common uses of the present perfect and contrasts this tense with the past simple. **2B** introduces SS to the present perfect continuous, through the context of life changes. SS also learn how to use 'strong' adjectives, e.g. *tiny, delicious.* In the final lesson of the file (**2C**) comparative and superlative adjectives and adverbs are revised and practised and the vocabulary of transport is introduced through the contexts of comparing forms of travelling and road safety.

Lesson plan

In this lesson SS revise the present perfect and the past simple and learn common words and phrases to talk about money. A song about today's money-obsessed society introduces some common words related to money, and a dialogue where two people are arguing about money provides the context for the grammar revision. In the second half of the lesson SS read about a woman who has decided to live without money. Finally, they practise saying and understanding numbers, fractions, and percentages, etc.

Optional lead-in (books closed)

Put SS in pairs and give them three or four minutes to brainstorm some titles of pop songs which are about money. Elicit the songs onto the board and for each one ask who sang it.

Some suggested titles: *Money* (Pink Floyd), *Money, Money, Money* (Abba), *Material Girl* (Madonna), *Can't buy me love* (The Beatles), *Money makes the world go round* (from 'Cabaret'), *Money for nothing* (Dire Straits), *If I were a rich man* (from 'Fiddler on the roof'), etc.

1 VOCABULARY & LISTENING money

a • 2.1 This song was originally recorded by the Canadian singer Shania Twain in 2002. For copyright reasons this is a cover version.

- Books open. Tell SS that they are going to listen to a song about money. Focus on the title (*Ka-ching!*) and tell SS that when they've heard the song they will know what it means.
- Now focus on the words in the list and ask SS which ones they know. Tell them not to worry about the words they don't know as they will focus on their meaning later when they see them in context in the song.
- Play verse one and then pause the tape / CD to give SS time to write in the missing words. Play the verse again if necessary. Then play the second verse and give SS time to try and write in the missing words. Check answers (marked in bold in the song).

2.1 CD1 Track 21

We live in a 1 **greedy** little world
that teaches every little boy and girl
to 2 **earn** as much as they can possibly,
then turn around and spend it foolishly.
We've created us a 3 **credit card** mess
we 4 **spend** the money that we don't possess.
Our religion is to go and 5 **blow** it all,
so it's shopping every Sunday at the 6 **mall**

All we ever want is more,
a lot more than we had before.
So take me to the nearest store. (Ka-ching!)
Can you hear it ring? (Ka-ching!)
It makes you want to sing. (Ka-ching!)
It's such a beautiful thing – Ka-ching!
(Ka-ching!) Lots of diamond rings, (Ka-ching!)
the happiness it brings, (Ka-ching!)
you'll live like a king,
with lots of money and things.

When you're 7 **broke** go and get a 8 **loan.**
Take out another 9 **mortgage** on your home,
consolidate so you can 10 **afford**
to go and spend some more when you get bored.

All we ever want is more, etc.

Ka-ching!

- Finally, ask SS what *Ka-ching* is (It's the sound of a shop till ringing a sale).

b • Put SS into pairs. Tell them to look at words 1–10 in the song and try to match them to their definitions A–J. Emphasize that the words in brackets (noun, verb, etc.) will help them make sure they choose the right word. Check answers. Model and drill the pronunciation of *mortgage* /mɔːgɪdʒ/ and elicit that the *t* is silent.

A spend	**F** credit card
B loan	**G** earn
C afford	**H** greedy
D mall	**I** blow
E broke	**J** mortgage

c • Give SS time to read the song and to understand it, and play the tape / CD again. Help with any difficult words and phrases, e.g. *foolishly* (= not intelligently), *a mess* (= when everything is untidy, not in its place), *possess* (= own, have), *consolidate* (= put all your debts together).

- Now focus on the three summaries of the song. Explain / elicit the meaning of *obsessed* (= when you are obsessed with something you think about it all the time). Tell SS to choose what they think is the correct summary of the song. Check answers.

2

d • Tell SS to go to **Vocabulary Bank *Money*** on *p.147* and to do section **1 Verbs.** Emphasize that they will have to put some of the verbs into the past tense. Set a time limit and then check answers. Model and drill pronunciation.

1 inherited	6 can't afford	11 invested
2 save	7 charged	12 earn
3 borrowed	8 took out	13 is worth
4 lent	9 cost	
5 waste	10 owe	

• Now focus on section **2 Prepositions** and emphasize that SS must write the preposition in the preposition column, not in the shaded gap in the sentence (This is so they can test themselves later). Check answers.

1 for 2 back 3 in, by 4 on 5 to 6 from 7 for

• Next, focus on section **3 Nouns** and give SS time to do the exercise. Check answers and model and drill the pronunciation of the words / phrases where necessary.

1 note	4 tax	7 cash machine
2 coin	5 loan	
3 salary	6 mortgage	

• Finally, focus on the instruction 'Can you remember the words on this page? Test yourself or a partner'.

Testing yourself

For **Verbs** SS can cover the list of verbs and the right-hand list of sentences and read sentences 1–13 to try to remember the verbs. They uncover, one by one, to check. For **Prepositions** they cover the **Preposition** column and read the gapped sentences and remember the prepositions. For **Nouns** they can cover the list and words 1–7 and try to remember the nouns.

Testing a partner

See **Testing a partner** *p.17*.

Study Link SS can find more practice of these words on the MultiROM and on the *New English File Intermediate* website.

• Tell SS to go back to the main lesson on *p.21*.

2 GRAMMAR present perfect and past simple

a • Put SS in pairs. Focus on the cartoon and dialogue and give SS time to read the dialogue and complete it with Ben's sentences. Tell SS that they have to guess Ben's last line.

b • **2.2** Play the tape / CD once for SS to check and correct their answers. Pause just before you get to the last line and elicit ideas from the class as to what Ben says.

2.2 CD1 Track 22

S = Shelley, B = Ben

S Is that a new camera?
B **Yes. I've just bought it.**
S What's wrong with our old camera?
B **It's old.**
S Old? How long have we had it? A year?
B **We've had it for at least three years. Maybe longer.**
S Three years? I'm sure we bought it last year. Look. We can't afford a new camera.
B **Why not?**
S Have you seen this?
B **No. What is it?**
S The gas bill. It arrived this morning. And we haven't paid the phone bill yet. Take it back to the shop and get your money back.
B **I can't.**
S Why not?
B **Because I've already used it.**

c • Focus on the instructions. Remind SS that the form of the present perfect is *have* + past participle. In pairs, give SS a couple of minutes to underline five examples of the present perfect and two of the past simple. Check answers and write the seven sentences on the board.

Present perfect	Past simple
Yes, I've just bought it. How long have we had it? We've had it for at least three years. Have you seen this? We haven't paid the phone bill yet.	I'm sure we bought it last year. It arrived this morning.

• Now tell SS to answer questions 1–4 in pairs. Tell them to look at the examples on the board to help them. Check answers using the examples on the board to exemplify the rules.

1 past simple (e.g. *We bought it last year.*)
2 present perfect (e.g. *We've had it for three years.*)
3 present perfect (e.g. *Have you seen this?*)
4 past simple (e.g. *It arrived this morning.*)

d • Tell SS to go to **Grammar Bank 2A** on *p.132*. Read the examples and go through the rules with the class. Model and drill the example sentences.

Grammar notes

• In **Grammar Bank 2A** the main uses of the present perfect are pulled together and contrasted with the past simple. This is all revision from the Pre-intermediate level but it is the first time SS have compared the two tenses in such detail. If you know SS' L1, some careful use of L1 / L2 contrast could help here.

Past simple

• The most important point to emphasize is that when we use the past simple, **a specific time in the past** is mentioned, e.g. *Did you see the match last night*?, or understood between the speakers, e.g. *Did you see the match?* (We both know it was last night.). So, a question beginning *When...*? will normally be in the past simple.

• Typical mistakes: ~~*Have you see the match last night?*~~ ~~*What time have you arrived?*~~

Present perfect

• SS will need more help with the various uses of this tense.

• The most important point to emphasize is that we use this tense for a past action where no specific time is mentioned or understood, e.g. *I've been to Paris twice* or when there is a connection with the present, e.g. *I've worked here for two years* (I'm still working here.). This second use is especially hard to remember for most nationalities, who would tend to use a present tense in their L1.

- Remind SS of the difference between *been* and *gone*. *He's been to Berlin* = He has visited Berlin and come back. *He's gone to Berlin* = He is in Berlin now.
- Typical mistakes: ~~*I've been to Paris last year. I work here for two years.*~~
- Refer SS to the **Irregular Verbs** list on *p.156* and test them periodically on the past and participle forms.

- Focus on the exercises for **2A** on *p.133*. Get SS to do exercise **a** individually or in pairs. Check answers. Then do the same for exercise **b**.

a 1 he hasn't arrived yet
2 We haven't seen each other
3 Have you ever written
4 She's never been to
5 I lent him €50
6 I've known them for ten years
7 What year did you leave
8 We have already been
9 she hasn't replied yet
10 They've lived in that house
b 1 have you been, started, lived, moved, 've lived
2 Has your brother found, 's just started
3 Have you ever been, went, was, cost

- Tell SS to go back to the main lesson on *p.21*.

3 SPEAKING

- This questionnaire practises the contrast between the past simple and present perfect and also provides an opportunity for free-speaking.
- Put SS in pairs and focus on the questionnaire and the example speech bubbles. Make sure SS understand *recently* and drill the pronunciation /riːsntli/.
- Point out that the questions in the questionnaire are in the present perfect because they are asking about your whole life until now (*Have you ever..?*) or about the recent past but without specifying a day or time (*Have you .... recently?).*
- However, if the answer is 'Yes' then the 'follow-up' questions asking for more information should be in the past simple, because you are now referring to a specific time in the past, e.g. *When (did you lose your credit card)? What happened?*
- Elicit all the questions to check that SS remember the past participles that they need to use.
- You could either get one student to ask all the questions and then SS change roles or SS can take turns to ask each other a question and the same question can be returned using *What about you?*
- Stop the activity when the time limit is up or if you think the activity is running down. If there's time, get some feedback by finding out, e.g. how many people in the class have sold something on the Internet. However, don't let this stage go on too long.

Extra support

You could model the activity first by getting SS to choose a couple of questions to ask you and eliciting follow-up questions.

4 READING

a • Focus on the three sentences and give SS a moment to choose the one that best describes their attitude to money. Find out with a show of hands the number of SS who have chosen each sentence.

b • Now focus on the photo of Heidemarie and the questions. Elicit some suggestions from the class (e.g. because she doesn't want to work, she begs in the street, she steals from shops, etc.).
• Set SS a time limit to read the whole article once (e.g. three or four minutes). Then check answers.

She wants to prove that money is not important; what is important is what kind of person you are.
She does things for other people and in exchange they give her what she needs to live.

c • Now tell SS to read the text again. When they have finished, they answer questions 1–8 either in pairs or individually. Check answers. Elicit / explain that *house-sit* (= look after another person's house while they are away, like babysit).

1 She was a psychotherapist.
2 A few clothes and a few personal belongings.
3 She set up a 'swapping circle'.
4 First she house-sat, now she lives in a student residence.
5 Yes, but she doesn't get paid.
6 She asks friends or she does something for someone.
7 That all jobs are equally important and that we shouldn't judge people according to how much they earn.
8 She gave it away.

d • SS now focus on the highlighted phrasal verbs, which they have to match to the dictionary definitions 2–6. Stress that although the verbs are in different tenses in the article, they should write them next to the definitions in the infinitive. Check answers.

2 give up	4 give away	6 look after
3 turn up	5 set up	

e • In pairs, SS answer the questions. Then feedback opinions from the class and try to find out what the class as a whole thinks about each question.

5 VOCABULARY & PRONUNCIATION
saying numbers

Pronunciation notes

Even though SS should already 'know' numbers 1–1000, this is an area where plenty of practice is always needed as it is never easy to understand and say numbers in a foreign language. Native speakers sometimes mishear the thirteen / thirty difference and ask for clarification.

a • 2.3 Get SS to write the missing numbers (in figures). Check answers by writing the numbers on the board in two columns to reflect the exercise.

15	750	75,000	1,000,000
50	1,500	750,000	7,500,000
100	7,500		

- Elicit from the class how each number is pronounced before playing the tape / CD and pausing before the next one.
- Emphasize:
  - the difference in stress between *fifteen* and *fifty* (*sixteen* / *sixty*, etc.) and the use and unstressed pronunciation of *and* /n/ in *seven hundred and fifty*.
  - that after a number we say *million*, not millions, e.g. *seven million*, *ten million*, etc.
  - that we usually say *a* before *hundred* and *thousand*. We only use *one* for a number bigger than a thousand, e.g. *one thousand five hundred*.

2.3 CD1 Track 23

fifteen
fifty
a hundred
seven hundred and fifty
one thousand five hundred
seven thousand five hundred
seventy-five thousand
seven hundred and fifty thousand
a million
seven and a half million

- Now get SS to practise saying the numbers themselves.

b • **2.4** Focus on the task. Get SS to try and fill the gaps and let them compare answers with a partner's. Then play the tape / CD for SS to check / correct their answers. Finally, check answers by writing the missing words on the board (see bold words in tapescript below).

- Point out:
  - with prices, e.g. $8.99, we usually say *eight dollars ninety-nine* NOT ~~ninety-nine cents~~.
  - the use and pronunciation of *per cent* to express percentages.
  - the use of 0 (= nought) and **.** (= point) in decimals.
  - the use of the indefinite article with fractions, e.g. *a half*.
- Give SS more practice by letting them repeat after the tape and by testing each other (**A** points at a figure and **B** says it, and vice versa).

2.4 CD1 Track 24

two **pounds** fifty	a **half**
eight **dollars ninety-nine**	a **third**
three **euros twenty**	a **quarter**
fifty **per** cent	three **quarters**
nought **point** five	six **and** a half
three point nine	

c • Focus attention on the numbers and get SS to practise saying them in pairs before getting feedback by asking individual SS or letting all SS call the numbers out.

6 LISTENING & SPEAKING

a • **2.5** Here SS listen to a news bulletin which features a whole range of numbers.

- Focus on the task. Play the tape / CD the first time for SS to simply count the number of news items and get a very general understanding of the bulletin.

There are four (a road accident, a protest by car workers, unemployment figures, house prices.)

Extra challenge

Get SS to also say briefly what each news item is about.

b • Focus on the questions and give SS time to read them. Then play the tape / CD again, this time in sections (item by item) and get SS to answer the two questions on each item. Play the recording (or parts of it) again if necessary. Then check answers.

1 17	**5** 150,263
2 85 mph (miles an hour)	**6** 1,490,000
3 2,600	**7** a third
4 8.5%	**8** £255,900

Extra support

If there's time, you could get SS to listen to the tape / CD with the tapescript on *p.123* so they can see exactly what they understood / didn't understand. Translate / explain any new words or phrases.

2.5 CD1 Track 25

(tapescript in Student's Book on *p.123*)
Good evening. I'm Peter Crane with the six o'clock news.

At least 17 people have been injured in the road accident that took place on the M1 near Leeds last night. The police said that the lorry which caused the accident was travelling at about 85 miles an hour, well over the 60 miles an hour speed limit for heavy goods vehicles.

2600 workers have walked out of the Peugeot car factory in Coventry in protest against the company's pay offer. The unions have asked for a rise of 8.5%. There'll be a meeting between their leaders and management later today.

The latest unemployment figures have been released for this year. They show an increase of 150,263 on last year's figures. This brings the total number of unemployed to approximately 1,490,000. The Employment Minister says this increase has been caused by the relocation of several factories from Britain to the Far East.

Estate agents are predicting that house prices will continue to rise this year, making it extremely difficult for first-time buyers to get onto the property ladder. It's estimated that house prices have increased by a third in the last five years. The average price of a three-bedroom house in south-east England is now £255,900.

And, the weather for the weekend…

c • Either do this in pairs and then get feedback from the whole class, or do it as a whole class activity and try to reach agreement on each figure.

Extra photocopiable activities

Grammar
present perfect and past simple *p.145*
Communicative
Numbers quiz *p.176* (instructions *p.165*)

HOMEWORK

Study Link **Workbook** *pp.14–16*

2 B

G present perfect continuous
V strong adjectives: *exhausted*, *amazed*, etc.
P sentence stress, strong adjectives

Changing your life

Lesson plan

People changing their lives through travel provides the context for introducing SS to the present perfect continuous (with *for* and *since*). They listen to a woman who took a year off from teaching to learn to draw in Lebanon and they read about two other women whose lives were changed for ever by a holiday. The lexical focus is on using strong adjectives, like *furious* and *exhausted*, and the pronunciation focuses on sentence stress. At the end of the lesson SS learn a second use of the present perfect continuous to talk about recently finished actions, e.g. *What have you been doing? You look exhausted. 'I've been doing exams all day.'*

Optional lead-in (Books closed)

- Ask the class if they know any foreigners living in their country.
- Then ask how long they have lived there and how well they speak the language.
- Finally, ask if they have any problems and what they are (e.g. adapting to different customs, food, etc.).

1 LISTENING

a • Books open. Put SS in pairs and get them quickly to discuss the three questions before getting some feedback from the whole class.

b • Focus on the photos and get SS to read the four lines about Karen. Elicit / explain that *took a year off* = stopped working for a year. Then get SS to say what they can see in each photo.

c • 2.6 Tell SS that they are going to listen to Karen talking about her life in Beirut. Before SS listen focus on questions 1–7 and make sure SS understand them (Belly dancing is a kind of Middle Eastern dance where women move their stomach and hips around).

• Focus on the questions. Then play the tape / CD once but tell SS just to listen.

d • Give SS a few minutes to compare with a partner what they have understood so far. Then play the tape / CD again for them to try and understand more details. Play all (or part of) the recording again if necessary. Check answers.

1 Because she and her husband (Mike) have always loved Arab culture and language.
2 She wanted a break from teaching / a change and she wanted to learn to draw (properly).
3 A fantastic art teacher, who speaks English.
4 Because of the pronunciation. / It takes a long time to learn to read and write.
5 For about six years.
6 They are happy that she loves Arabic music and understands something about their culture.
7 The people – the hospitality is amazing.

Extra support

If there's time, you could play the tape / CD again while SS read the tapescript on *p.123* so they can see what they understood / didn't understand. Translate / explain any new words or phrases.

2.6 CD1 Track 26

(tapescript in Student's Book on *p.123*)

I = Interviewer, K = Karen

I So, how long have you been living here?
K For about six months now.
I Why did you choose Beirut?
K Because, Mike – my husband – and I have always loved Arab culture and the language. Mike's an English teacher and he got a job here in a language school.
I Why did you want to take a year off?
K Basically I wanted a break from teaching. I love teaching children but I needed a change. Also I've been drawing and painting since I was little but I've never really had the chance to *study* drawing. So this seemed like the perfect opportunity to have a change and learn to draw properly.
I What have you been doing here since you arrived?
K Well, I found a fantastic art teacher, called Omayma and I've been having classes with her since October. She's great and she speaks English, which is lucky because I don't know much Arabic yet. But I am learning the language as quickly as I can.
I Is Arabic a difficult language to learn?
K Incredibly difficult! Especially the pronunciation. You have to learn to make a lot of new sounds. Also it takes a long time to learn to read and write in Arabic.
I You also teach belly dancing here?
K That's right.
I How did that happen?
K Well, I've been teaching belly dancing for about six years, and I love it so I wanted to continue doing it here. A lot of Lebanese women don't know how to belly dance and they want to learn. I give classes here in my living room. We have a lot of fun!
I Are your students surprised that an English person is teaching them belly dancing?
K Yes, very, but they're also really happy to find that a foreigner loves Arabic music and understands something from their culture.
I What's the best thing about living in Lebanon so far?
K The people! The hospitality of the people here is absolutely amazing.

2 GRAMMAR present perfect continuous with *for / since*

a • 2.7 Focus on the task and play the extracts from the interview with Karen twice. Check answers.

1 living 2 drawing and painting 3 doing
4 having 5 teaching

2.7 CD1 Track 27

1 How long have you been living here?
2 I've been drawing and painting since I was little.
3 What have you been doing here since you arrived?
4 I've been having classes with her since October.
5 I've been teaching belly dancing for about six years.

b • Get SS to look at sentences 1–5 and answer the three questions. You could do this as a whole class activity. Check answers.

1 action verbs
2 continuous / repeated actions
3 one which is still happening

c • Tell SS to go to **Grammar Bank 2B** on *p.132*. Go through the examples and rules for Present perfect continuous *for unfinished actions.* (NOT recent continuous actions). The second half of the grammar will be dealt with in the second part of the lesson.

Grammar notes

Present perfect continuous (with *How long...?* and *for / since*)

- For many SS, including those who used *English File Pre-intermediate*, this will be the first time they have seen the present perfect continuous.
- Point out to SS that in the same way that there is a 'simple' and 'continuous' form of the present and the past, there are also two forms of the present perfect (simple and continuous).
- The most important difference between the two forms for SS at this point is that with *How long…?* and *for / since* we normally use the continuous form with action verbs (e.g. *learn, go, play, do, wait*, etc.) and the simple form is used with non-action verbs (e.g. *be, have, know*).

⚠ Two common verbs which can be used in either tense are *live* and *work*.

- Some typical mistakes:
  – getting the form wrong, e.g. forgetting to include *been* ~~*How long have you learning English?*~~
  – depending on their L1, some SS may try to use the present tense instead of the present perfect continuous, e.g. ~~*I am learning English for a long time.*~~
  – using the continuous form of the present perfect with non-action verbs, e.g. ~~*I've been knowing my best friend for fifteen years.*~~
  – confusing *for* and *since*.

- Elicit that *'ve* = have and *'s* = has.
- Now get SS to do exercise **a** only on *p.133* (not **b**, which they will do later in the lesson) individually or in pairs. They will need to write the sentences in a notebook. Then check answers.

a 1 How long have they been going out together?
2 I've been studying English for two years.
3 He hasn't been feeling very well recently.
4 You've been reading that book for months!
5 Have you been waiting (for) a long time?
6 We haven't been spending much time together.
7 How long has she been living there?
8 I've been renting this flat for three years.
9 The lift hasn't been working since 10 o'clock.
10 Has she been working here (for) a long time?

- Tell SS to go back to the main lesson on *p.25*.

3 PRONUNCIATION sentence stress

Focus on the information box which reminds SS about this basic rule regarding stress patterns in English.

Pronunciation notes

As SS should already know, in English, words which are stressed more strongly are the ones which carry information, e.g. I WENT to the CINEMA on FRIDAY NIGHT. These are typically verbs, nouns, adjectives, and adverbs. The other 'non information' words (e.g. personal pronouns, articles and little words like *to, of, on, as*, etc.) are pronounced less strongly and these words often get shortened when we speak, e.g. *the* becomes /ðə/. It is this mixture of stressed and unstressed words which gives English its rhythm and SS need plenty of practice until correct stress and rhythm becomes instinctive.

a • 2.8 Tell SS that they are going to hear a dictation of five present perfect continuous sentences. The first time they listen they should try to write down any words they hear (these will probably be the stressed information words). Then they look at the words they have and try to remember or guess what the complete sentence is. The second time they listen, they try to fill in any gaps they have. These will probably be unstressed words. Play the tape / CD again if necessary. Check answers and write the sentences on the board.

2.8 CD1 Track 28

1 I've been learning English for six years.
2 Have they been living in Brazil for a long time?
3 How long has your brother been working for Microsoft?
4 How long have you been teaching Spanish?
5 My husband hasn't been sleeping very well recently.

b • 2.9 Play the tape / CD for SS to listen and repeat, copying the rhythm. Encourage them to pronounce the stressed (underlined) words more strongly and not to stress the other words. Remind SS that unstressed words are often contracted, e.g. *been* becomes /bɪn/ and *for* becomes /fə/.

2.9 CD1 Track 29

1 I've been living here for two years.
2 How long have you been learning English?
3 She's been working in Italy since October.
4 How long have you been waiting?
5 It's been raining all night.
6 We've been looking for a flat for ages.

4 SPEAKING

In this speaking activity, SS practise using both the present perfect simple and continuous.

a • Focus on the instructions and give SS time to write true information (e.g. *judo* in the first circle) in as many of the circles as they can. Go round the class making sure they have completed at least six of the circles.

b • Focus on the instructions and the ⚠ box. Emphasize that they should make the *How long…?* questions using the bold verbs. With an action verb, e.g. *play, do,* etc., they should use the present perfect continuous. With non-action verbs, they should use the present perfect simple, e.g. *How long have you known your best friend?* NOT ~~*How long have you been knowing...*~~

• Remind SS that with the verb *live* you can use either of the present perfect forms.

Extra support

Go through the circles before you start and elicit whether the verbs are action or non-action and the question that SS should ask in each case. You could demonstrate the activity yourself by copying a couple of circles on the board (one with an action verb, the other with a non-action verb) and writing something true in them. Then the class could ask you three questions about each one.

• Put SS in pairs. Focus on the speech bubbles. SS now compare their information and take it in turns to choose one of their partner's circles and ask him / her about the information in it. Remind them that one question must be *How long…?*

• Monitor and help or take part yourself if there is an odd number of SS.

• Bring the activity to a close before it starts running down. If there's time, get feedback from one person in each pair about an interesting piece of information about their partner.

5 READING

a • Focus on the question and elicit ideas, e.g. A holiday could relax you and make you feel happier / you could meet someone who becomes a good friend or even your partner / a holiday could make you decide to go and live in the place where you had the holiday, etc.

b • Focus on the task and go through the instructions. Then either read the introduction out loud or get SS to read it.

• Put SS in pairs, **A** and **B**. Set a time limit for SS to read their text (e.g. three or four minutes). Tell them not to worry about unknown words at this stage.

c • SS now take it in turns to tell their partner about the woman in their text using the four questions as a guide. Monitor and help SS.

Victoria
1 She's working at Monkey World (which looks after apes which have been ill-treated).
2 She was working as a manager in *Next*, a chain store.
3 She went on a working holiday to Borneo. She worked with apes and enjoyed it. When she came back she found it difficult to return to her old life. She decided go back to university to study biology.
4 She's really happy now. She feels that she's doing something important, not wasting her life.

Sally
1 She's living on the Greek island of Lipsi.
2 She was living in London, working for *American Express*. She had a good salary and social life but she didn't enjoy getting up early or the bad weather.
3 She went on holiday to Lipsi, a Greek island, with a friend and loved it – the people, the weather, the food, the mountains. She decided to apply for a job with the travel company who organized her holiday. She got a job as a tourist guide on the island.
4 She's very happy there. She can't imagine living in London again.

d • SS now read each other's texts.

Extra support

You could check SS' general understanding of both texts by asking individual SS the questions in **c**, first about Victoria, then about Sally.

e • Focus on the task. Still in pairs, SS look at each highlighted word in turn and try to guess its meaning. Then they match it to its dictionary definition. Check answers and model and drill pronunciation where necessary, e.g. *applied* /əˈplaɪd/, *tiny* /ˈtaɪni/.

1 trivial	6 the tube
2 mad	7 delicious
3 keeper	8 applied for
4 apes	9 blazing
5 ill-treated	10 tiny

f • Ask these two questions to the whole class and elicit opinions.

6 VOCABULARY & PRONUNCIATION

strong adjectives

a • Focus on the column headings and the two examples from the reading texts (1 and 2). *Tiny* and *delicious* are examples of 'strong' adjectives, i.e. adjectives which are used instead of using *very* + a normal adjective. Strong adjectives are more expressive than normal adjectives and are often used especially in conversation. Emphasize that you can't use *very* with these adjectives (although you can use *really* or *absolutely*).

• Give SS time to read the sentences which all contain a strong adjective. From the context or their previous knowledge, SS should be able to write synonyms for each one by writing the normal adjective. SS could work in pairs or they could compare answers when they finish.

- Check answers and model and drill pronunciation where necessary.

3 angry	8 big
4 afraid / frightened / scared	9 cold
5 tired	10 dirty
6 hot	11 good
7 hungry	12 bad

b • SS now cover exercise **a** and from memory complete the responses with a strong adjective.

c • 2.10 Play the tape / CD for SS to check their answers and ask SS to tell you how the strong adjectives are stressed (they are stressed strongly).

2 furious 3 tiny 4 exhausted 5 filthy 6 terrified

2.10 CD1 Track 30

1 **A** Are you hungry?
B Yes, I'm starving.
2 **A** Was your mother angry?
B Yes, she was furious.
3 **A** Is her flat small?
B Yes, it's tiny.
4 **A** Are you tired?
B Yes, I'm exhausted.
5 **A** Is the floor dirty?
B Yes, it's filthy.
6 **A** Are you afraid of spiders?
B Yes, I'm terrified of them.

- Play the tape / CD again pausing after each exchange for SS to repeat the questions and responses. Encourage SS to copy the strong stress on the strong adjectives.

d • Sit SS in pairs, **A** and **B**, preferably face to face. Tell them to go to **Communication** *Are you hungry? Yes, I'm starving!* **A** on *p.116*, **B** on *p.119*.
- Give SS a few moments to read their instructions and then demonstrate the activity with a student **B** (you take the part of student **A**).
- Point out that when a pair has finished the activity they should repeat it, this time trying to respond as quickly as possible and trying to stress the strong adjective strongly.
- Tell SS to go back to the main lesson on *p.27*.

7 GRAMMAR present perfect continuous (for recent continuous actions)

a • Get SS to look at the pictures. Ask them the two questions and elicit answers, e.g. *The girl looks angry and the boy too. Maybe they've been arguing*, etc.

b • 2.11 Play the tape / CD for SS to check their ideas and to complete sentences 1–3. Play the tape / CD again, stopping after each conversation. Check answers.

1 Sharon and Kenny **have been arguing**.
2 The man **has been reading by the pool** (without any suncream on).
3 The man and woman **have been sightseeing** and **walking all afternoon.**

2.11 CD1 Track 31

(tapescript in Student's Book on *p.123*)

1 **A** Hello?
B Hi Sharon. It's me... Kylie.
A Oh. Hi Kylie.
B Hey, you sound awful – what's been happening?
A Oh, nothing. Well, OK... Kenny and I have been arguing.
B What about? What's he been doing this time?
A He's been sending text messages to his ex-girlfriend again.
B No!
A I knew this holiday was a mistake. I shouldn't have come.
2 **A** You are so red! How long have you been sunbathing? All morning?
B I haven't been sunbathing. I've been reading.
A Yes, but in the sun! Didn't you put any suncream on?
B No.
A You'd better go and put some aftersun cream on now. You're going to feel terrible tonight…
3 **A** You two look exhausted. What have you been doing?
B We've been sightseeing in the town. We've been walking all afternoon.
C Yes, my feet are killing me.
A Well, come and sit down in the bar and have a nice cup of tea.

Extra support

Ask more questions to check comprehension, e.g. *Who's Sharon talking to?* (Kylie, maybe a friend or her sister.) *What has Kevin been doing?* (Sending text messages to his ex-girlfriend.), etc.

c • Tell SS to go to **Grammar Bank 2B** on *p.132*. Go through the rules for present perfect continuous for recent continuous actions.

Grammar notes

Present perfect continuous (for recent continuous actions)

- Here SS learn another use of the present perfect continuous, to talk about recent continuous actions which have often just stopped, e.g. if you phone a friend you haven't seen for a while, the conversation might be:
What have you been doing? I haven't seen you for a couple of weeks.
I've been doing exams (= he / she has either just finished or the exams are still in progress).

- Get SS to do exercise **b** on *p.133* individually or in pairs. Check answers.

b 1 Have … been crying, 've been watching
2 's been barking
3 haven't been sleeping
4 've been shopping
5 have … been doing, 've been playing

Extra idea

Give SS more practice of the rhythm of the present perfect continuous by getting them to read the dialogues in pairs.

- Tell SS to go back to the main lesson on *p.27*.

d
- Focus on the task and give SS time to think of a possible reason why they are *exhausted*, *filthy*, etc. Emphasize that their reason must be expressed using '*I've been ______-ing*.'
- Demonstrate the activity yourself with a student. First, focus on the exchange in speech bubbles. Then get the student to choose an adjective and ask you a question. (*Hi. You look .... What have you been doing?*). Then invent an answer with the present perfect continuous, and elicit more questions (*Why?*, etc.).
- Put SS in pairs and they take turns to have mini conversations using alternate adjectives. **A** asks **B** using *exhausted* and **B** asks **A** using *filthy*, etc. When they finish, they start at the beginning again but this time **B** starts, using *exhausted*.

Extra photocopiable activities

Grammar
present perfect continuous *p.146*
Communicative
How long have you been doing it? *p.177* (instructions *p.165*)

HOMEWORK

Study Link **Workbook** *pp.17–19*

G comparatives and superlatives
V transport and travel
P stress in compound nouns

2C Race to the sun

Lesson plan

In this lesson SS revise comparative and superlative forms and learn common words and phrases connected with travel and transport. In the first half of the lesson, the context is a race from London to the South of France to see which form of transport (car, plane, or train) is the quickest, cheapest, and most comfortable. In the second half of the lesson, the topic changes to safety and SS read and listen about some research which was done to determine which activities done while driving are the most dangerous (e.g. talking on the phone, opening a packet of crisps, etc.). This leads to SS talking about various aspects of road safety, such as speed limits and drinking and driving. The pronunciation focus is on word stress in compound nouns, e.g. *traffic jam*, *rush hour*, etc.

Optional lead-in (books closed)

- Do a quick class survey by writing these three questions on the board:
  1 How do you get to class?
  2 How long does it take you?
  3 Do you normally have a good or bad journey?
- First, get SS to ask the questions to the SS sitting nearest them. Remind SS that you can say *by car / train / underground*, etc. and either *on foot*, or more usually *I walk.*
- Then find out with a show of hands which is the most popular form of transport and who has the shortest / longest journey. Also try to establish who has the best or easiest journey and who has the worst.

1 READING

a • Books open. Put SS in pairs and get them to ask each other the two questions. Get some feedback from the class about which is the most popular of the three forms of transport.

b • Focus on the title of the article and make sure SS understand *race*. Tell SS that they are going to read about a race that was organized between three passengers who travelled either by train, car, or plane from London to the South of France. Tell SS to look at the map and the photos. Explain that many people in Britain go on holiday to the South of France and that people argue about which is the best way to get there, by train, car, or plane. Tell SS that they are going to read about the journeys by plane and train and that later they will listen to the car driver's journey.

• Get SS to read the introduction to the article. Check they understand the meaning of *cut price airline* (= a cheap airline which sells tickets on the Internet) and the phrasal verb *set off* (= to start a journey) and then get SS in pairs to answer the questions. (Try to avoid SS seeing that these questions are partially answered in exercise 2 on page 29!) Elicit some opinions from the class.

c • Explain the task and give SS a moment to look at the text to find out (but not to call out!) which paragraph they think is the first one for the plane. Elicit that the answer is paragraph E.

• Now set a time limit for SS to read the two jumbled texts and put the paragraphs in order. When they think they have completed the task, they should check their answers with another student. Check answers.

The plane	The train
1 E 2 A 3 C 4 G	1 D 2 H 3 B 4 F

Extra support

You could now go through the text with the SS, reading the two journeys aloud paragraph by paragraph. After each paragraph, ask SS which words told them that it was a plane or train journey, and focus on any other words related to travel in general, which SS could highlight or underline.

Travelling in general
travel (verb) set off, suitcase, luggage, taxi, ticket, journey, seat

Plane
airport flew (fly) airline check in window seat seat numbers security gate (48) board / get on (a plane) took off (take off) land

Train
inter city railway station platform buffet car

d • Focus on the instructions and get SS to read about the two journeys again, this time in the right order and to answer the questions by writing **T** or **P** in the boxes. Set a time limit and when SS finish, get them to compare their answers with a partner's, and then check answers.

1 P 2 T 3 P 4 T 5 T 6 P 7 P 8 T 9 T 10 T

Extra idea

You could get SS to underline or highlight five words or phrases they want to remember from the text. Get them to compare their words / phrases with a partner and then get some feedback from the class.

HOW WORDS WORK...

- Focus on the examples (taken from the text) and the explanation. Point out that:
  – *How long does it take...* (+ verb)*?* is often used to ask how much time is needed to complete a particular journey, e.g. *How long does it take to get to the city centre from here? It takes half an hour. How long does it take to fly from London to New York? It takes eight hours.*
- To ask somebody about their journey add *you* to the question:
  A: *How long does it take* ***you*** *to drive to work in the morning?*

B: *It takes **me** about half an hour.*

- We often use *How long does it take?* without a second verb, e.g.

  A: *Let's go to Manchester by train.*

  B: *OK. How long does it take?*

  A: *About six hours.*
- This construction can also be used to ask about other things, not just journeys, e.g. *How long does it take to learn to speak a foreign language?*
- Focus on the task. Put SS in pairs and get them to ask and answer the two questions. Encourage them to use *It takes me...* in their answers rather than just answering with a figure.

Extra support

If you think your SS need more practice of this structure, you could write some prompts on the board, e.g. *cook pasta, boil an egg, fly to London, walk to the town centre*, etc.

2 LISTENING

a • 2.12 Tell SS that they are now going to hear about the journey of the third person, the car driver, in the race to the South of France. Look again at the photo of Martin's car on *p.28*.

⚠ If this is a different lesson from when you did exercise **1 READING**, it would be a good idea to get SS to tell you what they can remember about the people who travelled by train and plane.

- Focus on the pictures of Martin's journey and the task. Then play the tape / CD the whole way through for SS to try to number the pictures in order.

Extra idea

Alternatively, you could pause the tape after each section and elicit which picture goes with it.

1 C 2 D 3 E 4 A 5 F 6 G 7 B

b • Get SS to read through sentences 1–9 and then play the tape / CD again for SS to mark the sentences T or F. Play the recording (or part of it) again if necessary. Get them to compare their answers with a partner's and then check answers. For false sentences elicit the correct information.

1 F (There was no rush hour traffic.)
2 T
3 T
4 T
5 F (The journey takes an hour and a half.)
6 T
7 F (It's 130 km/h.)
8 T
9 F (It's 960 km.)

2.12 CD1 Track 32

(tapescript in Student's Book on *p.123*)

I set off at six. It was still dark when I put my suitcase in the car and drove off. I had a good journey through London because it was Saturday so there was no rush hour traffic. Soon I was on the M20 motorway heading towards Folkestone on the south coast. I stopped at a service station for a cup of coffee and a sandwich. I didn't buy any petrol because it's much cheaper in France.
I arrived in Folkestone at 8.10. The problem with travelling by car from England to France is that Britain is an island. There are 35 kilometres of water between England and France. You can get across it by ferry, but there's a much better and quicker way – the Channel Tunnel!

The Channel Tunnel's only a train tunnel, not a road tunnel and so you have to put your car on a train. The journey takes an hour and a half, and drivers have to sit in their cars because there are no seats on the train for passengers. I arrived at the terminal and joined the queue of cars waiting for the next train.

At 10.30 the train arrived in Calais and I drove my car off the train and onto the road – a French road. I had to remember to drive on the right, not on the left!

The traffic in Calais was quite bad. Finally I got out of Calais and onto the motorway to the South of France. The speed limit on French motorways is 130 kilometres an hour and the road was clear so now I could travel quickly. But first I stopped at a service station to fill up with petrol.

Petrol's cheaper in France than in Britain but, on the other hand, you have to pay to travel on French motorways. In Britain they're free.

It's 960 kilometres from Calais to Avignon, and the journey on the motorway was boring. I listened to my favourite music to pass the time and I stopped again for lunch. At eight o'clock I finally arrived in Avignon. I found my hotel and I was looking forward to a lovely French meal.

c • 2.13 SS listen to the last part of Martin's journey and complete the chart. Check answers, and ask SS if they guessed correctly in exercise **1a**.

By car
14 hours £200 6/10 10/10

2.13 CD1 Track 33

At eight o'clock I finally arrived in Avignon. I found my hotel and I was looking forward to a lovely French meal. It took me 14 hours to get there, and cost a total of £200. I gave the journey ten out of ten for convenience but only six for comfort. I was exhausted.

Extra support

If there's time, you could get SS to listen to the tape / CD with the tapescript on *p.123* so they can see exactly what they understood / didn't understand. Translate / explain any new words or phrases.

d • Do this as a whole class activity. Agree on a city (preferably a good distance away). Elicit the different ways of travelling there and write them on the board, e.g. by car, by coach, by train, by plane. Elicit how long the journey takes by each form of transport and discuss which way is the best / worst.

3 GRAMMAR comparatives and superlatives

a • Focus on the task. Get SS to do this in pairs or individually and then compare answers in pairs. Check answers.

1 ✗ the quickest way
2 ✓
3 ✗ as cheap...as
4 ✓
5 ✗ less expensive than
6 ✗ the most comfortable hotel
7 ✓
8 ✓

b • Tell SS to go to **Grammar Bank 2C** on *p.132*. Read the examples and go through the rules with the class.

Grammar notes

Comparatives and superlatives

- SS will almost certainly have been taught the basic rules regarding comparative and superlative forms of adjectives and adverbs so this grammar focus should be mainly revision and consolidation. SS may still mix up comparative and superlative forms, e.g. ~~*This is the older building in the town*~~, and make mistakes with the rules for forming comparatives and superlatives.
- Typical mistakes include:
  - Always using *more* and *most*, e.g. ~~*more big*~~, ~~*the most fast*~~, etc.
  - mixing up comparative and superlative forms, e.g. ~~*This is the older building in the town*~~.
  - confusing *as* and *than*, e.g. ~~*The train isn't as cheap than the bus*~~.
  - omission of the definite article, e.g. ~~*He's best player in the team*~~.
  - confusing adjectives and adverbs, e.g. ~~*You drive more quick than me*~~.

• Get SS to do the exercises on *p.133* in pairs or individually. Check answers either after each exercise or after both.

a 1 as 2 the 3 than 4 ever 5 in 6 most 7 as 8 more 9 as 10 him
b 1 hotter 2 the most competitive 3 the laziest 4 better 5 the most boring 6 earlier 7 the worst 8 the most ambitious 9 safest 10 further

• Tell SS to go back to the main lesson on *p.30*.

c • Put SS in pairs. Focus on the task and demonstrate what SS have to do.

• First, SS have to decide, e.g. which is the safest of the three forms of transport, e.g. *Travelling by car is the safest. Travelling by motorbike is safer than travelling by bike.* Then they compare them again using each of the other two adjectives.

Extra challenge

Get pairs to compare with another pair to see if they agree, and get them to defend their choices.

4 VOCABULARY transport and travel

a • All the words appeared in the reading or listening texts. Give SS a couple of minutes to put them in the right column. Check answers.

train	**car**	**plane**
buffet car	motorway	check in
platform	rush hour	gate
station	speed limit	take off

b • Tell SS to go to **Vocabulary Bank *Transport and travel*** on *p.148* and do section **1 Plane**, either individually or in pairs. Check answers and model and drill pronunciation.

1 baggage reclaim	6 land
2 check-in desk	7 take off
3 (suit) case	8 luggage
4 gate	9 aisle
5 boarding card / pass	

• Point out that *baggage* and *luggage* mean the same (i.e. bags and cases) but that *luggage* is the more common word to use, and *baggage* the more technical word (used by the air industry). *Case* and *suitcase* are equally common. You may also want to teach the verb *check in*.

• Now get SS to do section **2 Train**. Check answers. Elicit and drill the pronunciation.

• Point out that you can just use *station* instead of *railway station*. You may want to point out that the London underground is commonly known as *the tube*.

10 ticket office	13 platform
11 (railway) station	14 carriage
12 the underground	

• Tell SS to do section **3a Road**. Check answers and pronunciation.

15 coach	20 car
16 motorway	21 helmet
17 bike	22 motorbike
18 van	23 tram
19 lorry	24 scooter

• Point out that *a bus* is usually a vehicle used within a town or city and *a coach* = an intercity bus.

• SS do **3b**. They could compare their answers in pairs before you check answers.

1 petrol station	8 speed limit
2 traffic lights	9 public transport
3 seat belt	10 pedestrian area
4 rush hour	11 cycle lane
5 car crash	12 road works
6 parking fine	13 taxi rank
7 traffic jam	14 car park

• Point out that the strong stress normally falls on the first syllable in compound nouns, e.g. *seat belt.*

• Finally, tell SS do section **4 Travel**. Check answers. Elicit the pronunciation of the words and model and drill if necessary.

1 journey 2 travel 3 flight 4 trip

• SS often confuse *travel* with *journey / trip* so emphasize that *travel* is often used as a verb and never as a countable noun. You can't say ~~*a travel*~~.

⚠ *travel* does exist as an uncountable noun, e.g. *travel broadens your mind* but it may be better not to focus on this at this level so as not to confuse SS.

- Finally, focus on the instruction 'Can you remember the words on this page? Test yourself or a partner'.

Testing yourself

For **Plane, Train and Road a)** SS can cover the words and look at the pictures and try to remember the words. For **Road b)** they can cover the list and the compound nouns 1–14. They look at the clues and remember the phrases, uncovering one by one to check. For **Travel** they cover the definitions and look at the words in the list and try to remember what they mean.

Testing a partner

See **Testing a partner** *p.17*.

Study Link SS can find more practice of these words on the MultiROM and on the *New English File Intermediate* website.

- Tell SS to go back to the main lesson on *p.30*.

5 PRONUNCIATION & SPEAKING stress in compound nouns

Explain to SS that compound nouns are very common in English. A compound noun is a two-noun phrase but where the first noun functions as an adjective that describes the second noun, e.g. a bus stop, a credit card. Sometimes they are one word, e.g. sunglasses, and occasionally they are hyphenated, e.g. can-opener.

a • 2.14 Focus on the task and play the tape / CD for SS to repeat the compound nouns one by one. Afterwards ask SS which of the two words carries more stress (the first one).

2.14 CD1 Track 34

traffic lights	pedestrian area
boarding pass	road works
car park	rush hour
car crash	seat belt
cycle lane	speed camera
parking fine	speed limit
traffic jam	ticket office

b • Put SS in pairs and tell them to answer the questions, which recycle compound nouns.

- Tell SS to take it in turns to ask the questions. Monitor that SS are stressing the compound nouns correctly.
- If there's time, get some feedback from the class.

6 LISTENING & SPEAKING

a • Focus on the instructions and check that SS understand all the vocabulary, e.g. *a packet of crisps, a can of drink*, etc. Give SS a few minutes to read the article and do questions 1 and 2. Get some class feedback.

b • 2.15 Focus on the task and play the tape / CD for SS to number the activities 1–6. To add suspense, you could pause the tape just before the expert says which thing is the most dangerous, second most dangerous, etc. and elicit from the class what they think is going to be next.

- Check answers.

1 Opening a packet of crisps or a can of drink.
2 Picking up a specific CD from the passenger seat.
3 Making a call on your mobile.
4 Listening to your favourite music.
5 Talking to other passengers.
6 Listening to music you don't know.

- Find out if anyone guessed the top three correctly.

c • Now SS listen for more detail. Tell SS to read questions 1–8. Play the tape / CD again pausing where necessary to give SS time to write the answers.

- Get SS to discuss what they heard with their partner and play the tape / CD again if necessary before checking answers.

1 Concentrate 100% on controlling the car.
2 Because you need both hands to do it (and you take your hands off the wheel for a second or two).
3 They take their eyes off the road for one or two seconds.
4 Their control of the car.
5 More quickly and less safely.
6 They drive more aggressively.
7 They don't pay (enough) attention to what is happening on the road.
8 Because it doesn't distract you as much.

- Finally, ask SS if any of the results surprised them.

2.15 CD1 Track 35

(tapescript in Student's Book on *p.124*)

T = TV host, E = Expert

T And this evening on *Behind the wheel* we talk to Brian Delaney, who's an expert on road safety. Brian, you did some tests to find out how dangerous it is to do other things when we're driving. According to your tests, what's the most dangerous thing to do?

E Well, the first thing I have to say is that doing any other things when you're driving is dangerous and can cause an accident. Because when you're driving you should concentrate 100% on controlling the car and anything else you do is a distraction.
The tests we did in a simulator showed that the most difficult and most dangerous thing is to try and open a packet of crisps or to open a can of drink. The reason is that most people actually need two hands to open a packet of crisps or a can of drink so they take both hands off the wheel for a second or two. And, of course, that's the most dangerous thing you can possibly do. In fact, one of the drivers in the simulator actually crashed when he did this.

T And which is the next most dangerous?

E The next most dangerous thing is to select a specific CD from the passenger seat. This is extremely dangerous too because to do this you have to take your eyes off the road for one or two seconds.

T And number three?

E Number three was making a phone call on a mobile. What we found in the tests was that drivers drove more slowly when they did this, but that their control of the car got worse.

T Yes, I can believe that. And number 4?

E Number four was listening to our favourite music. In the tests most drivers drove more quickly and less safely when they were listening to music they already knew. If the music was fast and heavy, some drivers even drove more aggressively.

T So no heavy metal when you're driving.

E Absolutely not.
T And in fifth place?
E In fifth place was talking to other passengers. The problem when we talk to other people in the car is that we pay too much attention to what we're saying or what we're hearing and not enough attention to what's happening on the road.
T So the least dangerous is listening to music you *don't* know.
E That's right. The least dangerous of all these activities is listening to unfamiliar music on the radio or on a CD player. It seems that if we *don't know* the music then we're less distracted by it. In this part of the tests, all drivers drove safely and well.

Extra support

If there's time, you could get SS to listen again with the tapescript on *p.124* so they can see exactly what they understood / didn't understand. Translate / explain any new words or phrases.

d • Give SS time to read the statements to decide if they agree or disagree with them and to think of their reasons.

e • Put SS into small groups of three or four. Appoint a group secretary, whose job it is to read out the sentence and then invite opinions from the other SS as well as giving his / her own opinion. The secretary should also note down how many people agreed or disagreed with each statement.

Extra support

Remind SS of expressions of agreement and disagreement (see *p.7*) by eliciting them and writing them on the board.

• Get feedback to find out if there was a general consensus of agreement or disagreement on each statement.

Study Link SS can find a dictation and a Grammar quiz on all the grammar from File 2 on the MultiROM and more grammar activities on the *New English File Intermediate* website.

Extra photocopiable activities

Grammar
comparatives and superlatives *p.147*
Communicative
Questionnaire *p.178* (instructions *p.166*)
Vocabulary
Split crossword *p.198* (instructions *p.195*)

HOMEWORK

Study Link **Workbook** *pp.20–22*

2 PRACTICAL ENGLISH IN THE OFFICE

Function Making requests, asking permission
Language *Could you...?, Would you mind...?, Is it OK if...?,* etc.

Lesson plan

In the first part of the lesson SS revise and extend ways of asking people politely to do things and asking permission. This language is presented through a series of exchanges between people in the office. In the second part of the lesson (**Social English**) Mark has a drink after work with Ben and Nicole.

Study Link These lessons are on the *New English File Intermediate* Video / DVD, which can be used instead of the Class Cassette / CD (see introduction *p.9*). The main functional section of each episode is also on the MultiROM with additional activities.

Optional lead-in (books closed)

- Revise what happened in the previous episode by eliciting the story from SS, e.g. *Who works in the MTC Paris office? What are their jobs? What happened when Mark arrived in the Paris office?*
  What did Mark and Allie talk about when they went for a walk in the evening? Do the people in the office know about their relationship? Do they want to keep it a secret?
- Also try to elicit the phrases they revised / learnt in the first episode for introducing people, e.g. *Let me introduce you to the team.* You could write these with gaps on the board to help SS remember.
- If you are using the video / DVD, you could play the previous episode again, leaving out the 'Listen and Repeat' sections.

REQUESTS AND PERMISSION

a • **2.16** Tell SS to cover the dialogue with their hand or a piece of paper (or write the questions on the board and get SS to close their books). Focus on the photo and the three questions.
• Play the tape / CD once the whole way through. Then play it again, pausing after the answer to each question to give SS time to answer. Check answers. Remind SS that *time off* = time when you don't have to work.

1 To send him the concert dates.
2 To help him (open a computer document).
3 If she can have tomorrow afternoon off.

b • Now get SS to look at the dialogue. In pairs, they read it and see if they can guess or remember the missing words. Emphasize that they shouldn't write the words in the dialogue but in pencil alongside or on a separate sheet of paper.

c • Play the tape / CD again for them to check. Then go through the dialogue line by line and check answers. Find out if SS had guessed the words correctly. Where they had not guessed correçtly, see if their alternative also fits.

> 2.16 CD1 Track 36
>
> **J = Jacques, M = Mark, B = Ben, A = Allie, N = Nicole**
>
> J Mark? Would you mind **sending** me those concert dates?
> M Of **course** not. Ben, are you busy?
> B Me? Never.
> M **Could** you help me? I can't open this document.
> B **Sure**.
> M Thanks.
> A Hi, Nicole.
> N Could you sign these, please?
> A Sure.
> N Is it **OK** if I take tomorrow afternoon off?
> A I'm **sorry**, but tomorrow's really difficult.
> N What about Friday afternoon?
> A Friday? That's fine. Do you **think** you could **send** me the request by email?
> N Er, yes, of **course**.
> A Hello. Hi, Mark...Could you hold a moment, Mark? Thank you, Nicole. **Can** you come and see me when you have a moment?

d • 2.17 Now focus on the key phrases highlighted in the dialogue. Play the tape / CD pausing after the beep for SS to repeat. Encourage them to copy the rhythm and intonation.

> 2.17 CD1 Track 37
>
> **J = Jacques, M = Mark, B = Ben, A = Allie, N = Nicole**
>
> J Would you mind sending me those concert date?
> M Of course not.
> M Could you help me?
> B Sure.
> N Is it OK if I take tomorrow afternoon off?
> A I'm sorry, but tomorrow's really difficult.
> A Do you think you could send me the request by email?
> N Yes, of course.
> A Can you come and see me when you have a moment?

e • Focus on the chart and the task and give SS time to complete the chart. Get them to do this in pairs or individually and then compare answers in pairs. Check answers.

Request	**Response**
Would you mind (sending me those concert dates)?	Of course not.
Could you (help me)? Do you think you could (send me the request by email)? Can you (come and see me when you have a moment)?	Sure. Yes, of course.
Permission	
Is it OK if (I take tomorrow afternoon off)?	I'm sorry but...

- Point out that:
  - The expression you use in a given situation often depends on, e.g. how big a favour you are asking or how well you know the person you are talking to.
  - You can also use *Can / Could / May I* to ask for permission, e.g. *May I use your phone?*
  - The verb after *Would you mind ...* must be the *-ing* form. This phrase requires a negative answer, e.g. *(No,) of course **not*** if you agree to the request.
  - Apart from *of course not*, the other responses can be used for all requests / permissions.

f • Tell SS to go to **Communication** *Requests* on *p.119* and focus on the task. Demonstrate if necessary. Set a time limit then get SS to move around the room and talk to as many SS as they can.
- At the end you could find out who got the most SS to help him / her.

SOCIAL ENGLISH Office gossip

a • 2.18 Focus first on the title and elicit / explain the meaning of *office gossip* (= talking about other people at work and their personal lives). Then focus on the photo and the task. Play the tape / CD once for SS to answer the question. Elicit answers.

Extra support

You might want to remind SS that *apartment* in American English is *flat* in British English.

> Ben, Jacques, Isabelle (Jacques's wife) and Allie.

> 2.18 CD1 Track 38
>
> (tapescript in Student's Book on *p.124*)
>
> **M = Mark, B = Ben, A = Allie, N = Nicole**
>
> N Have you started looking for an apartment?
> M No, I haven't had time yet.
> B Anyway, it's best to get to know Paris first.
> M Yeah – it's a big city.
> N Merçi.
> B Merçi.
> M Merçi beaucoup.
> N Very good, Mark!
> M Thanks. That's nearly all the French I know!
> B Hi, Beatrice. ... Yeah ... just a minute. Sorry.
> N How do you like the office?
> M Oh, it's great.
> N And the people?
> M Really friendly! I like Ben a lot. He's amazing with computers. And Jacques's a really nice guy!
> N Oh, Jacques, he's very charming. Everybody likes him. And he has a lovely wife. She used to be a pop star when she was young. Have you heard of Isabelle?
> M No, I'm sorry, I haven't.
> N She's very pretty. Allie is very attractive, too.
> M Allie? Yeah, I guess.
> N Although her clothes are very English. And she's very formal. You know, today, I asked if I could have a day off, and she wanted me to send her an email!
> M Well, the English have their funny ways.
> N Oh yeah. Oh, hello, Allie.
> A Hi.
> M Allie! Hi, let me get you a drink.
> A Thanks. I'll have a Diet Coke.

b • Focus on sentences 1–6 and go through them quickly. Then play the tape / CD for SS to mark them T or F. Play the recording again if necessary. Check answers getting SS to correct the false sentences.

> **1** T
> **2** T
> **3** F (She was a pop singer.)
> **4** F (She thinks her clothes are 'very English'.)
> **5** F (She says Allie is very formal.)
> **6** T

Extra support

If there's time, you could get SS to listen to the tape / CD with the tapescript on *p.124* so they can see exactly what they understood / didn't understand. Translate / explain any new words or phrases.

c • 2.19 Now focus on the **USEFUL PHRASES**. Give SS a moment to try to complete them, and then play the tape / CD to check.

2.19 CD1 Track 39

M = Mark, B = Ben, A = Allie, N = Nicole
N Have you started **looking** for an apartment?
M I haven't had time **yet**.
B **Just** a minute.
N **How** do you like the office?
N Have you **heard** of Isabelle?
M **Let** me get you a drink.
A Thanks. I'll **have** a Diet Coke.

Extra idea

Ask SS if they can remember who said each phrase (and in what context), e.g. *Ben says 'Just a minute'* (when his phone rings).

d • Play the tape / CD again, pausing for SS to repeat. In a monolingual class, you could elicit the equivalent expressions in SS' L1.

HOMEWORK

Study Link Workbook *p.23*

2 WRITING TELLING A STORY

Lesson plan

This second writing lesson focuses on using the past tenses practised in **File 1** to tell a story, and also on using common connecting expressions such as *so*, *because*, and *although*. The vocabulary from lesson **2C (Travel and transport)** is also recycled here. There is also a 'mini focus' on finding and correcting mistakes.

We suggest that you do exercises **a–c** in class, but set the actual writing (the last activity) for homework. If there's time, you may also want to do the planning in class.

a • Focus on the magazine article and tell the SS to read the story once without worrying about the mistakes or the gaps. Then ask them if the people caught their flight in the end (they did).

• Put SS in pairs and set a time limit. Tell them to read the article again and correct the six underlined mistakes. Check answers. Elicit that *felt* is the past of *feel*, not *fall* which is the verb here.

~~leaved~~ **left**	we ~~was~~ **were**
didn't ~~knew~~ **know**	we couldn't ~~to~~ check in **couldn't check in**
to ~~found~~ **find**	~~felt~~ over **fell**

b • Get SS in the same pairs to read the text again and complete the gaps with words from the list. Check answers.

1 when	**4** After	**7** so
2 but	**5** but	**8** Although
3 so	**6** because	**9** in the end

c • Focus on the **Useful language** box and make sure SS understand all the phrases. Then give them a few moments to decide if they refer to a car or plane journey. Check answers.

the flight was delayed P	there was a traffic jam C
you broke down C	you got a puncture C
you got lost C	you forgot your passport P
you missed your flight P	your flight was overbooked P

WRITE about a nightmare journey

Go through the instructions. Then either get SS to plan and write their story in class (set a time limit of 20 minutes) or get them to plan their story in class and write at home, or set both the planning and writing for homework.

If SS do the writing in class, get them to swap their stories with another student to read and check for mistakes before you collect them all in.

2 Revise & Check

For instructions on how to use these pages, see *p.32*.

GRAMMAR

a 1 already 2 long 3 Since 4 Have 5 yet
b 1 been working 2 just made
3 more expensive 4 carefully as 5 the most

VOCABULARY

a 1 bank (It's a place. The others are forms of payment.)
2 mortgage (It's a noun. The others are all verbs.)
3 hungry (The other adjectives are all 'strong' adjectives.)
4 awful (It has a negative meaning. The other three have a positive meaning.)
5 travel (It's a verb. The other words are nouns.)
6 helmet (You wear it. The other three are vehicles.)
7 railway station (It's related to rail travel. The other words are all related to road travel.)
b 1 filthy 2 tax 3 rush hour 4 lend 5 platform
6 inherit 7 boarding pass / card 8 tiny
c 1 off 2 out 3 for 4 back 5 by

PRONUNCIATION

a 1 coach (It's /əʊ/) 4 cycle (It's /s/)
2 tiny (It's /aɪ/) 5 earn (It's /ɜː/)
3 charge (It's /tʃ/)
b inv<u>e</u>st, sec<u>u</u>rity, l<u>u</u>ggage, ped<u>e</u>strian, t<u>e</u>rrified

CAN YOU UNDERSTAND THIS TEXT?

a 1 a 2 b 3 c 4 a 5 b
b **fortunate** = lucky
charity = an organization which collects money to help people who are poor, sick, etc.
volunteer = somebody who offers or agrees to do something without being forced or paid
orphanage = an institution where children without parents live and are looked after
deposit = a percentage of the price of something you are buying which you pay in advance
annoyed = made angry
adopted = taken by a family and looked after as if they were their own children
useful = having a practical use
definitely = certainly, without doubt

CAN YOU UNDERSTAND THESE PEOPLE?

a 1 b 2 c 3 b 4 c 5 a

b 1 £7,500 2 Three years 3 £261. 45 4 8½%
5 22nd March

2.20 CD1 Track 40

1 A What's the matter?
B I can't find my credit card. I must have dropped it somewhere.
A Well, think. When did you use it last?
B I bought some petrol on the way to work…Did I pay for lunch with the card? No, I paid cash. Oh, and this morning I went to the florist's. I got some flowers for Sally's birthday.
A Well, phone the shop then. Someone might have picked it up.

2 A How long have you been teaching?
B Well, I've been working here since last October, so that's a year and a half. And I taught for two years before that.
A Where was that?
B A school in Slovenia.
A Oh, that must have been nice.
B Yes, it was lovely.

3 Last night's heavy snow has made most main roads impassable.
At present, trains are still running normally but airports are closed, so it's definitely not a good day to be travelling. Business news now.
Wall Street closed 3 points down after yesterday's gains…

4 A Who are you flying to Munich with?
B We *were* going to fly with British Airways but then we saw these really cheap tickets with Euroflight on the Internet.
A I thought Anglo Air were the cheapest.
B They are, but we were too late. The flight was full.

5 A Why does your brother rent his flat? Why doesn't he buy one?
B He can't afford it.
A Yeah, but paying rent's just a waste of money. If you can afford to pay rent, you can afford to pay a mortgage.
B Yeah, but he's only got a temporary contract and his wife's unemployed at the moment.

2.21 CD1 Track 41

A Good morning, Ms Stevens. Do have a seat.
B Thank you.
A Now I understand you want a small loan.
B Yes, that's right. I want to buy a new car.
A What sort of amount were you looking for?
B I think I'm going to need about seven thousand five hundred pounds.
A OK and over what period of time do you want this loan?
B Three years.
A Well, over three years the monthly payments would be two hundred and sixty-one pounds and forty-five pence.
B So what's your interest rate at the moment?
A It's eight and a half percent.
B And might that change?
A No, that would be fixed for the period of the loan.
B OK.
A And when would you like the money?
B As soon as possible.
A By the end of next week?
B OK. And when will I start the repayments?
A Your first one will be on the 22nd March.
B Fine.
A OK. Well, I'll draw up the loan agreement and you'll receive that in the post in a couple of days.

Extra photocopiable activities

Quicktest 2 *p.217*

3 A

G *must, have to, should* (obligation)
V mobile phones
P sentence stress

Modern manners

File 3 overview

The grammatical focus of this File is on modal verbs. **3A** deals with modal verbs of obligation, **3B** looks at modal verbs of deduction or certainty (*must (be), may / might (be)* and *can't (be)*), and **3C** presents *can, could,* and *be able to* to express ability and possibility. By the end of the File, SS should have a clear understanding of how the common modal verbs work in English and when and how to use them.

Lesson plan

This lesson focuses on modern manners, which provides a context for SS to distinguish between different common ways of expressing obligation: *must / have to* and *should.* SS will have met these verbs separately, but will probably not have contrasted them before, and in this lesson the difference between a modal verb (*must, should*) and a normal verb (*have to*) is made clear. The vocabulary focus is on words and expressions related to phoning, and in pronunciation SS practise sentence rhythm.

Optional lead-in (books closed)

Do a quick survey to find how many students in the class are carrying a mobile phone. Then find out which make is the most popular. Take the opportunity to make sure everybody's mobile is switched off!

1 VOCABULARY & SPEAKING mobile phones

a • Books open. Focus on the instructions, and get SS to match in pairs. Check answers.

1 e 2 g (In German nouns always have a capital letter.) 3 b 4 a 5 f 6 d 7 c

• Ask the class which names they like most / least. You could get a show of hands for this.

b • **3.1** Now focus on the instructions and sentences A–G. Give SS a few moments to go through them in pairs and say what they think the bold words mean. Clarify the meaning of any words or phrases they don't know.

• Now play the tape / CD. Pause after the first sound effect, and elicit that the sounds they are hearing are different ring tones, so the answer is D. Now continue playing the tape / CD to the end and give SS time to compare answers. Play again if necessary and check answers.

Extra support

Alternatively, you could pause the tape / CD after each sound effect and let SS, in pairs, choose the right sentence.

1 D 2 C 3 G 4 F 5 A 6 E 7 B

3.1 CD1 Track 42

1 *Several different ring tones*
2 'Goodbye.'
3 *Engaged tone*
4 Jack Please leave a message after the tone.
Sandra Hi Jack, it's Sandra. I was just calling…
5 *Dialling tone and ring tone*
6 James Oh, hi. It's James. I phoned half an hour ago but Ann wasn't in. Is she there now?
7 *Texting*

• Get SS to close their books and play the tape / CD again. Pause after each sound effect and get the class (or individual SS) to say the sentences.

c • Focus on the questionnaire and go through the questions with SS. If you didn't do the lead-in, check that they understand *make* (e.g. *Nokia*, etc.), *hands free, switch off, speed dialling* (= when you programme numbers in the phone's memory so that you can dial just by pressing one number).

⚠ If there are SS in the class who don't have mobiles, get them to work in a group of three with two other SS and ask the questions.

Extra idea

Get SS to ask you the questions first (unless you don't have a mobile, in which case explain why).

2 GRAMMAR *must, have to, should* (obligation)

a • Focus on the picture of the man talking loudly on a mobile phone in a bus. In pairs, get SS to answer the questions together.

• Quickly check answers from SS but don't discuss question 3 too long as SS will be talking about bad mobile phone habits in **c**.

b • **3.2** Focus on the task and questions and quickly go through them. If necessary, explain / translate *complain* and *social occasions* and any other words SS don't understand.

• Play the tape / CD once pausing after each extract for SS to do the task.

• Check answers.

1 E 2 B 3 D 4 C 5 A

3.2 CD1 Track 43

(tapescript in Student's Book on *p.124*)

1 I'm a shop assistant and I work in a clothes shop and what really makes me angry is when I'm serving somebody and suddenly their mobile rings and they answer the phone and start having a conversation. It's really annoying. I think that if you're in a shop and talking to a shop assistant, then you shouldn't answer the phone.

2 What most annoys me is people who use their phones on a plane. I mean everybody knows that you have to switch off your mobile on a plane and that you mustn't use it until you get off the plane. But some people switch on their phones the moment the plane lands and they start making calls. Why can't they wait another fifteen minutes?

3 I hate it when people talk very loudly on their mobile phone in a public place. The other day I was in the waiting room at the doctor's and there was a man there whose mobile rang about every two minutes and we all had to listen to him talking loudly to his wife, then to his boss, then to a garage mechanic… I think that if you're in a public place and someone calls you, you should talk really quietly or go somewhere else. And you don't have to shout – the other person can hear you perfectly well.

4 What really annoys me are people who use their phones a lot when they're with other people – like when you're out having a drink or a meal with someone and they spend the whole time talking on their mobiles or texting other people to arrange what they're doing the next day. I think it's really rude.

5 I hate people who use their mobiles in the car, even if they're hands free. Whenever you see someone driving badly, nine times out of ten they're on the phone.

c • Focus on the instructions and get SS, in pairs or individually, to match 1–5 with A–E and then compare with a partner. Make sure SS understand *rule*, *law*, and *allowed* / *permitted*. Check answers.

1 D 2 C 3 B 4 A 5 E

• Finally, ask the class which of these things annoys them the most.

d • Tell SS to go to **Grammar Bank 3A** on *p.134*. Go through the examples and read the rules with the class. Model and drill pronunciation where necessary.

Extra idea

In a monolingual class, you could get SS to translate the example sentences and compare the forms / verbs they would use in their L1.

Grammar notes

Obligation and necessity: *have to* and *must*

- *have to* / *must* and *should* / *shouldn't* were taught separately in *New English File Pre-intermediate*.
  In this lesson they are revised and contrasted in more detail.
- Some typical mistakes are:
  – saying *must to*, e.g. ~~*I must to be on time tomorrow*~~.
  – confusing *mustn't* (prohibition) and *don't have to* (not necessary / not obligatory).
  – using *must* to talk about rules and laws (external obligation). *have to* is more common here.
  – using *must* (not *had to*) in the past tense, e.g. ~~*I must study last night*~~.

Advice or opinion: *should* / *shouldn't*

- The important point to emphasize here is that *should* isn't as strong as *have to* / *must* and it is normally used to express a personal opinion or give advice.
- Compare:
  You should talk to your teacher about the problem (= I think it's a good idea).
  You must talk to your teacher about the problem (= I think it's very important you do this).

• Focus on the exercises on *p.135* and get SS to do them individually or in pairs. Check answers either after each exercise or after they have done both.

a 1	don't have to	5	had to
2	must	6	Did you have to
3	didn't have to	7	shouldn't
4	Do you have to	8	mustn't
b 1	shouldn't go	4	should talk
2	they have to	5	mustn't go / drive
3	don't have to		

• Tell SS to go back to the main lesson on *p.37*.

3 PRONUNCIATION & SPEAKING sentence stress

a • 3.3 Focus on the sentences. Play the tape / CD and pause for SS to repeat, copying the rhythm.

3.3 CD1 Track 44

1 You mustn't use your phone on a plane.
2 I don't have to go to work tomorrow.
3 We have to do an exam in June.
4 You should switch off your mobile in class.
5 You shouldn't talk loudly on a mobile phone.
6 I must go to the bank this morning.

• Point out that:
  – in (+) sentences *should* is not usually stressed and is pronounced /ʃəd/.
  – the negative forms *mustn't*, *don't have*, and *shouldn't* are always stressed.
• Remind SS:
  – of the silent *l* in *should* /ʃʊd/ and the silent *t* in *mustn't* /mʌsnt/.
  – the weak form of *to* in *have to* /tə/.
  – *must* can have either a strong or weak pronunciation. It normally has a weak pronunciation unless we want to give special emphasis. Compare:
    1 I must go to the bank this morning. (= It is something I need to do.)
    2 I must go to the bank this morning. (= It is very important I do this.)

b • Focus on the definition of manners. Get SS to read it and make sure they understand it. In a monolingual class you could elicit a translation in their L1.
• Now focus on the instructions and the first sentence in **Manners or the law?** Ask SS if there is a law about not playing noisy games on a mobile in public, and elicit that there isn't. It is just good manners, so they have to mark this sentence M.
• Get SS in pairs to mark the rest of the sentences M or L. Check answers (some may vary from country to country).

Answers (in the UK)
1 M **2** L **3** L **4** L (if it is a class rule) **5** M
6 L **7** M **8** L

c • Now for sentence 1 elicit from the class *You shouldn't play noisy games on a mobile phone in public.* Get SS to practise saying it a couple of times to get the rhythm right.
• SS continue in pairs making sentences with *should / shouldn't, have to* or *mustn't.*

Possible answers according to the UK (may vary in different countries)
You shouldn't play noisy games on a mobile phone in public.
You mustn't send text messages when your car is stopped at traffic lights.
You have to switch off your mobile phone on a plane.
You have to switch off your mobile phone in class (if it's a school rule).
You shouldn't talk loudly on a mobile phone on public transport.
You mustn't use a hand held mobile while driving a car.
You shouldn't make very personal calls in public.
You mustn't use your mobile phone at a petrol station.

4 READING

a • Focus on the postcard and give SS a moment to read it. Then ask the class what they think it says about the English.

Being polite is very important to the English. If you want someone to do something, you must ask them politely.

• If you think the SS might have an opinion, ask if they think it's true and elicit ideas / experiences.

b • Focus on the article and the four summaries. Give SS time (at least five minutes) to read the article and then, with a partner, choose the best summary. Check answers.

The English and Russian idea of good manners is different.

Extra idea

An alternative and more 'interactive' way of dealing with this text would be to read the text with the class, paragraph by paragraph, asking SS to try and guess the meaning of new words from the context. After each paragraph, ask your SS questions to compare the English (or Russian) attitude to manners to that of people in their country (-ies). For example, after paragraph 1, you could ask if it is necessary in your SS' country to add words like *could you* and *please.*

c • Now get SS to read the article again and, in pairs, to mark sentences 1–10 T or F. Tell them to mark the part of the text that gave them the answer. Check answers and get SS to justify their answers.

1 F (She got angry because of the way he asked her to pour him some tea.)
2 T
3 T
4 F (He was <u>very</u> surprised, i.e. amazed.)
5 F (It was disgusting.)
6 F (She was angry.)
7 T
8 T
9 F (They thought she was mad.)
10 T

d • Focus on the instructions. SS should try to do the exercise from memory. Check answers.

1 step	**3** make	**5** translate
2 pour	**4** swallow	

e • Do this as an open class question and elicit ideas. Get SS to say why.
⚠ If you are teaching in Russia (or have Russian SS in the class), ask them if they agree with Alexander or not.

Extra idea

You could get SS to underline or highlight five words or phrases they want to remember from the text. Get them to compare their words / phrases with a partner and then get some feedback from the class.

5 LISTENING

a • 3.4 Focus on the instructions. Play the tape / CD once, pausing after each speaker to give SS time to write. You could also let them compare with a partner before moving on to the next speaker. Play the recording again if necessary.

1 Yes; they need to say what they think / be more direct.
2 Yes; they need to relax more.
3 No.
4 No.

b • Focus on the nine questions. Give SS time to read them. Then play the tape / CD again, pausing after each speaker to give SS time to write. Get SS to compare with a partner. Play the tape / CD again if necessary. Check answers.

1 They were doing a training course for teachers of English.
2 Pass, because the tutors were very polite when they gave their opinion about their teaching progress.
3 They failed – and they were very surprised! They didn't realize they were doing badly.
4 That they are cold / unfriendly.
5 Noisy and extrovert.
6 He thinks they are more polite than people from his country / have better manners.
7 English football hooligans and tourists who drink too much.
8 It rained a lot and people kept hitting her with their umbrellas and then saying sorry.
9 'Please stop saying sorry and be more careful.' She was tired of people saying sorry when they didn't mean it.

3.4 CD1 Track 45

(tapescript in Student's Book on *p.124*)

LÁSZLÓ Well, I think sometimes yes. English people can be so polite that you don't really understand them. For example, I went to London with some other teachers from Hungary to do a training course for teachers of English. It was a special course for foreign teachers. During the course the tutors, the people who were teaching us, talked to us a lot about our progress – and we thought we were all doing really well. So we were very very surprised when some of us failed the course! What had happened was that the English tutors were so polite when they gave their opinion about our teaching that we didn't realize we were doing things badly. I think that's typically English. I think sometimes they need to say what they think, to be more direct.

PAULA I think English people are so polite that it makes us Latin people think that they're cold. I mean we're very noisy and extrovert and so when they're quiet and polite we think that they don't like us, that they're being unfriendly. So maybe yes, they *can* be too polite. I think they need to relax more.

MELIK I think the English are very polite, but I don't think they are too polite – I mean I don't think it's a bad thing, I think it's a good thing. In my job, I have met a lot of English people and I think they're much more polite than we are both in the way they talk and also in the way they respect other people's opinions. And their manners in general are much better. OK, this isn't true about all English people. The football hooligans and some of the tourists that come here to Turkey and drink too much – they're not polite – but the majority are and I like it.

RENATA Well, I went to London a few years ago and one day, surprise surprise, it was raining and I was walking along the street and everybody had an umbrella and every time someone went past me they hit me with their umbrella and then said, 'Oh sorry,' or 'I'm awfully sorry,' or 'I'm terribly sorry'. And after the tenth time this happened, I just said to the person who hit me, 'Please stop saying sorry and just be more careful!' So in answer to your question, I don't think English people are too polite. They say 'sorry' and 'thank you' a lot, but it doesn't really mean anything.

Extra support

If there's time, you could get SS to listen to the tape / CD with the tapescript on *p.124* so they can see exactly what they understood / didn't understand. Translate / explain any new words or phrases.

- Now ask the class what they think, especially if they have been to England or met English people.

6 SPEAKING

- Divide SS into groups of three or four and focus on the instructions and the questionnaire.
- Then focus attention on the section **Greeting people** and the speech bubble. Elicit opinions from the whole class about what is good / bad manners in their country when meeting people for the first time.
- Let SS continue in groups. Monitor and help with vocabulary, and correct any misuse of modals of obligation, particularly confusion between *shouldn't* / *mustn't* and *don't have to.*
- When SS have finished, if there's time, get some feedback about one topic from each section.

Extra photocopiable activities

Grammar

must, have to, should p.148

Communicative

Are they true? p.179 (instructions *p.166*)

HOMEWORK

Study Link **Workbook** *pp.24–26*

3B Judging by appearances

G *must, may, might, can't* (deduction)
V describing people
P *-eigh, -aigh, -igh*

Lesson plan

In this lesson, SS begin by reading and talking about how people feel about their passport photos, which leads to them learning vocabulary to describe people physically. From this the topic develops into how we often judge people by their appearance – SS have to try and guess three women's jobs purely on how they look. This topic provides the context for learning modal verbs of deduction. SS have met all these modals (*can, must, might*) before, but have not used them to make logical deductions. The pronunciation focus in this lesson is on the tricky combination of letters *-eigh*, *-aigh*, and *-igh*.

Optional lead-in (books closed)

- Bring in any documents you have of yourself which have a photo, e.g. passport, ID card, driving licence, etc. or make an OHP transparency of them to project on the board.
- Ask SS what they do if they need a photo for ID. Elicit that you can ask someone to take a digital photo of you, or you can go to a photo studio or a photo booth. Ask SS which they think is best and why.
- Then show your ID card, etc. to SS. Ask them if they think it is a good photo / if you look different in the photo, and then tell them where you had it taken, if you think it looks like you, and if you like it or not and why.

1 READING

a • Books open. Focus on the questions, and, if you didn't do the lead-in, explain / translate *photo booth*. Give SS time to answer the questions in pairs. Tell them that they can show each other their photos if they have ID cards, etc. with them, but that they don't have to, especially if they truly dislike their photos!

b • Now focus on the instructions and the photos, and elicit SS' opinions as to whether the people look like their passport photos.

c • Focus on the instructions and the four questions. Make sure SS understand *vain* (= placing too much importance on your appearance). Give SS a minute to read the introductory paragraph of the article, and then get them to answer the questions in pairs. Check answers.

> 1 Because it's the photo of ourselves that we most often show other people.
> 2 The Italians.
> 3 The Norwegians.
> 4 The French.

• Now you could read the paragraph again with the class, eliciting / clarifying meaning of new vocabulary. Ask the class how they think people from their country feel about their photos.

d • Now set a time limit for SS to read the rest of the article. Get SS in pairs to answer the questions, and then check answers.

> **Ruth England** is happy with hers. She took time to get a good photo of herself.
> **Michael Winner** isn't happy with his. He thinks he looks like a drug dealer.
> **Toby Young** doesn't like his because it doesn't look like him, so people don't believe the passport is his.

Extra idea

Alternatively, instead of getting SS to read quietly, you could read the three paragraphs with the class and ask after each paragraph if the person is happy with their photo and why.

e • Focus on the instructions and the highlighted words and the two possible definitions for each one. Check answers, and if necessary, elicit an exact translation of each word. Model and drill the pronunciation. Get SS to underline the stress in *re<u>search</u>*, *em<u>bar</u>rassed* and *<u>hi</u>deous.*

> **1** a **2** a **3** b **4** a **5** b **6** a **7** b

HOW WORDS WORK...

• Focus on the sentences and then go through the rules. The common mistake here is for SS to use *look* with a noun (~~*He looks a businessman*~~) or *look like* with an adjective (~~*You look like happy*~~). Give SS a couple of minutes to do the exercise. Check answers.

> **1** look like **2** look **3** looks like **4** look

Extra support

If you think your SS need more practice, you could write these sentences on the board for them to complete.

1 He's forty but he only _____ thirty.
2 What's that building? It _____ a factory.
3 Your boss _____ a nice person. Is she?
4 This cake _____ delicious but it's horrible.

> **1** looks **2** looks like **3** looks like **4** looks

2 VOCABULARY describing people

a • Tell SS to go to **Vocabulary Bank *Describing people*** on *p.149*.

• Focus on section **1 Age** and get SS to do it in pairs. Check answers.

> **1** about **2** forties **3** mid- **4** late **5** early

Extra idea

Drill the expressions by asking SS how old various famous people are (i.e. people whose exact age SS are unlikely to know).

- Now focus on sections **2 Height and build** and **3 Hair**. Get SS to match the sentences and pictures, and check answers, either after each section or after the two sections. Model and drill pronunciation.

2
1 A 2 C 3 B
3
1 E 2 A 3 G 4 B 5 C 6 F 7 D

- Remind SS that:
  – we use the verb *be* with adjectives like *tall, short,* etc., and that we frequently use modifiers, e.g. *a bit, quite, very* / *really,* etc.
  – we use *have* + hair (except with the adjective *bald*), and that we don't use an article, e.g. ~~*she has **a** long blonde hair / **the** long blonde hair*~~.
  – when we describe a person physically height, build, and hair are the aspects we tend to concentrate on. We may also mention other features (eyes, nose, etc.) but usually only if they are in some way significant, e.g. *She has beautiful eyes.*
- Finally, focus on section **4 General adjectives**, which covers adjectives that describe various degrees of attractiveness. SS should first decide if they are positive or negative, and then if they are usually used for men, women, or both. Check answers and drill pronunciation if necessary.

attractive [+] [B]	plain [–] [B]
beautiful [+] [W]	pretty [+] [W]
good-looking [+] [B]	ugly [–] [B]
handsome [+] [M]	

- Point out that *ugly* is stronger than *plain.*
- Focus on the information box and point out the difference between the two questions. You could drill the questions by asking about members of the class, e.g. *What does Victor look like?* (e.g. *He's tall, he has dark hair,* etc., *What's he like?* (e.g. *He's friendly, funny,* etc.).
- Finally, focus on the instruction 'Can you remember the words on this page? Test yourself or a partner'.

Testing yourself

For **Age** SS can cover sentences 1–5 and just look at the definitions and try to remember the phrases. For **Height and build** and **Hair** SS can cover the sentences and look at the pictures only and remember the sentences. For **General adjectives** they can cover the right-hand column and try to remember if the adjectives are positive or negative or if they apply to men, women or both.

Testing a partner

See **Testing a partner** *p.17*.

Study Link SS can find more practice of these words on the MultiROM and on the *New English File Intermediate* website.

- Tell SS to go back to the main lesson on *p.41*.

b • 3.5 Now focus on the pictures. Explain that two women witnessed a robbery, and SS are going to hear them describing the man they saw to the police.
- Before listening, get SS in pairs to describe the people. Play the tape / CD once, and let SS discuss who they think the robber is and why. Then play the tape / CD again. Check answers, and get SS to tell you why it is the right person.

3

3.5 CD1 Track 46

(tapescript in Student's Book on *p.124*)

P = Policeman, W1 = Woman 1, W2 = Woman 2

P OK, ladies, now can you describe the man you saw in the bank?
W1 Well, he was, er, sort of medium height, you know, not short – but not tall either. And quite skinny, you know thin.
W2 Yes. And he had a beard and a little moustache.
W1 No, he didn't. He had a moustache but not a beard. It's just that I think he hadn't shaved.
W2 No, it was a beard, I'm sure.
W1 And anyway, Doris, you weren't wearing your glasses so you can't have seen him very well.
W2 I could see perfectly well.
P Ladies, ladies, please. So, no moustache then.
W1 No, he had a moustache but he didn't have a beard.
P And what about his hair?
W2 Dark.
W1 Yes, short, dark hair.
P Straight?
W1 No, curly, I'd say. Wouldn't you say, Doris?
W2 Yes, very curly.
P So, dark, curly, hair?
W1 Yes. That's what we said. Are you deaf or something?
P And what time was it when…?

Extra idea

You could give SS extra practice with the vocabulary by getting them to describe members of their family to each other, or to describe famous people for their partners to identify. Encourage them to begin with the person's age, then physical description, and then (to help them to identify the person) their job.

3 PRONUNCIATION *-eigh, -aigh, -igh*

Pronunciation notes

These combinations of letters can present problems for SS but in fact their pronunciation follows some clear rules:
-eigh is almost always /eɪ/. *Height* is an exception.
-aigh is always /eɪ/
-igh is always /aɪ/

a • Focus on the instructions and the words in the list. In pairs, SS try to put them in the right column. Get them to do this by instinct.

b • 3.6 Play the tape / CD once for SS to check. Then check answers and point out the spelling rules given above.

3.6 CD1 Track 47

train /eɪ/	bike /aɪ/
in his eighties	bright
neighbour	height
overweight	high
straight	light brown
weigh	might
	sight

Extra support

Play the tape / CD again pausing after each word for SS to repeat.

c • Focus on the questions and get the class to answer them. Tell SS that a good way to remember the pronunciation of *height* is to associate it with *high*.

> *-igh* is pronounced /aɪ/. *-eigh* is usually pronounced /eɪ/. *Height* is the exception.

d • 3.7 In pairs, SS now practise saying some sentences. Play the tape / CD for them to listen and check. For more practice you could get SS to repeat after each sentence.

3.7 CD1 Track 48

1 She has light brown hair. It's short and straight.
2 He's medium height and slightly overweight.
3 He's in his eighties, but his eyesight's very good.
4 She likes wearing tight straight-leg jeans.

Study Link SS can find more practice of English sounds on the MultiROM and also on the *New English File Intermediate* website.

4 GRAMMAR *must, may, might, can't* (deduction)

a • Focus on the title of the article and ask SS if they think it is true that we judge other people by their appearance.
• Focus on the photos and the three paragraphs. Tell SS that they are going to read part of an article from *Marie Claire*, where readers had to speculate which woman had which job, guessing only from their appearance.
• First, get SS to describe the three women using the vocabulary they learnt in the **Vocabulary Bank**, e.g. *She looks about 30. She's short and she has short dark hair*, etc.
• Then focus on the three jobs and get SS in pairs to guess who does what. Get feedback but don't tell them if they are right or wrong. Tell SS not to read the texts at this point.

Extra idea

You could write the three numbers on the board and have a show of hands to see how many people think, e.g. that 1 is the managing director, etc.

• Now give SS a couple of minutes to read the article and match each woman to a paragraph. Get SS to compare with a partner, and then check answers, getting them to say why.

> 1 C 2 B 3 A

b • Focus on the instructions and give SS a few minutes to read the article again. Get SS to discuss the questions in pairs and get feedback.

> 1 Laura, because people think she's too small to be a policewoman. Thea, because they think she's too young and dresses too casually to be a managing director.
> 2 Sam, because when people recognize her name they expect her to be a 'typical rich kid'.

c • Focus on the task and get SS to do this either individually or in pairs. Check answers.

> 1 can't be
> 2 must be
> 3 might be

d • Now tell SS to go to **Grammar Bank 3B** on *p.134*. Go through the examples and read the rules with the class. Model and drill the example sentences.

Extra idea

In a monolingual class, you could get SS to translate the example sentences and compare the forms / verbs they would use in their L1.

Grammar notes

modals of deduction: *must* (*be*), *may* / *might* (*be*), *can't* (*be*)

• SS are already familiar with these modal verbs in other contexts, e.g. *must* for obligation, and *can't* for permission. Here they are used in a different way to speculate and make deductions.
• Although these verbs are often used with *be* in the presentation, they can be used with any verb, e.g. *She must have a lot of money.*
• The most common mistakes are, e.g. using *mustn't* instead of *can't* for something that's impossible, (e.g. ~~*It mustn't be true.*~~) and using *can* instead of *might* / *may* for a possibility (e.g. *He's speaking Spanish.* ~~*He can be Spanish or South American.*~~).

• Now focus on the exercises on *p.135* and give SS time to do them individually or in pairs. Check answers either after each exercise or when SS have done both.

> **a** 2 G 3 A 4 D 5 J 6 C 7 F 8 E 9 B 10 H
> **b** 1 might / may 2 can't 3 might / may not 4 must 5 can't 6 can't 7 must

e • Now tell SS to go to **Communication** *Who do you think they are?* on *p.116*. Go through instructions a–d. Make sure SS remember the meaning of all the jobs.
• Tell SS to speculate with each person in turn, going through all the jobs, eliminating some and leaving a couple of possibilities (e.g. *The woman in A might be an X or a Y.*). Then when you think they've had enough time, tell them to make a final decision for each one. Monitor while they discuss and encourage them to use *He* / *She can't be*, *might be*, *must be*, etc.

- Check answers, eliciting from different pairs sentences with *We think he / she must be the...*, and see if any of the pairs guessed all five right.

Extra support

You could write *We think he / she must be the...* on the board.

A is a politician (Glenda Jackson. She used to be an actress).
B is a comedian (Rik Mayall).
C is a university professor (Shahriar Behboudi).
D is a boxer (Leila Ali, Muhammad Ali's daughter).
E is a violinist (Nigel Kennedy).

- Tell SS to go back to the main lesson on *p.43*.

5 LISTENING

a • Focus on the instructions and on the photo. Tell SS they must talk about each of the three possible answers, using *must be / might be / can't be*.
• After a few minutes, elicit sentences from each pair. If they use *can't be* or *must be*, encourage them to say why, e.g. *He can't be from Sweden. He's very dark.* **Don't tell them the right answers at this stage.**

b • **3.8** Focus on the instructions. Play the tape / CD for SS to check their answers to **a**. Get feedback to see who was right.

1 He's from England and Spain.
2 He's in his (late) thirties.
3 He's a musician (a flamenco guitarist).

3.8 CD1 Track 49
(tapescript in Student's Book on *p.125*)
I = Interviewer, R = Rafael
I Rafael Lloyd. A Spanish first name and a British surname?
R Yes. My mother was Spanish and my father's English.
I Is Rafael your real name then or your stage name?
R It's my real name: my mother was from Cordoba in Spain and Rafael's the patron saint of Cordoba. But it's also my stage name.
I What nationality are you?
R I'm British and Spanish. I was born in Spain and I was brought up there. I've spent a lot of time in Britain too. I've been living in Oxford for the last ten years.
I Oh, nice. Are you bilingual?
R Yes, I am.
I And, it's a strange question, do you feel more Spanish than British or vice versa?
R Well, I think I feel more Spanish in most respects, especially as a big part of my life revolves around Spanish culture. But I do like individuality, eccentricity, and tea. I must feel a little British too, I suppose!
I Do you think you look more Spanish than English?
R Well, I think I look Spanish, but when I travel, people always think I'm from their country and people have stopped me in the street, for example in Cairo and in Rome, to ask me for help, so I must have an international face...maybe I should be a spy!
I When did you start learning to play the guitar?
R I started when I was nine when my family lived in Madrid. A teacher used to come to our flat and give me lessons.
I I see, so how long have you been working professionally as a flamenco guitarist?
R I started when I was 17, I mean that's when I started to get paid for my first concerts. I'm now 39, so that's, erm, 22 years.

c • Focus on the instructions. Give SS time in pairs to look at the headings first to see if they can remember any of the information. Now play the tape / CD again. Then get SS to compare what they understood with their partner and make notes.
• Play the recording (or part of it) again if necessary, and then check answers. Try to elicit all the information Rafael gives for each heading.

Name: His name's Rafael Lloyd – he has a Spanish first name and an English surname. It's his real name and his stage name.
Parents: His mother was Spanish and his father's English. He was born in Spain but now he lives in England.
Languages: He's bilingual (English / Spanish).
Nationality: He *feels* more Spanish than English, partly because of his job.
He thinks he *looks* Spanish, but he says he must have an 'international face' because when he is abroad people always think he's from their country – e.g. if he's in Italy, people think he's Italian.
Profession:
He's a flamenco guitarist. He started playing the guitar when he was 9, in Madrid.
He's been working as a guitarist for 22 years. He started when he was 17.

d • **3.9** Now focus on questions 1–4. If necessary, check SS understand *make a living* and *stereotype*. Play the second part of the interview once and let SS compare what they think. Play it again if necessary, and check answers.

1 It's easier to make a living in Britain because there are fewer flamenco guitarists here.
2 In the USA, Germany, and Japan (but flamenco is popular all over the world).
3 The stereotype is of someone with long, dark hair (which he used to have).
4 In Spain (where they believe more in stereotypes). He thinks the British don't judge people by their appearance.

3.9 CD1 Track 50

(tapescript in Student's Book on *p.125*)

I = Interviewer, R = Rafael

I As a flamenco guitarist living in Britain, is it easy to make a living?

R I think life as a musician is never easy. But I think it's easier here than in Spain, because there are fewer flamenco guitarists here.

I And where's flamenco popular, apart from in Spain?

R Well, the biggest markets for flamenco outside Spain are really the USA, Germany, and Japan, but I've found that it's popular all over the world. It has a strong identity that people relate to in every corner of the planet.

I Now, you don't look like the stereotype of a flamenco guitarist. People imagine flamenco guitarists as having long, dark hair...

R That's true. I used to have really long hair, but I decided to cut my hair short.

I Are people in Britain surprised when they find out that you're a flamenco guitarist?

R No, not really. That's one of the things I like about Britain: no one judges you on appearance.

I And what about in Spain?

R Well, actually, in Spain people find it much harder to believe that I'm a flamenco guitarist. I think Spanish people believe in stereotypes more than in Britain. And they judge you more on your appearance. But as soon as people hear me playing the guitar, then they know that I'm the real thing.

I Could you play something for us?

R Of course.

Extra support

If there's time, you could get SS to listen to the tape / CD with the tapescript on *p.125* so they can see exactly what they understood / didn't understand. Translate / explain any new words or phrases.

e • Do this as an open class question. Elicit ideas / opinions, and tell SS what you think.

Extra photocopiable activities

Grammar

must, may, might, can't p.149

Communicative

Spot the difference *p.180* (instructions *p.166*)

HOMEWORK

Study Link **Workbook** *pp.27–29*

3 C

G *can, could, be able to* (ability and possibility)
V *-ed / -ing* adjectives
P sentence stress

If at first you don't succeed, ...

Lesson plan

The grammatical focus of this lesson is for SS to learn how to use *be able to* in the tenses / forms where *can / can't* cannot be used. The context is success and failure, and the language is presented through a magazine article about three people who have tried unsuccessfully to learn something. Later in the lesson, SS read about two women – a swimmer and a surfer – who have succeeded in their sport despite suffering enormous setbacks – they both lost a limb. The pronunciation focus is on sentence stress in sentences with *can / could / be able to*, and SS talk about different skills and whether they can do them or would like to be able to do them. The vocabulary focus revises *-ed* and *-ing* adjectives, which SS will have met before at Pre-intermediate level.

Optional lead-in (books closed)

- Write on the board:

Noun: **SUCCESS**	Opposite noun: ___________
Adj: ___________	Opposite adj: ___________
Verb: ___________	Opposite verb: ___________

- Put SS in pairs. First, elicit the meaning of *success* (= something well done), that it's a noun, and that the stress is on the second syllable. Then get SS to try to complete the chart. Check answers and drill pronunciation.

success	failure
successful	unsuccessful
succeed	fail

- Now ask SS whether they have ever tried to learn to do something, e.g. to learn a sport, and not succeeded. Get some feedback from the class finding out *why* the person failed to learn.

1 GRAMMAR *can, could, be able to*

a • Books open. Write the title of the lesson on the board: *If at first you don't succeed, ...* Focus on the instructions, and get SS, in pairs, to choose a sentence half to complete the sentence. Elicit answers from different pairs before telling them what the whole phrase is:

> If at first you don't succeed, try, try again.

• Now elicit ideas for which phrase SS think is the best advice.

b • Focus on the definition of *be able to*, and elicit that it is similar in meaning to *can*. Tell SS that now they are going to see how *be able to* is used and to compare it with *can*.

c • Focus on the task and on sentences A–G. Set a time limit for SS to read the text and to fill the gaps with the missing phrases. Tell them to read each text first before they try to complete it.

• Get them to compare their answers with a partner's and then check answers.

> 1 D 2 G 3 B 4 F 5 A 6 E 7 C

Extra support

Do the first text with the whole class.

d • Focus on the instructions and the question. Then take each phrase and elicit the answers.

A present perfect	**D** past simple
B past simple	**E** gerund
C future with *will*	**F** conditional
	G present simple

e • Tell SS to go to **Grammar Bank 3C** on *p.134*. Go through the examples and read the rules with the class. Model and drill where necessary.

Extra idea

In a monolingual class, you could get SS to translate the example sentences and compare the forms / verbs they would use in their L1.

Grammar notes

be able to

- SS should all be perfectly familiar with the verb *can* for ability, and possibility (or permission). *Can / can't* is a modal verb which has a past and conditional tense (*could / couldn't*) but has no present or past perfect forms nor does it have an infinitive or *-ing* form. In these situations *be able to* must be used.

⚠ For the near future you can often use *can* or *will be able to*, e.g. *I can't go to the meeting tomorrow / I won't be able to go to the meeting tomorrow.*

- Typical mistakes:
  – Trying to use *can* where they should use *be able to*, e.g. ~~*I want to can speak English well.*~~ / ~~*I won't can come to your party on Saturday*~~.
  – leaving out *to*, e.g. ~~*I won't be able help you.*~~

⚠ There is a small difference between *could* and *was able to*. In a (+) past simple sentence, if we want to refer to something difficult that someone succeeded in doing **on a specific occasion**, we use *be able to* (or *managed to*), e.g. *Although the space was very small, he was able to (or managed to) park there.* In this context it is not possible to use *could*. With a strong class you may want to point this out.

• Now focus on the exercises on *p.135* and give SS time to do them individually or in pairs. Check answers either after SS have done the first exercise or after they have done both of them.

a 1	haven't been able to	5	Will you be able to
2	be able to	6	'd be able to
3	won't be able to	7	'll be able to
4	to be able to	8	not being able to
b 1	can't	5	can
2	could	6	to be able to
3	to be able to	7	can
4	won't be able to	8	haven't been able to

f • Now put SS in pairs, **A** and **B**, preferably face to face. Tell them to go to **Communication** *Guess the sentence.* **A** on *p.116*, and **B** on *p.119.*

- Demonstrate the activity by writing in large letters on a piece of paper the following sentence:
  Sorry. I won't be able to see you tonight.
  Don't show the piece of paper to the SS yet. Then write on the board:
  Sorry. I won't ______________ you tonight.
- Tell SS that what's missing is a form of *be able to* + a verb. Tell them that they must guess the exact sentence that you have written on a piece of paper. Elicit ideas. If they are wrong, say '*Try again*', until someone comes out with the right answer. Then show them your piece of paper with the sentence on it.
- Tell SS to look at instruction **a**. Give them a few minutes to complete their sentences **in a logical way**. Emphasize that their partner has the same sentences already completed and the idea is to try and complete the sentences in the same way. Emphasize too that they must use a form of *be able to*. Monitor and help while they are doing this. **Tell SS not to show their sentences to their partner.**
- Now tell SS **A** and **B** to focus on their instruction **a** and tell **A** to read out his / her first sentence and for **B** to tell him / her if he / she has guessed the sentence correctly. If not, he / she has to guess again. When they finish, SS **B** read his / her sentences to SS **A**, etc.
- Tell SS to go back to the main lesson on *p.45*.

2 PRONUNCIATION sentence stress

Pronunciation notes

The first exercise here focuses on the strong and weak pronunciations of *can* and *could*.

SS will have been made aware of this before but it is an important point as it can cause communication problems, e.g. if a student says *I can do it* (incorrectly stressing *can*), a native speaker will probably understand *I can't do it*.

The second and third exercises are to help SS get the right rhythm when they make *be able to* sentences.

a • **3.10** Focus on the instructions and tell SS that they will hear the dictation twice.

- Play the tape / CD pausing between sentences to give SS time to write. Then play the recording again.
- SS may have difficulty distinguishing between *can* and *can't*. Check answers.

3.10 CD1 Track 51

1 He could read when he was four.
2 I can't play the guitar.
3 Where could we have dinner?
4 I can see what you mean.
5 We couldn't find the street.
6 What can you do there?

- Now remind SS that:
  – *can* and *could* are normally unstressed in positive (+) and interrogative (?) sentences when they are pronounced /kən/ and /kəd/. In negative (-) sentences *can't* and *couldn't* are stressed and are pronounced /kaːnt/ and /kʊdnt/. Emphasize the importance of not stressing *can* in positive sentences (see **Pronunciation notes**).
- Play the recording again for SS to listen and repeat the sentences.

b • **3.11** Here SS practise the rhythm of sentences with *be able to*. Play the tape / CD once the whole way through, and then play it again pausing after each sentence for SS to repeat it.

3.11 CD1 Track 52

1 I'd love to be able to ski.
2 We won't be able to come.
3 I've never been able to dance.
4 She hates not being able to drive.

c • **3.12** Go through the instructions. Explain (or show on the board) that they will first hear an example sentence, e.g. *I'd love to be able to ski.* Then they will hear a verb (e.g. **ride a horse**). SS then have to make a new sentence using that verb, i.e. *I'd love to be able to ride a horse.* At the same time they should try to copy the rhythm of the original sentence.

- When SS are clear what they have to do, play the tape / CD and get the whole class to respond. Repeat the activity for extra practice.

3.12 CD1 Track 53

1 I'd love to be able to ski. (**Ride a horse**)
I'd love to be able to ride a horse. (**Windsurf**)
I'd love to be able to windsurf.
2 We won't be able to come. (**Park**)
We won't be able to park. (**Do it**)
We won't be able to do it.
3 I've never been able to dance. (**Speak French**)
I've never been able to speak French. (**Play chess**)
I've never been able to play chess.
4 She hates not being able to drive. (**Cook**)
She hates not being able to cook. (**Swim**)
She hates not being able to swim.

3 SPEAKING

- Focus on the instructions and on the abilities in the circle, making sure SS understand them all.
- Now focus on the 'flow chart' and show SS the two possible routes depending on the answer to the first question. To demonstrate the activity, get SS to ask you about a couple of the abilities.

- Put SS in pairs, preferably face to face. If there is an odd number of SS in the class, you can take part yourself or have one group of three. Monitor and correct any misuse of *can / could / be able to.*
- Get some feedback afterwards to find how many people can, e.g. ride a horse or can't cook, etc.

HOW WORDS WORK...

Two different meanings of *so* are looked at here.

1 Focus on the two examples and get SS to match *so* to its meanings. Check answers.

1 to emphasize an adjective or adverb
2 to connect a cause and result

2 Give SS a minute in pairs to decide which use of *so* is exemplified in each sentence. Check answers.

A 1 B 2 C 1 D 1 E 2

- Point out that *so* (to connect a cause and result) is sometimes used in the middle of a sentence and sometimes at the beginning of a new sentence, e.g. *When we got to the station the train had already gone. So, we got a taxi home.*
- You could also tell SS that *so* is often used at the beginning of a question like this, *So, what happened in the end?*

4 VOCABULARY *-ed / -ing* adjectives

a • Focus on the picture and on the questions and elicit answers. Elicit / explain / translate the meaning of the two adjectives in each case.

1 The woman (C) is **bored** because the man is talking too much. He (A) is **boring**.
2 The little girl (B) is **embarrassed** because of the way her father is dancing. He (D) is **embarrassing**.

- Point out that:
  - the *-ed* adjective is used for the person who **has** the feeling. In other words, a *boring* person makes us feel *bored.*
  - the *-ing* adjective is used for a thing (or person) that **causes** the feeling.

b • Focus on the instructions and remind SS that these are all adjectives which have both *-ing* and *-ed* forms. Give SS a couple of minutes to choose the right adjective.

c • Tell SS to look back at the texts on *p.44* to check answers. Make sure SS know what the correct adjective means.
⚠ *Embarrassed* is a false friend in some languages, e.g. French, Spanish.

1 disappointed 2 embarrassing 3 frustrating

d • Now give SS a minute to complete the adjectives in the questions with *-ed* or *-ing*. Check answers.

1 exciting	6 bored
2 depressed	7 embarrassing
3 interesting	8 frightened
4 disappointed	9 tired
5 tiring	10 boring

e • Focus on the questions. Get SS to ask you a couple of questions first and get them to ask for more information. SS then ask and answer in pairs.

5 LISTENING

a • Focus on the instructions. Give SS a minute to match the three phrasal verbs and their meanings. Check answers.

1 c 2 a 3 b

Extra idea

You could quickly drill the verbs by asking SS: *Are you going to carry on with English next year? Is there anything you've just given up? Would you like to take up a new language or sport? Which one?*

b • 3.13 Focus on the instructions and give SS a few minutes to read the seven tips. The first time SS listen they must tick the **five** tips they hear the psychologist mention. Play the tape / CD the whole way through, and play again if necessary. Check answers.

1 3 4 5 7

3.13 CD1 Track 54

(tapescript in Student's Book on *p.125*)

I = Interviewer, P = Psychologist

I Hello and welcome to this week's edition of *All about you.* Today's programme's about taking up new activities, and how to succeed at them. With us is psychologist Dr Maggie Prior. Good afternoon.

P Good afternoon.

I Dr Prior, what tips can you give our listeners who are thinking of learning to do something new?

P Well, first of all, I would say **choose wisely**. On the one hand, **don't choose something completely unrealistic. For example, don't decide to take up sailing if you can't swim,** or parachute jumping if you're afraid of heights. But, on the other hand, **don't generalize and think that just because you aren't very good at one sport, you won't be able to do any sports at all. I mean, just because you were bad at gymnastics at school doesn't mean that you might not love playing tennis.**

I So think positive?

P Definitely. And never think you'll be bad at something before you've even tried it.

I OK, so, let's imagine I've started to learn to play tennis and I'm finding it very hard work.

P **Well, first don't give up too quickly, carry on for at least a few months.** It often takes time to begin to enjoy learning something new. Another thing that can help, **if you're having problems learning something, is to give it a break and then try again, perhaps a month or two later.**

I But what if I carry on and I find I really really don't have a talent for tennis?

P I think **the important thing is not to be too ambitious. I mean if you've never done much sport and you decide to learn to play tennis, don't expect to become the next Wimbledon champion. Just aim to enjoy what you're doing, not to be the best in the world at it.**

I But if even after all this, I still feel I'm not getting anywhere?

P Well, sometimes you do have to accept it and say, 'OK, this really isn't my thing,' and you need to give it up. But why not try something else? There are lots of other things you can learn to do. **But remember that if you take up an activity that you're really interested in, even if you aren't very good at it, you'll make new friends, because you'll be meeting other people who have similar interests to you.**
I So it might be good for my love life.
P Exactly.
I Dr Maggie Prior, thank you very much.

c • Now focus on the instructions and then play the tape / CD again. Pause after each tip and then let SS discuss in pairs exactly what they understood. Check answers, and then play the next tip, etc.

1 Don't take up sailing if you can't swim.
3 Just because you were bad at gymnastics doesn't mean you won't love tennis.
4 Carry on for at least a few months. / Have a break and then try again one or two months later.
5 If you take up tennis, don't expect to become Wimbledon champion.
7 You'll meet other people who have similar interests to you.

Extra support

If there's time, you could get SS to listen again with the tapescript on *p.125* so they can see exactly what they understood / didn't understand. Translate / explain any new words or phrases.

6 READING

a • Do this as an open class question. If you know someone yourself, tell SS about him / her.

b • Focus on the photos and ask what's unusual about the two women.
• Focus on the instructions, and make sure SS understand the questions in the chart.
• Put SS in pairs and give them time (e.g. five minutes) to each read their article, and complete the chart.

Natalie
1 A car hit her when she was going to a training session on a motorbike.
2 Three months after the accident.
3 Thrilled. It felt like her leg was there.
4 She qualified for the final at the Commonwealth Games in Manchester (for able-bodied swimmers).
5 She hopes to swim faster than she did before the accident.

Bethany
1 A tiger shark attacked her and tore off her arm.
2 As soon as she left hospital.
3 She was so happy she cried.
4 She finished 5th at the National Surfing Championship.
5 She accepts that she will never be world champion.

c • When SS have finished, get them to use the chart to tell each other about the person they have read about. Encourage them to give as much detail as they can. Monitor the pairs and help / correct.

d • Focus on the instructions. Give SS time to read the text they haven't read yet and to underline five words / phrases they don't know in either text. They can use their dictionary if they have one. Monitor and help with any problems.

e • Focus on the instructions and get SS to answer the two questions.

They are both sportswomen, who excelled in water sports. They both lost a limb, but have both gone back to their sports and have triumphed again, competing against able-bodied people.
Natalie still wants to improve as a swimmer and her dream is to swim faster than before she had the accident. Bethany, however, has accepted that she will never fulfil her dream to be world champion.

7 3.14 ♫ SONG *You can get it if you really want*

• This song was originally made famous in 1972 by the Jamaican reggae singer Jimmy Cliff. If you want to do this song in class, use the photocopiable activity on *p.208*.

3.14 CD1 Track 55

You can get it if you really want

You can get it if you really want,
You can get it if you really want,
You can get it if you really want,
But you must try, try and try,
Try and try,
You'll succeed at last.

Persecution you must bear,
Win or lose, you've got to get your share
Got your mind set on a dream
You can get it, though hard it seems
Now

You can get it if you really want, etc.

Rome was not built in a day,
Opposition will come your way
But the harder the battle you see,
It's the sweeter the victory
Now

You can get it if you really want, etc.

Study Link SS can find a dictation and a Grammar quiz on all the grammar from File 3 on the MultiROM and more grammar activities on the *New English File Intermediate* website.

Extra photocopiable activities

Grammar
can, could, be able to p.150
Communicative
Find someone who… *p.181* (instructions *p166*)
Vocabulary
Pictionary *p.199* (instructions *p.195*)
Song
You can get it if you really want p.208 (instructions *p.205*)

HOMEWORK

Study Link **Workbook** *pp.30–32*

3 PRACTICAL ENGLISH
RENTING A FLAT

Function Directions

Language *The easiest way is to get the metro. Take line 11 to...*

Lesson plan

In this lesson SS practise giving and understanding directions, which involve taking public transport (in this case the Paris metro). The language taught could also be used for journeys by bus or tram, e.g. *How many stops is it?*, etc.

In **Social English** Nicole takes Mark to see a flat. While they are looking at the flat, Allie calls Mark on his mobile but he tells Nicole that the caller was his daughter in the United States.

Study Link These lessons are on the *New English File Intermediate* Video / DVD, which can be used instead of the Class Cassette / CD (see introduction *p.9*). The main functional section of each episode is also on the MultiROM with additional activities.

Optional lead-in (books closed)

- Revise what happened in the previous episode by eliciting the story from SS, e.g. *What happened in the last episode?* (Mark chatted to Nicole in the bar after work.) *Who did they talk about?* (Ben, Jacques, and Allie.) *What did Nicole say about Allie?* (She is pretty but she dresses in a very English way. She is also very formal.) *Who arrived at the end?* (Allie.)
- Remind SS of the language that they learnt in the last lesson (ways of making requests and asking permission). You could write some of the key expressions on the board with gaps for SS to complete.
- If you are using the video / DVD, you could play the previous episode again, leaving out the 'Listen and Repeat' sections.

HOW TO GET THERE

a • 3.15 Focus on the photo and elicit that Mark is probably asking for directions. Then focus on the instructions and the three questions. Tell SS to cover the dialogue with their hand or a piece of paper.

Extra idea

You could write the questions on the board and get SS to listen with books closed.

- Play the tape / CD once and check answers.

The flat is in Belleville. The best way to go is by metro. Mark is going to drive there with Nicole.

b • Now get SS to look at the dialogue. In pairs, they read it and see if they can guess or remember the missing words. Emphasize that they shouldn't write the words in the dialogue but in pencil alongside or on a separate sheet of paper.

c • Play the tape / CD again for them to check. Then go through the dialogue line by line and check answers. Find out how many SS had guessed the words correctly. Where they had not guessed correctly, see if their alternative also fits.

- Point out the idiomatic phrase *I'll give you a lift* (third line from bottom of dialogue) which means *I'll take you in my car.* **NOTE**: the other common use of *lift* = machine to carry people up and down a building.

3.15 CD2 Track 2

M = Mark, J = Jacques, N = Nicole

M Where **exactly** is it? ...I'm sorry, I didn't catch that. OK. **How** far is it? ...OK, OK. Merçi. Au revoir.
J Any luck?
M I think I've found an apartment ... How do I **get** to Belleville?
J The easiest **way** is to get the metro at Pyramides. Take line 14 and **change** at Châtelet.
M OK.
J Then take Line 11 **towards** Mairie des Lilas.
M Where do I **get** off?
J At Belleville.
M How many **stops** is it?
J Six, I think.
M Oh, right, I've found it on the map. How long does it **take** to get there?
J About half an hour.
N Have you found a flat?
M Yeah ... in Belleville this time.
N When are you going to see it?
M This afternoon.
N If you can wait till six, I'll **give** you a lift. I live near Belleville so I'm driving that way.
M That's great. Thanks.

d • 3.16 Now focus on the key phrases highlighted in the dialogue. Play the tape / CD, pausing after the beep for SS to repeat. Encourage them to copy the rhythm and intonation.

⚠ Don't worry too much about how they pronounce the French place names.

3.16 CD2 Track 3

M = Mark, J = Jacques, N = Nicole

M Where exactly is it?
M How far is it?
M How do I get to Belleville?
J The easiest way is to get the metro at Pyramides.
J Take line 14 and change at Châtelet.
J Then take line 11 towards Mairie des Lilas.
M Where do I get off?
M How many stops is it?
M How long does it take to get there?
N If you can wait till six, I'll give you a lift.

e • Now get SS to cover the dialogue again and focus on the answers. Elicit the questions from the whole class.

1 How do I get to Belleville?
2 Where do I get off?
3 How many stops is it?
4 How long does it take to get there?

Extra support

You could give SS further practice of the rhythm of the phrases by getting them to read the dialogue in pairs.

f • Put SS in pairs, **A** and **B**. Tell them to go to **Communication** *How do I get there?*, **A** on *p.117* and **B** on *p.120.* Go through the instructions and focus on the speech bubbles. Give SS time to decide on the best routes from Marble Arch to wherever they are going to give directions to.

• **A** starts by asking **B** for directions. It is probably easier if **A** asks for directions for each of the four places, and they then swap roles, rather than asking alternately for directions. Monitor to check that SS are drawing the routes correctly.

• Finally, you could ask the class if anyone has ever used the London underground and if so, whether they found it easy / difficult to use.

SOCIAL ENGLISH What's going on?

a • 3.17 Focus on the photo and ask *Who can you see? Where are they? What are they doing?* Then focus on the question and play the tape / CD once and check answers.

Yes, he does.

3.17 CD2 Track 4

(tapescript in Student's Book on *p.125*)

L = Landlady, M = Mark, A = Allie, N = Nicole

L This is the apartment. Je vous laisse visiter. Je serai en bas.
M Merçi, madame. Sorry, Nicole. What did she say?
N She said that we can have a look at the flat. She's going to wait downstairs.
M Thanks. So, what do you think?
N Well, it's a long way from the station. And it's on the fourth floor. It's a pity there isn't a lift.
M Who needs one? The stairs are good exercise. Look, there's a great view from here.
N It's also very noisy.
M Sure, but it has character. It's just how I imagined an apartment in Paris.
N Everything's old, including the heating. It will be very cold in the winter.
M Oh, hi.
A [on phone] Well, what's it like?
M Nice – really Parisian.
A Are you going to take it?
M I think so, yeah…
A I can't wait to see it!
M Yeah…
A Are you OK? Are you on your own?
M No, I'm with the woman who owns the apartment. I'll call you back.
A OK, speak later. Love you.
M Love you too, bye. Sorry about that. That was…that was my… my daughter.
N Calling from America?
M You know. She's just taking an interest.
N Taking an interest. That's nice.

b • Focus on the questions. Then play the tape / CD again. Get SS to compare answers, and then play it one more time if necessary. Check answers, and elicit / explain the meaning of any words or expressions SS didn't understand.

1 **Advantages:** It's got a great view, it has character, it's very Parisian.
Disadvantages: It's a long way from the station, it's on the 4th floor and there's no lift, it's noisy, everything's old (including the heating).
2 He tells Allie he's with the owner of the flat because he doesn't want her to know he's with Nicole. He tells Nicole that it was his daughter on the phone, because he doesn't want her to know Allie phoned him. Nicole probably doesn't believe him.

Extra support

If there's time, you could get SS to listen to the tape / CD with the tapescript on *p.125* so they can see exactly what they understood / didn't understand. Translate / explain any new words or phrases.

c • 3.18 Now focus on the **USEFUL PHRASES**. Give SS a moment to try to complete them, and then play the tape / CD to check.

3.18 CD2 Track 5

So, what do you **think**?
It's a long **way** from (the station).
It's a **pity** (there's isn't a lift).
What's it **like**?
I can't **wait** (to see it)!
Are you on your **own**?
I'll call you **back**.

Extra idea

Ask SS if they can remember who said each phrase (and in what context), e.g. Mark says *So what do you think?* (When he asks Nicole about the flat).

d • Play the tape / CD again, pausing for SS to repeat. In a monolingual class, elicit the equivalent expressions in SS' L1.

HOMEWORK

Study Link Workbook *p.33*

3 Writing An informal letter

Lesson plan

In this third writing lesson, SS practise writing an informal letter. Although today most people tend to send emails where possible, there are some circumstances, for example to say thank you, where a handwritten letter might be more appropriate. Also, SS are sometimes required to write this kind of letter in external exams. The content and style are the same as for an email with just a couple of small differences.

a • Focus on the instructions. SS may remember Christelle, Claudia's friend (from **Writing 1**) who wanted to stay for a month in the UK.

• Go through A–G making sure SS understand *apologize*, *mention*, etc. Then give SS a few minutes to decide on a logical order for the letter. Don't check answers.

b • Now get SS to read the letter to see whether their order coincides with Christelle's. Check answers.

1 D **2** B **3** G **4** E **5** C **6** F **7** A

Extra idea

As you correct, ask SS a few questions about the content of the letter, e.g. after 1, *Why didn't she write earlier?* (Because she has been very busy), after 3, *What nice things does she mention?* (The weather, how her English got better, seeing Claire and Emma), etc.

c • Focus on the second paragraph of Christelle's letter and tell SS there are five punctuation mistakes. Elicit what kind of mistakes these might be, e.g. not using capital letters, leaving out apostrophes or putting them in the wrong place, or not using full stops or commas correctly.

• Give SS a few minutes to find the mistakes, individually or in pairs. Then check answers.

I'm writing to thank you for letting me stay with you in **August.** I had a fantastic time. The weather was perfect and I really think my **English** got better. **I** hope you think so too!

d • Give SS a moment to look back and compare the emails on *p.17* with the letter. Elicit that an informal email and an informal letter are almost identical in style / organization, etc. The only real difference is that:

– in letters you write your address. In an email you don't usually do that.

– you normally begin a letter with *Dear* (name). In emails people often use *Hi* (name) instead of *Dear.*

– in a letter you *enclose* a photo (i.e. put it in the envelope). In an email you *attach* a photo electronically.

• Finally, focus on the **Useful language** box and go through the expressions (which can be used in either informal letters or emails).

WRITE a letter to thank them

Go through the instructions. Then either get SS to plan and write the letter in class (set a time limit of 20 minutes) or get them just to plan in class, or set both the planning and writing for homework.

If SS do the writing in class, get them to swap their letters with another student to read and check for mistakes before you collect them all in.

3 Revise & Check

For instructions on how to use these pages, see *p.32*.

GRAMMAR

1 should join
2 can't be
3 be able
4 mustn't take / can't take
5 might not / may not
6 don't have
7 must be
8 might be / may be
9 have to
10 shouldn't drink

VOCABULARY

a 1 mid 2 length 3 straight 4 fringe 5 wears
b 1 interested 2 depressed 3 boring
4 embarrassing 5 frustrated
c 1 off 2 back 3 up 4 like 5 in

PRONUNCIATION

a 1 fifties (It's /ɪ/)
2 height (It's /aɪ/)
3 curly (It's /ɜː/)
4 fringe (It's /dʒ/)
5 moustache (It's /ʃ/)
b disappointed embarrassing interested mobile overweight

CAN YOU UNDERSTAND THIS TEXT?

a 1 b 2 a 3 c 4 a 5 b
b **burst into tears** = suddenly start crying
sympathetic = understanding other people's feelings / problems
I couldn't stand it = I couldn't bear / tolerate the situation
turned down = rejected, refused to publish
deeply hurt = (made to feel) very unhappy / upset

CAN YOU UNDERSTAND THESE PEOPLE?

a 1 b 2 c 3 a 4 c 5 b
b 1 Daniel 2 Gatti 3 Argentinian 4 Advanced
5 the States (the USA)

3.19 CDX Track 00

1 A Oh no. I can't find my mobile!
B Well, you had it when we were in the café. You were texting your friend.
A Yes, that's right. Maybe I left it in there.
B Do you want to go back and see?
A But can you phone me first? Then if my mobile's in the café, maybe someone will answer it.
B OK. Hey, I can hear it. It must be in your bag somewhere.
A No, it's in my jacket pocket.
2 A I'm starving. What time did you ask them to come?
B I said to come at eight o' clock for drinks, and then dinner at 8.30.
A Well, it's 8.15 now.
B Yes, they should be here any minute. They're usually very punctual.
A Ah – that must be them… Who was it?
B Somebody collecting money for charity. Honestly, I really think people should phone when they're going to be late. It's very inconsiderate. It's nearly twenty past now.
3 A No! Is that you? It doesn't look anything like you! I didn't know you used to have long hair!
B Well, this passport is nearly ten years old. Which reminds me, I'm going to have to renew it soon.
A Well, you definitely need a new photo. You look really awful.
B OK, let's see yours then.
A No, you can't see it. I hate showing people my passport photo.
B Come on! You've seen mine. That's not bad. It's a lot better than mine. In fact, I think I prefer your hair as it was then.
4 A So where did you meet him?
B At work. He's one of the designers.
A And what's he like?
B He's funny, intelligent...
A Yes, but what does he look like?
B Just like Pierce Brosnan, tall, dark, and handsome – no, I'm joking. He's got short dark hair and he's not very tall. But I think he's really good-looking.
5 A What happened? How did it go?
B No comment.
A Not again. What did you do this time?
B Nothing. I mean nothing wrong. It was really unfair. Just because I was going a tiny bit fast in the High Street.
A Oh well. You'll just have to take it again. Third time lucky.

3.20 CD2 Track 7

A Hello, sit down. I'm the secretary and you are...?
B Daniel.
A And your surname is?
B Gatti. G–A–double T–I.
A Are you from Italy?
B No, my grandparents were Italian but I'm Argentinian. But people always think I must be Italian because of my name.
A Oh, sorry. And what course were you thinking of doing?
B I'd like to do the Advanced course. I did an Upper Intermediate course in Buenos Aires last year so I think I'll be able to do an Advanced course here.
A Well, you'll have to do a level test first. You might find the Advanced course a bit difficult. Is this your first time in Britain?
B Yes, but I've been to the USA last year.
A I *went* to the USA last year, you mean. You see, maybe you're not quite ready for the Advanced after all. Now, the level test takes one hour.

Extra photocopiable activities

Quicktest 3 *p.218*

4 A

G first conditional and future time clauses + *when*, *until*, etc.
V education
P /ʌ/ or /juː/?

Back to school, aged 35

File 4 overview

This File revises and extends three structures which SS should have previously seen and were in *New English File Pre-intermediate*. However, second conditionals (**4B**) and *used to* (**4C**) are structures which SS are unlikely to be able to use accurately and confidently, and need thorough re-presentation in order for SS to now incorporate them into their active grammar. Lesson **4A** revises first conditional-type sentences and introduces future time clauses with *when*, *until*, etc. In **4B** second conditional sentences are presented again and contrasted with first conditionals. In **4C** *used to* to describe past states and habits is presented again and extended, and SS are reminded how to talk about present habits. The main lexical areas in this File are education, houses, and friendship.

Lesson plan

This lesson is about education and provides two different angles on the topic. An adapted text from *The Times* newspaper looks at the experience of a 35-year-old journalist who spent a week, as a pupil, at a UK secondary school to see if school today is easier than it used to be. In the second half of the lesson, SS hear about the results of another experiment (this time a TV programme) when some pupils from a modern day secondary school spent a month in a 1953-style boarding school. The grammar focus revises first conditional sentences and looks at the use of the present tense in other time clauses after *when*, *as soon as*, *until*, etc. In vocabulary SS learn high frequency words and phrases related to education, and practise pronouncing some of these in pronunciation which focuses on the letter *u*.

Optional lead-in (books closed)

Put SS in pairs. Write SCHOOL SUBJECTS on the board and give pairs three or four minutes to think of as many subjects as they can, e.g. *history*. When the time is up, write SS' ideas onto the board.

1 VOCABULARY education

a • Books open. Focus on the eight questions and set SS a time limit to answer them. Check answers.

1 1945	**5** Albert Einstein
2 Bogotá	**6** 22 1/2 (or 22.5)
3 William Shakespeare	**7** six
4 1,024	**8** hydrogen and oxygen

b • Now give SS a bit more time to match questions 1–8 with the school subjects by writing the correct number in each box. Check answers and model and drill pronunciation, especially *geography* /dʒiɒgrəfi/ and *literature* /lɪtrətʃə/.

chemistry [8]	**literature** [3]
geography [2]	**maths** [6]
history [1]	**physics** [5]
information technology [4]	**biology** [7]

c • Tell SS to go to **Vocabulary Bank *Education*** on *p.150*. Give them time to do section **1 Verbs** individually or in pairs. Check answers and elicit and drill pronunciation.

2 revise	**6** take (*do* is also possible)
3 learn	**7** start, leave
4 do	**8** pass, fail
5 cheat	**9** behave

• Now SS do section **2 Places and people**. Check answers and elicit and drill pronunciation of difficult items. Elicit / explain *priests and nuns* in definition 7 (= men and women who belong to a religious order) and the phrase *has a degree* in definition 12 (= has finished university and passed all the exams).

1 state school	**7** religious school
2 private school	**8** head teacher
3 nursery school	**9** professor
4 primary school	**10** student
5 secondary school	**11** pupil
6 boarding school	**12** graduate

• Finally, get SS to do section **3 School life** matching sentences and pictures. Check answers.

1 B
2 A
3 E
4 C
5 D

• Focus on the final instruction 'Can you remember the words on this page? Test yourself or a partner'.

Testing yourself
For **Verbs** SS can cover the list and the **Verb** column. They look at sentences 1–9 and try to remember the verbs. For **Places and people** SS cover the list and words 1–12. They read the definitions and try to remember the words, uncovering one by one to check. For **School life** SS cover the words and look at the pictures and try to remember the phrases.

Testing a partner
See **Testing a partner** *p.17*.

Study Link SS can find more practice of these words on the MultiROM and on the *New English File Intermediate* website.

• Tell SS to go back to the main lesson on *p.52*.

2 PRONUNCIATION & SPEAKING /ʌ/ or /juː/?

Pronunciation notes

The letter *u* has several different pronunciations but between consonants, or at the beginning of a word, it is usually (but not <u>always</u>) /ʌ/, e.g. *sun, luck, summer* or /juː/, e.g. *music, tune, student.*

SS often don't realize that there is a kind of 'hidden sound' – /j/ – in words like *music* and tend to pronounce them /muːzɪk/, or /stuːdənt/.

Students are also reminded here about the rule governing the use of the indefinite article *a* or *an* before words beginning with *u*. If the *u* is pronounced /ʌ/ (i.e. a vowel sound), then *an* is used, e.g. ***an** umbrella, **an** uncle* but if *u* is pronounced /juː/ (i.e. a consonant sound), then *a* is used, e.g. ***a** uniform, **a** university, **a** useful book.*

- Focus on the ⚠ box and point out the two common pronunciations of the letter *u*.
- You may want to point out here that *u* is also sometimes (but much less commonly) pronounced /ʊ/, e.g. *put* and *full.*

a • Focus on the task and make sure SS are clear how the two sounds are pronounced. Give SS a few moments in pairs to put the words in the right column (there are five in each column).

b • **4.1** Play the tape / CD once for SS to check their answers. Then play it again pausing after each word for SS to repeat.

4.1 CD2 Track 8

/ʌ/	/juː/
lunch	computer
nun	pupil
result	student
study	uniform
subject	university

- Finally, focus on the question about the article *a / an* before words beginning with *u* and elicit answers (See **Pronunciation notes**).

We use *a* when *u* is pronounced /juː/ and *an* when *u* is pronounced /ʌ/.

c • **4.2** Now SS practise saying sentences containing the two sounds. First, in pairs, get them to practise saying the sentences to each other. Then play the tape / CD for them to check their pronunciation (you could do this sentence by sentence). Then get individual students to say the sentences.

4.2 CD2 Track 9

1 What subject did you study at university?
2 Do pupils at your school wear a uniform?
3 Most students have lunch in the canteen.
4 I usually get good results in my music exams.

Study Link SS can find more practice of English sounds on the MultiROM and also on the *New English File Intermediate* website.

d • Education vocabulary is now put into practice in a free-speaking activity. SS interview their partner asking the questions in the questionnaire.

- Focus on the question prompts. Remind SS that if they are currently at secondary school, they should use the present tense (i.e. add *do* or *is / are* to the prompts). If they have finished school, they should use the past tense (i.e. add *did* or *was / were* to the prompts).

Extra support

Elicit the questions in the questionnaire before you start the activity.

- SS take turns to interview each other. Remind the student who is interviewing to react to the interviewee's answers and ask for more information where possible (*Really? / That's interesting, etc. / Why didn't you like it?*, etc.).
- Get some whole class feedback at the end by finding out, e.g. how many people liked / didn't like their school and what their best / worst subjects were.

3 READING

a • Focus on the photo on the right and elicit answers to the question.

One of the pupils is an adult.

b • Now get SS to read the introduction and find out the answers to the two questions. Check answers.

He's a journalist. He wanted to see if it was true that school is getting easier. He went to a large, state, secondary school.

- **NOTE**: 'High school' is what Americans call 'secondary school' but some UK schools use 'High school' in their name. This was the case with the school Damian attended to carry out the experiment.

c • Set SS a time limit to read the text, e.g. five minutes, and focus on the question. The first time they read, SS should just try to get a general understanding of the text. Tell them not to worry about the gaps. Check answers.

He finds school very different today because teaching methods have changed. He found it difficult to say if lessons are more difficult or easier than when he went to school, but he found being a pupil in today's school very hard work.

d • SS now read the text again and try to complete the gaps with phrases A–H. Focus on the phrases first and make sure SS understand, e.g. *crowd* (= a big group of people), *be involved* (= be part of or connected to something) and any other words from the phrases (i.e. not from the text, because they'll do these later) you think they may not know.

- Set a time limit again, e.g. five minutes, and then get SS to compare their answers in pairs before checking answers.

2 D **3** H **4** C **5** G **6** B **7** E **8** A

e • In pairs, SS focus on the highlighted words and phrases. Set a time limit. If SS don't have dictionaries, they should ask another pair to help with the meaning of unknown words *before* they ask you. Move around the class helping SS but then have a feedback stage at the end where you try to explain or translate any words or phrases SS aren't sure of.

interrogating = asking questions in an aggressive way
do up = fasten a button (or shoe laces)
in return = in exchange
canteen = a communal dining room, e.g. in a school or factory
spreadsheets = a computer programme used for financial planning
give it in = give sth to somebody in authority, e.g. a teacher
slightly dazed = (a bit) unable to think clearly
bell = a metal object shaped like a cup that makes a ringing noise when you move it

f • Focus on the task. Demonstrate the activity by talking about **French** and **Maths** at your own secondary school. Then SS work in pairs while you move around listening and helping. If there's time, get some general feedback.

Extra idea

Instead of **e** and **f** you could now read each paragraph aloud, eliciting the meaning of the highlighted words and any others that cause problems, and then ask the whole class after each paragraph in what way their experiences in each subject were different.

4 GRAMMAR first conditional and future time clauses

a • Focus on the task and get SS in pairs to answer the questions. Get some feedback from the class, and tell them how you feel or felt about exams.

b • 4.3 & 4.4 SS now listen to two interviews with people who have just taken important exams; in the interviews the speakers use several examples of time clauses with *if, when, as soon as*, etc.

• Focus on the photos of the two students. Explain that 'A-levels' (= Advanced level) are exams that UK secondary pupils take in their final year of school (usually in 3 or 4 subjects). University entrance depends on the 'grades' they get (A, B, C, D, etc.). FCE (= First Certificate in English) is an English exam usually taken by students at an upper intermediate level. Pass grades are A, B, and C.

• Tell SS that they are going to listen to Charlotte first. Focus on the questions and play the tape / CD once for SS to try to answer them. Play the tape again for SS to complete their answers. You could get them to compare their answers in pairs. Now check answers.

Charlotte
1 She is sure she has passed but is worried about her grades.
2 She gets her results tomorrow by post.
3 She doesn't want to plan any celebrations.
4 She will go to Cambridge University.
5 She will do another year at school and take the exams again next year.

4.3 CD2 Track 10

(tapescript in Student's Book on *p.125*)
J = Journalist, C = Charlotte
J What subjects did you take?
C Physics, chemistry, maths, and biology.
J Do you think you've passed?
C I'm sure I've passed, but I'm worried about what grades I'll get.
J Why?
C Because I want to study medicine at university – at Cambridge, and they won't give me a place unless I get three As and a B.
J Do you think you'll get them?
C I don't know. I think I did OK, but I'm a bit worried about maths.
J When will you get your results?
C Tomorrow, by post. I'm *really* nervous – and so are my parents! As soon as the post comes, I'll take the letter upstairs and open it.
J And how will you celebrate if you pass?
C I don't want to plan any celebrations until I get the results.
J And what will you do if you don't get the grades you need?
C I don't want to think about it. If I don't get into Cambridge, my parents will kill me. No, I'm joking. I suppose I'll do another year at school and take the exams again.
J Well, good luck!
C Thanks.

Extra challenge

You could ask SS a few more questions, e.g. *Which subjects did Charlotte take?* (Physics, chemistry, maths, and biology), *What does Charlotte want to study at Cambridge?*, etc.

• 4.3 Now repeat the process for Viktor.

Viktor
1 He thinks he has passed / he's quite optimistic.
2 Tomorrow morning, on the notice board at the school where he studies.
3 He will have a drink with other people in his class.
4 He will carry on studying and would like to take the CAE (Cambridge Advanced English) exam next year.
5 He will do the exam again in June.

4.4 CD2 Track 11

(tapescript in Student's Book on *p.125*)
J = Journalist, V = Viktor
J What exam did you take?
V FCE. First Certificate in English.
J Do you think you've passed?
V I think so. I'm quite optimistic. I think I did the exam quite well.
J When will you get your result?
V Tomorrow morning. I study at a language school and when I go to class tomorrow, the grades will be on the notice board. My name will be the first on the list because my surname begins with A.
J How will you celebrate if you pass?
V I'll go and have a drink with the other people in my class. Well, with the people who have passed.
J And what will you do if you pass? Will you carry on studying English?
V Yes, I'd like to take the CAE exam next year.
J And if you don't pass?
V I'll take the exam again in June.

c • 4.5 Focus on the five sentences from the interviews and elicit who said them (Charlotte said 1–4, and Viktor said 5). Then play the tape / CD, pausing after each one for SS to complete them. Check answers.

Extra challenge

Get SS to try and complete the sentences before they listen.

1 They won't give me a place **unless** I get three As and a B.
2 **As soon as** the post comes, I'll take the letter upstairs and open it.
3 I don't want to plan any celebrations **until** I get the results.
4 **If** I don't get into Cambridge, my parents will kill me.
5 **When** I go to class tomorrow, the grades will be on the notice board.

4.5 CD2 Track 12

1 They won't give me a place unless I get three As and a B.
2 As soon as the post comes, I'll take the letter upstairs and open it.
3 I don't want to plan any celebrations until I get the results.
4 If I don't get into Cambridge, my parents will kill me.
5 When I go to class tomorrow, the grades will be on the notice board.

- Elicit / explain the meaning of *unless* (= if not) and *as soon as* (= the moment when). Then ask SS what tense the verbs are after the bold words (present simple) and if they refer to the present or to the future (the future).

d • Tell SS to go to **Grammar Bank 4A** on *p.136*. Go through the examples and read the rules with the class.

Grammar notes

First conditionals and future time clauses

- SS should be familiar with basic first conditional type sentences (*if* + present, future (*will*)) from their Pre-intermediate course. Here they also learn to use *unless* (instead of *if…not*) in conditional sentences, and that other future time clauses (i.e. beginning with *when, as soon as, unless*, etc.) work in the same way as *if*-clauses, i.e. they are followed by a present tense although they actually refer to the future. This may be new for your students.
- Emphasize that in the other (main) clause the verb form is usually *will* + infinitive but it can also be an imperative, or *going to*.
- A typical mistake includes: using a future form after *when, unless*, etc., e.g. ~~*I'll call you when I'll arrive.*~~

- Focus on the exercises for **4A** on *p.137*. Get SS to do the exercises individually or in pairs. Check answers either after each exercise or when they have done both by getting SS to read the sentences aloud. Tell them to use contractions where possible.

a 1 before 2 until 3 as soon as 4 if
5 when / as soon as 6 unless 7 when 8 until
9 before 10 Unless
b 1 leave 2 finishes 3 won't get 4 'll tell
5 arrive 6 get 7 'll go 8 doesn't like 9 tell
10 'll be

- Tell SS to go back to the main lesson on *p.54*.

e • Put SS in pairs and focus on the task. Demonstrate yourself by making one or two true sentences.
- Give SS two or three minutes to choose their five sentences and complete them. Then SS take it in turns to tell each other their sentences. Get feedback from a few SS.

Extra challenge

Get SS to do **e** orally without writing the sentences down.

f • 4.6 Tell SS they are going to hear Charlotte and Viktor being interviewed again after getting their results. Focus on the task and then play the tape / CD twice. Get SS to compare what they heard and then check answers.

Charlotte passed but her grades weren't as good as she hoped (As in chemistry and biology but B in physics and C in maths.).
She's going to get in touch with Cambridge University to see if they will still accept her. If not, she will re-take her A levels.
Viktor passed with a grade B. He's going to celebrate with his friends (champagne and then dinner).

4.6 CD2 Track 13

(tapescript in Student's Book on *p.125*)
J = Journalist, C = Charlotte, V = Viktor
J Charlotte – I can see from your face that the results, er, weren't exactly what you wanted – am I right?
C Yeah. I got an A in chemistry and biology but only a B in physics and a C in maths.
J So what are you going to do now?
C Well, first I'll get in touch with the university. Perhaps they'll still accept me – but I don't think they will, so... I'll probably take my A levels again next year.
J Were your parents angry?
C No, my Mum and Dad have been really nice – they know how disappointed I am.
J Well Viktor, did you pass your FCE exam?
V Yes, I passed – and I got a B. I'm very pleased. I didn't think I'd get a B. I thought I'd get a C.
J And your friends?
V They all passed except one. But he didn't expect to pass – he didn't do any work.
J So are you going out to celebrate?
V Oh yes. We're going to have champagne in a bar and then we're going to have dinner together.

Extra support

Pause after Charlotte, and repeat if necessary. Then play Viktor twice.

5 LISTENING

a • Focus on the photo and the extract from the TV guide and get SS to read it. Explain that *'Em* in *That'll Teach 'Em* is a shortened form of *them*. Then focus on the questions and elicit answers from the whole class, but don't say if they are right or not at this stage.

Extra challenge

Get SS to discuss questions 1–4 in pairs, and then get feedback from the whole class.

b • 4.7 Tell SS they are going to listen to a TV critic talking about the programme *That'll Teach 'Em* (from exercise **a**). SS should listen and find the answers to questions 1–4 in **a**.

- Play the tape / CD once. Then tell SS in pairs to make notes alongside the questions and to circle the thing(s) which the pupils hated most.
- Check answers.

1 The idea was to compare education today with education in the 1950s.
2 The food (and the girls didn't like the cold showers).
3 Very strict. Silence all the time. If children misbehaved, they were caned (hit on the hand with a thin wooden cane) or had to stay behind after class and do extra work.
4 They did badly. Most of the pupils failed the exams. Only one pupil passed all the 1950s exams.

Extra support

Play the tape / CD in sections, pausing after each question is answered and playing again if necessary. Elicit the answers from the whole class.

c • SS listen again and this time they mark sentences 1–10 T or F. Get them to compare answers with a partner. Play the tape / CD again if necessary. Check answers, and get SS to say why the F ones are false.

1 F (30)
2 F (It was a boarding school.)
3 T
4 T
5 T
6 F (They didn't mind.)
7 F (Most of them found the classes interesting.)
8 F (They are different, but not necessarily easier.)
9 F (They were intelligent / bright children. They failed because the exams were so different from what they were used to.)
10 T

Extra support

If there's time, you could get SS to listen to the tape / CD with the tapescript on *p.126* so they can see exactly what they understood / didn't understand. Translate / explain any new words or phrases.

4.7 CD2 Track 14

(tapescript in Student's Book on *p.126*)

P = Presenter, M = Michael

P Hello and welcome to our review of the week's TV. With me today is the television critic Michael Stein… Michael, what did you think was the best programme of the week?

M Well, I've chosen the last programme in the Channel 4 series *That'll Teach 'Em*. I must say I found the whole series absolutely fascinating. For those of you who didn't see it, what the programme did was to take a group of 30 16-year-old children and send them – as an experiment – to a boarding school for one month. But it wasn't a modern boarding school, it was a 1950s boarding school. They recreated exactly the same conditions as in the 1950s – the same food, the same discipline, the same exams. The idea was to compare education today with education in the 1950s.

P I bet it was a shock for today's schoolchildren.

M Well, it was, of course. It wasn't just the classes – it was the whole atmosphere – I mean they had to wear the uniform from the 50s – horrible uncomfortable clothes – they hated them and they weren't allowed to leave the school once for the whole month, or watch TV, or use mobiles. And they had to have cold showers every morning, and go for cross-country runs!

P What was the worst thing for them?

M The food, definitely! Most of them hated it. They said it was cold and tasteless. And the girls didn't like the cold showers much either…

P What about the classes?

M Well, of course the biggest difference for the kids was the discipline. It was silence all the time during the lessons – only the teacher spoke. And anyone who misbehaved had to go to the headmaster and was either caned – hit on the hand – or had to stay behind after class and do extra work. And of course they couldn't use computers or calculators, but curiously the kids didn't really mind that, and in fact most of them found the lessons interesting – some of them said they were more interesting than their normal lessons. They had to work very hard though.

P So what happened in the end? Did they pass the 1950s exams?

M No. Most of them failed – although they were all really bright children. There was only one child who actually passed all the subjects.

P So, do you think that means exams really used to be harder in the 1950s?

M No, I think the kids failed because exams in the 1950s were very different. The children in the programme will probably do very well in their own exams. On the other hand, 1950s children would probably find today's exams very difficult.

P How did the kids themselves feel about the experiment?

M They were really positive. In general they had a good time and they all felt they learned a lot. I think it made them appreciate their own lifestyle more. Some of them actually said it was the best month of their lives. It was an interesting experiment and the programme was really well made. I very much enjoyed watching it.

d • Focus on the question and have a brief open class discussion.

6 SPEAKING

a • Put SS in small groups (three or four). Go through the discussion topics in the list, making sure SS understand them.

• Give SS time in their groups to each choose a different topic from the list. Then give them time (e.g. five minutes) to think of three reasons why they agree or disagree with the sentence. Help SS with any vocabulary they may need.

b • Now focus SS' attention on the **Useful language**. SS in each group now take turns to say whether they agree or disagree with the sentence they have chosen and why. The other SS should listen and say if they agree or disagree, and why.

• If there's time, you could have a brief open class discussion on each topic.

Extra photocopiable activities

Grammar

future time clauses: *if, when, etc. p.151*

Communicative

Sentence halves *p.182* (instructions *p.167*)

HOMEWORK

Study Link **Workbook** *pp.34–36*

4B In an ideal world...

G second conditional
V houses
P sentence stress

Lesson plan

This lesson revises second conditional type sentences with *if* and introduces SS to conditional sentences without *if*. In the **Grammar Bank** the second conditional is contrasted with the first. The initial context is provided by a questionnaire from a British newspaper where two famous people are asked hypothetical *What would you do / wear...?* type questions. In the second part of the lesson, SS learn the vocabulary of houses and listen to people describing their dream house. The theme of houses is continued with a reading text about a very personal house, that of the painter Frida Kahlo in Mexico City. The pronunciation focus in this lesson is on sentence stress in conditional sentences.

Optional lead-in (books closed)

Tell SS to imagine that they could live in another country. Ask them what country they would choose and why. Get feedback about SS' ideas and find out which country is the most popular and why. Tell SS that they are going to read a questionnaire from a British newspaper where famous people are asked similar questions.

1 GRAMMAR second conditional

a • Books open. Focus on the two photos and get SS to describe the people. Find out if they know anything about them. If they don't, use the notes below to tell SS about them.

> **Joaquín Cortés**
> Joaquín Cortés is Spanish and is a very well-known flamenco dancer. He began his dancing career in the Spanish National Ballet at the age of 15. He formed his own dance company in 1992 and became famous all over the world after the success of his show *Gypsy Passion*.
> **Isabella Rossellini**
> Isabella Rossellini is an actress and has appeared in several films including *Blue Velvet* (1986). She also modelled (for Lancôme Cosmetics) and has her own cosmetics company.

b • Focus on the questionnaire and explain that this is a weekly feature in a British newspaper in which famous people are asked the same hypothetical questions. Go through the questions making sure that SS understand them. SS should realize that the first four questions are second conditionals, but you could check this by asking them.

• Now focus on the answers which have been removed from the questionnaire and go through them making sure that SS understand them. Use the pictures to help deal with any difficult vocabulary, e.g. *fly*, *corset*.

• Remind SS that *I'd* = *I would* and that the answers are in the conditional too.

• Focus on the task and get SS to match two answers to each question. Then they should try and guess who each answer belongs to. Check answers.

> **1 B** (JC) and **J** (IR)
> **2 A** (IR) and **H** (JC)
> **3 D** (IR) and **F** (JC)
> **4 C** (JC) and **G** (IR)
> **5 E** (JC) and **I** (IR)

Extra idea

If you think they would enjoy it, you could now get SS to answer these questions themselves in pairs. However, question 3 may be a sensitive one with, e.g. younger SS, so be aware of this.

c • Focus on questions 1–4 and do this task as a whole class activity. Check answers.

> **1** The past tense.
> **2** The conditional form (*would* + infinitive).
> **3** There is no *if*-clause.
> **4** Imaginary situations.

d • Tell SS to go to **Grammar Bank 4B** on *p.136*. Go through the examples and read the rules with the class.

Grammar notes

Second conditional sentences

• SS who previously used *New English File Pre-intermediate* or a similar level course will have already been introduced to second conditional sentences (*if* + past, conditional (*would* / *wouldn't*)).

• What should be new here is the use of the conditional tense without *if* in sentences like *I would never buy a flat next to a pub or restaurant*. This use should not be too problematic as SS may well have a conditional form of the verb in their L1, and they have also already met this use of the conditional in the phrase *I would like...*

• After *I* / *he* / *she* / *it* you can use *was* or *were* (although *were* is more formal), e.g. *If I was / were younger, I'd have another child*. But, in the expression *If I were you*, ..., to give advice, you must use *were*, not *was*.

• Typical mistakes include:
  – Using *would* in both clauses, e.g. ~~*If I would have more time, I would learn another language*~~.
  – Mixing up the form of first and second conditionals, e.g. ~~*If I knew her mobile number, I'll call her*~~.
  – Using a first conditional where a second would be more appropriate or vice versa, e.g. ~~*If I am shorter, I can wear those shoes*~~.
  – ~~*If I was you*~~,...

• Now get SS to do the exercises on *p.137* individually or in pairs. Check answers either after each exercise or when they have finished both. Get SS to read the whole sentences aloud and encourage them to use contractions. In exercise **b** you could ask SS after each sentence if it is a first or second conditional.

a 1 It would be better for me if we met tomorrow.
2 She wouldn't treat him like that if she really loved him.
3 If I could live anywhere in the world, I'd / would live in New Zealand.
4 The kitchen would look bigger if we painted it white.
5 I wouldn't buy that house if I were you.
6 He'd / would be more attractive if he wore nicer clothes.
7 If we didn't have children, we'd / would travel more.
8 What would you do in this situation if you were me?

b 1 get 5 didn't live
2 'd / would feel 6 doesn't get lost
3 lost 7 gets
4 'll cook 8 'd / would enjoy

e • Sit SS in pairs, **A** and **B**, preferably face to face. Tell them to go to **Communication** *What would you do if…?* **A** on *p.117*, **B** on *p.120.*

• Go through the instructions and make sure SS understand what they have to do.

Extra idea

You could get an **A** and a **B** student to each choose a question to ask you first, before they start asking each other.

• Tell SS to go back to the main lesson on *p.57*.

2 PRONUNCIATION & SPEAKING sentence stress

Pronunciation notes

SS continue work on sentence stress and are given more practice in pronouncing more strongly the words in a sentence which convey important information (e.g. nouns, verbs, adjectives, and adverbs).

Other, shorter words (e.g. articles and pronouns) should be pronounced less strongly. Getting this balance right will help SS pronounce English with correct rhythm.

a • Focus on the task and give SS a minute or two to match the sentence halves. Get them to compare their answers in pairs.

b • 4.8 Play the tape / CD for SS to check their answers

1 F 2 D 3 E 4 C 5 A 6 B

4.8 CD2 Track 15

1 I wouldn't wear that hat if I were you.
2 If you did more exercise, you'd feel much better.
3 If it wasn't so expensive, I'd buy it.
4 I'd get married tomorrow if I could find the right person.
5 She'd play better if she practised more.
6 If you talked to her, I'm sure she'd understand you.

c • Ask SS why some words are underlined (Because they are the words which carry important information and so they are stressed.). Play the tape / CD for SS to listen and repeat, and encourage them to try to copy the rhythm by saying the underlined words more strongly and the unstressed words as lightly and quickly as possible.

d • Focus on the task and give SS time to choose their three sentences and complete them. Go round making sure that SS are writing correct sentences.

Extra idea

Before SS start writing you could focus on the pictures and ask SS what job, country, etc. the artist has illustrated (to China, a mini, cycling, an astronomer, to play the piano, a chalet in Switzerland). These were the artist's real answers to the questions!

• Put SS in pairs and they take it in turns to tell their partners their true sentences and to give reasons. Monitor and encourage them to get the right sentence rhythm.

3 VOCABULARY houses

a • Focus SS' attention on the cover of the magazine and explain that it is a well-known British magazine, which gives people ideas how to decorate and furnish their houses. Focus on the two questions and elicit answers.

It's a living room. You can see curtains, a sofa, cushions, a carpet, an armchair, a plant, a mirror.

b • Tell SS to go to **Vocabulary Bank** ***Houses*** on *p.151.* Focus on section **1 Types of houses**. SS do the exercise individually or in pairs. Check answers.

1 terraced house
2 block of flats
3 cottage
4 detached house

• Now focus on section **2 Where people live**, and give SS time to match the sentences. Check answers.

1 g 2 d 3 e 4 b 5 a 6 c 7 f

• Point out that *suburbs* does not have a negative connotation in English (it is a false friend in some languages); in fact, British suburbs are often expensive areas.

• Now get SS to match the words and pictures in section **3 Parts of a house**. Check answers.

1 chimney
2 roof
3 balcony
4 garage
5 wall
6 gate
7 garden
8 steps
9 terrace
10 path

- You may want to point out the difference between *balcony* and *terrace.* A balcony is always on a first or higher floor, whereas a terrace is on the ground floor.
- Finally, get SS to do section **4 Furniture**. Check answers after **a.**

bathroom	kitchen	living room	bedroom
washbasin	sink	coffee table	bedside table
shower	dishwasher	armchair	chest of drawers

Make sure SS know exactly what the words in **4a** mean by describing what each piece of furniture is used for or with drawings on the board.

- Now do **4b**. Give SS time to add words. Elicit words from SS and drill pronunciation.

Extra idea

When you check answers to **4**, copy the chart on the board. When you have checked **4a**, elicit SS' extra words (**b**) and write them on the board in the chart for other SS to copy down any new words.

- Finally, focus on the instruction 'Can you remember the words on this page? Test yourself or a partner'.

Testing yourself

For **Types of houses** and **Parts of a house** SS can cover the words and look at the pictures and try to remember the words. For **Where people live** SS can cover sentences 1–7 and look at sentences a–g and try to remember the words and phrases. For **Furniture** SS can cover the chart and try to remember the words in each column.

Testing a partner

See **Testing a partner** *p.17.*

Study Link SS can find more practice of these words on the MultiROM and on the *New English File Intermediate* website.

- Tell SS to go back to the main lesson on *p.58.*

c • Put SS in pairs, **A** and **B**. Give **A**s a few minutes to interview **B**s with the five questions before changing roles.

4 LISTENING & SPEAKING

a • 4.9 Focus on the task and play the tape / CD for SS to match the four speakers with their 'dream house' by writing numbers 1–4 in the appropriate box.

- Check answers. Elicit that *a penthouse flat* (4) is the top floor flat of a building, usually with a big balcony.

1 B 2 D 3 C 4 A

b • Now SS listen for more detail. Play the tape / CD again for SS to match the speakers to what they said by writing numbers 1–4 in the appropriate box. Check answers.

would not like to have other people living nearby [2]
would like to live somewhere that was partly old and partly modern [3]
would not spend much time inside their dream house [1]
doesn't think they will ever get their dream house [4]

Extra support

For **b**, play each person again and pause. Check which SS think is the corresponding sentence, and then ask SS a few more questions, e.g. for 1 *Where exactly would he like his house to be? What would the house be like? What view would he have?,* etc.

If there's time, you could get SS to listen to the tape / CD with the tapescript on *p.126* so they can see exactly what they understood / didn't understand. Translate / explain any new words or phrases.

4.9 CD2 Track 16

(tapescript in Student's Book on *p.126*)

1 When I retire, if I can afford it, I'd love to live in a cottage in a picturesque village somewhere in the country, not too remote. The most important thing for me would be the garden – I'd like a traditional English garden, with fruit trees and lots of flowers – not too big, though. I'd spend my life in the garden, especially in the spring and summer.

2 My dream house would be on the coast, by the sea, on a beautiful unspoilt beach. It'd be modern and quite simple, with wooden floors and big windows, and from every window you'd be able to see the sea. It'd be quite isolated, with no neighbours for miles and miles. Can you imagine – just the sound of the wind and the sea?

3 I'd love to have a big old town house in the centre of London, maybe one of those beautiful terraced houses with big rooms and high ceilings, and a lovely staircase going down to the hall. But the bathrooms and kitchens would have to be modern, because old ones are cold and a bit impractical. I'd need some help looking after it though so…

4 If I won the lottery, which of course I won't, I'd buy a big penthouse flat near the river with a great view, a really hi-tech flat, you know, with one of those intelligent fridges which orders food from the supermarket all by itself when you're running out and a huge TV and music system – but all very stylish and minimalist.

c • Focus on the speaking task and give SS a few minutes to think about what they are going to say. Go round the class helping SS with any vocabulary they might need which isn't in **Vocabulary Bank *Houses*.**

d • Put SS into small groups of three to five. They take turns to describe their dream house. They must also say which of the other houses they like best (not counting theirs). When the activity has finished, you could get feedback from each group to find out which house was the most popular.

5 READING

a • Ask the questions to the whole class and elicit answers. Be ready to answer the question yourself if SS are slow to volunteer anything.

- Focus on the photos. Elicit or tell the class who the woman is (Frida Kahlo) and where she was from (Mexico). Ask if any SS have seen the 2002 film *Frida* (about her life) starring Salma Hayek.

b • Focus on the task. Tell SS to read the article to find out which part of the house these things are connected to and why they are mentioned.

- Set a time limit and when it is up, elicit answers from the class.

Extra idea

Alternatively, you could read the text aloud to SS, as they follow it with you and look at the photos. After each paragraph stop and get a reaction from the class, e.g. after the first paragraph, ask SS if they have seen the film *Frida*, if they like her paintings, if anyone has ever been to Mexico, etc.; after paragraph two, ask what SS know about the various people mentioned. Deal with vocabulary as it comes up. When you get to the end, SS could do task **b** from memory, and then do **c**.

Two giant statues – **the entrance**: they guard it, and are nearly 7 metres tall.
Leon Trotsky – **the living room**. He was a political leader who was a friend of Frida Kahlo's and who visited the house.
A yellow floor – **the kitchen** has a yellow floor to stop insects from coming in.
A monkey and a parrot – **the kitchen**, where they used to have their meals. The monkey and parrot were Frida's pets. The parrot used to do tricks at the table in return for butter.
A pair of shoes – **Diego's bedroom**. They can be seen there today. They are enormous because Diego had very big feet.
A cupboard with a glass door – **upstairs in a bedroom**. It contains a colourful Mexican dress which Frida loved wearing.
July 7 1910 – this date is written **above the cupboard with the glass door**. It says that Frida was born on this day but she wasn't. She was born three years earlier.
1929-1954 – These dates are written on the walls of **the patio**. It says that Frida and Diego lived in the house for those years. In fact they lived separately for some of that time.

c • Focus on the task and get SS to work individually and then compare their answers with their partner. Check answers.

1 dresser	3 entrance	5 upstairs	7 shutters
2 glass	4 gallery	6 airy	8 patio

d • Focus on the two questions and get some feedback from the whole class.

6 4.10 ♫ SONG *Our house*

• This song was made famous by the British group Madness in 1982. If you want to do the song in class, use the photocopiable activity on *p.209*.

4.10 CD2 Track 17

Our house
Father wears his Sunday best
Mother's tired she needs a rest
The kids are playing up downstairs
Sister's sighing in her sleep
Brother's got a date to keep
He can't hang around

Our house, in the middle of our street
Our house, in the middle of our...

Our house it has a crowd
There's always something happening
And it's usually quite loud
Our mum she's so house-proud
Nothing ever slows her down
And a mess is not allowed

Our house, in the middle of our street, etc.
Something tells you that you've got to get away from it

Father gets up late for work
Mother has to iron his shirt
Then she sends the kids to school
Sees them off with a small kiss
She's the one they're going to miss
In lots of ways

Our house, in the middle of our street, etc.

I remember way back then when everything was true and when
We would have such a very good time such a fine time
Such a happy time
And I remember how we'd play, simply waste the day away
Then we'd say nothing would come between us two dreamers

Father wears his…, etc.

Our house, in the middle of our street
Our house, in the middle of our...
Our house, in the middle of our street
Our house, in the middle of our...

Our house, was our castle and our keep
Our house, in the middle of our street
Our house, that was where we used to sleep
Our house, in the middle of our street

Extra photocopiable activities

Grammar
second conditional *p.152*
Communicative
If you had to choose… *p.183* (instructions *p.167*)
Song
Our house p.209 (instructions *p.205*)

HOMEWORK

Study Link Workbook *pp.37–39*

4C Still friends?

G *usually* and *used to*
V friendship
P /s/ or /z/?

Lesson plan

Friends and friendship provides the main theme for this lesson which revises and consolidates *used to* to talk about habitual actions in the past, and states and actions which are no longer true.

The vocabulary focus of the lesson is words and phrases related to friendship and pronunciation focuses on the contrast between /s/ and /z/. The main context is the true stories (although the real names have been changed) of two people who contacted the *Friends Reunited* website to try and get back in touch with old friends from their past. In the second half of the lesson, SS read a provocative text which encourages us to 'edit' our friends and SS discuss various aspects of friendship.

Optional lead-in (books closed)

- Ask the class to think about how many of their friends from primary school they are still in touch with.
- Get feedback from the class to establish how many people they are in touch with and how often they meet. Find out who still has the most old friends from those years. If you are teaching adults, you could ask the same question about secondary school as well.

1 VOCABULARY & SPEAKING friendship

a • Books open. Focus attention on the photo of the two women and then on the task. Then give SS a few minutes to complete the text and to compare their answers with a partner's. Check answers.

1 known	**5** have a lot in common
2 met	**6** lost touch
3 colleague	**7** keep in touch
4 get on very well	**8** argue

b • Focus on the task and give SS a couple of minutes to think about a close friend and how they will answer the questions.

• Put SS in pairs and they take turns to interview each other about their close friend. While they are doing this, go round monitoring and helping if necessary.

Extra idea

You might also want to teach *workmate* as an alternative to *colleague*, and this use of *-mate*, e.g. *flatmate* (= someone who shares a flat / house with you), and *classmate* (= someone in your class at school).

2 GRAMMAR *usually* and *used to*

a • Ask SS the questions and elicit any experiences SS have had.

b • Get SS to read the information about *Friends Reunited* and answer the two questions.

It's for finding out what old friends are doing, and getting back in touch with them.
You find the web page for your old school or workplace and add your name to the list. You can also put a photo and some information. If you want to send a message to someone on the list, you do this via *Friends Reunited*, not personal emails.

• You could explain that *Friends Reunited* has been very successful in reuniting many old friends over the last few years. The inventors of the website have become millionaires.

c • Focus on the photos on *p.61* and tell SS that these are of two people who got back in touch with old friends through *Friends Reunited* (The photo of the couple is an old photo of Carol as a teenager with her boyfriend). They are true stories although the names have been changed. Tell SS to read both texts and to answer the two questions. Check answers.

Carol wanted to meet Robert, an old boyfriend. She lost touch with him when they broke up.
Alex wanted to meet his old school friends. He thought they might help him recover his memory, which he lost after a motorbike accident.

d • Focus on the *used to* phrases in the list and tell SS to read the texts again about Carol and Alex and to fill each gap with one of the phrases. SS can compare with a partner before you check answers.

1 We used to go out	**4** used to come
2 he used to go to	**5** I used to know
3 I used to live	

e • Focus on the task and the two questions. Do this as an open class activity. Elicit answers.

We use *used to* to talk about habitual actions or states in the past. We make negative sentences and questions with *did / didn't*, e.g. *Did you use to go to boarding school? I didn't use to have short hair.*

f • Tell SS to go to **Grammar Bank 4C** on *p.136*. Go through the examples and the rules with the class and drill the pronunciation of *used to*.

Grammar notes

usually* and *used to

• *Used to* is a grammar point which was presented in *New English File Pre-intermediate* and is revised and consolidated here. This is a 'late assimilation' structure as SS can express more or less the same idea by using the past tense + a time expression. Compare: *I used to go to that primary school* and *I went to that primary school (when I was a child)*. In that sense *used to* is a sophisticated structure and its correct use helps to give the impression of having a good level of English. In this lesson *used to* is contrasted with the use of the present simple with *usually* to talk about present habits.

- SS may have problems with *used to* as their L1 may either use a tense which doesn't exist in English for past habits, or may have a verb which can be used both for present and past habits, unlike *used to* which can only be used in the past.
- Emphasize the way we often don't repeat the main verb but just use the auxiliary verb with *any more* / *any longer* when we contrast the past and present habits, e.g. *I used to like cartoons but I don't any more.*
- Typical mistakes include:
  – Using *use to* instead of *usually* for present habits and states, e.g. ~~*I use to go to bed at 11.00 every night.*~~
  – Making mistakes of spelling, e.g. ~~*We didn't used to wear a uniform at my school.*~~
  – Confusing *used to* + infinitive with *be* / *get used to (doing something).*

- Now get SS to do the exercises on *p.137* individually or in pairs. Check answers either after each exercise or after both.

a 1 I **used** to get up
2 Did she always **use** to...?
3 Do you **usually** have breakfast...?
4 They didn't **use** to have
5 he **usually** drinks tea
6 He used **to** be a teacher
7 Do **you usually** wear...?
8 we **went** to
9 **Did** she use to live...?
10 we **didn't** use to wear

b 1 used to live
2 Did you use to have
3 didn't use to like
4 used to be
5 did you use to work
6 used to play
7 used to have
8 Did you use to argue
9 didn't use to be

- Tell SS to go back to the main lesson on *p.61*.

3 LISTENING

Tell SS that they are going to listen to what happened when Carol and Alex went to their reunions.

If this is a different lesson from when SS did exercise **2 GRAMMAR**, it would be a good idea to get them to read the texts again. Alternatively, you could read the texts aloud quite slowly to the class while they follow with books closed.

a • **4.11** Focus on the task. Play the tape / CD once, and tell SS they just have to listen if the meeting was a success or not. Elicit the answer.

Carol's reunion was not a success. They didn't have anything in common any more.

b • Now SS listen again for a more detailed understanding. Before SS listen, quickly go through questions 1–5 or give SS time to read them.

- Play the tape / CD once the whole way through. Then give SS time to discuss and answer the questions in pairs. Then play the tape once more if necessary, pausing to give SS time to complete their answers. Check answers.

Carol's story
1 He always said that he would hate to be a teacher.
2 She thought 'he always used to be late'.
3 People say she looks five years younger than she is. He looked like an old man. He was bald (and was wearing a hideous jacket).
4 That they didn't have anything in common any more.
5 He wasn't a rebel any more, he was boring and conventional.

c **4.12** Now do the same for Alex.

Alex's reunion was successful. He is now in touch regularly with the people he met and is going out with one of them.

d Now SS listen for the answers to questions 6–10.

Alex's story
6 No, he didn't recognize anyone.
7 He felt nervous.
8 All the things he used to do when he was at school (e.g. play in the football team, etc.).
9 He remembered that he used to wear glasses.
10 Anna is a girl who used to be at his school. They are now going out together.

4.11 CD2 Track 18
(tapescript in Student's Book on *p.126*)
CAROL
When Robert replied to my email I got really excited. He didn't actually say very much about himself. He just told me that he was now a teacher, which surprised me because he always used to say he would hate to teach. He also told me that he'd been married but was now divorced.
Anyway, I answered his email and we agreed to meet for lunch at a restaurant I like – it's a place where I often go at weekends.
When I got there I looked around to see if I could see him, but I couldn't, and I thought, 'Typical! Same old Robert,' because he always used to be late. So I sat down and ordered a drink. I was just sipping my wine when a man came over to my table and said, 'Carol, how are you?'. I could hardly believe it – I mean I know neither of us is young any more, but I think I look good for my age. People usually say I look five years younger than I am. But Robert looked like an old man. His lovely long hair was all gone – in fact he was bald, with a few strands of hair sort of combed over his head – and he was wearing the most *hideous* jacket. Well, I know you shouldn't judge by appearances, so I smiled at him and we started talking – and well, I quite enjoyed the lunch and we talked a lot about the past – but I knew as soon as I saw him that we didn't have anything in common any more. And I was right. Instead of the rebel he used to be, he was, well, now much more conventional than me. In fact, he seemed just like the sort of teachers we used to hate when we were young.

4.12 CD2 Track 19

(tapescript in Student's Book on *p.126*)

ALEX

I got to the pub late because I couldn't find it, but when I walked in I saw a whole group of young people at a table and I thought that must be them, though I didn't really recognize anybody. So I went up and they all said hello. They all recognized me, which was great though it felt a bit strange. I must admit I was feeling quite nervous. Anyway, I sat down and we started talking. They told me lots of things that I used to do when I was at school, like play in the school football team – they said I used to be really good – and they told me about all sorts of other things: places we used to go to, things like that. Some of my friends had even brought photos and we looked at them. I'd completely forgotten that I used to wear these really awful big glasses – and I sort of relaxed and I felt that I was getting to know them again, and getting to know more about myself and my past. Anyway, since we met that evening, we've all been emailing each other and I've started going out with Anna – one of the girls who was at the pub that night. She says she used to really like me at school, but that I didn't use to take any notice of her then! I can't remember any of that, but I know I like her a lot now!

4 PRONUNCIATION & SPEAKING /s/ or /z/?

Pronunciation notes

Many learners tend to pronounce the letters *se* as the unvoiced sound /s/ as in *bus*. In fact *se* is more often pronounced as a voiced sound /z/, e.g. *lose*, *revise*, etc.

a • **4.13** Focus on the two pronunciation pictures and elicit the two example words: *snake* and *zebra* and the /s/ and /z/ sounds. Focus on the task and point out that SS need to be careful with *se* because the pronunciation may be /s/ or /z/.

• Focus on the first sentence, and before playing the tape / CD, ask SS if *used to* is /s/ or /z/ (they should know that it is /s/).

• Play the tape / CD for SS to write *s* or *z* in the box after each sentence. Get them to compare their answers in pairs and then play the tape / CD again. Check answers, and elicit that the most common pronunciation of *se* is /z/.

1 /s/ 2 /z/ 3 /z/ 4 /s/ 5 /z/ 6 /z/ 7 /s/ 8 /z/

4.13 CD2 Track 20

1 I used to live in London.
2 I used my credit card to pay.
3 Excuse me. Can you help me?
4 You need to practise your pronunciation.
5 We won't win, we'll lose.
6 They advertise on TV.
7 They promised to keep in touch.
8 Could you close the window?

b • Get SS to practise saying the sentences in pairs and then ask individual SS to say them. You could also get SS to listen and repeat after the tape / CD before practising in pairs.

Extra challenge

You could also tell SS that in the same way that *used* is pronounced differently depending on its meaning, *close* also is /z/ when it's a verb but /s/ when it's an adjective as in a *close friend*.

c • Put SS in pairs, **A** and **B**. Focus on the task and give SS a few minutes to choose their three topics and plan what they are going to say.

• SS **A** start and tell **B** about their first topic, giving as much information as they can. **B** can ask for more information too. Then **B** tell **A** about their first topic, etc.

Extra support

Choose one of the topics and tell SS a little about it. This way you both demonstrate what you want them to do and give SS extra listening practice.

• As SS are talking, move round monitoring and helping.

Study Link SS can find more practice of English sounds on the MultiROM and also on the *New English File Intermediate* website.

5 READING

a • Ask the three questions one by one to the whole class and elicit some answers from individual SS.

Extra idea

Before doing **a**, you could write on the board A FRIEND, A COLLEAGUE, A CLASSMATE and ask SS what the difference is.

a friend = someone who you know and like
a colleague = someone who you work with in a job, especially in a profession
a classmate = someone who is in the same class as you

b • Focus on the task and the title of the article. Set SS a time limit to read the article once and find out what exactly 'editing your friends' means.

edit your friends = decide which of your friends are important, and stop seeing, spending time with the rest

c • Focus on the task. SS now read the article for more detail and choose the best summary for each paragraph. Get them to compare their answers with a partner before checking answers.

1 c 2 b 3 a 4 c

d • Focus on the task and give SS three or four minutes to do this. Feedback some of the words and phrases they have chosen.

e • Ask these questions to the whole class and elicit some reactions.

HOW WORDS WORK...

1 Focus on the instructions and give SS a few minutes, in pairs or individually, to match the *get* phrases, which have come up during the lesson, with definitions A–G. Check answers and make sure SS are sure what each *get* phrase means. Point out that the verb *get* has several different meanings and is one of the most common verbs in English. SS may already know or will come across other meanings, e.g. *I didn't get the joke* (here *get* = understand).

1 F **2** B **3** D **4** G **5** A **6** E **7** C

2 Focus on the task and give SS a minute or so to do it. Check answers and then get SS to quickly ask each other the questions in pairs.

1 get on with **2** get to know **3** get
4 get in touch **5** get rid of

6 LISTENING & SPEAKING

a • 4.14 Focus on the instructions and go through sentences A–F. Don't get your SS' opinions at this stage.
• Play the tape / CD and pause after the first speaker. Let SS discuss with a partner which sentence they think he is talking about. Check answers.

Speaker 1 B **Speaker 2** A **Speaker 3** D

b • Now play the tape / CD again, also pausing after each speaker. This time SS listen to see if the speakers agree or disagree with the sentence, and for the reasons and examples they give. Get SS to compare what they understood with their partner before eliciting answers.

1 Disagrees. He thinks it's easier because you can text, email, and chat online on the computer. He gives the example of several friends he met on holiday last year. He is still in touch with them.
2 Agrees. She thinks that men keep friends longer because their friendships are less intense (and less intimate) than women's – they don't talk about their personal lives much. As a result, they don't have arguments.
3 Agrees. He says that if you criticize your friend's partner while they are still together (and in love) you will lose the friendship. You should wait until they break up. He gives the example of how he once criticized his friend's girlfriend and now they aren't friends any more.

Extra support

If there's time, you could get SS to listen to the tape / CD with the tapescript on *p.126* so they can see exactly what they understood / didn't understand. Translate / explain any new words or phrases.

4.14 CD2 Track 21
(tapescript in Student's Book on *p.126*)
1 I don't agree at all. I think it's much easier. Today you can text, you can email, you can chat online on Messenger and things like that. I'm still in touch with some friends who I met on holiday last year even though they live miles away.
2 Actually, I think it's probably true. Because I know a lot of men who are still friends with people they went to primary school with, but I don't know many women who are. For example, my brother has a friend called Tim who he's known since they were three years old. But I think the reason why is because men's friendships are less intense, sort of less intimate than women's friendships. As men only ever talk about sport or superficial things, it doesn't matter if they've completely changed and don't have much in common any more – they can still talk about football.
3 You definitely shouldn't. I mean that's the quickest way to lose a friendship. If you don't like a friend's girlfriend, you should just keep quiet. You have to wait until they break up, and of course then you can say how awful you thought she was and your friend will agree and think you're being supportive. But if you say anything bad while they're still madly in love, it's a disaster. I know because it happened to me once with a friend of mine. I said something negative about his girlfriend. And now we're not friends any more.

c • Focus on the task and get SS to tick and cross the sentences according to their own opinions. Give SS a few minutes to think about their reasons. They can write notes if they want.

d • Put SS in groups and go through the expressions in **Useful language**. Then tell SS to discuss each sentence in turn giving their opinion. If there's time, get some feedback from the whole class.

Study Link SS can find a dictation and a Grammar quiz on all the grammar from File 4 on the MultiROM and more grammar activities on the *New English File Intermediate* website.

Extra photocopiable activities

Grammar
usually and *used to p.153*
Communicative
Am I telling the truth? *p.184* (instructions *p.167*)
Vocabulary
What's the difference? *p.200* (instructions *p.195*)

HOMEWORK

Study Link **Workbook** *pp.40–42*

4 PRACTICAL ENGLISH A VISIT FROM A POP STAR

Function Making suggestions
Language *Let's..., Shall we..?, Why don't we..?*, etc.

Lesson plan

In the first part of the lesson SS learn and practise ways of making suggestions. Allie and Mark discuss how they are going to entertain Scarlett, a 'difficult' young pop star who is in Paris for a concert that evening. In the second half of the lesson (**Social English**), they take Scarlett to an expensive restaurant, but Scarlett is not impressed.

Study Link These lessons are on the *New English File Intermediate* DVD / Video, which can be used instead of the Class Cassette / CD (see introduction *p.9*). The main functional section of each episode is also on the MultiROM with additional activities.

Optional lead-in (books closed)

- Revise what happened in the previous episode by eliciting the story from SS, e.g. *Where did Mark find a flat? How did he go to see it? What happened when Mark was looking at the flat? Did Mark decide to rent it?*
- Also try to elicit the phrases they learnt, e.g. *How far is it? How long does it take?* (You could write these with gaps on the board to help SS remember.)

  If you are using the video / DVD, you could play the previous episode again, leaving out the 'Listen and Repeat' sections.

MAKING SUGGESTIONS

a • 4.15 Focus on the photo and questions, and tell SS to cover the dialogue with their hand or a piece of paper. Alternatively, write the questions on the board and get SS to close their books.

• Play the tape / CD once the whole way through. Then play it again, pausing if necessary. Check answers.

> The problem is that Jacques is delayed in Rome so he can't look after Scarlett Scarpino, a young pop singer who will be in Paris that day. Jacques was going to look after her, but now Allie and Mark will have to. They decide to take her on a boat trip, then to the Eiffel tower and finally to lunch at the Renaissance (Jacques's favourite restaurant).

b • Now get SS to look at the dialogue. In pairs, they read it and see if they can guess or remember the missing words. Emphasize that they shouldn't write the words in the dialogue but in pencil alongside or on a separate sheet of paper.

c • Play the tape / CD again, pausing if necessary for SS to check or write answers. Then go through the dialogue line by line and check answers. Find out if SS had guessed the words correctly. Where they had not guessed correctly, see if their alternative also fits.

4.15 CD2 Track 22

A = Allie, J = Jacques, B = Ben, M = Mark
A I got a message this morning. It's from Jacques.
J (on the answerphone) Allie, it's Jacques. I'm in Rome. My return flight's been cancelled. There's a small problem. Scarlett Scarpino is in Paris for her concert this evening. I was going to look after her today. Could you possibly take care of her? Thank you. And see you later.
A You've met Scarlett Scarpino, haven't you, Ben?
B The punk princess? Yeah, I met her in London last year.
A What's she like?
B Let's say she's a bit…difficult.
A What are we going to **do** with her?
M Why **don't** you show her around Paris?
A I have a **better** idea. Why don't you show her around Paris?
M What, me? I'm new here!
A You can't leave me to do this on my own.
M OK, why **don't** we take her to Nôtre Dame? I mean, it's her first time in Paris, isn't it?
B I don't think churches are really her thing.
M How **about** taking her on a boat trip?
A Brilliant!
M And then we could go up the Eiffel Tower.
A **That's** a good idea. I'm sure she'll love the view.
B And she might fall off!
M Thanks for your help, Ben. **Shall** we have lunch after that?
A **Let's** go somewhere really nice. Do you have any recommendations, Ben?
B **What** about La Renaissance? It's Jacques's favourite.
A That sounds perfect. Er, Ben, do you want to come too?
B Sorry, Allie. I'm really busy. But I'm sure you'll have an unforgettable meal.

d • 4.16 Now focus on the key phrases highlighted in the dialogue. Play the tape / CD pausing after the beep for SS to repeat. Encourage them to copy the rhythm and intonation.

4.16 CD2 Track 23

A = Allie, M = Mark, B = Ben
A What are we going to do with her?
M Why don't you show her around Paris?
A I have a better idea.
M Why don't we take her to Nôtre Dame?
M How about taking her on a boat trip?
A That's a good idea.
M Shall we have lunch after that?
A Let's go somewhere really nice.
B What about La Renaissance?

e • Focus on the task. Give SS a few moments to try to memorize the highlighted phrases in the dialogue then get them to cover the dialogue and try to complete the gapped sentences. Get them to compare their answers in pairs before checking answers.

> **Why don't we** take her to Nôtre Dame?
> **How about** taking her on a boat trip?
> **Shall we** have lunch after that?
> **Let's** go somewhere really nice.
> **What about** La Renaissance?

- Point out that:
  - you can use either *What about..?* or *How about…?* in the second and fifth sentences. If you use a verb after *What / How about*, it must be in the *-ing* form.
  - *Let's...* is an abbreviation of *Let us...* and is a kind of imperative used to make a strong suggestion, i.e. when you have a clear idea of what you think is the best thing to do.
  - the other four ways of making suggestions are less strong, i.e. you use them to ask someone their opinion about what the best thing to do is.

f • Put SS in groups of three and focus on the task and then give them a few minutes to plan their evening. Encourage them to use the language of making suggestions that they have just learnt.
- Alternatively, you could do this as a whole class activity.

SOCIAL ENGLISH An unforgettable meal

a • 4.17 Focus on the photo and the task. Before they listen, ask SS to predict if they think Scarlett likes the restaurant.
- Play the tape / CD once. Ask SS if Scarlett liked the restaurant (she didn't until the end) and elicit what she had to eat in the end.

A pizza margherita.

b • Focus on sentences 1–7 and go through them quickly. Then play the tape / CD for SS to mark them T or F. Play the recording again if necessary. Check answers getting SS to correct the false sentences.

1 F (She's hungry but thinks that the food in the restaurant is 'horrible'.)
2 T
3 F (She's allergic to mushrooms, strawberries, and nuts.)
4 T (She was 'seasick'.)
5 F (Scarlett didn't want to because she can't stand heights.)
6 T (She thinks she's spoilt.)
7 T

4.17 CD2 Track 24

(tapescript in Student's Book on *p.126*)
M = Mark, S = Scarlett, A = Allie, W = waiter
M So … Scarlett. What would you like?
S Nothing.
M Aren't you hungry?
S Sure. But this food's really horrible.
A This is one of the finest restaurants in Paris.
S I can't eat this stuff. I never touch meat.
A The seafood looks good –
S Hey, fish have feelings, too.
M What about the mushroom risotto?
S Mushrooms? No way! Didn't they tell you guys about my allergies? I'm allergic to mushrooms, strawberries, nuts…
M Shall we go some place else?
S Whatever. I'm going to the restroom.
A Well, that was a disastrous morning. The boat trip made her feel sick and she wouldn't go up the Eiffel Tower. 'I can't stand heights.'
M It's a pity we didn't just take her shopping.
A She's so spoilt.
M Oh, come on, she's just a kid really.
A So, what are we going to do about lunch? Shall we leave now?
M No, hang on. I have an idea. Let me talk to the waiter.
W Monsieur?
M Do you think you could possibly do me a favour?
W Yes, of course, sir. What would you like?
M Well, I think this place is great. More wine, Allie?
A No, thanks.
W Mademoiselle…
S What's this?
M It's your lunch, Scarlett.
S But I didn't order anything.
W Voilà!
S Hey, pizza margherita! Cool!

Extra support

Let SS listen one more time with the tapescript on *p.126*. Help them with any vocabulary or expressions they didn't understand.

c • 4.18 Now focus on the **USEFUL PHRASES**. Give SS a moment to try to complete them, and then play the tape / CD to check.

4.18 CD2 Track 25

M = Mark, A = Allie, S = Scarlett
A What **would** you like?
M Aren't you **hungry**?
A The seafood **looks** good.
S I'm **allergic** to mushrooms, strawberries, nuts…
A **Shall** we leave now?
M No, **hang** on. I have an idea.
M Do you think you could **possibly** do me a favour?

Extra idea

Ask SS if they can remember who said each phrase (and in what context), e.g. Mark asks Scarlett *Aren't you hungry?* (Because she says she doesn't want anything to eat).

d • Play the tape / CD again, pausing for SS to repeat. In a monolingual class elicit the equivalent expressions in SS' L1.
- Finally, focus on the information box about US and British English. Scarlett said, '*I'm going to the restroom.*' In British English she would say, '*I'm going to the toilet / loo.*'

HOMEWORK

Study Link **Workbook** *p.43*

4 WRITING: DESCRIBING A HOUSE OR FLAT

Lesson plan

This fourth writing task focuses on describing a house or flat and recycles the vocabulary of **File 4**.

There is also a focus on using more expressive descriptive adjectives such as *magnificent*, *superb*, etc.

We suggest that you do exercises **a–c** in class, but set the actual writing (the last activity) for homework. If there's time, you may also want to do the planning in class.

a • Focus on the descriptions of the house and apartment, which are from adverts on a property rental website. Tell SS to quickly read both adverts once and then to decide which of the two they would prefer to rent for a two-week holiday.

b • Focus on the task and set a time limit. Tell SS to read only the first advert again and to highlight the adjectives which help to 'sell' the house. Check answers, and make sure SS understand all the adjectives.

Suggested answers
spacious, large, breathtaking, ideal, quiet, safe, warm, friendly, excellent, amazing, perfect

c • Focus on the task and the second advert. Explain that the adjective *nice* is not a very expressive word so is not a very good adjective to use in an advert when you are trying to persuade people to rent your place.

• Focus on the example and point out that *superb* is a much more positive adjective than *nice*. Ask SS if they could use any other of the adjectives in the list here, and elicit that, e.g. *magnificent* would also be possible.

• Now get SS to continue in pairs, and then check answers.

nice 150 square metre apartment	spacious / magnificent 150 square metre apartment
nice living room	magnificent / spacious living room
nice view	breathtaking / magnificent view
nice for people who…	perfect / ideal
nice for couples	perfect / ideal

• Focus on the **Useful language** box and make sure SS understand all the phrases.

WRITE a description of your house / flat

Go through the instructions. Then either get SS to plan and write their description in class (set a time limit of 20 minutes) or get them to plan their description in class and write at home, or set both the planning and writing for homework.

If SS do the writing in class, get them to swap their description with another student to read and check for mistakes before you collect them all in.

Extra idea

You could display SS' descriptions around the class and get SS to move around the class reading them and choosing one to rent.

4 REVISE & CHECK

For instructions on how to use these pages, see *p.32*.

GRAMMAR

a 1 will / 'll do
2 drank
3 are
4 would / 'd change
5 arrives

b 1 c
2 b
3 c
4 a
5 c

VOCABULARY

a 1 village (It's a place. The others are kinds of houses.)
2 shower (It's in the bathroom. The others are all in the kitchen.)
3 uniform (It's a noun. The others are all adjectives describing schools.)
4 exam (It's a noun. The others are all verbs related to exams.)
5 friendship (It's a concept. The others all describe people you spend time with.)

b 1 subjects 2 terms 3 private 4 professor 5 suburbs 6 chimney 7 roof 8 gate

c 1 about 2 in, with 3 in 4 on 5 at 6 in

PRONUNCIATION

a 1 student (It's /uː/)
2 punish (It's /ʌ/)
3 country (It's /ʌ/)
4 cottage (It's /ɪ/)
5 homework (It's /əʊ/)

b <u>u</u>niform, ex<u>a</u>m, s<u>e</u>condary, resi<u>den</u>tial, c<u>o</u>lleague

CAN YOU UNDERSTAND THIS TEXT?

a T 2 F 3 DS 4 T 5 F 6 F 7 T 8 DS 9 F

b **court** = the place where a judge or jury decide if someone has broken the law
royalties = money, e.g. a musician earns from the sales of a record, or when a song he / she wrote or performed is played on the radio
chorus = the part of a song which is repeated several times
kids = an informal word for children
banned = prohibited / didn't allow
regret = feel sorry for something (you did or didn't do)
degree = a university qualification

CAN YOU UNDERSTAND THESE PEOPLE?

a 1 b 2 a 3 c 4 c 5 a

b 1 18
2 400
3 gas and electricity
4 beginning of July
5 Parking

CD2 Track 26

1 **A** Good evening. I'm Mrs Connors... Sean Connors's mother.
B Oh hello. Nice to meet you. Please, sit down.
A So, what's the problem with Sean? He's a lazy so and so, isn't he?
B Yes, but that isn't what I wanted to talk to you about.
A (interrupting) Did he fail his maths exam again?
B Yes.
A What mark did he get?
B He got 90%.
A But that's good, isn't it?
B It would be excellent, except that he copied all the answers from the girl sitting in front of him. That's what we need to talk about.
A That Sean! Just wait till I get home!

2 **A** Do you see that woman over there? She used to go to my school.
B Which one? The tall one with long dark hair?
A No, the one next to her with short, blonde hair. What was her name? Janet. That's right. She's changed a lot. She's really slim now. She used to be quite fat. But it's definitely her.

3 **A** So what have you decided about these three houses?
B Well, we both loved the cottage…but not the price.
A And the detached house?
B That would be ideal…
A But…?
B The kitchen's tiny.
A And the terraced house?
B Could we see that one again?
A Certainly. How about tomorrow morning?

4 **A** And our next caller is…
B Dennis.
A Go ahead, Dennis. We're listening.
B Thank you. I used to go to a secondary school in North London and I'm trying to find an old friend of mine, called Eddie. We lost touch with each other after we left school.
A And when was that Dennis?
B Let me think. I started there when I was 11, so that's 1971 and I left school six, no, seven years later.
A So if you're listening Eddie, your old friend Dennis wants to make contact with you. If you hear this message, you can call the show or send us an email. The phone number is…

5 **A** Hi, this is Sophie.
B Oh hi, Sophie. Haven't heard from you for ages.
A Sorry. I've just been so busy.
B Me too. We never have time to see each other these days.
A That's why I'm calling. What about lunch next week?
B Great! What day?
A Monday?
B Can't. I've got a business lunch. Tuesday?
A I've got my yoga class at 1.00. Best day for me would be Thursday.
B Let me see. I've got a meeting at 12.30, but I should be finished by 2.00 at the latest. How about a late lunch?
A Fine. I'll come to you and meet you in the coffee bar downstairs.
B Perfect. I'll see you then.
A Bye!

4.20 CD2 Track 27

A Hello. Is that Nigel?
B Yes. It is.
A Oh, I'm ringing about the flat share.
B Oh right. Well…It's a three-bedroom house, kitchen, living room, bathroom, and a small garden.
A Where is it exactly?
B It's Bradley Road, number 18. Do you know this area?
A Yeah. I know where that is. How much is the rent?
B It's 400 hundred a month plus gas and electricity bills.
A OK. So how many other people will there be living in the house?
B Me and one other guy. We're both students at the university. Are you a student?
A Yes. I'm in my second year. Engineering. If I'm interested, when could I move in?
B Well, the guy who's leaving will stay till the end of this month, so the room's free from the beginning of July.
A Fine. I've got a car. What's the parking situation like?
B Er...that's a bit of a problem. You'll have to get a permit from the local council if you want to park in Bradley Road. It costs about ten pounds a month.
A OK. Well, thanks for all that. I'll think about it and I'll call you back. Is this a good time to call?
B Yeah, between six and eight there's usually someone here.
A OK. Bye then.

Extra photocopiable activities

Quicktest 4 *p.219*

5 A

G quantifiers
V noun formation
P *-ough* and *-augh*

Slow down, you move too fast

File 5 overview

Each lesson in this File either extends or brings together language points previously taught separately. **5A** focuses on quantifiers, **5B** on the use of articles, and **5C** on gerund and infinitive constructions. The File also looks at forming nouns from verbs and adjectives, the use of prepositions after certain verbs and adjectives, and vocabulary related to work.

Lesson plan

This lesson re-presents, and extends SS' knowledge of, quantifiers, e.g. *a lot / plenty of, too much, not enough*, etc. through the topic of modern lifestyles. The grammar is presented through the topic of people's work – life balance and how they feel about it. They also hear an expert giving tips on how we can slow down in our daily lives. In the second half of the lesson SS read and talk about the 'Slow movement'. This movement, which began in Italy but has since spread all over the world, aims to promote a slower, healthier world where people eat 'slow food' and live in 'slow cities'. The vocabulary focus is on word building, this time focusing on noun formation, and pronunciation focuses on the frequently problematic combinations *-ough* and *-augh*.

Optional lead-in (books closed)

- Write on the board:

  15 MINUTES 60 MINUTES 150 MINUTES
  30 MINUTES 90 MINUTES

- Ask SS *How can you say these times in another way?* and give them a couple of minutes in pairs to write the answers. Elicit and check answers. Remind SS of the silent *l* in *half* /hɑːf/ and the silent *h* in *hour* /aʊə/.

  a quarter of an hour
  half an hour
  an hour
  an hour and a half
  two and a half hours

1 GRAMMAR quantifiers

a • Books open. Focus on the instructions, and get SS to write down approximate times, and then compare.

Extra idea

You could start by getting SS to ask you the questions.

• Get feedback from the class. You could find out, e.g. who works / studies the most / least, etc.

b • Focus on the article and instructions and elicit / explain the meaning of *work – life balance* (= the amount of time you spend working compared to the amount of free time you have). Give SS a time limit to read the article to get an idea of the difference between the three people. Tell SS not to choose the correct grammatical form at this stage. Then ask the whole class the question (*Which of the three situations is most typical in your country?*) and get feedback.

c • Focus on the task and get SS, either individually or in pairs, to read the texts again and underline the correct phrases. Check answers.

2 long enough	7 plenty of
3 a lot of	8 quite a lot of
4 enough time	9 Lots of
5 much time	10 too hard
6 too many	11 too much
	12 a few

d • Tell SS to go to **Grammar Bank 5A** on *p.138*. Go through the rules and examples with the class. Drill pronunciation where necessary, e.g. *enough* /ɪˈnʌf/.

Extra idea

In a monolingual class, you could get SS to translate the example sentences and compare the expressions they would use in their L1.

Grammar notes

Quantifiers

- SS should have seen most or all of these forms previously but here they are brought together.

Large quantities

- *Lots of* is a colloquial equivalent of *a lot of*. Be careful SS don't say *a lots of*.

Small quantities

- *A little* and *very little* are quite different in meaning (the second is more negative). The same applies to *a few* and *very few*.

Zero quantities

- *not … any* is the most common way to talk about zero quantities, e.g. *I don't have any money; there isn't any milk.*
  However, you can also use *no* + noun after *there is* and *have*, e.g. *There's no milk.*
- *None* is a pronoun so is used on its own, e.g. *Is there any milk? No, I'm afraid there's none left.*

More / less than you need

- Typical mistakes are:
  – using *too much* + an adjective, e.g. ~~*I'm too much busy*~~.
  – the position of *enough*, e.g. ~~*I'm not enough tall to open the cupboard*~~.
  – mispronouncing *enough*.
  – some nationalities confuse *plenty of* and *full of* because of L1 interference.

- Focus on the exercises on *p.139* and get SS to do them individually or in pairs. Check answers.

a 1 too many	**2** very few	**3** ✓	**4** enough car parks
5 ✓	**6** a lot	**7** a little	**8** any time
b 1 plenty of time	**5** ✓		
2 too much work	**6** ✓		
3 ✓	**7** None		
4 old enough	**8** a lot of / lots of		

- Tell SS to go back to the main lesson on *p.68*.

e • Focus on the instructions and give SS a few minutes to talk in pairs or small groups. Monitor and correct any mistakes with quantifiers. Get some feedback.

2 PRONUNCIATION *-ough* and *-augh*

Pronunciation notes

The aim of these exercises is to help SS remember the pronunciation of a group of high frequency words which all contain *-ough* / *-augh* – a combination of letters which has rather anarchic spelling / pronunciation relationship.

a • Focus on the information box. Then focus on the five columns and elicit the sound word for each, e.g. *up*.

- Now get SS to put the words in the right column. They could do this in pairs. Encourage them to say the words out loud and to use their instinct to help them decide.

b • 5.1 Play the tape / CD once for SS to check. Check answers.

5.1 CD2 Track 28

up /ʌ/	horse /ɔː/	phone /əʊ/	car /ɑː/	boot /uː/
enough	bought	although	laugh	through
tough	brought			
	caught			
	daughter			
	thought			

- Now check answers to the two questions. Elicit that:
  - /ɔː/ is the most common pronunciation (especially when there is a *t* after *-ough* or *-augh*). This includes the past tense / participle forms (*bought, brought, caught, taught,* and *thought*).
  - *Enough, tough,* and *laugh* finish with the /f/ sound.
- Emphasize that this is a small group of very common (but slightly irregular) words and it is worthwhile for SS to memorize their pronunciation.
- Finally, play the tape / CD again for SS to listen and repeat the words in the chart.

c • 5.2 Focus on the sentences which all contain the target sounds. Give SS time to practise saying the sentences in pairs. Then play the tape for them to check, and let them say them again.

Extra support

Play the tape / CD first, pausing for SS to repeat. Then let SS practise saying them again.

5.2 CD2 Track 29

1 I bought some steak but it was very tough.
2 Although it was dark, we walked through the tunnel.
3 I thought I'd brought enough money with me.
4 I laughed when my daughter caught the ball.

Extra idea

Remember to test SS on the pronunciation of *-ough* / *-augh* words at the start of the next class and later in the course.

Study Link SS can find more practice of English sounds on the MultiROM and also on the *New English File Intermediate* website.

3 LISTENING

a • 5.3 Focus on the instructions and give SS a moment to read the five gapped tips.

- Now play the tape / CD once all the way through. Play again if necessary. Check answers.

1 sitting down	**4** in silence
2 gym, yoga	**5** bath, shower
3 long walk	

5.3 CD2 Track 30

(tapescript in Student's Book on *p.127*)

Tip number 1. Eat breakfast sitting down. Most people stay in bed until the last minute and then have a coffee and a piece of toast standing up. This is really bad for you, because it means that you start the day in a hurry. Your body and mind are already moving too fast. So do yourself a favour. Get up ten minutes earlier every day and have breakfast – nice and slowly.

Tip number 2. Forget the gym, and do yoga instead. Many people go to the gym after work to do exercise because they think that this relaxes them, but it doesn't, believe me. I really think that a gym is a very stressful place. Exercising hard, for example doing aerobics, makes your heart beat more quickly, so it doesn't relax your body at all. In fact, it does the opposite. So, forget the gym and try doing yoga. Yoga will not only help you to get fit, but it will also slow your body down and help you to think more clearly.

Tip number 3. Go for a long walk. Walking is the most traditional form of exercise but many people have just forgotten how to do it. These days we all just get into our cars. The great thing about walking is that you can't walk very fast, so walking actually slows you down. And when we walk, we look around us at the birds, the trees, the shops, other people. It reminds us of the world we live in and it helps us to stop, and think, and relax.

Tip number 4. Spend 10 minutes each day in silence. Meditation isn't new. People have been doing it for thousands of years and now it is becoming really popular again. In the United States now you can find meditation rooms in companies, schools, airports, and even hospitals. Meditation is a fantastic way to teach your mind to slow down and to think more clearly. And spending time in silence every day will also benefit your general health.

And finally, tip number 5. Have a bath, not a shower. Having a shower is very quick and convenient but it is another part of our fast-living culture. When you come home from work, instead of having a shower, have a bath and spend half an hour there. A bath is one of the most relaxing things you can do, and it will really help to slow you down at the end of a hard day.

b • Play Tip 1 again, then pause and give SS time to write down anything they understood about *why* you should do this. Get them to compare with a partner and play the tape / CD again if necessary. Check answers for Tip 1, then do the same for Tip 2, etc.

1 Eat breakfast sitting down – If you eat it standing up, you start the day in a hurry.
2 Forget the gym. Do yoga. The gym is stressful. Aerobics, etc. makes your heart beat quickly. Yoga helps you slow down (and get fit).
3 Go for a long walk. When we walk we can't do it fast. We have time to look at everything and everybody (birds, trees, shops, people, etc.). Helps us stop, think, and relax.
4 Spend ten minutes each day in silence. Meditation teaches your mind to slow down and think more clearly (good for your general health too).
5 Have a bath, not a shower. A half an hour bath is relaxing and will slow you down at the end of a hard day.

Extra support

If there's time, you could get SS to listen again with the tapescript on *p.127* so they can see exactly what they understood / didn't understand. Translate / explain any new words or phrases.

c • In pairs, get SS to choose what they think are the two best tips and say if they do them. Then get feedback from the class, and find out which are the two most popular tips.

4 READING & VOCABULARY

a • Focus on the leaflet and ask SS who they think wrote it (a politician). Then focus on the instructions and get SS in pairs to match the verbs to their dictionary definition. Check answers, and get SS to underline the stressed syllable.

1 encourage	4 promote
2 increase	5 reduce
3 ban	6 protect

b • Now focus on the question and the introduction to the article *Slow down, you move too fast.* Get SS to read it, or read it aloud yourself, and then elicit the answer from the whole class. Ask SS if they agree with the first paragraph.

The counter-revolution is a movement whose aim is to slow life down (so that we live in a happier and healthier way).

c • Put SS in pairs, **A** and **B**. Focus on the instructions and go through the questions. Make sure they understand the vocabulary in the questions, e.g. *aims* and *spread.* Set a time limit, e.g. four minutes, for **A** and **B** to read their text and answer the questions. Tell SS not to write their answers, but just to underline the relevant parts of the text.

A 1 Carlo Petrini, an Italian journalist. Because he saw that McDonald's had opened a restaurant in a beautiful square in Rome.
2 He thought it was tragic that people live too quickly to sit down to eat a proper meal and that they only eat mass-produced food.
3 To encourage people to stop during the day and eat slowly, to use local shops and markets, eat out in small family restaurants, cook with traditional recipes.
4 It is now a global organization and has members in 100 countries.
B 1 It was inspired by the Slow Food movement. It was started by the mayor of Greve in Chianti in Italy.
2 Its aims are to make our towns places where people enjoy living and working and to protect things that make the town different.
3 It has spread all over the world, e.g. Japan, Australia, etc.
4 Most people are very happy ('delighted') because they think it increases their quality of life. Teenagers aren't so happy. They have to travel 25 km to the nearest city if they want excitement.

d • Now get SS to cover the text and tell each other their answers to the questions giving as much detail as they can remember. Monitor and help.
• Then get SS to read the text they didn't read. Ask SS which words / phrases they had problems with in each text and elicit / explain / translate the meaning.

e • Ask this question to the whole class. Find out how many people would like to eat 'slow food' and live in a 'slow city' and why (not).

5 VOCABULARY noun formation

a • Focus on the information box and go through it with SS. Then, focus on the instructions and the words in the list and elicit word by word whether they are verbs or adjectives (*happy*, *mad*, and *similar* are adjectives; the others are verbs).
• Give SS time, individually or in pairs, to form nouns and to write them in the correct column.

b • 5.4 Play the tape / CD once for SS to check their answers. Then play it again, pausing after each word for SS to underline the stressed syllable. Check answers.
• Elicit the answer to the question *Which ending has a stressed syllable?* (*-ation* is the only noun ending here which is stressed.).

government	organization	discussion
movement	relaxation	reaction
proposal	happiness	possibility
survival	madness	similarity

5.4 CD2 Track 31

government	discussion	happiness
movement	reaction	madness
organization	proposal	possibility
relaxation	survival	similarity

6 SPEAKING

a • Focus on the instructions and go through the proposals. Give SS individually a few moments to tick or cross the proposals and think of a reason why they agree / disagree.

b • Focus on the instructions and go through the **Useful language**. Get SS to work in groups of three or four. They should discuss each proposal in turn, giving reasons for or against, and decide (by a vote) whether to support it or not.

• Monitor and help, encouraging them to use the **Useful language** expressions.

c • Get feedback from each group to find out which proposals they support. Write up the proposals supported by each group on the board to find out which are the most popular.

Extra idea

Ask SS if they think any of these things are happening or will happen in the future in their town / city.

Extra photocopiable activities

Grammar

quantifiers *p.154*

Communicative

Lifestyle survey *p.185* (instructions *p.168*)

HOMEWORK

Study Link **Workbook** *pp.44–46*

5B

G articles: *a* / *an*, *the*, no article
V verbs and adjectives + prepositions
P sentence stress, *the*, /ð/ or /θ/?

Same planet, different worlds

Lesson plan

In this lesson, SS practise when (and when not) to use an article, and which article to use. The rules given are the most common ones, for example the non-use of the definite article when generalizing. Other less common or more complex uses will be dealt with in subsequent levels of *New English File*. The topic of the lesson is a light-hearted look at men and women. In the first half of the lesson, the focus is on what men and women talk about, and in the second half their different attitudes to certain activities, e.g. visiting a spa. There is a focus on sentence stress, the sounds /ð/ and /θ/, and the two pronunciations of *the*. In vocabulary, SS learn common verb and adjective + preposition combinations.

Optional lead-in (books closed)

- Write the following sentences on the board:
  Where are my socks? I can't see them anywhere.
  You just relax. I'll organize the summer holidays this year.
  We need to talk.
  That wasn't a goal! He was definitely offside.
- Then ask SS who they think would probably say it, a man or a woman. Get them to say why.

1 GRAMMAR articles: *a* / *an*, *the*, no article

a • Books open. Focus on the instructions and give SS a couple of minutes to fill the gaps. Get them to compare with a partner before checking answers. Don't give any grammar explanations at the moment as this will come in **b**.

1 (-) **2** (-), the **3** a, the, an **4** (-), (-), (-) **5** a, (-)

b • Tell SS to go to **Grammar Bank 5B** on *p.138*. Go through the examples and rules with the class. In a monolingual class, you could get SS to compare what they use in their L1.

Grammar notes

Articles: *a*, *an*, *the*, no article

- SS have learnt rules for using articles before but here the main ones are brought together. Most nationalities will have some problems using articles correctly but especially those who don't have articles in their language.
- In this lesson the main rules are covered. Others will be introduced in subsequent levels of *New English File*.
- Typical mistakes include:
  – omission of the article, e.g. ~~*I saw old man with dog*~~.
  – incorrect use of definite article when generalizing, e.g. ~~*The*~~ *men usually love* ~~*the*~~ *football.*

- Focus on the exercises on *p.139* and get SS to do them individually or in pairs. Check answers.

a 1 the door, the house
2 a Russian, a lawyer
3 the theatre, a month
4 a beautiful day, the terrace
5 classical music, Italian food
6 the girl, the window
7 home, work
8 Men, women
9 dinner, bed
10 a lovely face, attractive eyes

b 1 the, (-), a
2 (-), (-), (-)
3 (-), an
4 a, an
5 the, the, (-)
6 the, a, the

- Tell SS to go back to the main lesson on *p.72*.

c • Focus on the instructions and on the sentences. Then get SS to complete them in pairs.
- Check answers.

1 a, the **2** the **3** the, the **4** the **5** (-), the, the

2 PRONUNCIATION sentence stress, *the*, /ð/ or /θ/?

Pronunciation notes

This pronunciation spot focuses first on the fact that articles typically have a weak pronunciation, e.g. *a* /ə/ and *the* /ðə/. Then the focus moves to the two different pronunciations of *the* depending on whether the following noun begins with a vowel or not.

Finally, there is a focus on the two possible pronunciations of *th*, /ð/ or /θ/. The actual difference between the two is small (the first is voiced, the second unvoiced) and the important thing is to make sure SS are not substituting another sound, e.g. /s/ or /d/.

a • **5.5** Focus on the instructions. Tell SS they are going to hear six sentences which all contain definite or indefinite articles. They will hear each sentence twice. The first time they should make sure they write down the key (stressed) words, and the second time the unstressed words.
- Play the tape / CD pausing after each sentence. Get SS to compare and then elicit the sentences onto the board.

5.5 CD2 Track 32
1 Shall we go for a walk in the park?
2 He's a doctor at the local hospital.
3 Is there a bookshop in the centre of town?
4 I'd like a ticket for the match on Thursday, please.
5 They have a big house in the country.
6 We can have a break at the end of this exercise.

- Elicit that articles are <u>not</u> normally stressed.

b • 5.6 Now focus on the instructions and the phrases. Play the tape / CD for SS to listen and repeat. Elicit that *the* is pronounced /ðə/ when the next word begins with a consonant sound (e.g. *the shop, the sun, the world*), and /ði/ when the next word begins with a vowel sound (e.g. *the address, the owner, the engineer*).

> 5.6 CD2 Track 33
> the shop
> the address
> the owner
> the sun
> the engineer
> the world

c • 5.7 Focus on the information box and remind SS of the two pronunciations of *th*. It can be pronounced /ð/ like *mother* or /θ/ like *thumb*.

- Emphasize that:
  - /ð/ is a voiced sound (i.e. it is made using the voice box in the throat). SS should feel their throat vibrate when they say it.
  - /θ/ is made in the mouth, not the throat (i.e. it's an unvoiced sound). SS should be able to feel air on their hand when they say it.
  - there are no rules for how *th* is pronounced, but SS can use their dictionary to check the pronunciation of new words.
- Then, play the tape / CD pausing after each sentence for SS to circle *th* if it is pronounced /ð/.
- Get them to compare with a partner and then play the tape / CD again. Check answers. (KEY See tapescript below)

> 5.7 CD2 Track 34
> 1 (Th)at man over (th)ere is very wealthy.
> 2 June is (th)e sixth month of (th)e year.
> 3 (Th)ere are three things you have to remember.
> 4 I threw it away (th)e o(th)er day.
> 5 We have maths in (th)e third term.
> 6 (Th)e athletics track is through (th)at gate.

- Play the tape again for SS to listen and repeat. Make sure SS don't pronounce *th* as /s/ or /d/.
- Then, get SS to practise saying the sentences themselves before asking individual SS to say them.

Study Link SS can find more practice of English sounds on the MultiROM and also on the *New English File Intermediate* website.

3 READING & SPEAKING

a • Before starting you might want to pre-teach a few key words or phrases in the text which you think your SS might not be able to guess from context, e.g. *gossip* (= chat, often about other people and their personal lives).

- Put SS in pairs. Focus on the instructions and do the first two or three subjects with the whole class. Then give SS time to mark the words **M** or **W**. Then get feedback from the class.

b • Now give SS a few minutes to read the first paragraph of the article. Check answers, and ask the class if they agree with the writer.

sport M	**films** W
work M	**politics** W
clothes W	**cars** M
health W	**their house** W
family W	**the opposite sex** M and W

c • Focus on the task. Set a time limit for SS to read the whole article and to choose a, b, or c.

- Get SS to compare their answers with a partner before you check answers. You could get SS to point out the relevant part of the text which gave them the right answer.

> 1 c 2 b 3 b 4 a 5 a

d • This speaking task is meant to be a light-hearted response to the text but will also provide practice of not using the definite article *the* when you generalize.

- Focus on the task. Put SS in pairs or groups of three. If you have a more or less equal number of men and women in your class, put them in mixed groups and get them to time each other.
- Monitor and correct, especially if SS use the article incorrectly when speaking in general (e.g. *I think the football is very boring*).
- Get feedback to find out which topic men or women found most difficult to talk about.

HOW WORDS WORK...

This exercise focuses on some common phrases which are often used to connect ideas in a text. SS should be familiar with *also* and *however*, but may not have met the other expressions before.

1 Give SS a few minutes in pairs to focus on the highlighted expressions and match them to their uses. Check answers making sure SS are quite clear about the meaning of these expressions.

> 2 however, on the other hand
> 3 also 4 according to

- Point out that:
  - *However* is usually used at the beginning of a sentence and is followed by a comma; *whereas* is usually in the middle of a sentence.
  - *On the other hand* is usually used at the beginning of a sentence to introduce an opposite argument and is followed by a comma. You might like to point out that when two arguments are being put forward we sometimes introduce the first one with *On the one hand,...* and the second with *On the other hand,...*

2 Now get SS to complete the sentences and check answers.

> 1 also
> 2 However / On the other hand
> 3 According to
> 4 whereas
> 5 On the other hand / However

4 LISTENING

a • Focus on the photo and ask SS where they think the people are and elicit that they're in a spa, having some kind of skin treatment.

• **NOTE:** A *spa* traditionally means a place where mineral water comes out of the ground and where people go to drink and bathe in the water to treat a variety of health problems. Nowadays, the meaning of spa also covers what are called 'health farms', i.e. places where you can receive various kinds of health and beauty treatments, e.g. massages, facials, manicures and pedicures, etc.

• Find out if anyone in the class has been to a spa and if they enjoyed it, etc.

b • Focus on the instructions and give SS a few minutes to read the introduction (including the treatments) and answer the questions. Check answers to the first question (to find out if men enjoy spas as much as women) and then elicit ideas for which treatment Joanna and Stephen will like best, getting SS to say why. Explain / translate any vocabulary as necessary.

c • 5.8, 5.9 and 5.10 Focus on the chart and the instructions. Play the first part (5.8), and get SS to complete the chart for Stephen and Joanna for the first treatment. Let SS compare answers and then play the tape / CD again for them to check.

• Do the same thing with the next two parts (5.9 and 5.10).

• Check answers and find out if any SS had guessed right in **b**. Try not to focus at this point on the meaning of the words which SS will listen for in **d** (below).

	Stephen **Marks / reasons**
The body polish	0: Horrible, uncomfortable; fruit is for eating.
The facial	4: Boring, long, too many creams
The foot treatment	9: His feet look great!
	Joanna **Marks / reasons**
The body polish	10: Smelled good, relaxing, etc.
The facial	9: Enjoyed it. Skin feels great / healthy
The foot treatment	9: A luxury, great nail colour.

5.8 CD2 Track 35

(tapescript in Student's Book on *p.127*)

V = Voice-over, J = Joanna, S = Stephen

V 1 The body polish

J So? What did you think?

S It was just horrible! Horrible. Fruit's for eating, not for putting on your body. It was hot and sticky and incredibly uncomfortable. And I felt so stupid. I'd never have that again. I give it zero out of ten.

J Sticky? It was fruit for goodness sake! I thought it was wonderful. It smells so good and it was incredibly relaxing. I mean how could anybody not like it? And the head massage was divine! That was one of my favourite spa treatments ever. Ten out of ten. OK, so now, the facial.

S Hmm. How long is this one?

J One hour 40 minutes.

S Oh you're joking? That's too long.

J Too long? It'll be heaven. See you later.

5.9 CD2 Track 36

(tapescript in Student's Book on *p.127*)

V = Voice-over, J = Joanna, S = Stephen

V 2 The facial

S Oh that was so boring. It went on forever.

J I loved it.

S Well, I must admit my face feels different – much smoother. But I'm not sure I really want a smooth face. And it was nearly two hours and she used about 12 different creams and things. It normally only takes me a minute to wash my face – and I just use soap and water – the therapist said I ought to buy *five* different products!

J Well, I enjoyed every second. My skin feels great – really healthy. I give it nine out of ten.

S Hmm… I give it four.

J Your problem was that you were hungry so you couldn't relax. We could have a fruit juice before the last treatment…

S A fruit juice? Oh, OK then…if you really want one.

5.10 CD2 Track 37

(tapescript in Student's Book on *p.127*)

V = Voice-over, J = Joanna, S = Stephen

V 3 The foot treatment

S Wow!

J Don't tell me you liked it!

S It was wonderful!

J I must say, your feet look…well, better. Clean anyway.

S Well, I've never liked my feet much to be honest, but now they look great. That was definitely worth the time and money. Nine out of ten. What do you think?

J Yes, it was great. A real luxury. And I love the colour they painted my nails. I agree – nine out of ten. You see…

d • 5.11 Focus on the instructions. Remind SS that just as they guess words from context when they read, they need to do the same when they listen.

• Play the tape / CD once, pausing after each sentence for SS to try and write the missing word. Then play it again and get SS to compare answers.

• Check answers by getting individual SS to guess how the missing words are spelt and what they mean.

1 sticky 2 divine 3 smoother 4 soap 5 nails

⚠ In a monolingual class, you can elicit a translation. In a multilingual class, use mime, drawings, or definitions, etc.

5.11 CD2 Track 38

S = Stephen, J = Joanna

1 S It was just horrible! Horrible. Fruit's for eating, not for putting on your body. It was hot and sticky and incredibly uncomfortable.

2 J The head massage was divine. That was one of my favourite spa treatments ever.

3 S I must admit my face feels different – much smoother. But I'm not sure I really want a smooth face.

4 S It normally only takes me a minute to wash my face – and I just use soap and water.

5 S What did you think?
J Yes, it was great. A real luxury. And I love the colour they painted my nails.

e • You could get the class to vote with a show of hands to see which of the treatments described in the introduction to the text is most popular. If you have a mixture of sexes in the class, get the women to vote first and then the men to see if they agree with Stephen and Joanna.

Extra support

If there's time, you could get SS to listen again with the tapescript on *p.127* so they can see exactly what they understood / didn't understand. Translate / explain any new words or phrases.

5 SPEAKING

- Put SS into groups of three or four. Focus on the task and quickly go through the ten activities.
- Now focus on the **Useful language** and get SS to underline the stress in *generally* / *general* and *common*. Focus too on the advice in the ⚠ box.
- Monitor and check as they discuss, correcting any misuse of articles and encouraging them to use the expressions in **Useful language**.
- Get quick feedback from a different group for each topic. Tell SS if you agree or not and why.

6 VOCABULARY verbs and adjectives + prepositions

a • Focus on the example sentences from the text and remind SS that they have to remember which prepositions to use after certain verbs and adjectives, e.g. you talk *to* a person *about* something / someone.
- Focus on the instructions and remind SS to write the prepositions in the column on the right, **not** in the sentence. Give them time to complete the column individually or in pairs.
- Check answers.

1 to, about	6 from	11 as	16 of
2 about	7 to	12 for	17 in
3 for	8 to	13 at	18 about
4 with	9 for	14 at	
5 for	10 for	15 from / to	

- Then get SS to quickly test their memory by covering the prepositions column with a book or piece of paper and looking at the gapped sentences and remembering the missing preposition. They can uncover the prepositions column sentence by sentence to check.

b • Focus on the instructions and put SS in pairs, **A** and **B**. Make sure they cover the prepositions column with a book or a piece of paper. They take turns to ask and answer the questions, adding the correct prepositions from memory.
- Get SS to swap roles.

7 5.12 ♫ SONG *Sk8ter Boi*

- *Sk8er Boi* was originally recorded by Avril Lavigne in 2002 and was a worldwide hit. For copyright reasons this is a cover version. If you want to do this song in class, use the photocopiable activity on *p.210*. The listening task helps to consolidate the grammar point in the lesson.

5.12 CD2 Track 39

Sk8er Boi

He was a boy, she was a girl
Can I make it any more obvious?
He was a punk, she did ballet
What more can I say?
He wanted her, she'd never tell
Secretly she wanted him as well
But all of her friends stuck up their nose
They had a problem with his baggy clothes

He was a skater boy
She said, 'See you later boy'
He wasn't good enough for her
She had a pretty face
But her head was up in space
She needed to come back down to earth

Five years from now, she sits at home
Feeding the baby, she's all alone
She turns on TV. Guess who she sees?
Skater boy rocking up MTV.
She calls up her friends, they already know
And they've all got tickets to see his show
She tags along, but stands in the crowd
Looks up at the man that she turned down.

He was a skater boy
She said, 'See you later boy'
He wasn't good enough for her
Now he's a superstar
Slamming on his guitar
Does your pretty face see what he's worth?

He was a skater boy
She said, 'See you later boy'
He wasn't good enough for her
Now he's a superstar
Slamming on his guitar
Does your pretty face see what he's worth?

Sorry girl but you missed out
Well tough luck, that boy's mine now
We are more than just good friends
This is how the story ends.
Too bad that you couldn't see,
See the man that boy could be
There is more than meets the eye
I see the soul that is inside.

He's just a boy, and I'm just a girl
Can I make it any more obvious?
We are in love, haven't you heard
How we rock each other's world?

I'm with the skater boy, I said see ya later boy
I'll be back stage after the show,
I'll be at the studio
Singing the song we wrote
About a girl you used to know.

I'm with the skater boy, I said see ya later boy
I'll be back stage after the show,
I'll be at the studio
Singing the song we wrote
About a girl you used to know.

5 B

Extra photocopiable activities

Grammar

articles: *a*, *an*, *the*, no article *p.155*

Communicative

Generally speaking *p.186* (instructions *p.168*)

Song

Sk8er Boi p.210 (instructions *p.206*)

HOMEWORK

Study Link **Workbook** *pp.47–49*

G gerunds and infinitives
V work
P word stress

5 C Job swap

Lesson plan

In this lesson, SS practise discriminating between gerunds (or *-ing* forms) and infinitives. The context is work, and SS look at two angles which hopefully will interest them whether or not they are working themselves. The first angle involves a questionnaire which helps people see what job would most suit their personality, and the second is a reality TV programme where contestants have to learn to do a new job in a month and then try to fool a panel of judges into believing that they are professionals. The vocabulary focus is on words and expressions related to work, and the pronunciation focus is on getting the correct word stress in multi-syllable words.

Optional lead-in (books closed)

- Jobs quiz. Put SS in pairs or small groups. Then read out the following quiz questions or write them on the board:
  Can you name…?
  – two jobs which people do in a restaurant
  – two jobs connected with transport
  – two jobs that people do at home
  – two jobs where you spend a lot of time outside
- Check answers, making sure SS can spell and pronounce the words correctly.
  Some possible answers
  waiter, chef, etc.
  taxi driver, pilot, bus driver, etc.
  housewife, writer, etc.
  police officer, farmer, footballer, etc.

1 VOCABULARY work

a • Books open. Focus on the pictures and sentences, and give SS, in pairs, a couple of minutes to match them.
• Check answers and model and drill pronunciation of the bold words.

1 E 2 B 3 H 4 F 5 A 6 D 7 G 8 C

• Point out that:
– we use *apply for* when we send a letter or a completed form to a company to ask for a job (usually in response to an advertisement).
– *CV* stands for Curriculum Vitae and means a document which shows your qualifications, experience and interests (SS will learn to write one in **Writing 5**).
– *overtime* = extra hours that you work over and above your normal working hours.
– *sacked* and *promoted* can be used with either *be* or *get*. If you are *sacked*, you lose your job. If you are *promoted*, you are given a better job in the same company.

b • Now get SS to cover the sentences and look at the pictures. Get them to retell the story in pairs from memory, **A** testing **B** and then swapping. Then elicit the story from the class by asking individual SS.

c • Now tell SS to go to **Vocabulary Bank *Work*** on *p.152*. Focus on section **1 Describing your job** and get SS to do the exercises individually or in pairs. Check answers and drill pronunciation where necessary.

a **A 1** is a librarian, **B 2** is a plumber.
b **2** experience **3** training course **4** working hours **5** self-employed **6** retire **7** resigned **8** temporary (permanent) **9** part-time (full-time) **10** qualifications

• Now focus on section **2 Saying what you do** and give SS a few moments to complete the **Prepositions** column. Remind SS **not** to write the prepositions in the sentences as later they can cover the **Prepositions** column and test their memory. Check answers.

1 for **2** as **3** in, of **4** in **5** for **6** at **7** in

• Now focus on section **3 People** and the typical endings for job words. In pairs, give SS time to add two more to each column.
• Write the column headings on the board and elicit the new words from different pairs. Write them on the board for the others to copy down. If you did the optional lead-in, SS could also add these words to the columns and drill pronunciation.

Some possible answers

-er	-or	-ist	-ian	other
builder	doctor	receptionist	musician	housewife
teacher	author	journalist	politician	nurse

• Focus on the box and drill the pronunciation of the two words.

• Finally, focus on the instruction 'Can you remember the words on this page? Test yourself or a partner'.

Testing yourself
For **Describing your job** SS can cover the words on the right and read definitions 1–10 and to try to remember the words. For **Saying what you do** SS can cover the **Prepositions** column and read sentences 1–7 and try to remember the prepositions. For **People** SS can cover the chart except for the endings (*-er*, etc.) and try to remember the jobs.

Testing a partner
See **Testing a partner** *p.17*.

Study Link SS can find more practice of these words on the MultiROM and on the *New English File Intermediate* website.

• Tell SS to go back to the main lesson on *p.76*.

2 PRONUNCIATION & SPEAKING
word stress

a • Focus on the words and phonetics and ask SS if they

can remember how the phonetics show them where the stress falls (the syllable after the apostrophe (ˈ) is the one which is stressed). Get them to underline the stressed syllable in each word using the phonetics to help.

b • 5.13 Play the tape / CD, pausing after each word to check answers. You could also ask SS to tell you how each word is pronounced just before you play it.

1 apply	6 permanent
2 contract	7 qualifications
3 employee	8 resign
4 experience	9 retire
5 overtime	10 temporary

• Now give SS a few minutes to practise saying the words. You could get them to practise saying them correctly by looking at the phonetics and also by repeating after the tape / CD.

5.13 CD2 Track 40

1 apply	6 permanent
2 contract	7 qualifications
3 employee	8 resign
4 experience	9 retire
5 overtime	10 temporary

c • Put SS in pairs. Focus on the questions and give SS a few minutes to read them and think whether they have a family member or friend who fits any of the categories. They should try to think of someone for as many of the questions as possible.

• SS work in pairs telling each other about people they know. Encourage them to give, and ask for, as many details as they can.

3 GRAMMAR gerunds and infinitives

a • Focus on the instructions and the questionnaire. Get SS to complete it, individually or in pairs, and check answers. They should be able to do this reasonably well from what they already know and by instinct. If SS ask for a reason why a particular verb has to be in the gerund or infinitive, tell them that they will see all the rules in the **Grammar Bank**.

2 helping	7 to work	12 improvising
3 not earning	8 managing	13 Doing
4 to work	9 expressing	14 solving
5 making	10 to follow	15 to understand
6 Taking	11 to be	16 to calculate

b • Now tell SS to read each sentence in the questionnaire carefully, and tick the sentences that they strongly agree with.

• When they have finished, get them to compare their answers with another student, explaining why they have ticked certain statements.

c • Focus on the instructions and get SS to read the 'answer' paragraph corresponding to the section where they have most ticks. Some SS may have an equal number of ticks in two sections in which case they should read both answer sections.

• Get feedback from some SS to find out what kind of job, according to the questionnaire, would suit them, and if this is the kind of job that they would actually like to do (or are actually doing).

d • Now focus on the rules and give SS a few minutes to complete them individually or in pairs. Check answers.

1 the gerund	4 the gerund
2 *to* + infinitive	5 the gerund
3 *to* + infinitive	

e • Tell SS to go to the **Grammar Bank 5C** on *p.138*. Go through the examples and rules, and get SS to compare what form they use in their L1.

Grammar notes

Gerunds and infinitives

• SS have learnt rules for using gerunds (or *-ing* forms) and the infinitive (with *to*) before, but separately. In this lesson they are brought together.

• SS will see in this lesson that there are three common verb forms in English: *to go* (infinitive with *to*), *go* (infinitive without *to*) and *going* (gerund or *-ing* form).

⚠ *Like* is listed as a verb which takes the gerund; however, SS may hear or see it used with the infinitive with *to*. There is a subtle difference in meaning which you may want to point out to your SS. Compare:
I like getting up early in the morning = I enjoy it.
I like to get up early in the morning = I think it is a good idea to do this (but I don't necessarily enjoy doing it).

• Verbs which can take either the gerund or infinitive but with a different meaning will be focused on in more detail in the next level of *New English File*.

• Emphasize the importance of learning which verb form to use after a particular verb or construction, and give SS plenty of practice. In time they will develop an instinctive feel for whether a gerund or infinitive is required.

• Focus on the exercises on *p.139* and get SS to do them individually or in pairs. Check answers.

a	1 to rent	5 failing	8 to find
	2 flying	6 dancing	9 learning
	3 to book	7 Being	10 To be able to
	4 not to make		
b	1 working	5 working	8 Working
	2 to work	6 working	9 to work
	3 work	7 to work	10 to work
	4 work		

• Tell SS to go back to the main lesson on *p.77*.

f • Focus on the instructions. Give SS a few minutes to choose five topics and to think about what they are going to say. Demonstrate the activity by talking about a couple of the topics yourself.

• Put SS in pairs and tell them to talk to each other about the topics they have chosen. Monitor to check that SS are using the right forms of the verbs.

• Get feedback from a few different SS.

4 READING

a • Focus on the instructions and on the title of the article and elicit some qualities from the class, e.g. *You need to be extrovert, self-confident*, etc.

b • Now focus on the photo of Jessica on *p.78* and on *p.79* where she is doing a TV interview and ask SS if she looks very different.

• Now focus on the instructions and the headings. Check SS understand *challenge* (= something difficult somebody has to do) and *contestant* (= person who takes part in a contest, e.g. a quiz show on TV).

• Read the first paragraph with the class, and check that they understand how the programme works. Then give SS a couple of minutes to read the rest of the text quite quickly and to match the other headings to the paragraphs. Check answers.

2 The contestant	4 The teachers
3 The challenge	5 The training

c • Focus on the definitions and get SS in pairs to find the words in the text. Check answers and get SS to underline the stressed syllables.

2 re<u>por</u>ter	5 MP
3 judge	6 poli<u>ti</u>cian
4 <u>jour</u>nalist	

d • Now set a time limit, e.g. four or five minutes, for SS to read the text again more carefully and tell them that they should try to remember the main facts. Help with any vocabulary problems.

• Then put them in pairs, **A** and **B**, and tell them to go to **Communication** *Test your memory*, **A** on *p.117* and **B** on *p.120*.

• Go through the instructions. SS should ask each other alternate questions, with **A** going first.

• Get feedback to see who had the best memory.

e • Ask the question to the whole class, and elicit ideas and reasons. Then tell them they are going to listen and find out what happened.

Extra idea

You could get SS to underline or highlight five words or phrases they want to remember from the text. Get them to compare their words / phrases with a partner and then get some feedback from the class.

5 LISTENING

To understand Jessica's mistake in **Week three** SS need to know that the British political system is essentially a two-party system in which power is held by one of the main parties. The two main parties are the Conservatives and the Labour party.

• 5.14, 5.15, 5.16 & 5.17 To create a bit of suspense it is best to do this activity section by section so that SS listen to one week at a time. Give SS a few minutes to look at questions 1–4 or read them aloud. Then play the tape / CD for **Week one** and get SS to answer the questions. Let them compare their answers in pairs, then play the tape / CD again. Then repeat the procedure for **Weeks two, three**, and **four**. For dramatic effect you could pause the tape / CD after Adam says, 'The judges gave their verdict…' and ask the class if they think Jessica passed the final test; then let them hear the verdict.

Week one
1 They thought she was nice.
2 He thought she was too shy and nice, not aggressive enough. Also she didn't know anything about politics.
3 Watch political interviews on TV, learn to speak more clearly, and read the political sections of all newspapers.
4 She felt exhausted.

Week two
5 She had her hair cut and got new, smarter clothes.
6 She learnt how to interview someone (in front of the camera).
7 She had to ask the Prime Minister a question.
8 No: the Prime Minister didn't hear the question.

Week three
9 He thought Jessica was finally making some progress and was more relaxed.
10 She had to interview a politician from the Conservative party.
11 She said 'Labour party' instead of 'Conservative party'.
12 She had to learn to carry on and not lose her confidence.

Week four
13 She had to interview the Minister of Education 'live'. She felt nervous, but well prepared.
14 Yes: she made him answer the question.
15 No. None of the three judges realized that Jessica wasn't the professional reporter. She passed the test!
16 No because she's much happier working in the library.

5.14 CD2 Track 41

(tapescript in Student's Book on *p.127*)
V = Voice-over, J = Jessica, A = Adam

V Week one.

J When I got to the studio on the first day, I was really nervous. I met my teachers, Adam and Sally, and they were very nice to me but I could see that they thought it was going to be impossible to teach me to be a reporter in just a month.

A The problem with Jessica at the beginning was that she was too shy and too nice. Political reporters need to be hard – almost aggressive sometimes – and I've never met anyone less aggressive than Jessica. And also she knew nothing about politics – she knew who the Prime Minister was but not much else!

J I spent the first week watching lots of political interviews on TV, and Adam and Sally taught me how to speak more clearly and more confidently. In the evenings they made me read the political sections of all the newspapers. It was very boring. At the end of the week I was exhausted.

5.15 CD2 Track 42

(tapescript in Student's Book on *p.127*)
V = Voice-over, J = Jessica, A = Adam

V Week two.

J Adam and Sally said I had to change my image for TV, so I had my hair cut and coloured, and I got new, smarter clothes. I must say I liked my new look. I spent the week learning how to interview someone in front of a camera.

A Then came Jessica's first big challenge. The Prime Minister was arriving home after a visit to the USA. She had to wait outside number 10 Downing Street with the other journalists and try to ask him a question.
J It was a disaster. I was so nervous I was shaking. There were a lot of other journalists pushing and shouting. They didn't let me get near the Prime Minister. I tried to ask my question, but he didn't hear me. I felt really stupid.

5.16 CD2 Track 43
(tapescript in Student's Book on *p.127*)
V = Voice-over, J = Jessica, A = Adam
V Week three.
A Jessica was finally making some progress. She was more relaxed. This week she had to interview a politician from the Conservative party in a studio.
J In the beginning it was fine. But then I made a stupid mistake.
[Flashback] *SFX* **JESSICA** *So could you tell us what the Labour party are going to do about...sorry, I mean the Conservative party...*
I said the 'Labour party' instead of the 'Conservative party'. And after that I was really nervous again.
A We all make mistakes sometimes. Jessica just has to learn to carry on, and not lose her confidence.

5.17 CD2 Track 44
(tapescript in Student's Book on *p.127*)
V = Voice-over, J = Jessica, A = Adam, M = Minister
V Week four.
J I spent the last week preparing for the test. It was going to be a live interview with the Minister of Education. There would be three professional reporters and me, all asking him questions. I'd done lots of research so although I was nervous, I felt well prepared.
J *Minister, many people think that the real reason why there aren't enough teachers is because their salaries are so low. Are you proposing to increase teachers' salaries?*
M *Well, let's not forget that salaries are much higher today than they were under the previous government.*
J *Yes, but you haven't answered my question. Are you going to increase them?*
M *Well, we're planning to spend a lot more money on education in the next two years.*
J *Is that a yes or a no?*
M *There are no immediate plans to increase teachers' salaries.*
J *So it's a no then. Thank you Minister.*
J When it was all over came the worst part. I had to wait while the judges decided which of us they thought *wasn't* a professional reporter.
A The judges gave their verdict – and incredibly *none* of the three realized that Jessica wasn't a professional! She did very very well.
Who knows, maybe one day soon you'll be seeing her on TV... and this time she'll be a real reporter, not pretending!
J It was a great experience and I was pleased how I did, but actually I *wouldn't* like to change jobs. I'm much happier working in the library.

Extra support

If there's time, you could get SS to listen again with the tapescript on *p.127* so they can see exactly what they understood / didn't understand. Translate / explain any new words or phrases.

6 SPEAKING

- Focus on the instructions and the jobs, and make sure SS understand what they are (*stuntman* = the person who does dangerous things in a film, e.g. car chases, instead of the main actors). Explain that these jobs were things that people spent a month learning to do in previous episodes of the programme.
- Now focus on the **Useful language**. Demonstrate the activity by talking about the first job (football coach), using some of the phrases in **Useful language**. Then get SS to talk, in pairs or small groups, about each of the jobs. Tell them that they must end up each choosing the one they would most and least like to learn to do.
- Get feedback to see which jobs SS would most / least like to learn to do.

Extra idea

If you have a class where several SS are working, you could get the rest of the class to interview them. Write their names and jobs on the board. Then get those with jobs to prepare a few notes about the pros and cons of their job. Meanwhile the other SS prepare a couple of questions for each person. Then get the SS with jobs to sit at the front of the class. Each should explain what he / she does and talk for a few minutes about the good and bad side of his / her job. Then the other SS ask their questions. This activity may take some time, but often provides real and motivating communication.

Study Link SS can find a dictation and a Grammar quiz on all the grammar from File 5 on the MultiROM and more grammar activities on the *New English File Intermediate* website.

Extra photocopiable activities

Grammar
gerunds and infinitives *p.156*
Communicative
Can you guess? *p.187* (instructions *p.168*)
Vocabulary
Pick a card *p.201* (instructions *p.196*)

HOMEWORK

Study Link **Workbook** *pp.50–52*

5 PRACTICAL ENGLISH MEETINGS

Function Giving opinions
Language *In my opinion..., Personally, I think...*

Lesson plan

In this lesson, SS practise asking for and giving opinions. The context is a meeting in the MTC office, where Allie, Mark, and Jacques discuss the best way to promote Scarlett's new CD. Mark and Jacques put forward their ideas and, to Mark's annoyance, both Allie and Scarlett agree with Jacques.

In **Social English** Mark and Allie go to the Louvre. At first Mark is tense because of the meeting but then he relaxes. They are enjoying themselves in the gallery when Mark suddenly sees Ben. Mark and Allie leave the gallery hoping that Ben hasn't seen them.

Study Link These lessons are on the *New English File Intermediate* DVD / Video, which can be used instead of the Class Cassette / CD (see introduction *p.9*). The main functional section of each episode is also on the MultiROM with additional activities.

Optional lead-in (books closed)

- Revise what happened in the previous episode by eliciting the story, e.g. *What did Mark and Allie have to do with Scarlett in the last episode? What happened when they took her to an expensive restaurant? What did Mark do to solve the problem?*, etc.
- Remind SS of the language that they learnt in the last lesson (ways of making suggestions). You could write some of the key expressions on the board with gaps for SS to complete.
- If you are using the video / DVD, you could play the previous episode again, leaving out the 'Listen and Repeat' sections.

GIVING OPINIONS

a • 5.18 Tell SS to cover the dialogue with their hand or a piece of paper. Focus on the photo and the questions. Alternatively, you could write the questions on the board and get SS to listen with books closed.

• Play the tape / CD once the whole way through and check answers.

> Jacques has the best idea. His idea is that Scarlett should tour clubs and festivals.

b • Now get SS to look at the dialogue. In pairs, they read it and see if they can guess or remember the missing words. Emphasize that they shouldn't write the words in the dialogue but in pencil alongside or on a separate sheet of paper.

c • Play the tape / CD again for them to check. Then go through the dialogue line by line and check answers. Find out if SS had guessed the actual words spoken correctly. Where they had not guessed correctly, see if their alternative also fits.

• Deal with any vocabulary problems. Point out that '*actually*' (line 10) = in fact. It doesn't mean *now*.

5.18 CD2 Track 45

A = Allie, S = Scarlett, M = Mark, J = Jacques

A That was a great concert last night, Scarlett.
S Thanks.
A As we know, Scarlett's got a new CD coming out soon. So let's have a look at the best way we can promote it in France.
M OK, well... I think Scarlett **should** visit the major music stores. In my **opinion**, that's the best way to meet her fans.
A I'm not so **sure**. What do you **think**, Jacques?
J Actually, I don't **agree** with Mark. Scarlett isn't commercial in that way.
A Scarlett? Scarlett?
S I agree **with** Jacques. I don't have a commercial image. It isn't my style.
M OK, but Scarlett needs more publicity. What about a series of TV and radio interviews? **Don't** you agree?
A Yes, but that's what everybody does. What we want is something different.
J **Personally**, I think Scarlett should tour clubs and summer festivals. She can DJ, play her favourite music, play the new CD, and meet her fans, too.
A Yes, **absolutely**! That's a much better idea. Mark?
M OK, why not?
A Scarlett?
S I think that's a **great** idea. Thank you, Jacques.

d • 5.19 Now focus on the key phrases highlighted in the dialogue. Play the tape / CD pausing after the beep for SS to repeat. Encourage them to copy the rhythm and intonation.

5.19 CD2 Track 46

A = Allie, S = Scarlett, M = Mark, J = Jacques

M I think Scarlett should visit the major music stores.
M In my opinion, that's the best way to meet her fans.
A I'm not so sure.
A What do you think, Jacques?
J Actually, I don't agree with Mark.
S I agree with Jacques.
M Don't you agree?
J Personally, I think Scarlett should tour clubs and summer festivals.
A Yes, absolutely.
S I think that's a great idea.

e • Focus on the chart and show SS how the first phrase has been written in each column. Give them time in pairs to write in the other phrases. Check answers.

Asking people what they think	Saying what you think	Agreeing / Disagreeing
What do you think?	I think...	I'm not so sure.
Don't you agree?	In my opinion...	I don't agree with Mark.
	Personally, I think...	I agree with Jacques.
	I think that's a great idea.	Yes, absolutely.

Extra support

You could give SS further practice of the rhythm of the phrases by getting them to read the dialogue in pairs.

f • Put SS in pairs, **A** and **B**, and get them to go to **Communication** *What do you think?*, **A** on *p.117* and **B** on *p.120*. Go through the instructions. Here SS should take turns to ask each other questions and give opinions.

Extra support

Remind SS to say *Sorry, could you repeat that?* if they don't understand the questions the first time.

• Get feedback from a few pairs to find out what the majority opinion is for one or two of the questions.

SOCIAL ENGLISH Why is she smiling?

a • 5.20 Focus on the photo and ask *Where are they? What's the painting?* (In the Louvre. The *Mona Lisa.*). Play the tape / CD once for SS to answer the question. Check answers.

They see Ben.

b • Focus on the questions. Then play the tape / CD again. Get SS to compare answers, and then play the recording again if necessary. Check answers, and elicit / explain the meaning of any words or expressions SS didn't understand, e.g. *self-portrait*…

1 No, it's his first time.
2 Because Allie agreed with Jacques's idea at the meeting.
3 That she had to do her job / She really thought Jacques's idea was better.
4 That she was the wife of a banker / That she's a self-portrait of Leonardo.
5 That she's the director of a music company!
6 Because they don't want Ben to see them.

Extra support

If there's time, you could let SS listen one more time with the tapescript on *p.128*. Help them with any vocabulary or expressions they didn't understand.

5.20 CD2 Track 47

(tapescript in Student's Book on *p.128*)
A = Allie, M = Mark
A It's great to be on our own again.
M Yeah.
A Is this the first time you've been to the Louvre?
M Uh huh.
A What's the matter? Is this about the meeting? Because I agreed with Jacques and not with you?
M Yeah, well, we knew it wouldn't be easy. Working together, I mean.
A It's difficult for me as well. But if I don't agree with you,…
M I know, I know, you're the boss.
A And I have to do my job. I really thought that Jacques's idea was better. And so did Scarlett.
M It's not a big deal, Allie. I'm fine, really. So who exactly was the Mona Lisa?
A I'm not sure. I think she was the wife of a banker…
M Is that why she's smiling? Because her husband has a good salary?
A I also read somewhere that she was a self-portrait of Leonardo.
M A self-portrait? You're kidding. Now I don't know much about art, but Leonardo Da Vinci was a man, right?
A Well, it's just a theory. Why do you think she's smiling?
M Well, in my opinion, she's the managing director of a music company.
A What?
M She lives in Paris, she's in love with her marketing director, and she has a lot of fun telling him what to do.
A That's really unfair!
M Hey, we're not in the office now – you can't tell me I'm wrong! Let's get a coffee.
A Good idea.
M Don't turn round!
A What is it?
M I've just seen Ben from the office.
A Where?
M I said don't look! I don't think he's seen us. Let's get out of here. Come on.

c • 5.21 Now focus on the **USEFUL PHRASES**. Give SS a moment to try to complete them, and then play the tape / CD to check.

5.21 CD2 Track 48

A = Allie, M = Mark
A What's the **matter**?
M It's not a big **deal**.
M You're **kidding**.
M Now I don't know much **about** art.
A That's really **unfair**!
M Don't **turn** round!
M Let's **get** out of here.

Extra idea

Ask SS if they can remember who said each phrase (and in what context), e.g. Allie says *What's the matter?* (Because Mark doesn't seem happy).

d • Play the tape / CD again, pausing for SS to repeat. In a monolingual class, elicit the equivalent expressions in SS' L1.

HOMEWORK

Study Link **Workbook** *p.53*

5 Writing: Formal letters and a CV

Lesson plan

In this fifth writing lesson SS practise writing a CV and a formal 'covering' letter, i.e. the letter you include with your CV when you send it to a company or organization in response to a job advertisement. The layout and style apply both to letters and emails.

a • Focus on the instructions. Give SS a minute to read the advertisement, and elicit answers. Deal with any vocabulary problems.

b • Focus on the CV and go through the headings. Check that SS understand *Career history* (= your working life, not your university course – *career* is a false friend in some languages). Then give SS a few minutes to match the headings. Check answers.

2 Career history	5 Computer skills
3 Education	6 Additional information
4 Languages	

Extra idea

Get SS to cover the CV and ask a few comprehension questions, e.g. *Where is he from? Is he married? Where has he worked before?*, etc.

c • Now focus on the covering letter. Explain that a covering letter is a letter you send when you also enclose something else, e.g. a CV or form, where you explain what you are sending and why. Remind SS that the letter is formal, and that they should circle the expression that they think is more formal from each pair. SS can do this individually or in pairs.

• Check answers.

1 I am writing
2 I have been working
3 I speak German fluently
4 I enclose
5 I look forward to hearing from you
6 Yours faithfully

d • Finally, focus on the **Useful language** box and get SS to complete it. Check answers.

You don't know the person's name: finish *Yours faithfully*
You know the person's surname: finish *Yours sincerely*

• Go through the rules, using the letter as an example, and remind SS that this format can also be used for a formal email.

WRITE your CV and a covering letter

Go through the instructions. SS could write the CV in class and the letter for homework, or write both for homework. If SS have not had any work experience, tell them to invent the details.

If SS do the writing in class, get them to swap their CVs and letters with another student to read and check for mistakes before you collect them all in.

5 Revise & Check

For instructions on how to use these pages, see *p.32*.

GRAMMAR

a 1 c 2 c 3 a 4 b 5 c
b 1 without locking 2 a few 3 getting up 4 to rent 5 big enough

VOCABULARY

a 1 government 2 reaction 3 happiness 4 possibility 5 qualifications
b 1 for 2 about 3 with 4 at 5 at 6 as
c 1 overtime 2 off 3 sacked 4 promoted 5 salary 6 contract 7 apply 8 self-employed 9 resign

PRONUNCIATION

a 1 movement (It's /uː/) 2 afraid (It's /eɪ/) 3 prefer (It's /ɪ/) 4 short (It's /ɔː/) 5 resign /(It's /z/)
b empl<u>oyee</u> unempl<u>oy</u>ed res<u>pon</u>sible <u>tem</u>porary ex<u>pe</u>rience

CAN YOU UNDERSTAND THIS TEXT?

a 1 F 2 T 3 T 4 DS 5 F 6 T 7 DS 8 T 9 F
b **a very advanced age** = be very old
single-handedly = by himself, without any help
centenarians = people who are a hundred years old or more
in the shade = in the area that isn't in direct sunlight and is darker and cooler
use up = use completely, expend (energy)
multiplying = increasing

CAN YOU UNDERSTAND THESE PEOPLE?

a 1 b 2 a 3 c 4 b 5 a
b 1 T 2 F 3 F 4 F 5 T

5.22 CD2 Track 49

1 A Excuse me, is there a bookshop near here?
B Er, sorry, I don't think so. Er...what are you looking for?
A I'm looking for a guidebook. Is there anywhere round here where I might be able to get one?
B Actually, there aren't very many bookshops in this town at all. I think there's one in the centre but that's all. But you might be able to get a guidebook at a newsagent's. There's one on the corner on the right, and another one a bit further on this way.
A Oh right, thanks very much.
2 A Where shall we have lunch?

B What do you think, Albert? You know the restaurants here.
C Well, you could go to Garibaldi's. The food's wonderful – home cooking. You need time though – they're a bit slow.
B We're in a bit of a hurry cos we're meeting Anna at 2.30.
C Well, there's Trattoria Marco – they do good pasta, and Roberto's. Their fish is very good.
A I had pasta last night.
B Me too. Let's go to the fish place then. Where exactly is it?

3 A There's nothing on TV tonight. Why don't you go and rent a DVD?
B Why don't you go?
A OK, but if I go, I choose the film.
B No way. I don't want to see another horror film in all my life.
A Well, you go then.
B We could both go and then get a takeaway for supper.
A OK then.

4 A Come in, sit down.
B Thank you.
A It's James Baker, isn't it?
B That's right.
A Tell me a bit about the last hotel where you worked. You were head of reception, is that right?
B Yes, I was a receptionist for two years and then I got promoted to head of reception.
A But you do realize that this hotel's much bigger than where you were before and the post vacant here is for a receptionist.
B Yes, yes, I know.
A Why did you decide to get a job straight after school? I mean, why did you decide not to carry on with your education?
B To be honest, I wanted to earn some money. But I'd like to do a diploma in tourism next year, maybe studying part-time.

5 A Have you applied for university next year?
B Yes. I've got a place at Manchester to do medicine.
A Medicine? You've always said you wanted to do biology.
B Yes, but I've changed my mind. I don't really want to work as a doctor, but I'd like to do medical research. And for that, the best thing is to study medicine.

5.23 CD2 Track 50

A So what do you think?
B I think I like the Volvo best. It's so comfortable. And I love the colour. It's a really nice shade of blue.
A Don't think about the colour. That's a ridiculous reason for buying a car. The question is, is the Golf big enough?
B There's not much space for luggage – the boot's much smaller than the Volvo's.
A Yes, but think about it – we only go on holiday once a year. The rest of the time we only use the boot for shopping. And the Golf would be much easier to park – that's the advantage of a smaller car. You know parking's not your strong point.
B I can park perfectly, thank you very much.
A Come on! What about last week when you scratched the mirror.
B That wasn't parking. It was when I was driving in the High Street. Anyway, Volvos are the safest cars on the road – everybody says so.
A The Volvo's quite a bit more expensive, you know. If we bought it, we'd have to get a bank loan.
B How much more expensive is it?
A About 20% more. We wouldn't be able to go to France this summer.
B What about the Peugeot? Over there. It's cheaper than the Volvo and the Golf. And it's a really sweet yellow.
A Look, we've been here more than an hour and I thought we'd agreed we were going to buy either the Volvo or the Golf.
B Yes, but now I'm not sure.

Extra photocopiable activities

Quicktest 5 *p.220*

G reported speech: statements, questions, and commands
V shopping
P consonant sounds: /g/, /dʒ/, /k/, /ʃ/, /tʃ/

6 A Love in the supermarket

File overview

This File has three quite different grammatical and lexical areas. **6A** focuses on reported speech: statements, questions, and commands. **6B** revises and extends SS' knowledge of the passive. **6C** focuses on defining and non-defining relative clauses. Lexical areas covered in the File are shopping, the cinema, and adjective formation.

Lesson plan

Shopping and complaining are the main themes for this lesson which revises and extends SS' knowledge of reported speech. The first half of the lesson focuses on reported statements and questions, which may be revision for some SS (it was covered in the last unit of *New English File Pre-intermediate*). SS learn vocabulary related to shopping which they put into practice in a questionnaire. In the second half of the lesson, reported commands are introduced through the context of complaining about things you've bought or bad service in a restaurant or hotel. The pronunciation focus in this lesson is common consonant sounds.

Optional lead-in (books closed)

- Write these questions on the board:
  Do you ever go to a supermarket? Which one?
  How often do you go there?
  Why do you go to that supermarket?
  What do you like or don't you like about it?
  Do you ever talk to other people who are shopping there?
- Put SS in pairs and get them to answer the questions. Get some feedback from the class.

1 GRAMMAR reported speech: statements and questions

a • Books open. Focus on the short story and the pictures. Tell SS to read the story and try to guess the missing last word (they can use the pictures to help them). Elicit ideas and then give them the right answer. The missing word is *over* (i.e. their relationship was finished).

b • Focus on the task and give SS time to complete the speech bubbles in the pictures with the lines of conversation A–K. Get them to compare answers with their partners.

c • **6.1** Play the tape / CD for SS to check answers. Make sure SS finish with the speech bubbles correctly filled with the lines of dialogue.

1 F, H **2** I, D **3** J **4** A, C **5** G, K **6** E, B

6.1 CD3 Track 2

A Do you need any help?
B Thanks. My name's Olga.
B I'm a student. What do you do?
A I work in advertising.
A Olga, I'm falling in love with you.
A Will you marry me?
B Yes, I will.
A Do you know how many calories there are in a bar of chocolate?
B Are you saying I'm fat?
B I don't think you're really my type.
A I'll see you around. Bye.

d • Remind SS what 'reported speech' is by asking them what a 'reporter' does (He / She works for a newspaper or TV company and interviews people and writes down what they say.). 'Reported speech' is when we say or write what another person said.
• Focus on the task and get SS to find and compare the two lines of 'direct speech' (the actual words that the man spoke) and how they are 'reported' (written down) in the story. Give them a few moments to complete the sentences then check answers.

He told her (that) he was falling in love with her.
He asked her if she would marry him.

• Ask SS what differences they can see between 'direct' and 'reported' speech:

sentence: the verb *tell* is used + *that* + person, *is* changes to *was*, *you* changes to *her*
question: the verb *ask* is used, *will* changes to *would*, *if* has been added

e • Tell SS to go to **Grammar Bank 6A** on *p.140*. Read the examples and go through the rules for **reported speech: statements and questions** with the class.

Grammar notes

Reported speech: statements and questions

- This is a structure which may be new for some students and not for others (it was introduced in *New English File Pre-intermediate* in File 9). The basic principle of reported speech is quite straightforward – when you report what someone else said you move the tenses 'backwards', i.e. present to past, *will* to *would*, etc. Making the link between a 'reporter' who reports (i.e. tells other people what someone has said) and 'reported speech' may help SS understand both the grammatical term and concept.
- Point out that the use of *that* after *say* and *tell* is optional.
- You should point out that when direct speech is reported at a later time or in a different place from when it was originally said, some time / place words may change as well, e.g. *tomorrow* may change to *the next day*, *this* to *that*, etc.

⚠ In conversation people often do not change the past to the past perfect.

- Typical mistakes are:
  - SS sometimes confuse *tell* and *say*, e.g. ~~*He said me that he was ill*~~.
  - they forget to change the tenses, e.g. ~~*The waiter said he will call the manager*~~.
  - they forget to change the word order in reported questions, e.g. ~~*She asked him what was his name*~~.

- Get SS to do exercise **a** (**not b**) on *p.141* in pairs or individually. Check answers.

a 1 The waiter said (that) he would call the manager.
2 Jack said (that) he had passed all his exams.
3 They said that we should get to the airport early.
4 Jack said (that) he might be late.
5 Mary said (that) she hadn't told anybody.
6 She asked us if we could help her.
7 He asked me if I wanted to dance.
8 I asked her if she had been there before.
9 She asked me what music I liked.
10 I asked her where the nearest bank was.

- Tell SS to go back to the main lesson on *p.84*.

f • Focus on pictures 1–6 and choose individual SS to change the direct speech in each speech bubble to reported speech. Remind SS that they should use *He / She said...* or *He / She told him / her...* but not ~~*He / She said him / her*~~.
- Then get SS to retell the story in pairs in reported speech. Elicit each sentence back from individual students.

He asked her if she needed any help. She said thank you and (told him) said that her name was Olga. She said (told him) that she was a student and she asked him what he did. He said (told her) that he worked in advertising. He said (told her) that he was falling in love with her and he asked her if she would marry him. She said that she would. Then he asked her if she knew how many calories there were in a bar of chocolate. She asked him if he was saying she was fat. She said (told him) that she didn't think he was really her type. He said (told her) that he would see her around and he said goodbye.

Extra support

Simply elicit the story round the class rather than in pairs.

2 VOCABULARY shopping

a • Focus on the task. Give SS a few minutes to talk in pairs and then check answers.

A **supermarket** is a large shop which sells food, drink, and cleaning materials for the house, etc.
They are often owned by big companies.
A **market** is a place, often outside, where people can buy and sell things. There are usually a lot of individually owned 'stalls'.
A **chemist** (or **chemist's**) and a **pharmacy** are the same thing: a shop which sells medicine, etc.
A **shopping centre** is a place where there are many shops together (sometimes outside a town).
A **department store** is a large shop divided into departments, which sell a lot of different things.
A **shopping centre** is the same as **a shopping mall** but **mall** is American English.
A **library** is a place where you can borrow (but not buy) books to read.
A **bookshop** is a shop where you can buy books.

b • Get SS to answer the questions with a partner, and then elicit answers from individual SS.

c • Tell SS to go to **Vocabulary Bank *Shopping*** on *p.153*. Get them to do section **1 Places** individually or in pairs. Check answers and model and drill pronunciation where necessary. Point out that the apostrophe *s*, e.g. in *baker's* or *butcher's* is because *baker* is the job, and *baker's* is short for the *baker's shop*.

a 1 street market **2** shopping centre
3 department store **4** supermarket
b 5 stationer's **6** newsagent's **7** chemist's
8 baker's **9** bookshop **10** shoe shop
11 butcher's **12** travel agent's

- Now get SS to do section **2 In the shop**. Check answers and model and drill pronunciation if necessary.

1 sales	**7** trolley
2 bargain	**8** refund
3 shop window	**9** basket
4 receipt	**10** customer
5 discount	**11** manager
6 shop assistant	**12** till

- Now get SS to do section **3 Verbs and phrases**. Check answers and model and drill pronunciation, e.g. *online* /ɒnˈlaɪn/ and *queue* /kjuː/.

1 c **2** g **3** d **4** h **5** a **6** e **7** b **8** f

- Finally, focus on the final instruction 'Can you remember the words on this page? Test yourself or a partner'.

Testing yourself
For **Places** SS can cover the words and look at the pictures and try to remember the words. For **In the shop** they can cover the list and words 1–12. They read the definitions and try to remember the words. For **Verbs and phrases** they cover sentences 1–8 and read sentences a–h and try to remember the verbs and phrases.

Testing a partner
See **Testing a partner** *p.17*.

Study Link SS can find more practice of these words on the MultiROM and on the *New English File Intermediate* website.

- Tell SS to go back to the main lesson on *p.85*.

3 PRONUNCIATION consonant sounds: /g/, /dʒ/, /k/, /ʃ/, /tʃ/

Pronunciation notes

The problems your SS have with these sounds will depend on whether similar sounds exist in their own language. You could go through these rules when SS go to the **Sound Bank** in **c**.

Remind SS that:

/g/ - The letter *g* is usually pronounced /g/, e.g. *goal*, with the exceptions below in /dʒ/.

/dʒ/ - The letters *j* and *dge* are always pronounced /dʒ/, e.g. *jacket, bridge* and *g* before *i* or *e* is often /dʒ/ too, e.g. *manager, German.*

/k/ - The letters *ck* and *k* are always /k/ and the letter *c* is often /k/, e.g. *come, across.*

/ʃ/ - This sound occurs in *sh*, e.g. *wash* and in words with *ti-*, and *ci-*, e.g. *patient, information, delicious, special.*

/tʃ/ - This sound occurs in words with *ch, tch,* and in the ending *-ture*, e.g. *future.*

a • 6.2 Focus on the five sound pictures and elicit the words and sounds: *girl* /g/, *jazz* /dʒ/, *key* /k/, *shower* /ʃ/, *chess* /tʃ/.

• Now play the tape / CD for SS to try and cross out the word with a different sound.

• Play the tape / CD again and check answers. Get SS to tell you how the highlighted letter in the different word is pronounced.

1 newsagent's – the *g* sound is /dʒ/.
2 gift shop – the *g* sound is /g/.
3 receipt – the *c* sound is /s/.
4 cereals – the *c* sound is /s/.
5 chemist's – the *ch* sound is /k/.

6.2 CD3 Track 3

1 girl	/g/	bargain newsagent's argument ground floor
2 jazz	/dʒ/	vegetables manager change gift shop
3 key	/k/	discount baker's queue receipt
4 shower	/ʃ/	shoe shop stationer's cereals washing powder
5 chess	/tʃ/	butcher's chemist's cheese choose

Extra support

Play the tape / CD again for SS to repeat the sounds. Then get them to practise individually or in pairs.

b • 6.3 Focus on the task and play the tape / CD for SS to repeat. Then get them to practise saying them individually or in pairs.

6.3 CD3 Track 4

1 You can't get cheese at a chemist's!
2 I had an argument with the manager of the gift shop.
3 I had to queue for ages at the baker's.
4 Could you give me the receipt for the shoes, please?
5 My new green jacket was a bargain.

c • Tell SS to go to the **Sound Bank** on *p.159* and go through the possible spellings for these sounds. (See **pronunciation notes**)

Study Link SS can find more practice of English sounds on the MultiROM and also on the *New English File Intermediate* website.

• Now tell SS to go back to the main lesson on *p.85*.

4 SPEAKING

• Focus on the questionnaire and quickly go through the questions with the whole class.

• Put SS in pairs, preferably face to face. **A** (book open) asks **B** (book closed) the questions in the questionnaire. When they change roles, tell **B** to ask the questions in a different order.

• Monitor and help SS with any more vocabulary they may need. When they have finished, get some feedback from some individual SS.

Extra idea

Get the class to interview you first with some or all of the questionnaire.

5 READING

a • Ask this question to the whole class and elicit some opinions / experiences. Tell SS what you usually do.

b • Focus on the article and task and give SS a time limit to read it and number the paragraphs. Check answers.

2 A 3 G 4 B 5 D 6 F 7 C

c • Focus on the task. SS now read the text again with the paragraphs in the right order and complete the chart. Get SS to compare their answers with a partner's and then check answers. You could write the answers on the board.

	Mr Thomas	Mr Oakley
1 What did he complain about?	His laptop computer.	A (recordable) DVD player.
2 What was the problem?	It was getting slower.	They didn't have one in stock.
3 How did he try to solve it?	He took it to a local repairer and then to a computer shop.	He went back to the shop and phoned many times to reserve one.
4 Why wasn't he successful?	It was too expensive to repair.	Because they just told him to come back but it never arrived.
5 Who did he write to?	Toshiba.	The Managing Director of Argos.
6 What happened as a result?	Toshiba collected the laptop, repaired it and returned it free of charge.	He got his DVD player + ten discs.

d • Focus on the task and give SS a few minutes to do this. Check answers and drill pronunciation of new words, e.g. *staff* /stɑːf/ and *guarantee* /gærənˈtiː/.

1 branch	5 services
2 staff	6 compensation
3 goods	7 guarantee
4 in stock	

Extra support

Go through the text (reading it aloud) paragraph by paragraph with the class making sure SS understand it. If necessary, use SS' L1 to clarify.

e • Focus on the last part of the article 'Top tips for complaining' and on the five phrases (*Be reasonable*, etc.). Make sure SS understand what they mean. Get SS to read the text and complete it with the phrases. Get them to compare their answers with a partner's and then check answers. Deal with any vocabulary problems SS may have.

• Finally, get SS to vote on which two tips they think are most important and why.

1 Act quickly
2 Always go to the top
3 Keep a record
4 Don't lose your temper
5 Be reasonable

6 GRAMMAR reported speech: commands

a • Focus on the two sentences from the article in **5 READING**, and ask SS to imagine what the actual words used by the shop assistants were. You could refer SS to the cartoon in the text for the first one.

Possible answers
1 '(If you want my advice,) buy a new one.' / 'If I were you, I'd buy a new one.' / 'I think you should buy a new one.'
2 'Come back in a week, sir.' / 'Could you come back next week?'

• Emphasize that when the shop assistants' words were 'reported', i.e. turned into 'reported speech', the construction was *They told him* + the infinitive (with *to*).

b • Focus on the instructions, and the four cartoons and speech bubbles. Tell SS to complete the four sentences using the positive or negative infinitive of a verb. Put SS in pairs and set them a time limit. Check answers.

1 She asked the shop assistant to give her a refund.
2 He told the people at the next table not to make so much noise.
3 She asked the receptionist to change her room.
4 He told the taxi driver not to go / drive so fast.

c • Tell SS to go to **Grammar Bank 6A** on *p.140*. Read the examples and go through the rules for **Reported speech: commands**.

Grammar notes

Reported speech: commands

- This structure is not difficult but can be a problem for SS who use, for example, a subjunctive in their L1.
- Some typical mistakes are:
  – not using an infinitive, e.g. ~~*He told me I not worry / that I don't worry*~~.
  – forgetting to use the infinitive with *to*, e.g. ~~*He told me not worry*~~.

• Get SS to do exercise **b** on *p.141* either individually or in pairs. Check answers.

b 1 to be quiet
2 not to smoke
3 to open my mouth
4 not to tell anyone
5 to show him my driving licence
6 to switch off our mobiles
7 not to eat with her mouth open
8 to bring him the bill
9 to get off at the next stop
10 not to wait

• Tell SS to go back to the main lesson on *p.87*.

7 LISTENING & SPEAKING

a • 6.4 Focus on the questions and go through them. Then play the tape / CD and pause after the first story (the taxi). Give SS time to answer the questions in pairs. Then play this story again if necessary. Check answers, and ask a few more comprehension questions, e.g. *Where were they? Where was the speaker going?*, etc. Then repeat the process for the other two stories.

The taxi
1 Because the taxi driver said that all English people were football hooligans.
2 He asked him to stop the taxi.
3 He got out and he didn't pay anything.

The hotel
4 It wasn't clean / It was in a mess. The bed hadn't been made, there were dirty towels on the floor and the bathroom was filthy.
5 He said that she had to wait half an hour while they cleaned her room.
6 She told him to give her another room. He did this.

The restaurant
7 Because there was a black hair in it.
8 Because they had charged him for the ravioli. He thought they shouldn't charge for it.
9 He complained and they didn't have to pay for the ravioli.

6.4 CD3 Track 5

(tapescript in Student's Book on *p.128*)

1 I was in a taxi in Greece, in Athens, and I was going into the centre to do some shopping and the taxi driver started chatting to me. He asked me where I was from. When I said I was English, he started getting really aggressive. He said that he didn't like the English and that all English people were football hooligans. He went on and on – he just wouldn't stop. I got really annoyed. I mean I thought, 'Why do I have to listen to all of this?'. So I asked him to stop the taxi and let me get out. Luckily, he stopped and I got out – and of course, I didn't pay him anything.

2 This happened to me recently when I was travelling around France on business. I was really tired because I'd been working and travelling all day. Anyway, when I got to the hotel in Toulouse – it was the evening – I checked in and the receptionist gave me the key to my room. So I went up to my room and opened the door, but it was a complete mess! The bed wasn't made, there were dirty towels on the floor and the bathroom was *filthy*. I went downstairs and told the receptionist and he said that I would have to wait for half an hour while they prepared the room. But I was exhausted and needed to rest, so I told him to give me another room straightaway. Luckily, he did.

3 This happened to me last week. I went to a restaurant in London with my family to celebrate my dad's birthday. Anyway, my dad ordered ravioli and when his dish arrived he saw that it had a long, black hair in it. So he asked the waitress to take it back and bring him another one. She brought him another plate of ravioli and it was fine, and we finished our meal. But when my dad asked for the bill, he saw that they had charged us for the ravioli. He didn't think that was right. He thought the ravioli should be free because he had found a hair in it. So he asked the waitress to take it off the bill. She went away and spoke to the manager, and he came and apologized and he took the ravioli off the bill.

Extra support

If there's time, you could get SS to listen to the tape / CD with the tapescript on *p.128* so they can see exactly what they understood / didn't understand. Translate / explain any new words or phrases.

b • Put SS in pairs and focus on the task. Get SS to discuss questions 1 and 2 for a few minutes. Then get feedback from the class.

Extra idea

Get SS to ask you the questions first and tell them about any experiences you have had.

c • Put SS in pairs, **A** and **B**, preferably face to face. Tell them to go to **Communication** *I want to speak to the manager*, **A** on *p.118* and **B** on *p.121*. Go through the instructions for the first roleplay situation. Remind SS that in the first roleplay student **A** is the customer and **B** is the shop assistant. Tell **A** to start first saying *Excuse me, I bought…*

- When they have finished roleplaying the first situation, tell them to read the instructions for the second situation. This time **A** is the restaurant manager and **B** is the customer. **B** starts *Good evening. Are you the manager?*
- Get feedback to see whether different customers achieved their objectives or not.

Extra photocopiable activities

Grammar

reported speech *p.157*

Communicative

Who asked what? *p.188* (instructions *p.168*)

HOMEWORK

Study Link **Workbook** *pp.54–56*

G passive: *be* + past participle
V cinema
P sentence stress

6 B See the film...get on a plane

Lesson plan

The topic of this lesson is the cinema. In the first half of the lesson there is an article about exotic film locations, which have inspired people to visit them. This provides the context for revision and extension of the passive form. In the second half of the lesson, cinema vocabulary is presented and then put into practice in a questionnaire where SS talk about their own preferences and experiences. Finally, SS listen to the true story of a young student who met, and then worked for, a world famous film director.

Optional lead-in (books closed)

- Put SS in pairs or threes.
- Write on the board the names of some famous films you think your SS will know which are set in a different country from where your SS are studying.
- Then teach SS the question *Where is the film set?* (= In which country does the action take place?).
- Set a time limit, e.g. three minutes. Tell each pair or group to write down the country in which each film is set.

  Some possible films (but try to include some recent, famous films):

  Casablanca (Morocco), *Zorro* (Mexico), *Harry Potter* (England), *Braveheart* (Scotland), *Independence Day* (USA), *Brokeback Mountain* (USA), *Memoirs of a Geisha* (Japan), *The Da Vinci Code* (France)

1 READING

a • Books open. Focus on the question and elicit answers from the class.

b • Ask SS to read the article once and try to guess the name of each film and where it was filmed. Tell SS to write the name of the film next to the numbered gap and the name of the country in which it was filmed in the gap in the texts. Set a time limit, e.g. five minutes. Check answers.

1 *The Beach*, Thailand
2 *Out of Africa*, Kenya
3 *The Lord of the Rings*, New Zealand

Extra support

There are many clues both in the texts and photos to help SS identify the films and countries. However, if you think that your SS will still have problems, you could write in jumbled order the three film titles and countries on the board to help them.

c • Focus on the questions and make sure SS understand everything, especially:
were based on a book = when a film is made using a story or novel (e.g. the Harry Potter books)
was set at the beginning of the 20th century / was set in a place where... = the film was situated at a particular time and in a particular place. Point out that *set* is an irregular verb (*set-set-set*).

• Set a time limit for SS to read the article again and answer the questions (with the name of the film). Sometimes they need to answer with more than one film. Get SS to compare their answers with a partner's and then check answers.

1 *The Lord of the Rings*
2 All three films
3 *Out of Africa*
4 *The Beach*
5 *Out of Africa*
6 *The Beach*
7 *Out of Africa*
8 *The Lord of the Rings*

Extra support

You could now go through the whole article, dealing with any vocabulary problems.

d • Do this as a whole class activity. Ask the class about each film and find out how many people have seen it and how many liked it. Then, with a show of hands, find out which of the three countries they would most like to visit.

Extra idea

You could get SS to underline or highlight five words or phrases they want to remember from the text. Get them to compare their words / phrases with a partner and then get some feedback from the class.

2 GRAMMAR passive: *be* + past participle

a • Focus on the instructions. Ask SS which is the first example of a passive in *The Beach* (*is set*). Then, give SS a few minutes to underline more examples. Check answers by eliciting and writing the sentences (or parts of sentences) on the board. Elicit the rule for making the passive.

Possible answers
Present simple passive: It is based on a best-selling book.
Past simple passive: It was directed by the British director, Danny Boyle. / The film was shot on the island of Phi Phi Leh. / Most of the hotels were destroyed in 2004 by the tsunami.
Present perfect simple passive: ... they have now been rebuilt.

The passive is formed with the verb *be* (in the appropriate tense) and the past participle.

Extra challenge

You could get SS to underline more examples of the passive in the other two texts.

b • Focus on the chart and get SS to underline the verbs in the active chart and tell you the tense of the verb.

inspire: present simple
directed: past simple
are making: present continuous
will release: future
have visited: present perfect simple

• Put SS in pairs and get them to complete the chart with passive verbs. Emphasize that they have to use the verb *to be* first (in the correct tense) and then a past participle. Check answers by writing the passive verbs on the board.

Passive
The film **is being made** on location.
The film **will be released** next year.
The country **has been visited** by thousands of fans.

c • Tell SS to go to **Grammar Bank 6B** on *p.140*. Read the examples and go through the rules with the class.

Grammar notes

The passive: *be* + past participle

- If your SS previously used *English File Pre-intermediate*, they will already have had an introduction to the passive although only in the present and past tenses.
- The form of the passive (*be* + participle) is quite straightforward and the easiest way to approach this grammar point is to emphasize that there are two ways of saying the same thing (active and passive) but sometimes with a change of emphasis or focus.

  Active: Peter Jackson directed The Lord of the Rings (The focus is on Jackson.).

  Passive: The Lord of the Rings was directed by Peter Jackson (The focus is on the film.).
- Depending on your SS' L1 it may be worth pointing out that we often use the passive in sentences like *It's made in…*, and *They're grown in…*, where some languages use an impersonal subject. Some contrasting with their L1 may help SS to see when to use the passive.
- Typical mistakes include:
  - using the active instead of the passive, e.g. ~~*The tickets sell at a newsagent's*~~.
  - SS thinking they always have to use *by (somebody)* when they make a passive sentence.
  - problems of form, e.g. leaving out the verb *be* or not using the participle correctly.

• Now get SS to do the exercises on *p.141* in pairs or individually. Check answers either after each exercise or when SS have finished both.

a **1** is being built
2 was / is based on
3 was watched by
4 was stolen
5 were written by
6 my computer was being repaired
7 You will be taken
8 has been cancelled
9 is spoken
10 must be worn
b **1** are subtitled
2 were thrown away by mistake
3 is being painted
4 have been sold
5 will be played tomorrow
6 must be paid tomorrow

• Tell SS to go back to the main lesson on *p.89*.

3 PRONUNCIATION sentence stress

Pronunciation notes

Remind SS that information words are the ones which are usually stressed. These are the words which you hear more clearly when somebody speaks to you. The unstressed words are heard much less clearly.

a • 6.5 Focus on the task and tell SS that they are going to hear six passive sentences which they have to try to write down.

• Play the tape / CD, pausing after each sentence to give SS time to write down the sentences.

• Play the tape / CD again for SS to check their answers. Check answers by writing the correct sentences on the board (see tapescript below). Leave the sentences on the board for the next exercise.

b • Play the tape / CD again and get SS to tell you which words to underline in the sentences. Point out that it is the words which carry the most important information (usually nouns, adjectives, and verbs) which are stressed more strongly. Finally, play the tape / CD again pausing for SS to repeat and copy the rhythm.

6.5 CD3 Track 6

1 How's <u>this</u> <u>word</u> <u>pronounced</u>?
2 <u>My</u> <u>car's</u> been <u>stolen</u>.
3 <u>When</u> was this <u>house</u> <u>built</u>?
4 Our <u>television's</u> <u>being</u> <u>repaired</u>.
5 I've been <u>offered</u> the <u>job</u>.
6 <u>When</u> will the <u>new</u> <u>airport</u> be <u>finished</u>?

c • Focus on the task. Play the tape / CD, pausing after each sentence for SS to repeat. Encourage them to use the correct rhythm by stressing the underlined words more strongly.

4 VOCABULARY cinema

a • Focus on the task and give SS a couple of minutes to see if they can remember (without turning back to the previous page) the words from the article related to the cinema.

b • Get SS to compare with a partner before telling them to look back at text 2 on *p.88* to check their answers. Then elicit and write the answers on the board.

1 the soundtrack	**4** the film crew
2 the director	**5** on location
3 the cast	**6** the screen

c • Tell SS to go to **Vocabulary Bank *Cinema*** on *p.154* and do section **1 Kinds of film** either individually or in pairs. Check answers and drill pronunciation of any difficult words. You could elicit famous films of each type from your SS.

1 Western	**5** Thriller
2 Action film	**6** Comedy
3 Musical	**7** Science fiction
4 Horror film	

Extra challenge

Elicit other kinds of films, e.g. war film (e.g. *Apocalypse Now / Platoon / Jarhead*), romcom (= romantic comedy, e.g. *Love Actually*), musicals (e.g. *Chicago*), etc.

• Get SS to do section **2 People and things** and then check answers. Elicit and drill the pronunciation of any difficult words (e.g. words where the phonetics are given).

1 cast	**5** plot	**9** special effects
2 star	**6** scene	**10** script
3 director	**7** audience	**11** extra
4 soundtrack	**8** sequel	**12** subtitles

• Finally, get SS to do section **3 Verbs and phrases** and then check answers. Elicit and drill the pronunciation of any difficult words.

1 b **2** e **3** f **4** a **5** c **6** d

• Now, focus on the final instruction 'Can you remember the words on this page? Test yourself or a partner'.

Testing yourself

For **Kinds of film** SS can cover the words and look at the pictures and try to remember the film types. For **People and things** they can cover the list and words 1–12. They look at the definitions and remember the words, uncovering one by one to check. For **Verbs and phrases** they can cover the phrases 1–6 and look at the definitions a–f and try to remember the phrases.

Testing a partner

See **Testing a partner** *p.17*.

Study Link SS can find more practice of these words on the MultiROM and on the *New English File Intermediate* website.

• Tell SS to go back to the main lesson on *p.90*.

5 SPEAKING

a • Focus on the cinema questionnaire and quickly go through the questions. Give SS two or three minutes to think about their answers.

b • Put SS in pairs and they take turns to interview each other to find out if they have similar tastes.

Extra idea

If there's time, you could get the class to interview you.

6 LISTENING

This interview is with a Polish woman, Dagmara, who became Steven Spielberg's interpreter in the film *Schindler's List*, and the person speaking on the tape / CD is Dagmara herself, so you may like to tell your SS in advance that she speaks with a light Polish accent.

Schindler's List was partly shot in Krakow, where Dagmara lives, and is based on the true story of Emil Schindler, a Pole who saved the lives of many Jews during the Second World War by employing them in his factory. The film stars Liam Neeson and Ben Kingsley and won nine Oscars in 1993.

a • Focus SS' attention on the photograph and the task. Get SS to quickly discuss the four questions. Don't check answers at this stage.

b • **6.6** Play the tape / CD for SS to check their answers. Elicit answers from the class.

The man is Steven Spielberg and the woman is Dagmara, a Polish student.
They are on a film set.
The film is *Schindler's List*.
They are talking to the Polish 'extras'. Dagmara is interpreting for Spielberg, i.e. he is speaking in English and Dagmara will then give his instructions in Polish.

c • Focus on the questions and go through them quickly. Tell SS not to try to write answers while they listen but to wait until the end. Play the tape / CD again. Then let them discuss the answers in pairs.

• Play the tape / CD again if necessary, pausing after each of Dagmara's answers, and then check answers.

1 In Krakow in Poland.
2 She was working in the film company's office, translating documents and parts of the script.
3 No, she was a student at the time.
4 At a party, just before the shooting started.
5 She had to translate Spielberg's speech because the girl who was going to do it didn't come.
6 She was very nervous and she made some mistakes but she got to the end.
7 Spielberg thanked her and asked her to be his interpreter for the film.

6.6 CD3 Track 7

(tapescript in Student's Book on *p.128*)

I = Interviewer, D = Dagmara

I So how did you get involved in the film, Dagmara?

D Well, as you probably know, a lot of the film *Schindler's List* was shot in Krakow, in Poland, which is where I live. And before the actual shooting of the film started, the film company had an office in Krakow and I got a job there translating documents and parts of the script – things like that – I was a university student at the time.

I But how did you get the job as Spielberg's interpreter in the film?

D It's a funny story. I didn't think I would ever get to meet Spielberg or any of the actors. But then, just before the shooting started, there was a big party in one of the hotels in Krakow and I was invited.
At first, I wasn't going to go – I was tired after working all day, and I didn't think I had anything suitable to wear. But in the end, I borrowed a jacket from a friend and I went. But when I arrived at the party, the producer – who was Polish – came up to me and said, 'Dagmara, you're going to interpret for Steven Spielberg. You have to translate his opening speech, because the girl who was going to do it couldn't come.'
I How did you feel about that?
D I couldn't believe it! I was just a student – I had no experience of interpreting – and now I was going to have to speak in front of hundreds of people. I was nervous so I drank a couple glasses of champagne to give myself courage. But when I started speaking, I was so nervous that I confused the dates of the Second World War – but luckily I managed to get to the end without making any more mistakes.
And afterwards, during the party, Spielberg came up to speak to me to say thank you – he was really nice to me and said he was impressed by the way I had interpreted. And then he said, 'I'd like you to be my interpreter for the whole film.' I couldn't believe it. I had to pinch myself to believe that this was happening to me.

d • 6.7 Focus on the task and go through the headings under which SS have to take notes. Tell them just to listen and to make notes after they have heard the tape. Play the tape / CD.

e • Get SS to compare their notes and then play the tape / CD again for them to check / complete their notes. Play again if necessary, pausing after each section. Elicit answers and write them on the board.

The most difficult thing about the job
When they had to shoot a scene many times. She thought it was her fault – maybe she hadn't translated correctly.
The worst moment
Once when they repeated a scene many times Spielberg got angry and shouted at her. Later he apologized.
What it was like to work with Spielberg
He was demanding but he treated her well – like a daughter, e.g. he made sure she was warm enough. It was hard work but she enjoyed it.
Her opinion of the film
She thinks it's great, a masterpiece. The actors were brilliant. She likes the way it was mainly shot in black and white.
How she feels when she watches the film
She can't be objective. She remembers where she was in each scene, perhaps hiding under the bed.

• Finally, ask SS if they have seen *Schindler's List* and what they thought of it – if they agree with Dagmara. You could also ask them if they would like to have done Dagmara's job, or which director they would like to interpret for.

Extra support

If there's time, get SS to listen to the whole interview with Dagmara with the tapescript on *p. 128* so they can see exactly what they understood / didn't understand. Translate / explain any new words or phrases.

6.7 CD3 Track 8
(tapescript in Student's Book on *p.128*)
I = Interviewer, D = Dagmara
I So what exactly did you have to do?
D I had to go to the film set every day. A car came every day to pick me up from my house – I felt really important! And then what I had to do was to translate Spielberg's instructions to the Polish actors, as well as the extras. I had to make them understand what he wanted. It was really exciting – sometimes I felt as if I was a director myself.
I Was it a difficult job?
D Sometimes it was really difficult. The worst thing was when we kept having to shoot a scene again and again because Spielberg thought it wasn't exactly right. Some scenes were repeated as many as 16 times – and then sometimes I would think that maybe it was my fault – that I hadn't translated properly what he wanted, so I'd get really nervous. I remember one scene where we just couldn't get it right and Spielberg started shouting at me because he was stressed. But in the end we got it right and then he apologized, and I cried a little, because I was also very stressed – and after that, it was all right again.
I So, was Spielberg difficult to work with?
D Not at all. I mean he was very demanding – I had to do my best every day – but he was really nice to me. I felt he treated me like a daughter. For instance, he was always making sure that I wasn't cold – it was freezing on the set most of the time – and he would make sure I had a warm coat and gloves and things. It was hard work but it was fascinating – an amazing experience.
I What did you think of the finished film?
D I believe that *Schindler's List* is truly a great movie, a masterpiece. I think the actors were brilliant, especially Liam Neeson and Ben Kingsley – and I love the way it was shot in black and white, with colour in just one scene.
But, as you can imagine, I can't be very objective about it – I mean, I lived through nearly every scene. And when I watch it – and I've seen it a lot of times – I always remember exactly where I was at that moment. I can't help thinking, 'Oh there I am, hiding under the bed, or standing behind that door.'

Extra photocopiable activities

Grammar
passive: *be* + past participle *p.158*
Communicative
Cinema quiz *p.189* (instructions *p.169*)

HOMEWORK

Study Link **Workbook** *pp.57–59*

6C

G relative clauses: defining and non-defining
V what people do
P word stress

I need a hero

Lesson plan

The theme of this lesson is heroes and icons. The first half of the lesson focuses on one of the most iconic figures of the 20th century: the revolutionary Che Guevara (whose face has adorned many students' walls and T-shirts). This context is used to revise and extend SS' knowledge of relative clauses. They should be familiar with defining clauses but probably won't be familiar with non-defining clauses. The second half of the lesson focuses on people who *Time* magazine consider to be heroes and icons of the 21st century. The lexical and pronunciation focus is on nouns describing what people do. At the end of the lesson, SS talk about people (dead or alive) who they admire.

Optional lead-in (books closed)

- Put SS in pairs. Tell SS to imagine that they are going to sell T-shirts to raise money for the school. The T-shirts will have on them the face of a famous person. Each pair has to choose whose face they want to have on their T-shirt and be ready to explain why.
- Give SS a few minutes to do this and then ask each pair who they have chosen and why.

1 GRAMMAR relative clauses

a • Books open. Focus on the picture and the quiz and put SS in pairs. Set them a time limit and then check answers.

1 c **2** b **3** a **4** a **5** a **6** b **7** b

b • Tell SS to cover texts A–E on *p.93*. Focus on the photos on *pp.92–3* and tell SS to try and guess what the connection is between the photos and Che Guevara. Elicit ideas from SS (e.g. *I think the motorbike is the one which Che Guevara rode in the film 'The Motorcycle Diaries'*, etc.) but don't tell them if they are right or wrong yet.

c • Get SS to read texts A–E to find out the connection between the photos and Che Guevara. Feedback answers. Go through the texts (you could read them aloud). Translate / explain any words or phrases that caused problems.

d • Tell SS to cover the texts and look at sentences 1–6 (which are all taken from the texts). They should complete the gaps with a relative pronoun. Check answers.

1 whose, which **2** which, which **3** who **4** where
5 which **6** who, who

e • Now focus on the instructions and get SS to compare sentences 1 and 2 with the almost identical sentences in text **A** and find three differences. Elicit the answer from the class.

The text says '*...the motorbike journey Che made with his friend Alberto across South America*' (the relative pronoun **which** is omitted), '*...it was the poverty he saw on this trip...*' (the relative pronoun **which** is omitted) and, '*...it was the poverty he saw on this trip* ***that*** *made him...*' (**that** is used instead of *which*).

- Tell SS that they will learn the rules for when they can leave out the relative pronoun and when they can use *that* instead of *who / which* in the **Grammar Bank**.

f • Tell SS to go to **Grammar Bank 6C** on *p.140*. Read the examples and go through the rules with the class.

Grammar notes

Relative clauses

- SS who used *New English File Pre-intermediate* will have already had an introduction to defining relative clauses but not to non-defining ones. In writing it is always clear which is which because of the comma(s) which always separate off the extra information in a non-defining clause.
- Although *that* is a common alternative to *who / which* in defining relative clauses, it cannot be used in non-defining clauses. For this reason, it may be advisable to train your SS to always use *who / which* in both kinds of clauses to avoid error.
- *Whom* is also sometimes used as a relative pronoun instead of *who* to refer to the object of the verb in the relative clause, or after prepositions, e.g. *She's the woman whom I met yesterday. He's the man to whom I spoke yesterday.* It is much less common and more formal than *who*. You may wish to point out its use to SS.
- Typical mistakes include:
  - confusing *who* and *which*, e.g. ~~*She's a friend which lives near her.*~~
  - using a personal pronoun, e.g. ~~*He is the man who he works with my father.*~~
  - using *that* in non-defining relative clauses, e.g. ~~*This film, that won an Oscar in 1999, will be shown on TV tonight for the first time.*~~

- Get SS to do exercise **a** on *p.141*, in pairs or individually. Check answers.

1 where	**4** which	**7** whose	**10** which
2 who	**5** which	**8** who	
3 whose	**6** where	**9** which	

- Now get SS to do exercise **b** in pairs or individually. Check answers. Point out that this exercise is based on defining clauses.

The following sentences should be ticked: 5 and 10

- Now get SS to do exercise **c** in pairs or individually. This exercise is based on both defining and non-defining clauses. Check answers.

1 ✓
2 ✗ **who** you met...
3 ✓
4 ✓ **which** is...
5 ✓ **whose** garden...
6 ✓
7 ✓
8 ✗ who ~~they~~ come from...

- Tell SS to go back to the main lesson on *p.92*.

g • Now get SS to cover the text and look only at the photos. Ask them if they can remember what the connection was between each photo and Che Guevara. SS will probably use a relative clause in some of their answers, e.g. *It's the town where Che Guevara was born. / It's the motorbike which was used in the film.*

2 LISTENING & SPEAKING

a • **6.8** Focus on the task and explain the meaning of *icon* (= a famous person that people see as a symbol of a particular idea, way of life, etc.). Put SS in pairs and explain that they are going to hear a quiz programme, which is a series of clues to identify eight famous people. Point out that the presenter of the programme always gives the first letter of each person's name as an extra clue. So, for example if the person was Nelson Mandela, the letters would be N and M. Emphasize that SS **mustn't call out answers** but that they should write them down on a piece of paper.

- Play the tape / CD once the whole way through, and then again. Alternatively, you could pause the recording after each question and give SS time to discuss with a partner who they think the person is.
- Then ask how many pairs think they have correctly identified all eight people. If there are several, check answers. If nobody seems to have got all of them, then play the recording again before checking answers.

1 Bill Gates	**5** Jackie Onassis
2 Pope John Paul II	**6** Martina Navratilova
3 Madonna	**7** George Clooney
4 Giorgio Armani	**8** Maria Callas

Extra support

If there's time, you could get SS to listen to the tape / CD again with the tapescript on *p.128* so they can see exactly what they understood / didn't understand. Translate / explain any new words or phrases.

6.8 CD3 Track 9

(tapescript in Student's Book on *p.128*)

It's 12.00 noon and so it's time for today's competition. Today the topic is 'Heroes and Icons'. As usual, the rules are very simple. I'm going to give you eight clues and you have to identify the people. If you know all the answers, send them to me straightaway by email. The first person who sends me the correct answers wins a prize. Today's prize is two plane tickets to ... the Big Apple, New York!

OK, so let's get started with those clues. I'll say each one twice only. And remember, I always give you the first letter or letters of the word I'm looking for. Today they are all people's names.

Let's start with an easy one. Two letters, B and G. It's a man who's probably the richest man in the world, the founder of Microsoft. That's BG, the man who started Microsoft.

Number 2. Two letters again, J and P, although this isn't the name he was born with. A man whose humanity made him an icon for millions of people all over the world. This religious leader was born in Poland but he died in Rome in 2005.

Number 3 begins with M, just one word. It's the name of a woman who has had a lot of different jobs. She's been an actress, she's even written children's books, but she's most famous as a singer. One word beginning with M.

And number 4. This time it's a man, and the letters are G and A, though many people just know him by his surname. He's an Italian designer, whose clothes are considered among the most elegant in the world, and whose name is also on perfume bottles everywhere. G and A, for an Italian fashion designer.

On to number 5. Two letters, J and O. It's the name of a famous American woman, whose first husband was president of the USA and whose second husband was a Greek millionaire. Although she died in 1994, she is still admired for her style all over the world. Two letters, J and O.

And number 6. It's a woman again and the letters are M and N. She's the woman who changed the shape of women's tennis, and is possibly the greatest female player of all time. She was born in Prague but later became a US citizen. M and N for the greatest ever woman tennis player.

Number 7 is an American actor. He was born in Kentucky in 1961 and he is often called the most attractive male actor in Hollywood today. He first became famous in a TV hospital drama in which he played the part of a doctor. His first name begins with G and his surname with C. So that's a Hollywood actor, G and C.

And finally, number 8. Two letters. M and C. She was born in Greece and died in Paris, and she is the woman whose voice is familiar to lovers of opera all over the world. Nicknamed 'La Divina' her life was tragic, but her voice will never be forgotten. MC, la Divina.

So, if you think you've got the eight correct answers, email them to me now at this address, Guessthenames@BT.com, that's Guessthenames@BT.com. And the first person with the correct answers will win those two tickets to New York.

Time for some music.

b • Put SS in pairs, **A** and **B**, preferably face to face. Tell SS to go to **Communication** *Relatives quiz*, **A** on *p.118* and **B** on *p.121*.

- Go through their instructions and make sure SS understand what they have to do. You could demonstrate the activity by doing number 1 (for **A** and **B**) with the whole class, before getting them to write their questions. Monitor to make sure SS are writing sensible questions.
- SS then take it in turns to ask their questions to their partner.

Extra Challenge

You could encourage SS to make their clues a bit cryptic, so that they are more difficult to get, e.g. if the word was *generous*, instead of defining it as *a person who likes giving presents*, they could define it as, e.g. *a person who is always the first to take out his wallet in a restaurant when the waiter brings the bill.*

3 READING

a • Focus on the task and get SS to try to match the photos and people. Check answers, and for each person ask the class what he / she is famous for. Elicit ideas but don't tell them if they are right or wrong.

> Aung San Suu-Kyi 5
> Bono 1
> Thierry Henry 2
> Bernard Kouchner 3
> Queen Rania of Jordan 4

b • Get SS to read the article and match the five names with the texts. Check answers.

> **A** Thierry Henry
> **B** Queen Rania of Jordan
> **C** Bono
> **D** Aung San Suu-Kyi
> **E** Bernard Kouchner

Extra idea

Alternatively, you could read each paragraph aloud to the class and elicit who the person is, and also the meaning of any new words or phrases.

c • Set a time limit, e.g. six or seven minutes, and get SS to read the article again and answer the questions. Check answers.

> 1 Bono. He couldn't take the child with him.
> 2 Queen Rania of Jordan, by getting children vaccinated.
> 3 Aung San Suu-Kyi. She chose her job.
> 4 Bernard Kouchner. He participated actively himself in aid work.
> 5 Bono and Thierry Henry. Bono is trying to free Africa of hunger and poverty, and Henry is trying to eradicate racism from sport.

d • Focus on the task and get SS to read the article again to find the nouns. Check answers, and get SS to underline the stressed syllable.

2 modernity	5 choice
3 hunger	6 operation
4 poverty	7 sale

e • In pairs, tell SS to cover the article and try to remember as much as they can about each person.

Extra support

Do this as a whole class activity.

4 VOCABULARY & PRONUNCIATION what people do, word stress

Focus on the information box and remind SS that these are the common endings for words which tell us what someone's profession or occupation is.

a • Now focus on the chart and the four examples. SS do the exercise in pairs or individually and then compare with a partner.
• Check answers.

-er	-or	-ian	-ist
leader	*actor*	*politician*	*physicist*
composer	conductor	musician	cyclist
designer	director		guitarist
footballer	inventor		scientist
painter	sculptor		violinist
photographer			
presenter			

b • 6.9 Play the tape / CD for SS to underline the stressed syllable in each word. Check answers, and get SS to practise saying the words. Remind them that endings added to words are usually not stressed.

Extra challenge

You could get SS to underline the stressed syllable first and then listen to check.

6.9 CD3 Track 10

leader	actor	politician	physicist
composer	conductor	musician	cyclist
designer	director		guitarist
footballer	inventor		scientist
painter	sculptor		violinist
photographer			
presenter			

5 SPEAKING

a • This is a free-speaking activity which gives SS a chance to talk about their own heroes.
• Give SS time to write a name in three of the categories and give them a few minutes to prepare to talk about them (who they are, what they have done, and why they admire them). Monitor and help SS with any vocabulary they may need.

b • Put SS into small groups of ideally three SS (or if this is impractical, in pairs).
• SS take it in turns to talk about the people they admire (i.e. each student talks about one person, then the next student speaks about one of their people, etc.).
• If there's time, get some feedback from the whole class on which people SS chose.

Extra idea

Begin by telling SS about a couple of people that you admire and explain why.

6 6.10 ♫ SONG *Holding out for a hero*

- This song originally recorded by Bonnie Tyler in 1982 was used as the theme song in the film *Shrek* 2 (2004). For copyright reasons this is a cover version. If you want to do this song in class, use the photocopiable activity on *p.211*.

6.10 CD3 Track 11

Holding out for a hero

Where have all the good men gone and where are all the gods?
Where's the streetwise Hercules to fight the rising odds?
Isn't there a white knight upon a fiery steed?
Late at night I toss and I turn and I dream of what I need

I need a hero
I'm holding out for a hero till the end of the night
He's gotta be strong and he's gotta be fast
And he's gotta be fresh from the fight
I need a hero
I'm holding out for a hero till the morning light
He's gotta be sure and it's gotta be soon
And he's gotta be larger than life
Larger than life

Somewhere after midnight
In my wildest fantasy
Somewhere just beyond my reach
There's someone reaching back for me
Racing on the thunder and rising with the heat
It's gonna take a Superman to sweep me off my feet

I need a hero
I'm holding out for a hero till the end of the night
He's gotta be strong and he's gotta be fast
And he's gotta be fresh from the fight
I need a hero
I'm holding out for a hero till the morning light
He's gotta be sure and it's gotta be soon
And he's gotta be larger than life

I need a hero
I'm holding out for a hero till the end of the night

Up where the mountains meet the heavens above
Out where the lightning splits the sea
I could swear there is someone somewhere watching me
Through the wind and the chill and the rain
And the storm and the flood
I can feel his approach like a fire in the blood

I need a hero
I'm holding out for a hero till the end of the night
He's gotta be strong and he's gotta be fast
And he's gotta be fresh from the fight
I need a hero
I'm holding out for a hero till the morning light
He's gotta be sure and it's gotta be soon
And he's gotta be larger than life

Study Link SS can find a dictation and a Grammar quiz on all the grammar from File 6 on the MultiROM and more grammar activities on the *New English File Intermediate* website.

Extra photocopiable activities

Grammar
relative clauses *p.159*
Communicative
Which definition is right? *p.190* (instructions *p.169*)
Vocabulary
Alphabet race *p.202* (instructions *p.196*)
Song
Holding out for a hero p.211 (instructions *p.206*)

HOMEWORK

Study Link **Workbook** *pp.60–62*

6 PRACTICAL ENGLISH BREAKING NEWS

Function Giving and reacting to news
Language *You'll never guess what's happened! You're joking! Are you serious?*, etc.

Lesson plan

In the first part of the lesson, SS learn and practise ways of giving and reacting to news. Ben tells the other people in the office that he saw Mark and Allie together in the Louvre and they express their surprise and disbelief. In the second part of the lesson (**Social English**), Mark arrives at work and Ben questions him about his weekend. Then Allie, by mistake, sends a personal email to everyone in the office.

Study Link These lessons are on the *New English File Intermediate* Video / DVD, which can be used instead of the Class Cassette / CD (see introduction *p.9*). The main functional section of each episode is also on the MultiROM with additional activities.

Optional lead-in (books closed)

- Revise what happened in the previous episode by eliciting the story from SS, e.g. *Why did they have a meeting with Scarlett? Who did Allie agree with, Mark or Jacques? Where did Mark and Allie go in Paris at the weekend? Why did they have to leave the art gallery quickly?*, etc.
  If you are using the video / DVD, you could play the previous episode again, leaving out the 'Listen and Repeat' sections.
- You could also try to elicit from the SS the phrases they revised / learnt in the previous episode for giving opinion, e.g. *Personally, I think Scarlet should..., I agree with Jacques*, etc. (You could write the phrases with gaps on the board to help SS remember.).

GIVING AND REACTING TO NEWS

a • 6.11 Tell SS to cover the dialogue with their hand or a piece of paper. Focus on the photo and the two questions. Alternatively, write the two questions on the board and get SS to close their books.
• Play the tape / CD the whole way through. Check answers.

> Ben's news is that he saw Allie and Mark together in the Louvre, holding hands.
> Jacques is more surprised than Nicole, who already suspected that Mark and Allie were going out together.

b • Now get SS to look at the dialogue. In pairs, they read it and see if they can guess or remember the missing words. Emphasize that they shouldn't write the words in the dialogue but in pencil alongside or on a separate sheet of paper.

c • Play the tape / CD again for them to check. Then go through the dialogue line by line and check answers. Find out if SS had guessed the words correctly. Where they had not guessed correctly, see if their alternative also fits.

> **6.11** CD3 Track 12
> **B = Ben, N = Nicole, J = Jacques, M = Mark**
> B Hi.
> N / J Hi. / Hello.
> N Did you have a nice weekend?
> B Oh yeah. You'll never **guess** who I saw on Saturday.
> N Who?
> B Allie...and Mark. In the Louvre...together.
> N **Really**?
> J You're **joking**.
> B It was definitely them. And they looked really close. I think they were holding hands.
> J No! I don't **believe** it.
> B It's true, I'm **telling** you! And I think they saw me because they turned and left really quickly.
> J Are you **serious**?
> N You know, I'm not surprised. I think they've been seeing each other ever since Mark arrived. Or maybe even before.
> J That's **incredible**. What makes you say that?
> N When I went to look at Mark's new apartment, I'm sure Allie called him on his mobile. And I've seen her looking at him...in a certain way...
> B Hey, quiet everyone. It's Mark.
> M Hi.
> B Hi.
> J / N Good morning.

d • 6.12 Now focus on the key phrases highlighted in the dialogue. Play the tape / CD pausing after the beep for SS to repeat. Encourage them to copy the rhythm and intonation.

> **6.12** CD3 Track 13
> **B = Ben, N = Nicole, J = Jacques**
> B You'll never guess who I saw on Saturday.
> N Really?
> J You're joking.
> J No! I don't believe it.
> B It's true, I'm telling you!
> J Are you serious?
> J That's incredible.

e • Get SS to cover the dialogue and try to remember five ways of reacting to news with surprise or interest. You could get SS to work with a partner or do it as a whole class activity.

> Really?
> You're joking.
> I don't believe it.
> Are you serious?
> That's incredible.

Extra support

You could write the first letter of each phrase on the board to help SS.

f • Focus on the instructions and demonstrate the activity by inventing a piece of news to tell the class, e.g. about a politician or local celebrity. Encourage SS to react with surprise, and ask for details to which you should invent answers (Don't forget to tell SS after that your news isn't really true!).

- Then put SS in pairs and give them a few minutes to invent their piece of news. You could remind them that we often use the present perfect to give news, e.g. *The Prime Minister has resigned / X and Y have broken up*, etc.
- They then take turns to tell the class their news. The class should react using the expressions from **e**. If they are enjoying the activity, let them continue inventing more news for a few minutes.

SOCIAL ENGLISH For your eyes only

a • 6.13 Focus on the email and the question. Play the tape / CD, replaying the relevant line if necessary. Check the answer.

Thank you for the information. And thank you, darling, for a wonderful weekend.

b • Now focus on sentences 1–5 and go through them quickly. Then play the tape / CD for SS to mark the sentences T or F. Play the recording again as necessary. Check answers. Get SS to correct the wrong sentences.

1 F (He said it was 'very quiet'.)
2 F (He says 'one evening'.)
3 F (He says he went on his own.)
4 F (He says he didn't see Mark.)
5 T

6.13 CD3 Track 14
(tapescript in Student's Book on *p.129*)
M = Mark, B = Ben, J = Jacques, N = Nicole
M Dear all
Please find attached a copy of the latest sales report from the USA. Mark.
M So, did you guys have a good weekend?
B Yes, fine.
J Not bad. Very quiet.
B What about you, Mark?
M Oh, I spent most of the time at home…just being domestic, you know. The apartment's looking pretty nice, now. You must come round for a meal one evening.
J That would be very nice.
B So didn't you go out at all?
M Oh sure. I went to the Louvre on Saturday. I felt like getting a bit of culture.
J On your own?
M Yeah. I kind of prefer going to museums and galleries on my own. You can look at everything at your own pace.
B That's funny. I went to the Louvre on Saturday, too.
M Really? I didn't see you.
B Well, it's a big place. I didn't see you either.
N I've just had an email from Allie.
J So have I.
M Me, too...
N Dear Mark,
Thank you for the information. And thank you, darling, for a wonderful weekend.
Allie.

Extra support

Let SS listen one more time with the tapescript on *p.129*. Help them with any vocabulary or expressions they didn't understand.

- Finally, ask SS what they think Mark and Allie will do now.

c • 6.14 Now focus on the **USEFUL PHRASES**. Give SS a moment to try to complete them, and then play the tape / CD to check.

6.14 CD3 Track 15
M = Mark, B = Ben, J = Jacques
M You must come **round** for a meal one evening.
J That **would** be very nice.
B So didn't you go out at **all**?
M I felt **like** getting a bit of culture.
B That's **funny**. I went to the Louvre on Saturday, too.
B I didn't see you **either**.

Extra idea

Ask SS if they can remember who said each phrase.

d • Play the tape / CD again, pausing for SS to repeat. In a monolingual class, elicit the equivalent expressions in SS' L1.

HOMEWORK

Study Link **Workbook** *p.63*

6 Writing A film review

Lesson plan

This writing task focuses on writing a film review. The task recycles both the grammar and vocabulary from **File 6**. There is also a 'mini focus' on using prepositions correctly. We suggest that you do exercises **a–c** in class, but set the actual writing (the last activity) for homework. If there's time, you may also want to do the planning in class.

a • Focus on the title of the film and the photos, and ask SS if anyone has seen it and if they liked it.

b • Now focus on the task and tell SS to first read the review through once without worrying about the gaps. Ask SS if the review makes them want to see the film. Then, give them a few minutes to complete the task. Get them to compare in pairs before checking answers.

Paragraph 1	The name of the film, the director, etc.
Paragraph 2	Where and when it was set
Paragraph 3	The plot
Paragraph 4	Why you recommend this film

c • Get SS to read the text again and complete the gaps with prepositions from the list. Check answers.

2 for **3** about **4** At **5** back **6** In **7** about **8** as **9** to **10** in

⚠ For number 4 you may need to explain the difference between *in the beginning* and *at the beginning*. We say ***in** the beginning* when it is a phrase on its own (= At first), followed by a comma, e.g. *In the beginning, nobody understood what was going on.* We say ***at** the beginning* when it is followed by *of* sth, e.g. *At the beginning of the book / programme / class*, etc.

d • Focus on the question and elicit that we normally use the present tense to tell the plot of a film or book.

• Finally, focus on the **Useful language** box and make sure SS understand all the phrases. Tell them to imagine they are writing, e.g. about *The Lord of the Rings* and elicit the sentences from them, e.g. *It was directed by Peter Jackson.*

Extra idea

If there's time, you could get SS to practise the **Useful language** phrases by using them to tell a partner about the film they are going to write about.

WRITE a film review

Go through the instructions. Then, either get SS to plan and write their film review in class (set a time limit of 20 minutes) or get them to plan their review in class and write at home, or set both the planning and writing for homework.

If SS do the writing in class, get them to swap their film reviews with another student to read and check for mistakes before you collect them all in.

6 Revise & Check

For instructions on how to use these pages, see *p.32*.

GRAMMAR

1 I wanted	**6** was made
2 she would	**7** being built
3 he was	**8** been bought
4 to open	**9** whose son
5 not to	**10** which cuts

VOCABULARY

a **1** shop window (The others are types of shops.)
2 sales (It's a noun. The others are verbs related to shopping.)
3 special effects (The others are all people who are involved in making a film.)
4 sequel (It's a film made as a continuation of an earlier one. The others are all specific kinds of films.)
5 plot (It's a noun. The others are participles related to the cinema.)

b **1** butcher's **2** receipt **3** queue **4** trolley **5** subtitles **6** soundtrack **7** audience **8** bargain

c **1** on **2** on **3** about **4** back **5** on **6** by **7** in

PRONUNCIATION

a **1** special (It's /ʃ/) **2** manager (It's /æ/) **3** scene (It's /s/) **4** window (It's /əʊ/) **5** chemist's (It's /k/)

b s<u>u</u>btitles, compl<u>ai</u>n, rec<u>ei</u>pt, s<u>ou</u>ndtrack, c<u>u</u>stomer

CAN YOU UNDERSTAND THIS TEXT?

a **1** c **2** c **3** b **4** a **5** b

b **manipulative tactics** = ways of controlling or influencing people
trust their own tastes = believe in their own opinions and judgement about what to wear
use your skill = use your ability to do something well
to take risks = do something that you know might fail or be dangerous
exorbitant prices = much more expensive than they should be

CAN YOU UNDERSTAND THESE PEOPLE?

a **1** c **2** c **3** b **4** a **5** b

b **1** 1812 **2** factory **3** separated **4** Friend **5** 58

6.15 CD3 Track 16

1 **A** Did you go to that new restaurant last night?
B Yeah, but I wouldn't recommend it.
A Why not?
B Well, our soup was cold and then I asked for my steak well done but it was burnt. So I asked the waiter to take it back, and then I had to wait ten minutes for another one, by which time my husband's meal was cold.

2 **A** What did you think of it, then?
B I was a bit disappointed, to be honest.
A Yeah? I loved it. What didn't you like?
B Well, I thought Scarlett Johansson was good and the one who played her husband…
A Orlando Bloom.
B Yeah, he was good too. But the story was just ridiculous. I mean the bit when he went to see his ex-wife. A man would never do that.
A Oh I don't agree. I thought it was completely believable. I loved the soundtrack too.
B Yeah, that was all right.

3 **A** Oh I like your sweater. Is it new?
B Yeah. I bought it in the sales.
A How much?
B What do you think?
A 80, 100?
B No. It was originally £90 but then it had a 25% percent discount.
A £70?
B Less! 67. It was a real bargain.

4 **A** You were an extra in a film once, weren't you?
B Yeah. It was when I was studying at university in Leeds and they were making *Chariots of Fire* – the one about the two athletes.
A Oh yeah. I remember.
B Anyway, I saw an advertisement in the paper saying that they were looking for extras. So I went along and I was in a scene that was being filmed in a pub.
A What did you have to do?
B Nothing. I was just sitting at a table, pretending to drink beer. I didn't have to say anything, but I was still quite nervous. When I saw the film at the cinema, I waited and waited for the pub scene but it wasn't there.
A They cut it?
B Yeah, I suppose the film was too long or something.
A What a pity!
B Yeah.

5 **A** I saw a fascinating programme on TV last night.
B What was it?
A It was about Brunel. Did you see it?
B No. Who's Brunel? Isn't he that boxer?
A A boxer? That was Frank Bruno.
B Oh yeah.
C Brunel was a famous architect, wasn't he?
A Well, you're a bit closer than Susan. He built lots of famous bridges, like that one in Bristol.
C Oh that's right – he was an engineer, wasn't he?
A Yes. Not exactly a boxer.

6.16 CD3 Track 17

This is Poets' Corner. It's the place in the cathedral where many famous British novelists and poets are buried. And as you can see this is the tomb of the great novelist Charles Dickens. He was born on February 7th 1812, the second of seven children. He had a very unhappy childhood. His parents had money problems – his father owed a lot of money and so at the age of twelve Dickens was sent to work in a factory. When Dickens was older he started working as a journalist and later he began writing his wonderful novels. Probably the most famous of them is *David Copperfield*, which has been translated into almost every language in the world. Dickens was unhappily married and in 1858 he and his wife Catherine separated. But not before they had had ten children. Dickens' last novel *Our Mutual Friend* was unfinished when he died suddenly at home at the age of 58. Now, if you follow me through here, we can see the tomb of a very famous British poet…

Extra photocopiable activities

Quicktest 6 *p.221*

7 A

G third conditional
V making adjectives and adverbs
P sentence stress

Can we make our own luck?

File 7 overview

In **7A** SS practise using the third conditional, which they may or may not have studied in their previous course. In lesson **7B** SS look at some new ways of asking questions (using question tags and indirect questions). This will probably be new to most SS. In the final lesson of the course, the focus is on phrasal verbs, which SS should already be quite familiar with. Here SS learn more high-frequency verbs and revise and extend their knowledge of separable and non-separable verbs.

Lesson plan

This lesson presents the third conditional, in the context of two true, good and bad luck stories. This conditional has the most complex form of the three conditionals but the concept (speculating hypothetically about a past situation) is not difficult to put across to SS.

In pronunciation SS focus on the rhythm of third conditional sentences. The vocabulary focus is on word building and SS learn to use suffixes and prefixes to form adjectives and adverbs. The topic of luck is further developed through a text which argues that we are not born lucky or unlucky, but that we can make ourselves lucky.

Optional lead-in (books closed)

- Draw a horseshoe on the board with the open part at the top. Ask SS what it is, and tell them that in Britain and America people believe that if you find a horseshoe, it will bring you good luck, and people often hang them up on the wall. Ask if it also means good luck in SS' country.
- Then put SS in pairs and ask them to think of things which in their country are believed to bring either good luck or bad luck.
- Get feedback and write them in two columns GOOD LUCK / BAD LUCK on the board. Then ask SS if they really believe in this.

1 READING & LISTENING

a • Books open. Focus on the article and photos. Tell SS that the man and woman in the first story had very bad luck, and the woman in the second had very good luck.

• Now focus on **Bad luck?** and set a time limit (e.g. three minutes) for SS to read it. Then elicit ideas about what happened next, but don't tell them the answers and try to build suspense. Deal with any vocabulary problems.

Extra idea

Alternatively, you could read the text aloud, asking SS the meaning of words / phrases as you go along.

b • 7.1 Focus on the instructions and tell SS they are going to hear how the story ended. Play the tape / CD once. Get SS to compare what they understood and see whether they had guessed right.

c • Play the tape / CD again. Get SS in pairs to write a couple of sentences to explain what happened. Check answers. Ask a few more comprehension questions, e.g. *Who was Eddie? What happened in Singapore? What was Ian's 'special reason' for going to England?*, etc.

Amy had travelled to Sydney to surprise Ian at exactly the same time he was travelling to the UK to surprise her. When they spoke on the phone, Ian asked her to marry him and she said yes.

7.1 CD3 Track 18

(tapescript in Student's Book on *p.129*)

N = Narrator, I = Ian, A = Amy

N Ian thought Amy had gone out for the evening and sat down to wait for her to come back. Tired after his long journey, he fell asleep. When he woke up, the phone was ringing. Ian answered the phone. It was Amy.

I I said, 'Where are you?' She said, 'Ian, I'm sitting in your flat in Australia.' At first I didn't believe her but then she gave the phone to Eddie, who lives in my flat in Sydney, and he told me it was true. I was so shocked I couldn't speak.

N Amy had had the same idea as Ian. She had flown from London to Sydney via Singapore at exactly the same time Ian was flying in the opposite direction. Incredibly, both their planes stopped in Singapore at the same time. Ian and Amy were sitting in the same airport lounge but they didn't see each other.

A I had saved all my money to buy a ticket to Sydney. I wanted it to be a fantastic surprise for Ian. I couldn't wait to see his face when I arrived. You can't imagine how I felt when I arrived at his flat and his friend Eddie told me he'd gone to England! I just couldn't believe it! When I spoke to Ian on the phone, he told me that he had flown back to England for a special reason and then he asked me to marry him. I didn't know whether to laugh or cry but I said 'yes'.

I It was just bad luck. If one of us had stayed at home, we would have met. It's as simple as that.

d • 7.2 Now follow the same procedure for the second story **Good luck?** For dramatic effect you could briefly pause the tape / CD after '…but they didn't.' Comprehension questions could include *Where was the medical conference? Where did the plane land? What happened when Mrs Fletcher got back to England?*, etc.

⚠ When SS read the text make sure they understand what a *call bell* is in the last line (= the bell a passenger rings on a plane if he wants, e.g. a drink of water, or needs help).

There were 15 cardiologists from different countries on the plane all going to a conference. They then gave her emergency treatment, and they managed to save her, so she was able to go to her daughter's wedding.

7.2 CD3 Track 19

(tapescript in Student's Book on *p.129*)

N = Narrator, MF = Mrs Fletcher

N The cabin crew put out a desperate call to the passengers: 'If there's a doctor on the plane, could you please press your call bell...'
The cabin crew were hoping to hear this [*sound effect of a bell*], but they didn't. They heard this [*sound effect of lots of bells*]. Incredibly, there were *fifteen* doctors on the plane, and *all* of them were cardiologists. They were from different countries and they were travelling to Florida for a medical conference.
Four of the doctors rushed to give emergency treatment to Mrs Fletcher. At one point, they thought she had died, but finally they managed to save her life. The plane made an emergency landing in North Carolina and Mrs Fletcher was taken to hospital. After being in hospital for four days, she was able to go to her daughter's wedding.

MF I was very lucky. If those doctors hadn't been on the plane, I would have died. I can't thank them enough.

N But now that she's back in England, Mrs Fletcher has been less lucky with British hospitals.

MF I had *fifteen* heart specialists on that plane, but I'll have to wait three months until I can see *one* in this country!

Extra support

If there's time, you could get SS to listen again with the tapescript on *p.129* so they can see exactly what they understood / didn't understand. Translate / explain any new words or phrases.

2 GRAMMAR third conditional

a • Focus on the two sentences and get SS in pairs to complete them. They probably won't find this easy.

Extra support

You could write *have, would, hadn't,* and *stayed* on the board and get SS to put them in the right place in the sentences.

b • 7.3 Play the tape / CD for SS to check. Check answers.

1 stayed, would 2 hadn't, have

7.3 CD3 Track 20

IAN If one of us had stayed at home, we would have met.

MRS FLETCHER If those doctors hadn't been on the plane, I would have died.

c • Focus on the questions and get SS to answer orally in pairs. Check answers and elicit / explain that in both sentences they are imagining how something in the past could have been different.

1 No, no. 2 Yes, no. 3 Something that didn't happen.

d • Tell SS to go to **Grammar Bank 7A** on *p.142*. Go through the examples and the rules with the class. Model and drill the example sentences.

Extra idea

In a monolingual class, you could get SS to translate the example sentences and compare the tenses they would use in their L1.

Grammar notes

The third conditional

- If SS have a similar tense in their own language, they may not have too many problems with the concept but most SS will have problems with the 'mechanics' of the structure, i.e. remembering which verb form goes in each part of the sentence and also in understanding and producing contracted forms.
- Typical mistakes are:
  - using *would have* in the *if*-clause, e.g. ~~*If I would have known, I would have done something about it.*~~
  - using the past perfect in both clauses, e.g. ~~*If I had known, I had done something about it.*~~

- Focus on the exercises on *p.143* and get SS to do them, individually or in pairs. Check answers either after each exercise or when they have done both.

a 2 G 3 H 4 K 5 C 6 J 7 A 8 E 9 D 10 B 11 F
c 1 would have won, hadn't been
2 'd known / had known, wouldn't have married
3 would have lent, 'd asked / had asked
4 'd had / had had, would have spent
5 would have been able, 'd told / had told
6 'd asked / had asked, would have changed
7 'd have enjoyed / would have enjoyed, had come

- Tell SS to go back to the main lesson on *p.101*.

3 PRONUNCIATION sentence stress

Pronunciation notes

The main focus here is on getting SS to say third conditional sentences with good rhythm, by stressing the information words. You may also want to encourage your SS to produce the weak forms of *would, have, been,* and *had* in these kinds of sentences. These forms are commonly used by native speakers but SS at this level will find these tricky to imitate and produce.

a • 7.4 Focus on the instructions and give SS a moment to read the sentences.
• Play the tape / CD once for SS to listen. Then play it again pausing after each sentence for SS to repeat.

7.4 CD3 Track 21

1 If you'd told me earlier, I would have gone too.
2 If the weather had been better, we would have stayed longer.
3 If I hadn't stopped for petrol, I would have arrived before he left.
4 We would have been late if we hadn't taken a taxi.
5 She wouldn't have come if she'd known he was here.
6 It would have been cheaper if we'd booked last month.

- Remind SS that:
  – the stressed words in the sentence are the information words.
  – negative auxiliaries, e.g. *wouldn't* and *hadn't* are always stressed.
  – *would, have been* and the contracted form of *had* (*'d*) have a weak pronunciation.

b • Put SS in pairs, **A** and **B**, and tell them to go to **Communication** *Guess the conditional*, **A** on *p.118* and **B** on *p.121*.

- Demonstrate the activity. Write on a piece of paper *If I had known it was your birthday, I would have bought you a present.* Don't show the sentence to your SS.
- Then write on the board *If I had known it was your birthday, I* ____________ (+). Tell SS that you have this sentence completed on a piece of paper, and they have to try to guess what it is.
- Elicit possible completions with a positive (+) verb phrase (e.g. *would have said happy birthday / sent you a card*). Say 'try again' if they say something different, until someone says the phrase *I would have bought you a present*, and say 'that's right'.
- Now go through the instructions. Emphasize that SS should write their ideas next to the sentence but not in the gap, and only complete the gap when their partner says '*That's right*'.
- SS continue in pairs. Monitor and help.

4 SPEAKING

a • Point out that this questionnaire was created by a British psychologist (see article on *p.102*).

- Focus on the questionnaire and go through the statements. Help SS with new vocabulary like *anxious, instinct*, and '*the bright side of life*'...
- Then give SS a few minutes to mark their answers. Stress that they shouldn't read the interpretation yet.

b • Get SS to compare and explain their answers. Demonstrate by saying what you would put for 1 and why, e.g. *I put 1 because I'm quite shy and I'm not very good at talking to people I don't know. I certainly don't enjoy it.*

c • SS now check their scores, compare with a partner, and say if they agree or not. Get feedback to find out how many people agree with their score and how many fall into each category.

5 READING

a • Focus on the title. Then ask SS if they think people are born lucky, or if they make their own luck. Don't expect SS to be able to explain why exactly, just find out whether they agree or not.

- Read the first two paragraphs aloud with SS, and establish that Dr Wiseman thinks that people who <u>think</u> they are lucky create good luck for themselves.

b • Now tell SS that they are going to learn how to become luckier! Explain that there are four pieces of advice about how to become luckier and four 'exercises' that you can do to put the advice into practice. The exercises A–D have been separated from the pieces of advice 1–4.

- Focus on the task and give SS two minutes to read tip 1 and to match it to its exercise. Elicit the answer.

1 B

- Now set a time limit (e.g. five minutes) for SS to read tips 2–4 and to match them to the other three exercises. Get SS to compare their answers with a partner before you check answers.

2 D **3** A **4** C

c • Focus on the instructions and give SS a minute to read the article again (not the exercises). Then get them to complete the expressions with the missing verb. Check answers and model and drill pronunciation. Then get SS to test themselves by covering the left-hand column.

1 seem	**5** make an effort
2 achieve	**6** convince
3 vary	**7** realize
4 bump into	

d • Now get SS in pairs to read exercises A–D again and choose which one they think is best. Get feedback from the class to find out which one is the most popular.

HOW WORDS WORK...

- Focus on the examples and then explain the difference between *what* and *which* as relative pronouns. Emphasize that *what* is generally used after a verb or preposition, whereas *which* is used after a noun or noun phrase. If you know your SS' L1, point out what they would use in their language.
- Now give SS a few minutes to do the exercise and check answers.

1 what **2** which **3** which **4** what **5** which **6** what

6 VOCABULARY making adjectives and adverbs

a • Focus on the sentence from the text, and elicit that *lucky* is an adjective, and *luck* is a noun.

- Now focus on the chart. Then get SS in pairs to complete it. Check answers.

fortunately, unfortunately
comfortable, uncomfortable, comfortably, uncomfortably
patient, impatient, patiently, impatiently
careful, careless, carefully, carelessly

- Point out that:

  - the suffixes *-y* and *-able* are both typical adjective endings.

  - the prefixes *un-* and *im-* are common to make an adjective negative, but adjectives formed with the suffix *-ful*, e.g. *careful* normally make the opposite adjective with *-less*, e.g. *useful, useless.*

  - the suffix *-ful* = *full of* or *with.*

  - the suffix *-less* = *without.*

  - sometimes there are spelling changes, e.g. the final *e* is dropped before an *-ly* suffix in *comfortably*, and the *y* changes to *i* in *luckily*.

b • Focus on the three two-syllable nouns, *fortune, comfort* and *patience* and elicit that they are all stressed on the first syllable. Now ask SS how this will help them stress the adjectives and adverbs correctly.

> The stressed syllable doesn't change even when you add a prefix (e.g. *un-*) or a suffix (e.g. *-ly*).

- Now give SS a few moments in pairs to practise saying the words with the right stress.

Extra support

Get SS to underline the stressed syllable in all the words in the chart.

c • Focus on the instructions. Tell SS to first decide if they need an adjective or an adverb, and then if it should be positive or negative. You could do the first one or two with the whole class.

- Either get SS to do the exercise in pairs or individually and then compare with a partner. Check answers and drill pronunciation.

1 unfortunately	6 luckily
2 comfortable	7 patiently
3 carelessly	8 careful
4 unlucky	9 fortunately
5 impatient	10 comfortably

7 7.5 ♫ SONG *Ironic*

- *Ironic* was originally recorded by the Canadian singer Alanis Morissette in 1995. For copyright reasons this is a cover version. If you want to do this song in class, use the photocopiable activity on *p.212*.

7.5 CD3 Track 22

Ironic

An old man turned ninety-eight
He won the lottery and died the next day
It's a black fly in your Chardonnay
It's a death row pardon two minutes too late
And isn't it ironic...don't you think?

It's like rain on your wedding day
It's a free ride when you've already paid
It's the good advice that you just didn't take
And who would've thought...? It figures.

Mr Play-It-Safe was afraid to fly
He packed his suitcase and kissed his kids goodbye
He waited his whole damn life to take that flight
And as the plane crashed down he thought
'Well isn't this nice...'
And isn't it ironic...don't you think?

It's like rain on your wedding day
It's a free ride when you've already paid
It's the good advice that you just didn't take
And who would've thought...? It figures

Well life has a funny way of sneaking up on you
When you think everything's okay and everything's going right
And life has a funny way of helping you out when
You think everything's gone wrong and everything blows up
In your face

A traffic jam when you're already late
A no-smoking sign on your cigarette break
It's like ten thousand spoons when all you need is a knife
It's meeting the man of my dreams
And then meeting his beautiful wife
And isn't it ironic...don't you think?
A little too ironic... yeah, I really do think

It's like rain on your wedding day
It's a free ride when you've already paid
It's the good advice that you just didn't take
And who would've thought...? It figures

Well life has a funny way of sneaking up on you
And life has a funny, funny way of helping you out,
helping you out.

Extra photocopiable activities

Grammar

third conditional *p.160*

Communicative

Third conditional game *p.191* (instructions *p.169*)

Song

Ironic p.212 (instructions *p.206*)

HOMEWORK

Study Link **Workbook** *pp.64–66*

7 B Murder mysteries

G question tags, indirect questions
V compound nouns
P intonation in question tags

Lesson plan

In this lesson, SS learn two new ways of making questions, using question tags, and indirect questions. They will probably have seen both types before, but won't have focused on how they are formed and used. The context is murder mysteries; first the true story of Jack the Ripper and a detective novelist's theory as to who he was, and then an extract from a detective novel by Donna Leon. The vocabulary focus is on compound nouns, and SS also revise other compound nouns that have come up in previous Files.

Optional lead-in (books closed)

- Write up the word MURDER on the board and elicit what it means and how it's pronounced /mɜːdə/. Then give SS, in pairs, three minutes to brainstorm ten words connected with murder. Write their suggestions up on the board.
  Possible words include
  murderer, kill, victim, detective, knife, gun, police, police station, body, blood, suspect, crime, witness, etc.
- Finally, ask SS if they can think of a famous British murderer from the past. Give clues if necessary to elicit Jack the Ripper.

1 READING & LISTENING

a • Books open. Focus on the instructions and set a time limit (e.g. five minutes) for SS to read the article and answer the questions. They could either answer them orally in pairs, or in writing.
• Check answers. Deal with any vocabulary problems.

1 In London in the autumn of 1888.
2 He sent the police letters signed Jack the Ripper.
3 Seven.
4 For three months.
5 A doctor, a businessman, a painter, and a member of the royal family.
6 She's a crime writer.
7 By analyzing DNA samples.

Extra idea

You could read the article paragraph by paragraph together with SS, asking them to guess the meaning of new words as you go, and explain / translate the meaning of any that they can't guess.

Alternatively, you could get SS to underline or highlight five words or phrases they want to remember from the text. Get them to compare with a partner and then get some feedback from the class.

b • 7.6 Focus on the three photos of the suspects, and the task. Then play the tape / CD once all the way through. Get SS to compare with a partner and play the tape / CD again, pausing after each person if necessary. Check answers.

Prince Albert, Queen Victoria's **grandson**
James Maybrick, a cotton merchant
Walter Sickert, an **artist** ✓

7.6 CD3 Track 23
(tapescript in Student's Book on *p.129*)
I = Interviewer, K = Ken
I Good morning and thank you for coming, Mr Morton – or should it be Inspector Morton – you were a detective with Scotland Yard, weren't you?
K Yes, that's right. For twenty-five years. I retired last year.
I People today are still fascinated by the identity of Jack the Ripper, more than a hundred years after the crimes were committed. It's incredible, isn't it?
K Well, it's not really that surprising. People are always interested in unsolved murders – and Jack the Ripper has become a sort of cult horror figure.
I Who are the main suspects?
K Well, there are a lot of them. But probably the best known are Prince Albert, Queen Victoria's grandson, the artist Walter Sickert, and a Liverpool cotton merchant called James Maybrick.
I Patricia Cornwell in her book 'Jack the Ripper – case closed' says that she has identified the murderer. Who does she think it was?
K Well, she's convinced that Jack the Ripper was Walter Sickert, the painter.

c • 7.7 Focus on the instructions and give SS time to read the sentences first. Make sure they understand *evidence*, *confess*, and *serial killer*. Then play the tape / CD a couple of times. Get SS to compare their answers with a partner, explaining why they think they are true or false.
• Check answers, getting SS to say why the F ones are false.

1 T
2 F (From a painting)
3 T
4 T
5 F (A diary)
6 F (He thinks it's a ridiculous theory.)
7 F (He doesn't know.)
8 T

7.7 CD3 Track 24
(tapescript in Student's Book on *p.129*)
I = interviewer, K = Ken
I What evidence did she discover?
K Well, she mainly used DNA analysis. She actually bought a painting by Sickert at great expense and she cut it up to get the DNA from it – people in the art world were furious.
I I can imagine.

K And then she compared the DNA from the painting with DNA taken from the letters that Jack the Ripper sent to the police. Patricia Cornwell says that she's 99% certain that Walter Sickert was Jack the Ripper.
I But you don't think she's right, do you?
K No, I don't. I don't think her scientific evidence is completely reliable and there's a lot of evidence which says that Sickert was in France *not* London when some of the women were killed.
I There's been another recent theory, hasn't there? About James Maybrick? Do you think he was the murderer?
K Well, somebody found a diary which is supposed to be his, where he admits to being Jack the Ripper. But nobody has been able to prove that the diary is genuine and, personally, I don't think he was the murderer.
I And Prince Albert, the Queen's grandson?
K This for me is the most ridiculous theory. I can't seriously believe that a member of the royal family could be a serial murderer. In any case, Prince Albert was in Scotland when at least two of the murders were committed.
I So, who do *you* think the murderer was?
K I can't tell you because I don't know.
I So you don't think we'll ever solve the mystery?
K No, I wouldn't say that. I think one day the mystery *will* be solved. Some new evidence will appear and we'll be able to say that the case of Jack the Ripper is finally closed. But at the moment it's still a mystery, and people like a good mystery.

Extra support

If there's time, you could get SS to listen again with the tapescript on *p.129* so they can see exactly what they understood / didn't understand. Translate / explain any new words or phrases.

2 GRAMMAR question tags

a • 7.8 Focus on the instructions and questions 1–4. Play the tape / CD, pausing to give SS time to write. Check answers.

1 weren't you 2 isn't it 3 do you 4 hasn't there

Extra challenge

You could elicit ideas first for what the two missing words are.

7.8 CD3 Track 25

1 You were a detective with Scotland Yard, weren't you?
2 It's incredible, isn't it?
3 But you don't think she's right, do you?
4 There's been another recent theory, hasn't there?

b • Ask the whole class the questions, and elicit that the interviewer thinks he knows what the inspector is going to answer and is just checking what he knows to be true. This is probably because he has already discussed Patricia Cornwell's theory with the inspector *before* the interview.

c • Tell SS to go to **Grammar Bank 7B** on *p.142*. Read the examples and rules for question tags, and get SS to compare what they use in their L1.

Grammar Notes

Question tags

- Question tags are difficult for SS to use with any fluency because they need to use the correct auxiliary each time depending on the tense or modal verb they are using. Getting the right intonation can also be tricky. This lesson provides SS with a gentle introduction and focuses on their most common use, which is to check information.

- Focus on exercise **a** only on *p.143* and get SS to do it individually or in pairs. Check answers.

a 1 do you	6 wasn't she
2 aren't they	7 haven't we
3 can he	8 did you
4 doesn't she	9 wouldn't you
5 will you	10 isn't it

- Tell SS to go back to the main lesson on *p.105*.

3 PRONUNCIATION & SPEAKING

intonation in question tags

Pronunciation notes

The normal intonation for a question tag when we say something that we think is right or true, and that we expect the other person to agree with, is a falling tone. Examples would include *It's hot today, isn't it? You're Spanish, aren't you?* (I'm sure you're Spanish).

⚠ Question tags can sometimes be used as real questions with rising intonation, normally to express surprise, or to check information that we are not very sure about. This use is not focused on here.

a • 7.9 Focus on the dialogue between a policeman and a suspect.
• Point out that the policeman probably already has the information and is just checking. Play the dialogue once for SS to listen. Then give them a few minutes to complete the question tags, and then play the tape / CD again for them to check. Check answers.

7.9 CD3 Track 26

P = Policeman, S = Suspect
P Your surname's Jones, **isn't it**?
S Yes, it is.
P And you're 27, **aren't you**?
S Yes, that's right.
P You weren't at home last night at 8.00, **were you**?
S No, I wasn't. I was at the pub.
P But you don't have any witnesses, **do you**?
S Yes, I do. My brother was with me.
P Your brother wasn't with you, **was he**?
S How do you know?
P Because he was at the police station. We arrested him last night.

b • 7.10 Play the tape / CD, pausing for SS to repeat the policeman's questions.

7.10		CD3 Track 27
1	POLICEMAN	Your surname's Jones, isn't it?
2	POLICEMAN	And you're 27, aren't you?
3	POLICEMAN	You weren't at home last night at 8.00, were you?
4	POLICEMAN	But you don't have any witnesses, do you?
5	POLICEMAN	Your brother wasn't with you, was he?

Extra support

Give SS extra practice by getting them to read the dialogue in pairs.

c • Put SS in pairs, **A** and **B**, preferably face to face. Tell them to go to **Communication** *Just checking*, **A** on *p.118* and **B** on *p.121*. If there is an odd number of SS, you should take part in the activity yourself. Go through the instructions. Make sure SS are clear that first **A** (as police inspector) will ask **B** some questions and try to remember the answers, and then he / she will check them with question tags. Then they swap roles. Demonstrate the activity by taking **A**'s role and asking one student the questions and then checking.

• Monitor and help SS to form the question tags correctly. When both have done their interviews, get feedback to find which 'police inspectors' had the best memory.

• Tell SS to go back to the main lesson on *p.106*.

4 GRAMMAR indirect questions

a • Ask the whole class the questions, and tell them about yourself and your tastes. Focus on the book cover and ask SS if any of them have read any Donna Leon books (they are translated into many languages).

b • 7.11 Focus on the instructions. Then play the tape / CD. Get SS to listen and read, and underline the inspector's questions as they read. Check answers.

Could you tell me how long you and your husband were married?
How many children do you have?
Are they in school in Venice?
Would you say yours was a happy marriage?
Could you tell me if your husband had any particularly close friends or business associates?
Other friends?

7.11 CD3 Track 28

'I'd like to ask you some questions about your personal life, signora.'
'Our personal life?' she repeated, as though she had never heard of such a thing. When he didn't answer this, she nodded, signalling him to begin.
'Could you tell me how long you and your husband were married?'
'Nineteen years.'
'How many children do you have, signora?'
'Two. Claudio is seventeen, and Francesca is fifteen'.
'Are they in school in Venice, signora?'
She looked up at him sharply when he asked this.
'Why do you want to know that?'
'My own daughter, Chiara, is fourteen, so perhaps they know one another,' he answered and smiled to show what an innocent question it had been.
'Claudio is in school in Switzerland, but Francesca is here. With us. I mean,' she corrected, rubbing a hand across her forehead, 'with me.'
'Would you say yours was a happy marriage, signora?'
'Yes', she answered immediately, far faster than Brunetti would have answered the same question, though he would have given the same response. She did not, however, elaborate.
'Could you tell me if your husband had any particularly close friends or business associates?'
She looked up at this question, then as quickly down again at her hands. 'Our closest friends are the Nogares, Mirto and Graziella. He's an architect who lives in Campo Sant'Angelo. They're Francesca's godparents. I don't know about business associates: you'll have to ask Ubaldo'.
'Other friends, signora?'
'Why do you need to know all this?' she said, voice rising sharply.
'I'd like to learn more about your husband, signora'.
'Why?' The question leaped from her, almost as if beyond her volition.
'Until I understand what sort of man he was, I can't understand why this has happened'.
'A robbery?' she asked, voice just short of sarcasm.
'It wasn't robbery, signora. Whoever killed him intended to do it.'

c • Ask SS if they think Brunetti is aggressive or polite when he interviews Signora Trevisan, and elicit that he is very polite and that Signora Trevisan is nervous and worried. Then ask SS if they think she murdered her husband and elicit ideas (She didn't murder him herself, but is involved in the murder.).

• Now go through the text quickly with SS and help SS with any words or phrases they find difficult.

Extra idea

You could then play the tape / CD again with books closed so that SS can just listen and try to enjoy it.

d • Focus on the four questions and ask SS which two they think are more polite (the two beginning *Could you tell me…*).

• Then write on the board:
How long were you and your husband married?
Did your husband have any particularly close friends…?

• Get SS to compare the two direct questions with the indirect ones. Elicit that after '*Could you tell me…*', the word order is normal subject + verb (not inverted as in a normal question) and there is no auxiliary verb.

e • Tell SS to go back to **Grammar Bank 7B** on *p.142*. Go through the examples and rules for **Indirect Questions**.

Grammar notes

Indirect questions

• In many ways, indirect questions are the same as reported questions, which SS have worked on recently, the only difference being that the tense of the verb doesn't change.

• SS mainly have problems remembering not to invert the subject and verb, typical mistakes being, e.g. ~~*Could you tell me where is the station?*~~

- Focus on exercise **b** on *p.143* and get SS to do it individually or in pairs. Check answers.

b **1** where they live
2 if there's a bank near here
3 where I can buy some stamps
4 if this bus goes to the castle
5 what time the shops open
6 where the toilets are
7 if Susan's (is) at work today
8 if Milan won last night
9 where we parked the car
10 what the time is

- Tell SS to go back to the main lesson on *p.107.*

f • **7.12** SS now practise transformations from direct questions they hear. Demonstrate by giving them a couple more questions to transform, e.g.

T: Where's the bus stop?
SS: Could you tell me where the bus stop is?
T: Is this the town hall?
SS: Could you tell me if / whether this is the town hall?, etc.

- Now play the tape / CD, pausing after each question for SS to complete the indirect question. Check answers.

7.12 CD3 Track 29

1 How much does it cost? [PING] [Pause]
Could you tell me **how much it costs**?
2 Is there a bank near here? [PING] [Pause]
Do you know if **there's a bank near here**?
3 What time does the next train leave? [PING] [Pause]
Could you tell me **what time the next train leaves?**
4 Does the museum open on Saturdays? [PING] [Pause]
Can you tell me if **the museum opens on Saturdays?**
5 Where's the bus station? [PING] [Pause]
Can you tell me **where the bus station is**?
6 Does this bus go to the beach? [PING] [Pause]
Do you know if **this bus goes to the beach?**

Extra challenge

You could do this again with books closed or covered and SS have to do the tranformations orally.

g • Focus on the situation. If you were interviewing someone in the street, it would be natural to use a polite question form.

- Elicit the first question from the class (*Could you tell me what your name is?*). Now SS practise in pairs. One student should ask all the questions, and then they swap roles.

5 VOCABULARY compound nouns

a • SS have already met compound nouns (in lesson **2C**). Remind them that these phrases are two nouns but the first noun (always singular) describes the second one, i.e. it functions as an adjective. Usually they are written as two words, but occasionally with a hyphen (e.g. *can-opener*) or occasionally as one word (e.g. *sunglasses*).

- Focus on the instructions and the example (detective novel). Give SS time to match the words in the two ovals to make five other compound nouns.

b • **7.13** Play the tape / CD for SS to check answers, and ask them which word is normally stressed more (the first one).

7.13 CD3 Track 30

detective novel
horror film
murder mystery
police inspector
crime writer
police station

c • This activity revises compound nouns that have come up during the course. Focus on the race and set a time limit, e.g. two minutes. SS can do it individually or in pairs / groups. When the time is up, check answers. Encourage SS to use articles and prepositions as in the key.

1 A credit card.
2 At a railway station / train station.
3 He's a film director.
4 The rush hour.
5 Your seat belt.
6 A department store.
7 On a tennis court.
8 A boarding pass.
9 A state school.
10 At a petrol station / service station.
11 The ring tone.
12 A traffic jam.

Extra photocopiable activities

Grammar
question tags, indirect questions *p.161*
Communicative
The scariest places in London *p.192* (instructions *p.170*)

HOMEWORK

Study Link **Workbook** *pp.67–69*

7C Switch it off

G phrasal verbs
V television, phrasal verbs
P revision of sounds, linking

Lesson plan

Television is the context for revising and extending SS' knowledge of phrasal verbs. First, SS talk about their TV watching habits and then the grammar is presented through three amusing newspaper stories, which all feature TV in some way. In the second part of the lesson, SS read about a couple who lived for 37 years without electricity and say which modern electrical devices they would not want to live without. Pronunciation focuses on TV words and common phrasal verbs and revises some common sounds and sound linking.

Optional lead-in (books closed)

- In a monolingual class, you could ask SS what they think is the best TV programme on their country's state channels at the moment. Write the suggestions on the board and then have a class vote. Then repeat the process for the worst programme on TV at the moment.
- In a multilingual class, ask SS to evaluate from 1–10 (10 = fantastic) the quality of TV programmes in their country. Get feedback to find out which country's TV is rated the best.

1 VOCABULARY & SPEAKING television

a • Books open. Focus on the TV survey and go through the questions making sure SS understand them. Focus especially on the meaning and pronunciation of the bold words.

• Clarify meaning, e.g. by asking SS to name the state channels in their country. Use the photos to help you with the meaning of the different types of TV programmes and ask SS to give you examples.

⚠ *Soap operas* (often called *soaps*) = a weekly or daily drama series usually about everyday life in different families. Point out that they were originally called *soap operas* because when this kind of programme was invented they were used to advertise soap powder (the advertisements were shown in programme breaks).

b • Give SS a few moments to think about their answers to the questions. Get them to write L, H, or DM in the boxes next to the kinds of programmes.

• Put SS in pairs and get them to interview each other using the questionnaire. They could either take it in turns to ask the questions (**A** book open, **B** book closed) or get them to look at, and answer, the questions together.

Extra idea

Get the class to ask you the questions first.

• Get some feedback by asking the last question to the whole class and eliciting examples.

2 GRAMMAR phrasal verbs

a • Focus on the task and give SS one clear example of a phrasal verb (= verb + preposition) related to TV, e.g. *switch on.*

Some possible answers
switch on / off **or** turn on / off
turn up / down (NOT *switch*)
plug in (opposite *unplug)*
switch / turn over *(to another channel)*

b • Focus on the task and the list of verbs A–H. Then tell SS that they should first read each true story on *p.109* before they complete the gaps. Set a time limit, e.g. five minutes.

• Get SS to compare with a partner before checking answers. Point out that *turn on / off* and *switch on / off* are identical in meaning. *Pass away* is a polite / formal way of saying *die. Look out* = be careful. You can also use *watch out.*

• Deal with any other voacbulary problems SS may have.

1 E looking forward to
2 D or F turn / switch it off
3 D or F turn / switch off
4 B sold out
5 G find out
6 H passed away
7 C picked up
8 A Look out

c • Focus on the task and get SS to read the texts again trying to memorize the main details.

• Put SS in pairs and tell them to cover the texts and look at the pictures. Then together they try and remember the stories. Finally, elicit the three stories from the class.

Extra support

Instead of putting SS in pairs simply get them to close their books and elicit the stories from the whole class by asking questions, e.g. *Who was Mitch Altman? Where did he go with his friends? What happened?*, etc.

d • Remind SS that with some phrasal verbs there are two possible word orders, e.g. *switch off the TV* or *switch the TV off.*

• Focus on the task and the dictionary extract and elicit answers.

When the abbreviation *sth* (= something) goes between the verb and the particle (*off, on*, etc.) then the verb and particle can be separated.

• Point out too that *sth* is used in dictionaries as an abbreviated form of *something.*

e • Tell SS to go to **Grammar Bank 7C** on *p.142*. Go through the examples and the rules with the class. Model and drill the example sentences.

Grammar notes

Phrasal verbs

- Phrasal verbs (a verb + particle, i.e. a preposition or adverb) are a feature of English and it is important that SS can recognize and use a limited number of high frequency verbs like *turn on*, *look after*, but it is also important not to make them seem like an obstacle for SS.
- Although we have pointed out for reference the three most common grammatical groups, SS will probably already 'have a feel' for when they can separate the particle from the verb.
- Some useful points to emphasize:
  - Phrasal verbs often have a more formal (often Latin-based) synonym, e.g. *fill in* (this form) can be replaced by *complete* (this form), *come back* has the same meaning as the more formal *return*.
  - Other phrasal verbs have no easy equivalent, *e.g. I get on* (with my boss) would require a long phrase to paraphrase it, e.g. *I have good, friendly relations* (with my boss). These are the phrasal verbs which it is essential for SS to learn and be able to use.
  - The same phrasal verb sometimes has more than one meaning, e.g. *take off your coat* / *the plane took off*. A dictionary will give these different meanings.
  - Sometimes the particle (*up*, *on*, etc.) has a clear, literal meaning, e.g. *go away* and sometimes it doesn't, e.g. *go on* (= continue).
  - Phrasal verbs are an area of English that SS will pick up bit by bit. They should aim at slowly increasing their knowledge, and not worry about 'learning them all'.
  - When phrasal verbs are non-separable (groups 1 and 2) they cannot be separated by an adverb either, e.g. you can't say ~~*I go often out with my friends*~~.
- Typical mistakes include:
  - confusing the particle, e.g. *It's hot.* ~~*Take away your coat*~~.
  - problems of word order, e.g. ~~*Turn off it. We set early off*~~.

• Now get SS to do the exercises on *p.143* either individually or in pairs. Check answers after each exercise or after SS have done both.

a 1 up 2 back 3 up 4 over 5 out 6 out 7 up 8 up 9 up 10 out
b 1 Take them off.
2 Could you look after them?
3 Do you get on with her?
4 Switch them off.
5 I'm looking for them.
6 Please pick it up.
7 Turn it down!
8 I'm really looking forward to it.
9 Can I try it on?
10 Don't throw it away!

• Tell SS to go back to the main lesson on *p.110*.

3 PRONUNCIATION revision of sounds, linking

Pronunciation notes

In the first exercise, SS revise some common sounds and try to remember how these sounds are transcribed using phonetic symbols found in dictionaries. Once again emphasize the importance of being able to use this system to check pronunciation. It is well worth the investment of time to learn the sound words and symbols in the **Sound Bank** on *pp.158–9*.

In the second exercise, SS practise understanding and saying short phrases spoken quite fast where some of the words become joined or linked together (a common characteristic of spoken language).

a • To demonstrate the activity focus on the pink letters in the first sentence and the examples.

• Put SS in pairs and get them to try and complete the chart. SS may not remember all the symbols but tell them not to check in the back of the book until you tell them.

b • Now tell SS to go to the **Sound Bank** on *p.157* to check their answers, before returning to the main lesson on *p.110*.

• Elicit answers from the class and write the completed chart on the board.

Sound word	Symbol
2 bike	/aɪ/
3 horse	/ɔː/
4 up	/ʌ/
5 chess	/tʃ/
6 flower	/f/
7 bull	/ʊ/
8 mother	/ð/

c • 7.14 Play the tape / CD for SS to listen and repeat the sentences. Play again for extra practice.

7.14 CD3 Track 31

1 We can't go. They've sold out.
2 I'd like to find out about train times.
3 I'm looking forward to August.
4 I was talking to my mother but we were cut off.
5 In future, remember to switch off the kitchen lights.
6 Philip's not old enough to look after a five-year-old.
7 We put on our seat belts before the flight took off.
8 They don't get on with each other.

Extra support

Get SS to practise saying each sentence in pairs. They take turns to say the sentence.

Study Link SS can find more practice of English sounds on the MultiROM and also on the *New English File Intermediate* website.

d • 7.15 Focus on the task and quickly run through the six sentences. Tell SS that they are going to hear each sentence plus another three-word phrase (which contains a phrasal verb). They have to write the second phrase. Explain that the first phrase will help them by giving the context and that the phrases will be said quite quickly so that most of the words will be linked together (making the phrase more difficult to understand).

- Play the tape / CD once all the way through and let SS just listen to the six sentences without writing anything.
- Now play the recording again, preferably pausing after each sentence, for SS to write down the phrases.
- Play again if necessary. Check answers by eliciting the six phrases onto the board.

7.15 CD3 Track 32

1 There's a towel on the floor. **Pick it up**.
2 I hate this music. **Switch it off**.
3 Your jacket's on the chair. **Put it away**.
4 You don't need a coat. **Take it off**.
5 I can't hear the TV. **Turn it up**.
6 Coffee is bad for you. **Give it up**.

- Finally, play the tape / CD again pausing after each sentence for SS to repeat.

4 VOCABULARY & SPEAKING

a • Tell SS to go to the **Vocabulary Bank *Phrasal verbs*** on *p.155*. Focus on the instructions in **a** and demonstrate the activity by doing sentence 1 with the whole class.

- SS uncover the first sentence to check their answer. They then continue, looking at each sentence with the particle covered and testing themselves to see if they can remember it.
- Finally, focus on the ⚠ box below and go through the information and examples.
- Now, focus on the instruction 'Can you remember the words on this page? Test yourself or a partner'. Tell SS to test themselves regularly on these verbs.

Testing yourself

SS can cover the **Particle** column and look at sentences 1–40 and try to remember the particle (*for*, *out*, *up*, etc.). They can uncover, one by one, to check.

Testing a partner

See **Testing a partner** *p.17.*

Study Link SS can find more practice of these words on the MultiROM and on the *New English File Intermediate* website.

- Tell SS to go back to the main lesson on *p.110.*

b • Focus on the task and give SS time to choose their six questions. Deal with any vocabulary problems.

c • Put SS in pairs and focus on the task emphasizing that they should try and keep the conversation going where possible by asking more questions and giving more information.

Extra support

Demonstrate by getting SS to choose some questions to ask you, and elicit follow-up questions to keep the conversation going.

- Get SS to ask and answer their questions in pairs. If there's time, get some feedback from the class.

5 READING

a • Focus on the task and tell SS to choose two things. Elicit ideas from the class but don't give answers at this stage.

b • Focus on the article and set a time limit, e.g. three or four minutes, for SS to read the article once to check their answers to **a**. Find out if anybody guessed the two things.

An iron and a vacuum cleaner. No, they don't.

c • Give SS a few minutes to read the article again more carefully. Then tell SS to cover the article and see if they can remember what the numbers in the list refer to. Make sure they don't look at the numbers while they are reading the text for the second time. Elicit answers from the class.

37 - The number of years they lived without electricity.
74 and 72 - The ages of the couple.
19,000 - It will cost £19,000 to install electricity.
200 - The house is 200 years old.
3 - The house has three bedrooms.
9 - The couple have nine children.
24 - The couple have 24 grandchildren.
8 - They have eight great-grandchildren.

d • Focus on the questions and give SS a few minutes to answer them. Then get them to compare their answers with a partner. Check answers.

1 Yes, one.
2 She's happy ('looking forward to it') but she doesn't think they missed anything by not having electricity in the past.
3 No (They 'got by').
4 From the land (their garden).
5 Because they played together, made up games or read stories.
6 It was a very healthy way of life. They were never ill.

e • Focus on the task and give SS, in pairs, a few minutes to complete the chart. Remind them that if *sth* / *sb* are in the middle of the gap, it means that the verb is separable. If it's at the end, it means that the verb is non-separable. Check answers.

Phrasal verbs

1 grow up	5 make sth up
2 get by	6 live off sb / sth
3 put sth in	7 bring sb up
4 move back	

- Point out the difference between *bring up*, which is what parents do to their children (i.e. look after them, feed them, teach them things) and *grow up*, which is what the children do (i.e. get older, bigger until they are an adult).

6 LISTENING

a • 7.16 Focus on the task and play the tape / CD once the whole way through for SS to find out the two things the people would miss the most. Check answers.

Claire:	1 fridge	2 laptop (computer)
Andy:	1 mobile	2 MP3 player
Julia:	1 dishwasher	2 iron
Tyler:	1 mobile	2 lights

b • Play the tape / CD again, pausing after each speaker for SS to listen why they would miss these things. Get them to compare in pairs before checking answers.

Claire
(fridge) She would miss cold drinks and would have to go shopping every day.
(laptop) She wouldn't be able to work.
Andy
(mobile) He needs his mobile to keep in touch with people.
(MP3 player) He needs his music.
Julia
(dishwasher) She has a family and lots of washing up.
(iron) Everybody in the family would look terrible without one.
Tyler
(mobile) There are some numbers he only has in his mobile.
(lights) It's often dark early in the morning and in the afternoon.

Extra support

If there's time, you could get SS to listen again with the tapescript on *p.129* so they can see exactly what they understood / didn't understand. Translate / explain any new words or phrases.

7.16 CD3 Track 33
(tapescript in Student's Book on *p.129*)
CLAIRE Well, it wouldn't be electric light because I love candles. And I could live without a washing machine for a week – I often do when I'm on holiday. I think I would miss a fridge though – I'd hate not to have cold drinks, and it would mean having to go shopping every day for food or it would go off. So a fridge would be one thing, and then probably my laptop. It has a battery, but I could only use it for three hours or so without charging it. So I wouldn't be able to do much work.
ANDY Er well, it depends. I'd quite miss the TV, but I suppose I could live without it for a week if I had to. And, er, what else – oh no, my mobile. I wouldn't be able to charge it. I couldn't *live* without my mobile. I mean that's how I keep in touch with all my friends. And my MP3 player. I need my music. Yes, definitely those two.
JULIA I think for me it would have to be first and foremost the dishwasher. Because with a family and so much washing up, I would just be over the sink for ever. It would be a nightmare for me to have no dishwasher and I've got so used to it. So that would be the first thing. And the second thing, probably again because of having a family, a young family, would be an iron, because there's so much ironing and if I had to go without that, everyone would look terrible. Nobody would look smart. So those would be my two things.
TYLER Well, I suppose the first thing I'd miss most would be my mobile phone, because I couldn't charge it up, so I couldn't use it, and I'd get very upset about that. There are some people's numbers that are only stored in the phone. I haven't got them written down, and I wouldn't be able to get in touch with those people. So mobile phone. And the other thing I'd miss would be, electricity, em if the electricity had gone, would be the lights, at this time of year especially, when the days are short, the mornings are dark, early afternoon, late afternoon's dark too. I'd miss lights as well. So mobile phone and lights.

c • Focus on the task. Give SS a minute to talk about what they would miss and then elicit some answers from whole the class. You could also tell SS what you would miss most.

Study Link SS can find a dictation and a Grammar quiz on all the grammar from File 7 on the MultiROM and more grammar activities on the *New English File Intermediate* website.

Extra photocopiable activities

Grammar
phrasal verbs *p.162*
Communicative
Phrasal verbs race *p.193* (instructions *p.170*)
Vocabulary
Split crossword *p.203* (instructions *p.196*)

HOMEWORK

Study Link **Workbook** *pp.70–72*

7 PRACTICAL ENGLISH EVERYTHING IN THE OPEN

Function Apologizing, giving excuses
Language *I'm really sorry. I did it without thinking*, etc.

Lesson plan

This is the last **Practical English** lesson. In the first part of the lesson SS learn and practise ways of apologizing and giving excuses. Mark tells Allie that she has mistakenly sent a personal email intended for his eyes only to everyone in the office. Allie then apologizes to everyone in the office for not being completely honest about her relationship with Mark.

In the second part of the lesson (**Social English**), Mark and Allie go for a walk by the river Seine and discuss how the people in the office discovered their secret. Then Mark asks Allie to marry him.

Study Link These lessons are on the *New English File Intermediate* Video / DVD, which can be used instead of the Class Cassette / CD (see introduction *p.9*). The main functional section of each episode is also on the MultiROM with additional activities.

Optional lead-in (books closed)

- Revise what happened in the previous episode by eliciting the story from SS, e.g. *What did Ben tell Jacques and Nicole about his weekend? Who didn't believe him at first? Why did Nicole believe him?*, etc.
- If you are using the video / DVD, you could play the previous episode again, leaving out the 'Listen and Repeat' sections.
- You could also try to elicit from the SS the phrases they revised / learnt in the previous episode for expressing surprise and interest, e.g. *Really? You must be joking. I don't believe you* (You could write the phrases with gaps on the board to help SS remember.).

APOLOGIZING, GIVING EXCUSES

a • 7.17 Tell SS to cover the dialogue with their hand or a piece of paper. Focus on the photo and the two questions, or write the questions on the board and do the first listening with books closed.

• Play tape / CD once the whole way through. Then play it again, pausing after each question to give SS time to answer. Check answers.

> To Mark. Because she sent a personal email to everyone in the office (She pressed 'Reply to all' by mistake.).

b • Now get SS to look at the dialogue. In pairs, they read it and see if they can guess or remember the missing words. Emphasize that they shouldn't write the words in the dialogue but in pencil alongside or on a separate sheet of paper.

c • Play the tape / CD again for them to check. Then go through the dialogue line by line and check answers. Find out if SS had guessed the words correctly. Where they had not guessed correctly, see if their alternative also fits.

> **7.17** CD3 Track 34
> **M = Mark, A = Allie, N = Nicole**
> M Mark Ryder.
> A Mark, can you come in?
> M Sure.
> A Thanks for the sales report.
> M I think there's something more important to talk about right now.
> A What do you mean?
> M That message you sent me. You hit 'reply to all'. You sent it to everyone in the office.
> A Oh no. You're joking. Oh, Mark. I'm **so** sorry. I did it without **thinking**.
> M It's **all right**, Allie. It's an easy mistake to make.
> A How could I be so **stupid**? I just wasn't **concentrating**.
> M Allie…
> A I'm **really** sorry.
> M Don't **worry** about it. It doesn't **matter**. But I think we should talk to the others.
> A Yes, you're right. I'll do it. It was my **fault**. Listen everybody. I just want to say that I'm **terribly** sorry. I haven't been honest with you. Erm, we… Mark and I…
> N That's OK, Allie. We had already guessed. It wasn't really a surprise.

d • 7.18 Now focus on the key phrases highlighted in the dialogue. Play the tape / CD pausing after the beep for SS to repeat. Encourage them to copy the rhythm and intonation.

> **7.18** CD3 Track 35
> **A = Allie, M = Mark**
> A I'm so sorry.
> A I did it without thinking.
> M It's all right, Allie.
> A How could I be so stupid?
> A I just wasn't concentrating.
> A I'm really sorry.
> M Don't worry about it.
> M It doesn't matter.
> A It was my fault.
> A I'm terribly sorry.

e • Get SS to look at the highlighted phrases in the dialogue and use them to complete the chart. Check answers.

Apologizing	Admitting… / Explaining	Responding to an apology
I'm so sorry.	I did it without thinking.	It's all right (it's an easy mistake to make).
I'm really sorry.	How could I be so stupid?	It doesn't matter. Don't worry about it.
I'm terribly sorry.	I just wasn't concentrating.	That's OK. It was my fault.

• Point out that:
 – I'm *so / really / terribly sorry* are stronger forms of apology than *I'm sorry.*
 – As well as *It's OK* and *That's OK* you can also use *It's all right* and *That's all right.*

f • Put SS in pairs, **A** and **B**, preferably face to face. Tell SS to go to **Communication** *I'm so sorry!* **A** on *p.118* and **B** on *p.121*. Give SS a minute or so to read their instructions. Then demonstrate the activity by taking the part of first student **A** then **B**, and do the first situation for both. Try to elicit a reasonable sounding excuse, and then accept it with, e.g. *That's OK.*

• Now get SS to work together in pairs and complete the task.

SOCIAL ENGLISH A walk by the Seine

a • 7.19 Focus on the photo and the question. Play the tape / CD once for SS to answer the question. Elicit the answer.

Mark asks Allie to marry him. She says yes.

b • Focus on questions 1–5 and go through them quickly. Then play the tape / CD. Play the recording again if necessary. Check answers.

1 She thinks Mark said something to the people in the office (He's bad at keeping secrets.).
2 No. He thinks they guessed (because the French are experts on love affairs).
3 No, because now they don't have to pretend any more.
4 Because a boat on the river makes a noise (a boat horn).
5 He asks her to send him her answer in an email (He's joking.).

7.19 CD3 Track 36

A = Allie, M = Mark
A I still can't work out how they knew about us. I was always really careful not to treat you differently.
M You were really hard on me.
A Mark, I wasn't.
M Oh, you were just being fair and very British.
A So if it wasn't me, it must have been you.
M What?
A I've got my own office. You're with them all the time. You must have said something. You're hopeless at keeping secrets!
M Don't blame me. This wasn't my fault. They probably just guessed.
A How?
M You know the French, they're experts on love affairs.
A Maybe.
M Actually, I think it's great that everyone knows. Now we don't have to pretend any more.
A Yeah. That's true.
M Allie, there's something I've been wanting to ask you for a long time... I just haven't said anything. But... it's now or never.
M Allie, will you marry me?
A Sorry, Mark. I didn't hear a word you said.
M I said...Will you marry me?
A Yes, I will.
M Was that a 'yes'?
A Yes!
M Can you confirm that in an email for me? Just don't send it to everyone in the office this time.

c • 7.20 Now focus on the **USEFUL PHRASES**. Give SS a moment to try to complete them, and then play the tape / CD to check. Elicit / explain that *hopeless at* = very bad at.

7.20 CD3 Track 37

A = Allie, M = Mark
A So if it **wasn't** me, it must have been you.
A You're **hopeless** at keeping secrets!
M Don't **blame** me.
M But it's now or **never**.
A I didn't hear a **word** you said.
M Can you **confirm** that in an email?

Extra idea

Ask SS if they can remember who said each phrase and what they were talking about.

d • Play the tape / CD again, pausing for SS to repeat. In a monolingual class, elicit the equivalent expressions in SS' L1.

HOMEWORK

Study Link **Workbook** *p.73*

7 Writing: An article for a magazine

Lesson plan

This final writing task focuses on writing a 'for and against' article for a magazine. This is the kind of writing task SS are often asked to do if they sit official exams. The task focuses on the organization of ideas and on the use of connecting phrases like *Firstly,... On the other hand,... In conclusion,...*.

There is also a mini focus on using error correction.

We suggest that you do exercises **a–d** in class, but set the actual writing (the last activity) for homework. If there's time, you may also want to do the planning in class.

a • Focus on the article and on the task. Give SS five or six minutes to read the article and correct the ten mistakes. Check answers.

1 has	**6** programmes
2 talking	**7** documentaries
3 fitter	**8** what's (or what is)
4 different	**9** although
5 their	**10** off

b • Focus on the task and put SS in pairs. Tell them to read the article again and then cover it and answer the questions together from memory. Then check answers.

> **1** Families spend time talking to each other. They do more creative things like reading. They are usually fitter.
> **2** Children who don't have a TV may feel different from their friends. They might know less about what is happening in the world.
> **3** The writer is for having a TV but thinks we should only watch good programmes.

c • Focus on the task and put SS in pairs. Give them a few minutes to make a list of advantages and disadvantages.

> **Some possible answers**
> **advantages:** very convenient – you always have a phone to use wherever you are / people can always contact you wherever you are / very useful in a crisis – you can call for help / very useful when you are trying to meet someone, e.g. in a crowded place, etc.
> **disadvantages:** more expensive than normal phones / people can phone you at inconvenient times, e.g. when you are driving or having a meal in a restaurant / it can be annoying when people talk loudly on their phone in a public place or answer their phone when they are talking to you, etc.

d • Focus on the task and get SS to number their advantages and disadvantages 1–3.
• Now focus on the **Useful language** box and make sure SS understand all the phrases.

WRITE an article

Go through the instructions. Then either get SS to plan and write their article in class (set a time limit of 20 minutes) or get them to plan their article in class and write it at home, or set both the planning and writing for homework.

If SS do the writing in class, get them to swap their article with another student to read and check for mistakes before you collect them all in.

7 Revise & Check

For instructions on how to use these pages, see *p.32*.

GRAMMAR

a 1 c 2 b 3 c 4 a 5 b
b 1 hadn't got 2 you arrived 3 if ... stops
4 doesn't it 5 forward to

VOCABULARY

a 1 unfortunately 2 impatient 3 comfortable
4 lucky 5 carelessly
b 1 station 2 horror 3 nursery 4 fine 5 cash
c 1 look 2 up 3 back 4 up 5 take 6 Slow
7 get 8 on 9 up 10 broke

PRONUNCIATION

a 1 put (It's /ʊ/) 2 patient (It's /eɪ/) 3 down (It's /aʊ/) 4 careful (It's /eə/) 5 machine (It's /ʃ/)
b impatient, comfortable, documentary, cartoons, detective

CAN YOU UNDERSTAND THIS TEXT?

a 1 F 2 T 3 F 4 DS 5 T 6 T 7 T 8 DS
b **give up** = stop
carried on = continued, didn't stop
picked out = chosen
going back = returning to
turn up = arrive, appear

CAN YOU UNDERSTAND THESE PEOPLE?

a 1 a 2 c 3 a 4 b 5 c
b 1 spiders 2 Detective 3 9.15 4 BBC 1
5 Happy Days

7.21 CD3 Track 38

1 **A** So then I spoke to the manager...Hey, my computer's not working.
B The electricity's just gone off. It'll come back on in a minute.
A Oh no. I don't know if I've saved the article I was writing.
B Doesn't it save automatically?
A Yes, but only every half hour. Oh – it's back on again. Now we'll see. Yes, thank goodness, it's all there. If I hadn't saved it, I would have had to look up all that information again.
B You were lucky. So tell me what the manager said…

2 **A** Why do you always wear that yellow T-shirt when you play?
B It's my lucky shirt. I put it on under my football shirt.
A Do you really believe it brings you luck?
B Well, I suppose it's just superstition really. But the one time I wasn't wearing it we lost.
A Why weren't you wearing it?
B Because I'd left it out the night before on my chair, but my wife thought it looked dirty and put it in the washing machine.

3 **A** What are you reading?
B *The Minotaur* by Barbara Vine.
A She's a detective writer, isn't she?
B Yes, she's brilliant.
A You're always reading detective novels. Don't you ever read anything else?
B Of course I do. I read lots of classics, and science fiction too. It's just that when I'm on a train or a bus I need something light. And anything's better than reading the sports papers like you do. Anyway, shut up now and let me read. I'm just about to find out who the murderer is.

4 **A** OK, now I'm going to ask you a few questions. And just so that you know, this interview will be recorded. This is detective inspector David Hawkins interviewing Gerald Carter on Thursday May the 20th. OK, let's start with what you were doing last night?
B I was at home.
A Any witnesses?
B My mum. She was there. You can ask her if you like.
A So you didn't go out at all?
B No, I stayed in and watched TV. Well, I went to the corner shop to get some milk. But that was just five minutes.
A Did you watch anything in particular? On TV?
B Yeah, the football. England and Denmark. Rubbish match.
A So you weren't anywhere near the pub? The Kings Head?
B The pub? Me? No way.
A So you'd be surprised to hear that three people saw you there.
B They're lying. And I'm not going to answer any more questions without a lawyer.

5 **A** Could you turn the TV off, please?
B But Mum, it hasn't finished yet.
A What hasn't finished?
C The film. It's *Star Wars. The Return of the Jedi.*
A But you've seen it before. I know you have.
B Yes, but it's so good. And it's nearly finished, I promise. Just five more minutes.
A I don't care. It's 10 o'clock and it's time to go to bed. It's already half an hour past your normal bedtime.
C But yesterday you said we could watch it if we'd finished our homework.
A Yes, but I didn't know it was on so late. Bedtime and that's that.

7.22 CD3 Track 39

And finally, tonight's TV – a word about what's on television this evening. At 8.00 p.m. on BBC2 you can see *Eight-legged Wonders*, a documentary about those fascinating insects – well, arachnids I should say – spiders. It's a must for anyone who's interested in nature and wildlife.
However, if you suffer from arachnophobia, you'd be better off watching ITV, as at the same time as *Eight-legged Wonders*, there's the first episode of a new crime series called *The Silent Detective*, starring Amanda Hobbs.

Then after that on ITV, at 9.15 there's this week's edition of *Who wants to be a millionaire?* Note that the time has changed for this quiz show as it used to be on at 9.30. On BBC1 a bit later, at 10.05 the film in the *All-time Greats* series is the wonderful Ingmar Bergman film *Fanny and Alexander*, so if you're a fan of European cinema, don't miss it.
And finally, a change of programme on ITV. Instead of tonight's episode of *Hospital Life*, at 10.30, as a tribute to the late John Miller, ITV will be screening his Oscar winning film, *Happy Days*. So if you're waiting to find out what's going to happen to Doctor Hammond and Nurse Marshall, you'll have to wait till next week. And now...

Extra photocopiable activities

Grammar
revise and check *p.163*
Communicative
Revision *p.194* (instructions *p.170*)
Vocabulary
Revision *p.204* (instructions *p.196*)
Quicktest 7 *p.222*
End-of-course test *pp.223–225* (tapescript *p.215*)

CONTENTS

Photocopiable material

- There is a **Grammar activity** for each main (A, B, and C) lesson of the Student's Book.
- There is a **Communicative activity** for each main lesson of the Student's Book.
- There is a **Vocabulary activity** for each File of the Students Book.
- There are six **Song activities**. These can be used as part of the main lesson in the Student's Book or in a later lesson. The recording of the song can be found in the main lesson on the Class Cassette / CD.
- There is a **Quicktest** for Files 1–7. These are short tests of the main Grammar, Vocabulary, and Pronunciation to be used at the end of each File.
- There is an **End-of-course test**, which tests Grammar, Vocabulary, and Pronunciation from the course as well as Reading, Listening, and Writing.

Using extra activities in mixed-ability classes

Some teachers have classes with a very wide range of abilities, and where some students finish Student's Book activities much more quickly than others. You could give these fast-finishers a photocopiable activity (either Communicative or Grammar) while you help the slower students. Alternatively, some teachers might want to give faster students extra oral practice with a communicative activity while slower students consolidate their knowledge with an extra grammar activity.

Tips for using Grammar activities

The Grammar activities are designed to give students extra practice in the main grammar point from each lesson. How you use these activities depends on the needs and abilities of your students and time you have available. They can be used in the lesson if you think all of your class would benefit from the extra practice or you could set them as homework for some or all of your students.

- All of the activities start with a writing stage. If you use the activities in class, get students to work individually or in pairs. Allow students to compare before checking the answers.
- Many of the activities have a final section that gets students to cover the sentences and to test their memory. If you are using the activities in class, students can work in pairs and test their partner. If you set them for homework, encourage students to use this stage to test themselves.
- If students are having trouble with any of the activities, make sure they refer to the relevant Grammar Bank in the Student's Book.
- Make sure that students keep their copies of the activities and that they review any difficult areas regularly. Encourage them to go back to activities and cover and test themselves. This will help with their revision.

Tips for using Communicative activities

- We have suggested the ideal number of copies for each activity. However, you can often manage with fewer, e.g. one copy per pair instead of one per student.
- When SS are working in pairs, if possible get them to sit face to face. This will encourage them to really talk to each other and also means they can't see each other's sheet.
- If your class doesn't divide into pairs or groups, take part yourself, get two SS to share one role, or get one student to monitor, help and correct.
- If some SS finish early, they can swap roles and do the activity again, or you could get them to write some of the sentences from the activity.

Grammar activity answers

introduction

a **2** a **3** b **4** c **5** c **6** a **7** b **8** c **9** a **10** a **11** a **12** b **13** a **14** b **15** a **16** c **17** c **18** b **19** b **20** a

b **3** I have / 've lived **4** My **husband's** name's Pedro **5** We don't have **any** children **6** ✓ **7** we'd like **to have** **8** We are looking **for a flat** **9** ✓ **10** Pedro is **an** engineer **11** work very **hard** **12** we don't have **to** do **13** ✓ **14** **much** free time **15** ✓ **16** ✓ **17** I don't have **enough time** **18** I want **to** be **19** ✓ **20** I **often make** mistakes **21** ✓ **22** **to** do

1A present simple and continuous

a **2** I'm doing **3** do you come **4** do you have **5** It depends **6** Are you going **7** Do you mean **8** I need **9** I'm moving **10** are you living **11** I'm staying **12** are you doing **13** want **14** I'm meeting

b **2** 'm visiting **3** don't mind **4** are you staying **5** 'm going home **6** do you like **7** Do you know **8** comes **9** are you doing **10** 're waiting **11** do you live **12** aren't doing **13** Are you carrying **14** have **15** Do you want **16** says

1B past tenses

2 hadn't studied **3** was raining **4** arrived **5** had already started **6** couldn't answer **7** had ever given **8** was sitting **9** was writing **10** looked **11** was standing **12** wasn't looking **13** threw **14** had already finished **15** called **16** was holding **17** had / 'd both failed **18** had / 'd written

1C future forms

2 c **3** b and c **4** b and c **5** a **6** a **7** c **8** a and c **9** a and c **10** a **11** c **12** b and c

2A present perfect and past simple

a **2** I've been **3** did you go **4** finished **5** I've already been **6** did you go **7** went

b **2** taught **3** 've just come back **4** have you been **5** was **6** started **7** haven't finished **8** have you been married **9** had **10** did you meet **11** went **12** 've known **13** got **14** were you **15** 've just met

2B present perfect continuous

2 A How long has it been raining?
B It's been raining since yesterday morning.
3 A How long have you had that jacket?
B I've had it for ten years.
4 A How long has he been working / has he worked here?
B He's been working / He's worked here since he left school.
5 A How long have they been married?
B They've been married for 60 years.
6 A How long have you been learning Russian?
B I've been learning Russian for three years.

b **2** Have you been waiting **3** have you been doing **4** I've been shopping **5** 've been playing **6** 've been watching a (sad) film.

2C comparatives and superlatives

2 **more nervous** than **3** ✓ **4** ✓ **5** **nicer** than **6** the **worst** one **7** ✓ **8** ✓ **9** ✓ **10** **lazier** than **11** the highest divorce rate **in** the world **12** **more slowly** **13** the **best** chocolate cake **14** ✓ **15** as cold **as** **16** **the** most affectionate **17** **hotter** than **18** ✓ **19** same school **as** **20** ✓

3A *must, have to, should*

a **2** mustn't **3** ✓ **4** had to **5** ✓ **6** don't have to

b **2** don't have to **3** must / have to **4** should **5** mustn't **6** must / have to **7** shouldn't **8** don't have to

3B *must, may, might, can't*

a **2** might **3** must **4** can't **5** may

b **1** must **2** might not / may not, must **3** might / may, can't, must **4** might / may, can't, must

3C *can, could, be able to*

a **2** ✓ **3** be able to **4** be able to **5** ✓ **6** will be able to **7** ✓ **8** ✓ **9** being able to **10** ✓

b **2** be able to **3** can't **4** been able to **5** could **6** be able to **7** being able to **8** can **9** couldn't **10** could **11** be able to

4A future time clauses: *if, when*, etc.

2 finish **3** 'll text **4** finishes **5** Come **6** can **7** don't phone **8** get **9** 're / are **10** are **11** won't be able to **12** pass **13** meet **14** don't study **15** won't have

4B second conditional

a **2** had, could **3** would be, didn't go out **4** wouldn't argue, didn't borrow **5** went, wouldn't be **6** painted, wouldn't look **7** would feel, went **8** shared, would get on **9** didn't have to, could **10** did, would improve

b **2** could **3** don't reduce **4** see **5** were **6** doesn't have **7** had **8** wouldn't drive **9** won't eat **10** would look

4C *usually* and *used to*

2 don't live **3** used to dream **4** used to be **5** didn't use to worry **6** used to share **7** don't go **8** didn't use to like **9** don't ride **10** used to ride **11** spend **12** didn't use to eat **13** didn't use to be **14** used to have

5A quantifiers

2 too much **3** a lot of **4** little **5** How many **6** None **7** a lot of **8** enough time **9** any **10** plenty **11** A few **12** little **13** too **14** few **15** too much **16** enough **17** no

5B articles: *a, an, the*, no article

a **2** a **3** a **4** The **5** the **6** a **7** The **8** a **9** a **10** (–) **11** (–) **12** the **13** The **14** (–)

b **1** (–) **2** (–) **3** a **4** a **5** a **6** the **7** a **8** a **9** the

c **1** (–) **2** (–) **3** The **4** (–) **5** a **6** (–) **7** a **8** a **9** (–) **10** the **11** a **12** (–) **13** (–) **14** the

5C gerunds and infinitives

a **2** spending **3** to talk **4** to be able **5** to explain **6** going **7** to spend **8** to know **9** to ask **10** to read **11** guessing **12** to do

b **2** to do **3** Getting **4** losing **5** to wait **6** being **7** thinking **8** to ask **9** to go **10** to book

c **2** to go **3** to go **4** go **5** go **6** to go **7** go

6A reported speech

a **2** would have to **3** were going to **4** this could **5** 'd / had just come **6** 'd / had agreed **7** hoped **8** would agree **9** had to

b **1** who he thought would be the next President of the UN
2 if more countries would be present at the next meeting
3 if he had discussed that with the US President
4 what the rich countries should do to eliminate world poverty

c **1** asked us to put our seatbelts on **2** told her boyfriend not to worry **3** told us not to cheat **4** asked his friend to slow down **5** asked me not to tell

6B passive: *be* + past participle

a **2** were used **3** will be seen **4** have been made **5** was nominated **6** was paid **7** was being made, was asked **8** had been murdered **9** were used **10** are being made

b **2** was directed **3** is set **4** is sent **5** takes **6** speaks **7** falls **8** is rescued **9** learns **10** was written **11** have been sold

6C relative clauses

a **2** which **3** which **4** which **5** who **6** which **7** where **8** who **9** whose

b 2, 3, 4, 5, 6, 8

c 3, 6

d **2** whose best-known painting is *Guernica*
3 which is the capital of Australia
4 where I used to work
5 whose daughter is the local doctor
6 who died in 2005
7 which was the worst for over 75 years
8 who is a clothes designer

7A third conditional

a **2** I wouldn't have won this Oscar if it hadn't been for my wonderful director.
3 If you had / 'd listened to me, you wouldn't have married him.
4 I would have / 've passed my test if I hadn't driven through a red light.
5 If I had / 'd known that the letter was important, I wouldn't have thrown it away.
6 He wouldn't have forgotten their anniversary if he had / 'd written it in his diary.

b **2** would have / 've arrived, hadn't got
3 had / 'd known, would have / 've taken
4 would have / 've done, hadn't been
5 hadn't taken, would have / 've got
6 hadn't sat, would never have met

7B question tags, indirect questions

a **2** are you **3** aren't you **4** are you **5** have you **6** wouldn't you **7** don't you **8** didn't I **9** can't you **10** isn't it **11** didn't you

b **2** what time the bank opens **3** if this train goes **4** how this photocopier works **5** if there's a hotel near here

7C phrasal verbs

a **2** out **3** in **4** on **5** up **6** out **7** down **8** off

b **2** going **3** growing **4** get **5** calm **6** set **7** go

c **2** ✗ write **them down** **3** ✓ **4** ✗ is looking **for a new job** **5** ✓ **6** ✗ I pick **you up** **7** ✗ **look after** my little sister **8** ✓ **9** ✓ **10** ✗ Give **it back**

revise and check

1 finishes
2 studying
3 hadn't locked
4 was raining
5 have you been learning
6 won't be able to
7 did
8 see
9 've / have had
10 need
11 didn't watch
12 Shall I make
13 be
14 to go
15 not to tell
16 works
17 would have seen
18 will win / is going to win
19 's / is being repaired
20 've / have been working

Circle the correct answer, a, b, or c.

1 My brother __________ a job at the moment.
a hasn't b don't have (c) doesn't have

2 __________ Mr S Roberts live here?
a Does b Is c Do

3 My dad __________ at the university.
a teachs b teaches c teach

4 I __________ to the cinema with Katie tonight. I've bought the tickets.
a go b will go c 'm going

5 I __________ back from New York this morning.
a flied b flown c flew

6 He didn't __________ the holiday very much.
a like b liked c likes

7 I __________ a shower when the water stopped working.
a had b was having c were having

8 **A** I'm thirsty.
B __________ get you a drink?
a Will I b Am I going to c Shall I

9 **A** I have a new mobile.
B I'm sure you __________ it, just like your last one.
a 'll lose b 're losing c lose

10 **A** Would you like something to eat?
B No, thanks, __________ lunch.
a I've already had b I already have had
c I've had already

11 Have you ever __________ to Paris?
a been b gone c went

12 The traffic is __________ than it used to be.
a badder b worse c more bad

13 Cycling isn't as dangerous __________ skiing.
a as b than c that

14 What __________ you do if there was a snake in your room?
a will b would c did

15 I'll come to your party if I __________ work early enough.
a finish b will finish c finished

16 You drive much __________ than me.
a slowly b slowlier c more slowly

17 If I __________ you, I'd look for a new job.
a was b am c were

18 My bike __________ last week.
a is stolen b was stolen c stole

19 We were too late. When we arrived at the station, the train __________.
a already left b had already left
c has already left

20 'I love you.' He said he __________ her.
a loved b love c is loving

a Read about Maria José. Then look at the **bold** phrases. Tick (✓) the sentences that are right and correct the wrong ones.

My name's Maria José. **I'm 26** and I'm from Brazil.	1 ✓	
I am born in São Paulo and **I live** there all my life.	2 *I was born*	3 ______
I'm married. **My husband name's Pedro**. He's from São Paulo, too.	4 ______	
We don't have some children. We live with Pedro's parents in	5 ______	
their flat, **and I get on with them** very well, but	6 ______	
we'd like having our own place. **We are looking a flat for** at	7 ______	8 ______
the moment. **I work for** a bank and **Pedro is engineer**.	9 ______	10 ______
We both **work very hardly**, but **we don't have do** the housework.	11 ______	12 ______
Pedro's parents are retired, so **they look after** the house.	13 ______	
I don't have **many free time**, but when I have the chance	14 ______	
I enjoy listening to music. **I used to play** the piano,	15 ______	16 ______
but now **I don't have time enough**. I'm learning English because	17 ______	
I need it for my job. My speaking is OK, but **I want be**	18 ______	
better at writing. **I have to write** letters and emails in English	19 ______	
and **I make often mistakes.**	20 ______	
Next summer **I'm going to go to** the USA **for do** a finance course.	21 ______	22 ______

b Write a similar paragraph about yourself, where you live, your work and / or studies, your hobbies, and why you are learning English.

a Circle the correct form of the verbs.

NOEMI 1 What **do you study** / (**are you studying**)?
VICTOR Political Science.
NOEMI 2 **I do / I'm doing** Social Anthropology. Where 3 **do you come / are you coming** from?
VICTOR I'm from Coimbra, in Portugal.
NOEMI How many hours of classes 4 **do you have / are you having** a day?
VICTOR 5 **It depends / It's depending** on the day, but usually four. 6 **Do you go / Are you going** to the party tonight?
NOEMI 7 **Do you mean / Are you meaning** the one for new students? I can't, because 8 **I need / I'm needing** to get organized tonight. 9 **I move / I'm moving** to a rented flat tomorrow.
VICTOR Where 10 **do you live / are you living** at the moment?
NOEMI 11 **I stay / I'm staying** in a bed and breakfast.
VICTOR What 12 **do you do / are you doing** on Sunday afternoon? If you 13 **want / are wanting**, we could meet and look around the city.
NOEMI 14 **I meet / I'm meeting** some friends in the afternoon. What about Sunday morning?
VICTOR Fine. Where shall we meet?

b Complete the dialogues with the correct form of the verbs: present simple or present continuous.

DRIVER So, What 1 *are you doing* (do) here in Chicago, mister?
MAN I 2 __________ (visit) some clients.
DRIVER Where are you from? You 3 __________ (not mind) me asking, do you?
MAN Not at all. From Inchon, in Korea.
DRIVER Good place to be! Me, I'm from Idaho. How long 4 __________ (stay) here?
MAN Three days. I 5 __________ (go) home on Saturday.
DRIVER OK. Hey, 6 __________ (like) steak? 7 __________ (know) where the best steak in all of America 8 __________ (come) from? That's right – Idaho!

POLICEMAN What 9 __________ (do) here?
JOSH Nothing. Why?
POLICEMAN We ask the questions here.
JOSH We 10 __________ (wait) for someone.
POLICEMAN Where 11 __________ (live)?
JOSH 151 Churchill Road.
POLICEMAN What are your names?
JOSH I'm Josh and he's my brother, Wayne. We 12 __________ (not do) anything illegal, are we?
POLICEMAN 13 __________ (carry) any form of identification?
JOSH Yes. I 14 __________ (have) my driving licence. 15 __________ (want) to see it? Here!
POLICEMAN It 16 __________ (say) Dean Allen on this licence.
JOSH Does it? Oh yes, it's my dad's.

a Complete the text with the correct form of the verbs in brackets: past simple, past continuous, or past perfect.

My exam **nightmare**

I [1] *woke up* (wake up) on the morning of the maths exam with a horrible feeling in my stomach. I knew that I [2] __________ (not study) enough the night before and that I was going to fail.

When I left home it [3] __________ (rain) and there was a lot of traffic. I [4] __________ (arrive) five minutes late and the exam [5] __________ (already / start). I sat down quickly and looked at the questions. I [6] __________ (not can) answer any of them! It was the most difficult exam the teacher [7] __________ (ever / give) us.

I [8] __________ (sit) next to one of my friends called Sophie and I could see that she [9] __________ (write) very quickly. She was great at maths. Suddenly I had an idea. I [10] __________ (look) at the teacher, Mr Everitt. He [11] __________ (stand) by the window and he [12] __________ (not look) at us. I wrote a message on a piece of paper and [13] __________ (throw) it to Sophie. It said 'I need help.' Sophie [14] __________ (already / finish) the exam. She copied the answers on a piece of paper and quickly passed it to me.

The following day Mr Everitt [15] __________ (call) us both to his room. We saw that he [16] __________ (hold) my exam paper, and Sophie's, too. He told us that we [17] __________ (both / fail) the exam. We [18] __________ (write) exactly the same answers for every question, including several wrong answers.

b Cover the text and try to remember the story.

Circle the best answer. Sometimes two answers are possible.

1 A __________?

B Tomorrow. My flight is in the morning.

a When will you leave
(b) When are you leaving
(c) When are you going to leave

2 A You must bring the money tomorrow.

B Don't worry, __________.

a I'm not forgetting
b I'm not going to forget
c I won't forget

3 A Do you have any plans for tonight?

B Yes, __________.

a I'll meet some friends
b I'm going to meet some friends
c I'm meeting some friends

4 A The interviews for the new manager were yesterday.

B I think __________.

a Bob is getting the job
b Bob is going to get the job
c Bob will get the job

5 A This suitcase is too heavy for me.

B __________.

a I'll carry it for you
b I'm carrying it for you
c I'm going to carry it for you

6 A What would you like to drink?

B __________.

a I'll have a cappuccino, please
b I'm going to have a cappuccino, please
c I'm having a cappuccino, please

7 A Here's my email address.

B Thanks. __________ tomorrow.

a I'm going to send you the photos
b I'm sending you the photos
c I'll send you the photos

8 A __________ this weekend?

B No, I have to work on Saturday.

a Are you going to go away
b Will you go away
c Are you going away

9 A England are playing Brazil tomorrow.

B I'm sure __________.

a they'll lose
b they're losing
c they're going to lose

10 A My train arrives at 2.15.

B OK, __________ by the information desk.

a I'll meet you
b I'm going to meet you
c I'm meeting you

11 A What time does the film start?

B I don't know. __________ phone the cinema and check?

a Will I
b Am I going to
c Shall I

12 A Do I need to bring an umbrella?

B No, I don't think __________.

a it rains
b it'll rain
c it's going to rain

11–12 Excellent. You can use different future forms very well.
7–10 Quite good, but check the rules in the Grammar Bank (Student's Book *p.130*) for any questions that you got wrong.
0–6 This is difficult for you. Read the rules in the Grammar Bank (Student's Book *p.130*). Then ask your teacher for another photocopy and do the exercise again at home.

2A Grammar **present perfect and past simple**

a Circle the correct verbs.

STEVE So, where shall we go for our honeymoon?
NATALIE I don't know. [1]Have you ever **been** / **gone** to Thailand?
STEVE Yes, [2]**I've been / I went** there twice.
NATALIE I didn't know that. When [3]**have you been / did you go** there?
STEVE The year after I [4]**have finished / finished** university.
NATALIE What about Vietnam?
STEVE [5]**I've already been / I already went** there, too.
NATALIE Yes? Who [6]**have you been / did you go** with?
STEVE With an ex-girlfriend. But we only [7]**have been / went** to Hanoi. Let's go there.
NATALIE No, let's go somewhere else.

b Complete the dialogues with the correct form of the verbs in brackets: past simple or present perfect.

A [1] *Have you taught* (you / teach) English abroad before, Mr Cooper?
B Yes, I [2]__________ (teach) from 2001 to 2003 in Saudi Arabia, and I [3]__________ (just / come back) from a six-month job in Bahrain.
A How long [4]__________ (you / be) a language teacher?
B For eight years. Before that I [5]__________ (be) a state school teacher for two years.
A Do you have any post-graduate qualifications?
B I [6]__________ (start) a part-time MA at Aston University two years ago, but I [7]__________ (not finish) it yet.

A How long [8]__________ (you / be) married, Dave?
B Ten years. Anna and I [9]__________ (have) our anniversary last month.
A Where [10]__________ (you / meet) Anna? At work?
B No, we [11]__________ (go) to the same school. We [12]__________ (know) each other since we were five years old. What about you?
A I'm divorced. I [13]__________ (get) divorced last year.
B How long [14]__________ (you / be) married?
A Only three years.
B So you're on your own now?
A Yes, but I [15]__________ (just / meet) someone new. We're going out this weekend.

a Complete the questions and answers with the present perfect continuous **or** present perfect simple and *for* or *since*.

1 **A** How long *have they been playing together*? (they / play together)
B They *'ve been playing together since* 1985.

2 **A** How long ______________________? (it / rain)
B It ______________________ yesterday morning.

3 **A** How long ______________________? (you / have that jacket)
B Let me think. I ______________________ _____ ten years.

4 **A** How long ______________________? (he / work here)
B He ______________________ he left school.

5 **A** How long ______________________? (they / be married)
B They ______________________ 60 years.

6 **A** How long ______________________? (you / learn Russian)
B I ______________________ three years.

b Look at the pictures. What have they been doing? Write present perfect continuous sentences.

1 He 's *been cooking*.

2 Sorry I'm late. ______________________ for a long time?

3 You're filthy. What ______________________?

4 I'm exhausted. ______________________ all morning.

5 They ______________________ for an hour.

6 They______________________.

c Cover the sentences. Look at the pictures and remember the sentences.

Grammar **comparatives and superlatives**

● Tick (✓) the sentences that are right and correct the wrong ones.

1 This painting looks ~~**the same than**~~ (the same as) the other one.

2 Coffee makes you **nervouser than** tea.

3 Chile is **the most beautiful country** I've ever been to.

4 He doesn't speak English **as well as** his wife.

5 Are those jeans new? They're **more nice than** your other ones.

6 Her last novel was **the worse** one she has written.

7 Rugby players earn **less money than** footballers.

8 This club is very expensive. Shall we go somewhere **a bit cheaper**?

9 Do you think Americans **work harder than** British people?

10 Madison is **more lazy than** her sister.

11 The USA has **the highest divorce rate of the world**.

12 Can you speak **slowlier** please? I can't understand you.

13 That was delicious. It's **the better chocolate cake** I've ever eaten.

14 Which athlete has won **the most Olympic medals**?

15 I hope this winter isn't **as cold than** the last one!

16 Ben is **most affectionate** of all my nieces and nephews.

17 July is usually **hoter than** June here.

18 Do girls learn languages **more easily than** boys?

19 I go to **the same school that** your sister.

20 Driving is **much more dangerous than** flying.

18–20 **Excellent**. You can use comparatives and superlatives very well.
13–17 **Quite good**, but check the rules in the Grammar Bank (Student's Book *p.132*) for any questions that you got wrong.
0–12 **This is difficult for you**. Read the rules in the Grammar Bank (Student's Book *p.132*). Then ask your teacher for another photocopy and do the exercise again at home.

a Circle the correct verb. Tick (✓) if both are possible.

1 **A** Did you see that film last night?
B Yes, it was brilliant. You **must / should** go and see it. ✓

4 Until the early 1960s, in Britain, young men **must / had to** do military service.

2 When you open the photocopier, you **mustn't / don't have to** touch this part here; it's very hot.

5 You **mustn't / shouldn't** be late. Once the concert has started, you can't go in.

3 You **must / have to** get a visa if you want to go to Russia.

6 When you drive across many European Union borders, you **mustn't / don't have to** show your passport.

---

b Complete the sentences with *must, mustn't, have to, don't have to, should,* or *shouldn't.*

1 You *have to* pay for food and drinks separately.
2 You __________ leave a tip in this restaurant.
3 You __________ fasten your seat belt now.
4 You __________ drink this wine at between 14 and 16°C.
5 Hotel staff __________ go into this room.
6 If you're in transit, you __________ go to the Alitalia desk.
7 You __________ eat this after March 4th.
8 You __________ have any experience to work here.

3 B Grammar ***must, may, might, can't***

a Circle the correct verbs.

A Isn't that Grant Duncan, over there?
B No, it [1](**can't**) / **must** be. He lives in New York now.
A I'm sure it's Grant.
B Well, I suppose it [2]**can't / might** be him. But his hair is very grey. Grant doesn't have grey hair.
A But it [3]**must / can't** be three years since we last saw him. A man's hair can go grey in three years.
B Who's the woman he's with? She [4]**can't / mightn't** be his wife, can she?
A No, I'm sure it isn't his wife. I think it [5]**may / can't** be his daughter. She looks just like him. Shall we go and say hello?

b Complete the dialogues with *must*, *might*, *might not*, or *can't*.

1 A This pizza ___*can't*___ be for me. It looks like a Margherita and I ordered a Four Seasons.
B It __________ be mine, then. I ordered a Margherita.

2 A What time is Jane coming?
B She wasn't sure. She's working late. She said she __________ be here until 8.30 or 9.00.
A She __________ be very busy, then.

3 A Which city is this?
B I'm not sure. It __________ be Rome.
A No, it __________ be Italy. The street sign is in French.
B It __________ be Paris, then. That's the only place I've been to in France.

4 A Can you help me finish this crossword? I can't do eight across.
B Let's see. An animal found in Australia. It __________ be *kangaroo* or maybe *crocodile*.
B It __________ be *kangaroo*. It ends in a y. I know! It __________ be *wallaby*.
A That's right. Well done!

a Circle the correct verbs. Tick (✓) if both are possible.

Tango dancing

I decided to try to learn tango about six months ago. I've never [1](**been able to**) / **could** dance well, though both my parents are good dancers. I thought: well, if they [2]**could / were able to** do it, I should [3]**can / be able to** learn, too. But the tango's not an easy dance to learn, because the steps aren't fixed, and every eight steps the man has to decide what move he's going to make, and he has to [4]**can / be able to** transmit that to his partner. My first partner and I [5]**weren't able to / couldn't** understand each other at all, so she changed partner. I think my new partner understands me better, so I hope we [6]**will can / will be able to** dance well soon.

Irish

As my family's Irish, I thought I should learn to speak the language. I found a school and started going to classes, but the first problem was that I [7]**couldn't / wasn't able to** go to class every week, and the second was that it's a very difficult language. Also I [8]**wasn't able to / couldn't** find the time do much homework, and trying to learn a language without [9]**can / being able to** study between classes is almost impossible. If [10]**I can / I'm able to** find time to go to Ireland in the summer, I'll definitely try again.

b Complete the sentences where possible with *can* / *can't* or *could* / *couldn't*. If neither is possible, complete with a form of *be able to*.

1 I started reading *War and Peace*, but I *couldn't* finish it. It was too long.

2 I've invited Mark to the party, but I don't think he'll __________ come.

3 You __________ park there. There's not enough room.

4 I want to buy a new car next year, but I haven't __________ save much money yet.

5 He __________ play the piano when he was only four years old.

6 If that car was a bit cheaper, I'd __________ buy it.

7 I like __________ do what I want when I'm on holiday.

8 We don't have to buy the tickets now – we __________ get them on the train.

9 I didn't enjoy the film because I __________ understand what was going on.

10 Excuse me, do you think you __________ help me with my cases?

11 We won't __________ meet tonight, I'm working.

● Complete the emails with the verbs in the correct form: present simple, imperative, or *will* + infinitive.

Time: 23.05
Sender: Corinne
Subject: Final exams!

Hi Elena,

How's it going? I'm studying hard, but I need a break. We could meet tomorrow night for dinner. I [1] *'ll call* (call) you when I [2] __________ (finish) class tomorrow, OK?

Love, Corinne

Time: 23.07
Sender: Elena
Subject: RE: Final exams!

Hi Corinne,

I'm studying too. My first exam is tomorrow afternoon. I'm really worried about it. OK for tomorrow night, but not too early. I [3] __________ (text) you when the exam [4] __________ (finish).

Love, Elena

Time: 23.08
Sender: Corinne
Subject: RE: Final exams!

OK. [5] __________ (come) to my place as soon as you [6] __________ (can). We can phone for a takeaway pizza or something.

Time: 23.09
Sender: Elena
Subject: RE: Final exams!

OK, but [7] __________ (not phone) until I [8] __________ (get) there. I might be late. I've been thinking, if you [9] __________ (be) free when all our exams [10] __________ (be) over in June, why don't we go away for a few days?

Time: 23.10
Sender: Corinne
Subject: RE: Final exams!

Great idea! But I [11] __________ (not be able to) go away unless I [12] __________ (pass) all the exams! We can talk about it when we [13] __________ (meet) here tomorrow night.

Time: 23.11
Sender: Elena
Subject: RE: Final exams!

OK. Time to go back to work. If I [14] __________ (not study) a bit more tonight, I [15] __________ (not have) any chance of passing biology tomorrow. See you tomorrow, and wish me luck!

a Complete the sentences with the correct form of the verbs in brackets to make second conditional sentences.

1 I *wouldn't be* (not be) so broke if I *spent* (spend) a bit less on going out.

2 If I __________ (have) more money, I __________ (can) travel next summer.

3 My parents __________ (be) happier if I __________ (not go out) so much.

4 Maybe if I __________ (share) a flat with friends, I __________ (get on) better with my parents.

5 If I __________ (go) to bed earlier, I __________ (not be) so tired all the time.

6 If I __________ (paint) my room white, then it __________ (not look) so depressing.

7 I __________ (feel) a lot better if I __________ (go) to the gym more.

8 I __________ (not argue) with my brother if he __________ (not borrow) my things all the time.

9 If my girlfriend __________ (not have to) work so hard, we __________ (can) see each other more often.

10 If I __________ (do) something with my life instead of just thinking about it, maybe things __________ (improve).

b First or second conditional? Complete the sentences with a verb from the list in the correct form.

can   be   ~~catch~~   not drive   not eat   not have   look   have   not reduce   see

1 If we hurry, *we 'll catch* the earlier train. It leaves in three minutes.

2 If it wasn't so windy, we __________ have lunch in the garden.

3 They'll never sell their house if they __________ the price.

4 If you __________ James, tell him to phone me. I need to speak to him urgently.

5 If I __________ you, I'd buy the black dress. It's much more 'you'.

6 He won't pass his driving test if he __________ a few more lessons.

7 If I __________ more time, I'd do it myself.

8 I __________ to work if public transport was better in this town.

9 Gavin __________ that soup if it has meat in it. He's a strict vegetarian.

10 Your sister __________ much better if she cut her hair a bit shorter.

Nacho and Luciana as students

Nacho and Luciana today

● Look at the table and complete the sentences with a correct form of *used to* or the present simple.

	then	now
Occupation	university students	Nacho: journalist, Luciana: psychologist
Residence	Buenos Aires, Argentina	Barcelona, Spain
Hopes and dreams	go into politics	that their son is happy and successful
Personality	relaxed, quite lazy	very worried about work; hard-working
House	shared a flat with other students	apartment, with 18-year-old son
Holidays	hitchhiking	go to small apartment on the Costa Brava
Musical tastes	pop and rock; Luciana: disco	jazz, classical, tango
Vehicle	bikes; Nacho: an old scooter	cars; son has motorbike
Clothes	informal	similar, but more expensive taste
Body type	slim	getting a bit overweight
Food	vegetarians	omnivores
Friends	lots of friends	just a few close friends

1 Nacho ___*works*___ as a journalist. **work**
2 They ______________ in Argentina any more. **not live**
3 They ______________ of going into politics. **dream**
4 They ______________ quite lazy. **be**
5 They ______________ about work. **not worry**
6 They ______________ a flat with other students. **share**
7 They ______________ hitchhiking any more. **not go**
8 Luciana ______________ listening to jazz. **not like**
9 They ______________ bikes any more. **not ride**
10 Nacho ______________ an old scooter. **ride**
11 They ______________ more on clothes than before. **spend**
12 Luciana ______________ overweight. **not be**
13 They ______________ meat, but they do now. **eat**
14 They ______________ lots of friends. **have**

The Prime Minister and the Leader of the Opposition are having a debate on live television.

a Circle the correct answer for each gap.

A After four years in government, what have you done? Look at the state of the country: there isn't ______ money for	**1** no / (enough)
pensions, there's ______ unemployment, and	**2** too many / too much
______ children are failing at school.	**3** a lot of / a lot
B Our problem is that we have had very ______ time to	**4** few / little
repair the damage that your government did before us.	
______ people were happy with the Education system	**5** How much / How many
when you were in government? ______!	**6** Any / None
A Nonsense! You don't know what you're doing! And	
______ people in your own party are now saying that,	**7** much / a lot of
too. You say you haven't had ______? I say you don't	**8** enough time / time enough
have ______ ideas!	**9** any / no
B We have ______ of ideas, and they're working!	**10** plenty / many
______ years ago our economy was getting worse; not any	**11** A few / A little
more. We have very ______ unemployment now,	**12** few / little
compared to when you were in government. The people of this	
country are ______ intelligent to believe your ideas again.	**13** enough / too
A Really? Well, I think very ______ of them will be	**14** few / little
convinced by your arguments.	
B The problem is that your party spends ______ time	**15** too much / too
insulting the government, and not ______ time thinking	**16** many / enough
of new ideas.	
C Thank you very much, gentlemen I'm afraid we have	
______ more time today...	**17** any / no

b Now cover the words and look at the conversation. Try to remember the missing words.

Complete the texts with *a*, *an*, *the*, or – (no article).

a

Flat to rent

Located close to Gaudí's masterpiece, [1] *the* Sagrada Familia, this apartment was built in 1993 and is ideal for three people.
There are two bedrooms, one with [2] ______ double bed and one with [3] ______ single bed. [4] ______ windows of [5] ______ large bedroom look onto [6] ______ small terrace.
[7] ______ living room also has [8] ______ terrace, with [9] ______ table and [10] ______ chairs so you can have [11] ______ breakfast in [12] ______ sun.
[13] ______ apartment has [14] ______ air conditioning and central heating.

b

Move your account to **24/7**

24/7 is [1] ______ one of Europe's leading 24-hour personal banks. You can take care of all your banking needs by [2] ______ telephone or online, at [3] ______ time and place that is convenient for you, 24 hours [4] ______ day, 365 days [5] ______ year. We haven't closed since [6] ______ day we opened in 2004. Our friendly and professional staff are always here to help you. You can call or just click to check your account, pay [7] ______ bill, or arrange [8] ______ personal loan.

24/7

Why not do it today? Just complete [9] ______ application form below and return it to: **24/7**, FREEPOST, Manchester MA98 2AJ.

c

Hi Marian,
Hope all is well. Here [1] ______ life is a bit hectic. Jim and I are really busy at [2] ______ work – we hardly ever have time to talk to each other. [3] ______ children are all busy too. Mark has his driving test [4] ______ next Thursday. He should pass, because he has lessons three times [5] ______ week. Tom is working hard at [6] ______ school – he has suddenly decided he wants to be [7] ______ doctor! What [8] ______ surprise! Anna is fine – she's just finished [9] ______ primary school. I must say she is definitely [10] ______ easiest of the three. I suppose that's because she's [11] ______ girl. There's no question that [12] ______ girls are less work than [13] ______ boys.
Can't write more just now, I've got to go to [14] ______ shops before they close.
Love, Sue

a Circle the correct form.

JENNY So how's it going with Luke?
EMILY Well, not bad. He's given up [1]**(smoking) / to smoke** , so that's good.
JENNY What about his friends?
EMILY They're OK. I don't mind [2]**to spend / spending** time with them. They're quite nice really.
JENNY But?
EMILY The thing is, although he says I'm easy [3]**to talk / talking** to, we don't seem [4]**to be able / being able** to communicate very well.
JENNY For example?
EMILY Well, it's difficult [5]**to explain / explaining**. But for example, when I suggested [6]**to go / going** away together, he was very enthusiastic, but when my family invited us [7]**spending / to spend** a week in France with them, he said 'no', but he didn't say why. I need [8]**knowing / to know** where this relationship is going.
JENNY Well, you need [9]**to ask / asking** him. Don't expect him [10]**to read / reading** your mind. Men aren't very good at [11]**to guess / guessing** what other people are thinking.
EMILY Well, I tried [12]**to do / doing** that last Saturday oh, there's my phone. Oh, it's him. Hi, Luke...

b Complete the dialogue with the verbs in the gerund or infinitive with *to*.

ALEX So, have you decided [1] *to ask* (**ask**) her, Luke?
LUKE Well, I was planning [2]__________ (**do**) it yesterday, but then I didn't. What if she says 'no'? [3]__________ (**get**) engaged is such a big step. She might think it's too soon. I'm worried about [4]__________ (**lose**) her.
ALEX You can't afford [5]__________ (**wait**) for ever. You love her, don't you?
LUKE Er, yes, of course. And I love [6]__________ (**be**) with her, I can't stop [7]__________ (**think**) about her.
ALEX Then do it. Phone her now. Invite her out for meal, somewhere really romantic.
LUKE You're right. I'll phone her now. ...Hi, Emily. I just called [8]__________ (**ask**) you if you're doing anything on Friday night. Would you like [9]__________ (**go**) out for a meal?...At Café du Marché...OK. Great. I'll pick you up at 8.00...No, I won't forget [10]__________ (**book**) a table...

c Complete with *to go* or *go*.

1 I really should *go* now. It's getting late.
2 I have ________ to the bank before it closes.
3 When I was a child I used ________ to the beach every summer.
4 Shall I ________ to the supermarket, or will you?
5 My dad won't let me ________ to the Halloween party tonight.
6 Will you be able ________ to the party next weekend?
7 My parents always made me ________ to bed early.

a Read the journalist's interview. Then complete her report with the **bold** verbs in the correct tense.

JOURNALIST Dr Makele, now you said recently in New York that big changes are necessary if we want to avoid a global catastrophe. What changes were you thinking of?

DR MAKELE Well, firstly, we [1]**cannot** continue to use up the world's natural resources at the present rate. Secondly, the richer countries [2]**will have to** allow developing countries to export more. And thirdly, we [3]**are going to** have to devote more resources to fighting diseases such as AIDS.

JOURNALIST And how [4]**can this** be done, Dr Makele?

DR MAKELE Well, [5]**I've just come** from a top-level meeting in Mexico City and there we [6]**agreed** on a series of proposals to take to next month's G8 meeting in Berlin. I [7]**hope** the richer nations [8]**will agree** to help eliminate poverty in the next 20 years. At the same time, we [9]**must** promote responsible government in the developing world.

'Dr Paul Makele of the United Nations told me that we [1] *could not* continue to use up the world's natural resources. He said that rich countries [2] __________ allow developing countries to export more. He added that we [3] __________ have to devote more resources to fighting AIDS. When I asked him how [4] __________ be done, he said that he [5] __________ from a top-level meeting in Mexico City where they [6] __________ on a series of proposals to take to next month's G8 summit in Berlin. Dr Makele said that he [7] __________ the richer nations [8] __________ to help eliminate poverty in the next 20 years. He said that we [9] __________ promote responsible government in the developing world.

b Write some other questions journalists asked Dr Makele in reported speech.

BBC: Who do you think will be the next President of the UN?
1 The BBC asked Dr Makele __________________________.

FOX: Will more countries be present at the next meeting?
2 Fox News asked him __________________________.

RTVE: Have you discussed this with the US president?
3 RTVE asked him __________________________.

RAI: What should the rich countries do to eliminate world poverty?
4 RAI asked him __________________________.

c Complete the reported imperatives / requests using *asked* or *told*.

Can you put your seatbelts on, please?
1 The pilot __________ us __________________.

Don't worry, Toni. Alex is only a friend.
2 She __________ her boyfriend __________________ because Alex was only a friend.

Don't cheat!
3 The teacher __________ us __________________.

Can you slow down, please?
4 He __________ his friend __________________.

Please don't tell anybody.
5 My friend __________ me __________________ anybody.

a Complete the sentences by putting the verbs into the correct passive tense.

DID YOU KNOW...?

1. The country with the smallest film industry is Iceland, where only three films *are made* every year. (**make**)
2. More than 26,000 costumes ____________ in the 1963 film *Cleopatra.* (**use**)
3. In the near future more films ____________ on computers than at the cinema. (**see**)
4. The most filmed character is Sherlock Holmes. Until now, more than 200 different films ____________ about him. (**make**)
5. Spielberg's film *The Color Purple* ____________ for 11 Oscars in 1985, but didn't win any. (**nominate**)
6. Macaulay Culkin ____________ $4.5 million dollars for his role in *Home Alone* in 1990. (**pay**) This was a record for a child at the time.
7. The director Stanley Kubrick died while his film *Artificial Intelligence* ____________ (**make**). Spielberg ____________ to finish the film. (**ask**)
8. When the actress Marilyn Monroe died of a drugs overdose in 1962, many people believed that she ____________ by the CIA. (**murder**)
9. Over 300,000 extras ____________ for the crowd scenes in the film *Gandhi.* (**use**)
10. At this very moment, thousands of films ____________ all over the world. (**make**)

b Active or passive? Circle the correct form.

Films to collect on DVD: *The Piano*

The Piano [1](won) / **was won** the Palme d'Or at the Cannes Film Festival in 1993. It [2]**directed / was directed** by Jane Campion, and it starred Holly Hunter and Harvey Keitel. It [3]**set / is set** in New Zealand in the 19th century, and is about a Scottish woman, Ada, who [4]**sends / is sent** there by her parents to marry a local man. She only [5]**takes / is taken** two things with her: her daughter and her piano. Ada never [6]**speaks / is spoken**, and has a very unhappy time with her new husband, who is a violent man. Ada [7]**falls / is fallen** in love with a neighbour and finally she [8]**rescues / is rescued** by him from her husband, and in her new life she [9]**learns / is learned** to speak again. The unforgettable soundtrack [10]**wrote / was written** by Michael Nyman, and millions of copies of the CD [11]**have sold / have been sold** all over the world.

a Complete the text with *who*, *which*, *where*, or *whose*.

A place? A song? A number? An object? A person? An animal? A shop? A photo?

We ask readers to tell us about things which have a special meaning for them. This week, the TV actor Gavin Jones.

'Well, I've chosen Paris because it's the place [1] ___*where*___ I lived for the first ten years of my life. A song? Well, that has to be Eurythmics singing *Sweet dreams are made of this* because it was the song [2]__________ was playing in the background in the pub at the exact moment when I met my girlfriend. My number is 13. It's a number [3]__________ some people think is unlucky, but it's my date of birth and it's lucky for me. For the object in my house I have chosen an antique camera [4]__________ was a present from my parents. The person is Kenneth Branagh. He's the actor [5]__________ inspired me when I was a student. My animal is a cat, because they are the animals [6]__________ I like most in the world. A shop? That was easy – one called Blackwell's, in Oxford Street in London, because it's the place [7]__________ I worked for a year after finishing university. And the last thing is a photo, a photo of someone [8]__________ is very important in my life but [9]__________ name I'm not going to tell you.'

b In which sentences could you also use *that*?

c In which sentences could you leave out *who*, *which*, etc.?

d Combine the two sentences using a non-defining relative clause.

1 Our neighbours are both chemists. They work for the same pharmaceutical company.
Our neighbours, ___*who are both chemists*___, work for the same pharmaceutical company.

2 Pablo Picasso's best-known painting is *Guernica*. He was born in Málaga in 1881.
Pablo Picasso, ____________________, was born in Málaga in 1881.

3 Canberra is the capital of Australia. It's smaller than Sydney and Melbourne.
Canberra, ____________________, is smaller than Sydney and Melbourne.

4 Our local post office has closed down. I used to work there.
Our local post office, ____________________, has closed down.

5 Mrs Bradbury is my mother's best friend. Her daughter is the local doctor.
Mrs Bradbury, ____________________, is my mother's best friend.

6 George Best was possibly the most talented British footballer of his generation. He died in 2005.
George Best, ____________________, was possibly the most talented British footballer of his generation.

7 The hurricane caused millions of dollars' worth of damage. It was the worst for over 75 years.
The hurricane, ____________________, caused millions of dollars' worth of damage.

8 My sister is a clothes designer. She's opening her own company next month.
My sister, ____________________, is opening her own company next month.

a Put the words in the correct order to make conditional sentences.

1 would / ~~he~~ / scored / ~~if~~ / had / the / they / have / won / match

If he *had scored, they would have won the match*.

2 have / my / it / wonderful / won / hadn't / this / director / if / ~~I~~ / been / for / wouldn't / Oscar

I ________________________________.

3 married / ~~you~~ / you / him / wouldn't / ~~if~~ / listened / me / have / had / to

If you ________________________________.

4 test / driven / passed / red / ~~I~~ / light / would / I / have / my / if / a / hadn't / through

I ________________________________.

5 known / that / I / thrown / ~~if~~ / was / important / ~~I~~ / had / wouldn't / it / away / have / the letter

If I ________________________________.

6 in / had / their / ~~he~~ / diary / if / his / forgotten / written / it / he / wouldn't / anniversary / have

He ________________________________.

b Put the verbs in brackets in the correct tense to make third conditional sentences.

1 I *would have enjoyed* (enjoy) university more if I *had chosen* (chose) a different subject.
2 We __________ (arrive) half an hour earlier if we __________ (not get) lost.
3 If I __________ (know) how cold it was going to be in London, I __________ (take) a warmer coat.
4 Andrea __________ (do) much better in the exam if she __________ (not be) so nervous.
5 It was raining a lot. If we __________ (not take) a taxi, we __________ (get) completely wet.
6 If we __________ (not sit) next to each other on the plane, we __________ (never / meet).

7B Grammar **question tags, indirect questions**

a Complete the dialogues with the correct question tags.

MOTHER What is it, Paula? What's wrong, love?
PAULA Nothing.
MOTHER It's not school, 1 *is it* ?
PAULA No, it's not school. School's OK.
MOTHER You aren't having problems with the other children, 2 ________?
PAULA No, I'm not. Everything's fine, Mum.
MOTHER And you're enjoying school, 3 ________?
PAULA Enjoying school? I don't know; it's OK.
MOTHER You're not feeling sick, 4 ________?
PAULA I feel fine, Mum.
MOTHER You haven't had an argument with one of your friends, 5 ________?
PAULA Of course not. We never argue.
MOTHER Paula, you would tell me if something was wrong, 6 ________?
PAULA Yes, Mum. Now will you please leave me alone?

FATHER You know how to print digital photos from the computer, 7 ________?
EMILY Yes, Dad, I told you how to do it you last week, 8 ________?
FATHER But you can tell me how to do it again, 9 ________? I've done everything you said, but nothing's happening.
EMILY OK. The computer's switched on, 10 ________?
FATHER Of course it is. I'm not stupid.
EMILY And the printer?
FATHER What?
EMILY Oh Dad, you forgot to turn the printer on again, 11 ________? Parents! They never learn.

b Complete the indirect questions that these people ask strangers.

1 Excuse me, could tell me *what this says* ?

2 Excuse me, could you tell us ________________________?

3 Excuse me, could you tell us ________________________ to Edinburgh?

4 Excuse me, do you know ________________________?

5 Excuse me, could you tell us ________________________?

a Complete the text with the correct particles from the list.

on ~~back~~ down off in out (x2) up

'Hello, Dave? I tried phoning earlier and you told me to call you 1 *back*. Yes, I bought this computer yesterday and it doesn't work. And neither do the speakers nor the webcam. Can you help me sort it 2 __________? What? Of course I've plugged it 3 __________! And yes, I've turned it 4 __________, too. I tried to read the instructions, but I gave 5 __________. They don't make any sense. I can't find 6 __________ how to start it up. Dave, I can't hear you, can you turn 7 __________ the music, please?...What? You want me to switch it 8 __________ and start all over again? OK. Here we go...'

b Complete the text with the correct verbs from the list.

calm get go going growing ~~looking~~ set

'Oh yes, leaving the city and coming to live here was the best thing we've ever done. I have to tell you, I wasn't 1 *looking* forward to it at all. I thought that I'd miss 2 __________ out in the evenings, the cinemas, the theatres and all the things you can do in a city. But we love it here. The kids are 3 __________ up in a clean, healthy environment, and they 4 __________ on very well with the other kids in the village school, so that's good. And we don't have to rush everywhere any more, I've managed to 5 __________ down, which is exactly what my doctor told me to do. And Tom, that's my husband, has been able to 6 __________ up his own business, and work from home. I wouldn't want to 7 __________ back to the city now.'

c Are the **bold** phrases right (✓) or wrong (✗)? Correct the wrong ones.

1 I'm broke. **Can you pay me back** the money I lent you? ✓

2 These words are all new, so please **write down them**.

3 Your room's in a mess. Please **put your clothes away**.

4 My sister **is looking a new job for**.

5 The match **will soon be over**.

6 Shall **I pick up you** at the airport?

7 I usually **look my little sister after** when she gets home from school.

8 Are you going **to try that dress on**? I think it'll look great on you.

9 **Could you fill this form in**, please, before the plane lands.

10 That's my book! **Give back it**!

Put the verbs in brackets in the correct form.

1 Do you know what time the film ________________? (**finish**)
2 Are you going to carry on ________________ Italian next year? (**study**)
3 Five minutes after we left, I remembered that I________________ the back door. (**not lock**)
4 When I woke up this morning, I could hear that it ________________ very hard. (**rain**)
5 **A** How long ________you ________ English? (**learn**)
B Since October.
6 I'm sorry, but I ________________ come to the meeting on Wednesday. I'm away until Friday. (**be able to**)
7 He asked me what I ________________ and I told him I was a lawyer. (**do**)
8 I'll tell him as soon as I ________________ him. (**see**)
9 I ________________ this computer for at least six years. I need a new one. (**have**)
10 I'm really tired at the moment. I ________________ a holiday! (**need**)
11 If you ________________ so much TV every night, you would have more time for reading. (**not watch**)
12 **A** I'm really hungry.
B ________ I ________ you a sandwich? (**make**)
13 You've been travelling all day. You must ________________ exhausted. (**be**)
14 We can't afford ________________ to that restaurant. It's much too expensive. (**go**)
15 I told Jane ________________ anybody, but of course she told everyone. (**not tell**)
16 He won't pass his exams unless he ________________ a lot harder. (**work**)
17 You ________________ them if you'd arrived five minutes earlier. They've just gone. (**see**)
18 Who do you think ________________ the match tonight? (**win**)
19 We can't use the lift because it ________________ at the moment. (**repair**)
20 **A** You look exhausted!
B I am. I ________________ in the garden all morning. (**work**)

18–20 **Excellent**. You can use the verb tenses from *New English File Intermediate* very well.
13–17 **Quite good**, but check the rules in the Grammar Bank (Student's Book *p.130*) for any questions that you got wrong.
0–12 **This is difficult for you.** Read the rules in the Grammar Bank (Student's Book *p.130*). Then ask your teacher for another photocopy and do the exercise again at home.

Getting to know you

A pairwork activity

This photocopiable 'getting to know you' activity can be used together with the Grammar activities on pages 140 and 141 as a first-day class, especially if your SS do not yet have the Student's Book.

SS write information about themselves. They then swap with a partner and ask each other to explain the information.

Copy one page of questions and spaces (**A** or **B**) per student.

LANGUAGE	General revision of pre-intermediate grammar and vocabulary

- Put SS in pairs and give each student a chart and a sheet of instructions (**A** or **B**).
- Give SS five minutes to write answers in the appropriate spaces. When they have finished, take back the instruction sheet or tell them to turn it over.
- Now get SS to swap charts. Demonstrate the activity by taking a chart from a student and asking him / her *Why did you write…?* Ask follow-up questions too, to continue the conversation.
- SS now do the activity in pairs. Make it clear to them that they had different instructions, and stress that they can ask about the information in any order. Monitor and help where necessary. Stop the activity when most SS have asked about all their partner's information.

1A A time for everything

A pairwork information gap speaking activity

SS read different parts of a text about chronobiology (the best time of day to do certain activities), and then share the information with their partner to establish the 'ideal' daily routine. Copy one sheet per person.

LANGUAGE	Present simple Daily routine: *What time do you usually have lunch?*

- Put SS in pairs and give out the sheets.
- Focus on **a** and the chart. Highlight that we are talking about when it is best for your body to do these activities, not when it suits you best. Elicit ideas for the first one (*have a big meal*) and tell SS to complete the chart with what they think.
- Set a time limit, e.g. five minutes, for SS to talk and complete the **We think** column.
- Now focus on the text, and read the introduction aloud with SS. Then get **A** to read the first part of the article, and **B** the second part. **Tell SS not to read each other's text**.
  Monitor and help with any unknown vocabulary.
- Now in pairs, SS look at the chart and help each other complete the **Expert opinion** column with an exact time (e.g. 7–8 a.m.), i.e. they must tell each other what is the best time (and why) to do the things they read about in *their* text.
- Check answers. Then get SS to compare the answers with what they had predicted.

1 12–2 p.m.	**7** 8–10 p.m.
2 10–11 p.m.	**8** 7–9 a.m.
3 4–6 p.m.	**9** 6–8 p.m.
4 9–10 a.m.	**10** 6–8 p.m.
5 11 p.m.–7 a.m.	**11** 3–5 p.m.
6 10 a.m.–12	**12** 7–9 a.m.

Extra support SS could now swap and read the other part of the article that they didn't read.

d Now ask SS how many of them have their big meal between 12 and 2, and find out what time the others have it and why. SS continue in pairs, saying when they do each thing.

- Finally get feedback to find out which SS do most things at the 'best' time.

Extra idea You could as a final activity tell the class about yourself and when you do some of these things and why.

1B What a cheat!

A pairwork activity

SS complete different texts about cheating in sport with verbs in the right tense (past simple, continuous, or perfect) and then memorize and tell each other their story. Copy one sheet per pair and cut into **A** and **B**.

LANGUAGE	Past tenses Sport vocabulary

- Put SS into pairs and get them to sit face to face if possible. Give out the sheets. Explain that they each have a different true story about cheating in sport.
- Focus on **a**. Give SS a few minutes to read the story, and then complete the numbered spaces with the verbs in the box.
- Check answers by copying the key onto the board.

Rosie Ruiz	Ben Johnson
1 came	**1** was competing
2 won	**2** were waiting
3 became	**3** noticed
4 noticed	**4** began
5 wasn't sweating	**5** had won
6 investigated	**6** had beaten
7 had seen	**7** said
8 said	**8** lasted
9 had seen / saw	**9** had taken / took
10 took	**10** took
11 had finished / finished	**11** gave
12 had cheated / cheated	**12** discovered

Extra support You could get two **A**s and two **B**s to work together to complete their stories.

- Focus on **b**. Explain that SS are now going to tell each other their stories, and ask their partner a final question about the story.
- Give SS time to re-read and memorize the story.
- Now get **A** to tell **B** from memory about Rosie Ruiz, and then ask **B** the final question (instruction **c**). They should try to tell the story from memory but can use their texts as prompts where necessary.
- **B** then does the same for Ben Johnson and asks the final question **c**.
- Get feedback by asking SS who they think was the worse cheat and why.

1 C Future questions

A group activity

SS pick questions about the future to ask other people in their group. Copy and cut up one set of cards per 3 or 4 SS.

LANGUAGE	Future forms (*going to*, *will* and present continuous)

- Put SS in groups of 3 or 4 and give each group a set of cards face down.
- SS take turns to pick a card and ask the question to the other people in the group. Remind them to use *What about you?* when they repeat the question to the second or third student.
- Demonstrate by picking a card yourself and asking one group. Ask extra questions for more information, to encourage SS to do the same.
- SS then continue. Monitor and correct any mistakes with future forms.
- Stop the activity when one group has asked all the questions, or when you think it has gone on long enough.

Non-cut alternative Copy one sheet per pair of SS, and cut in half. Put SS in pairs (preferably sitting face to face) and give them one half each. **A** asks **B** his / her first question. **B** answers, and then returns the question by saying *What about you?* Then **B** asks **A** his / her first question.

2 A Numbers quiz

A pairwork activity

SS practise saying big numbers, percentages, etc. Copy one sheet per pair and cut into **A** and **B**.

LANGUAGE	Numbers, fractions, percentages, etc.

- Focus on **a**. Put SS into pairs and give out the sheets. Explain that they should circle what they think is the right answer to each question.
- Quickly go through all the questions to make sure SS understand everything, e.g. *bones*, *snail*, *MP* (member of parliament), *cheetah*. Refer SS to the pictures.

Extra support You could put SS in groups of four and have two **A**s and two **B**s.

- Focus on **b**. **A** now checks his / her answers saying to **B**, e.g. *I think the population of London is three million five hundred thousand.* **B** has to decide if **A** has said the number correctly. **A** gets one point for choosing the right number, and one point for saying the number correctly, so there is a possible total of 16 points for the whole quiz.
- Now **B** checks his/her answers in the same way.
- Get feedback to see if any SS got 16 points!

Extra idea You could divide the whole class in two and do this as a team game.

2 B How long have you been doing it?

A class mingle

SS have a question which they use to survey the rest of the class. Copy and cut up one sheet per 12 SS.

LANGUAGE	Present perfect simple and continuous: *How long have you been driving? For ten years.*

- If you have more than 12 SS, divide the class into two groups and make them move to different sides of the class. Give each student a different question card. Tell SS to work out what the second question is (they must use either the present perfect simple or continuous), but not to write it. Elicit and check the questions before SS start the activity.

Driving: How long have you been driving?
Glasses: How long have you been wearing them?
Close friend: How long have you known him / her?
Exercise: How long have you been going there?
Home: How long have you lived/have you been living there?
Languages: How long have you been learning it?
This school: How long have you been coming here?
Musical instrument: How long have you been playing it?
Sport: How long have you been playing it?
Restaurant: How long have you been going there?
Book: How long have you been reading it?
Car: How long have you had it?

Extra support You could let SS write down their second question on the card.

- Now tell SS they have to ask their question to all the other SS in the class or group and make a note of the answers.
- SS stand up and mingle, asking their questions. If you have two groups, get them to mingle in different halves of the classroom. Take part in the mingle yourself, and monitor.
- When SS have asked everyone their questions, get them to sit down.
- Get feedback for each card to find out who has been doing each activity the longest.

Non-cut alternative Copy one sheet per pair of SS, and cut in half. Put SS in pairs (preferably sitting face to face) and give them one half each. **A** asks **B** his / her first question. **B** answers, and then returns it, saying *What about you?* Then **B** asks **A** his / her first question. They find out between the two of them who has been doing each thing the longest.

2C Questionnaire

A pairwork questionnaire

SS revise comparatives and superlatives by completing a questionnaire with comparatives or superlatives and then asking and answering the questions. Copy one sheet per pair and cut into **A** and **B**.

LANGUAGE	Comparatives and superlatives

- Put SS into pairs and give out the questionnaires.
- Focus on the adjectives / adverbs and tell SS to complete each question with a comparative or superlative of the adjective / adverb.

⚠ Tell SS that there may be two comparatives or two superlatives – it is not always one of each.

- Check answers. You could copy the key onto the board, so that SS don't actually hear each other's questions yet.

A	B
more active	harder
the most unhealthy	more healthily
more often	more enjoyable
the furthest	the worst
the most useful	the most difficult
easier	higher
the most relaxing	the most often
the best	the best
more safely	closer
the most talkative	the laziest

- Now focus on **b**. Get SS (sitting face to face if possible) to ask and answer the questions. They can either ask alternate questions, or **A** can interview **B** and they then swap roles. If there's time, they could also return the questions asking *What about you?*

3A Are they true?

A pairwork speaking activity

SS read about laws and customs from around the world. Together they have to discuss and then decide whether they are true or not. Copy one sheet per pair.

LANGUAGE	*You have to… You don't have to…* *You should… You shouldn't…* *You must… You mustn't…*

- Put SS into pairs and give out the sheets. Focus on **a**. Highlight that four of the laws and customs are false.
- Give SS a few minutes to read all the laws and customs. Then set a time limit, e.g. ten minutes, for pairs to discuss each law and custom one by one and to decide if it is true or false.
- Check answers and see if any pair correctly identified the four false laws. The false ones are 3, 5, 16 and 19. The othes are all true (as far as we know!)
- Focus on **b**. Tell SS to go through each law / custom and decide which three laws they would like to have in their country.
- Get feedback to decide which three are the most popular.

3B Spot the difference

A pairwork information gap activity

SS describe their pictures and find ten differences between them. Copy one sheet per pair and cut into **A** and **B**.

LANGUAGE	Appearance / age: *He's short and a bit overweight.*

- Pre-teach any words that you think SS may have forgotten for clothes or appearance, and remind SS that to refer to each person they will need to say, e.g. *the first / second man on the left / right*, etc.
- Put SS in pairs, ideally face to face, and give out the sheets. **Make sure SS can't see each other's sheets.**
- Explain that they both have the same picture, but it has been changed so that there are ten differences.
- Get **A** to start by describing the first person on the left e.g. *She's quite short. She has shoulder-length hair…* **B** should listen, and ask questions if necessary, to see if there are any differences. Then **B** describes the next person.
- SS continue in pairs. When they have found the differences they can show each other the pictures to make sure they have identified the differences correctly.
- Check the differences orally with the class.

1. In picture **A** the woman on the left has **shoulder-length hair**. In **B** she has **long straight hair.**
2. In picure **A** the woman **isn't carrying a bag**. In **B** she **is.**
3. In picture **A** the man on the left has **a beard and a moustache.** In **B** he only has **a moustache.**
4. In picture **A** the woman in the middle has **short, curly hair**. In **B** she has a **ponytail and a fringe.**
5. In picture **A** the woman in the middle is wearing **trousers.** In **B** she is wearing a **skirt**.
6. In picture **A** the man in the middle is **quite tall.** In **B** he is **quite short**.
7. In picture **A** the man in the middle has **short dark hair.** In **B** he is bald.
8. In picture **A** the tall woman on the right **isn't wearing glases.** In **B** she **is.**
9. In picture **A** the man on the right is quite **slim.** In **B** he is **well-built.**
10. In picture **A** the man on the right is **wearing a watch.** In **B** he **isn't.**

3C Find someone who…

A class mingle

SS ask each other questions to complete a survey. Copy one sheet per student.

LANGUAGE	*can, could,* and *be able to*: *Would you like to be able to travel more?*

- Elicit the questions 1–10.

1. Would you like to be able to travel more?
2. Will you be able to come to the next class?
3. Could you swim before you were four years old?
4. Have you been able to speak English outside class this week?
5. Can you park in very small spaces?

6 Would you like to be able to speak another language?
7 Can you make good cakes?
8 Have you been able to do all the homework this week?
9 Can you ski?
10 Do you need to be able to speak English in your job (or in a job you'd like to do)?

⚠ Make sure SS don't try and ask negative questions for questions 2, 5, 8 and 9.

- Focus on the **More information** column and elicit follow-up questions for questions 1 and 2 to help SS get the idea, e.g. *Where to? Why can't you travel now?*
- Demonstrate the activity. Ask a student the first question: '*Would you like to be able to travel more?*. Elicit 'Yes, I would.' or 'No, I wouldn't.' If the student answers 'Yes', write their name in the column on your sheet, then ask a follow-up question, and write the answer under **More information**. If the student answers 'No' then say 'Thank you' and ask another student until somebody answers 'Yes.'
- Tell SS to try to find and write the name of a different student for each question. SS mingle, asking each other the questions, follow-up questions, and writing in names and more information.
- Get feedback to find out who in the class would like to be able to travel more, etc. You may need to teach *nobody*.

4A Sentence halves

A class mingle

SS mingle and try to match their sentence halves to others. Copy and cut up one sheet per 18 SS. Each student should have one beginning and one end of a sentence. If you have more than 18 SS give the same cards to two students, or invent some more. If you have a very small class give more cards to each student.

⚠ Make sure that all beginnings and ends are given out. If you have an odd number of SS you could take some cards yourself.

LANGUAGE	First conditionals and future time clauses: *As soon as I know anything, I'll call you.* *We won't get a cheap flight unless we book early.*

- Give out two cards to each student, one beginning and one ending of a sentence. The endings are all on shaded cards. Explain or demonstrate the activity. SS must move around the class saying their sentence beginnings to each other, and seeing if it matches an ending. When they think they have found a match, the student who has the ending of the sentence should give it to the student who has the beginning.
- The activity finishes when everyone has found their matching ending, and has one complete sentence (or more if you have given each student more than one beginning).
- Get SS to sit down, and check by getting each student to read out his / her sentences.

As soon as I know anything, I'll call you.
We can't go out until it stops raining.
Hannah will be really angry when she finds out.
You'll feel better if you take an aspirin.
I'll never finish this today unless you help me.
Write that down before you forget it.
He would like to retire when he's 55.
I'm not going to start the class until everyone stops talking.
I'll go to the bank as soon as it opens.
Jack won't leave home until he gets a job.
I can't buy the food until I know how many people are coming to lunch.
We won't get a cheap flight unless we book early.
If you make a noise, you'll wake the baby up.
Unless we run we won't catch the bus.
Turn off all the lights and lock the door before you go to bad.
We won't catch the 6 o'clock train unless we get a taxi to the station.
You can go home as soon as you finish the exercises.
When I leave school I want to go to university.

Non-cut alternative Copy one sheet per student (or pair of SS). In pairs, SS have to match the sentence halves (by writing '1' next to the first beginning and then '1' next to its ending, etc.). When they have finished, check answers. Then **B** puts his / her sheet face down, and **A** reads the first nine beginnings to see if **B** can remember the endings. Then **B** does the same with the final nine.

4B If you had to choose...

A pair or groupwork activity

SS ask questions about preferences, either to a partner or small group. SS have to say which alternative they would prefer and why. Copy one sheet per pair or small group. You can personalize the activity if you want by inventing more alternatives yourself.

LANGUAGE	Second conditionals: *I would prefer to live in a small village, because it would be quieter and more healthy.*

- Put SS in pairs or small groups and give out the sheets.
- Demonstrate the activity by getting a student to ask you one of the questions. Answer in as much detail as possible. SS then continue either asking their partner the question or asking all the people in the group. Tell the other student(s) to return the question using *What about you?*
- While SS are talking, go round and monitor, correcting any mistakes with conditionals.
- When the activity finishes, get feedback from a few pairs or groups.

4C Am I telling the truth?

A pairwork activity

SS talk about their childhood, sometimes inventing information and sometimes telling the truth. Their partner asks questions to find out if their partner is telling the truth or inventing their answers. Copy one sheet per pair and cut into **A** and **B**.

LANGUAGE	*used to*: *I used to love playing 'Monopoly.'* *Who did you use to play with?*

- Put SS in pairs, ideally face to face, and hand out the sheets. Focus on instruction **a**. Give SS a few moments to complete the circles with real or invented information.
- Focus on **b** and **c** and get SS to read the instructions. Then demonstrate the activity. Get one student to tell you about

his / her first circle. Then ask several questions, and finally say *I think you're telling the truth* (or *I don't think you are telling the truth*). You could also choose one circle and tell SS your own answer, and get them to ask you questions.

- SS continue in pairs, each speaking about one circle alternately.
- Get feedback from some of the pairs to find out if they were good at spotting when their partner wasn't telling the truth.

5A Lifestyle survey

A pairwork activity

SS compare information about their diet, lifestyle, etc. and practise using quantifiers. Copy one sheet per pair and cut into **A** and **B**.

LANGUAGE	Quantifiers: *How much free time do you have? Not enough.*

- Put SS into pairs and give out the sheets. Focus on **a**, and give SS a few moments to read all their question prompts. Then focus on **b** and on the expressions SS should use in their answers.

Extra support Drill all the questions with the whole class.

- Demonstrate the activity by getting an **A** and a **B** to ask you their first question. Answer with an expression from the box, and then explain it, and elicit follow-up questions.
- SS ask and answer in pairs. Get them to ask alternate questions, and, if there's time, to return the questions with *What about you?*
- Get some feedback from the class.

5B Generally speaking

A group discussion

SS practise generalizing by discussing topics in small groups. Copy one sheet per group of 3 or 4 and cut into cards.

LANGUAGE	Not using *the* for generalizing: *I think dogs make the best pets because…*

- Put SS in groups of 3 or 4. Try to have a mixture of sexes where possible, as this always helps to promote disagreement. Give out one set of cards to each group and put face down.
- Pick up the top card from one group and read it out. Say whether you agree or disagree, and give a reason.
- SS continue in groups. One student picks a card and reads it out, says whether he / she agrees or not, giving reasons, and the others then say what they think. Monitor and correct any misuse of the definite article.
- Get some feedback to see whether, generally speaking, SS agree or disagree with the sentences.

Extra support You could write some useful expressions on the board for SS to use, e.g. *I agree / don't agree, (Personally,) I think…, In my opinion…, For example,….* Remind SS not to use the definite article the when they generalize.

Non-cut alternative Give one sheet to each pair or group and get them to discuss the statements one by one.

5C Can you guess?

A pairwork activity

SS complete sentences by guessing real information about their partner. Copy one sheet per pair and cut into **A** and **B**.

LANGUAGE	Gerunds and infinitives: *(I think) you would like to learn to ski.*

- Demonstrate the activity by writing on the board: *When you go away on holiday, you love… .* Elicit that you need to continue with a gerund. Then tell SS to gues what *you* love doing on holiday. Elicit answers and then tell the class what you *really* love doing.
- Sit SS in pairs, ideally face to face, and give out the sheets. **They must not look at what their partner writes.** Tell them to complete the sentences, trying to guess how their partner would complete each sentence. Monitor and check that they are using gerunds and infinitives correctly.
- Now SS take turns to read their completed sentences to their partner, who tells them if they have guessed correctly or not. Encourage them to react by contradicting what their partner has said, and then giving the real answer if the guess is wrong, e.g. *No, I don't. I hate sunbathing! But I love walking / reading,* etc.
- Get feedback from several pairs and find out who, in the pair, had more correct guesses.

Extra challenge If you want to give more practice, get SS to repeat the activity but swapping roles **A** and **B**.

6A Who asked what?

A group mingle

SS survey each other with one question each. Then the rest of the class have to remember which question each person asked, and the person reports the answers. Copy and cut up one set of cards per 20 SS. If you have a bigger class, invent a few more questions or give one question card to two SS.

LANGUAGE	Reported speech: *Jacek asked me if I had a pet.*

- Give each student a card with a question, and tell them to memorize it. Then tell them they have to survey the rest of the class by asking everyone the question. They should quickly and briefly note down everyone's answers.
- SS mingle, asking all other SS their question and making a note of the answers.
- When all SS have asked everyone, tell them to sit down.
- Now put SS in pairs, and have them try to remember which question each person asked, and then write it in reported speech (see LANGUAGE box). Set a time limit.
- Check answers. Point to one SS, and then ask somebody else in the class *What did (Jacek) ask you?*

Extra idea If there's time, you could get each student to briefly give the result of his / her survey. They should just give the most significant fact, e.g. *Ten people in the class have never changed a wheel on a car. Eight people said that oranges were their favourite fruit.* It will help to give the class a couple of examples.

Non-cut alternative Copy one sheet per pair and cut in half. SS ask and answer the questions. Then take away the sheets and give SS five minutes to try to write down in reported speech the ten questions they were asked.

6 B Cinema quiz

A pair or group quiz

SS answer questions about the cinema. Copy one sheet per pair or group.

LANGUAGE	The passive Cinema vocabulary

- Divide the class into pairs, small groups or teams. If you think your SS know a lot about the cinema, they could do the quiz in pairs. If not, groups of 4 or even teams may work better.
- Give out one quiz to each pair or group, and place it face down. Big teams may need more than one copy.
- When you say 'Go' SS turn over the sheet. Set a time limit for them to choose the right answers.
- Check answers, where possible making SS give you the whole sentence (not just saying **a**, **b**, or **c**).

Films
1 b **2** c **3** a
Places
1 Paris c, Tokyo a, London b **2** b **3** a
Music
1 b **2** a **3** b
People
1 c **2** a **3** b (Quentin Tarantino)
Famous lines
1 e **2** b **3** d **4** c **5** a
Film titles
1 Close Encounters of the Third Kind
2 The Chronicles of Narnia: The Lion, the Witch and the Wardrobe
3 Dead Poets' Society
4 Crocodile Dundee
5 Four Weddings and a Funeral
6 The Godfather
7 A Hundred and One Dalmatians
8 Kill Bill
9 Mission Impossible
10 Silence of the Lambs

6 C Which definition is right?

A group card game

SS play a definitions game in groups of 4 or 6. Copy and cut up one set of cards per 12–18 SS (see below). You will need at least two cards per group.

LANGUAGE	relative clauses: *a thing which… a person who…*

- Put SS into small groups of 4–6. The group then divides into two teams, **A** and **B** (two or three SS in each).
- Demonstrate the activity. Write the following word and phonetics on the board: **A broom** /bru:m/.
- Explain that you are going to give three possible definitions of the word. SS have to listen and decide which they think is correct. Now read out the following definitions:

1 It's a small room which is both a bedroom and a sitting room, which students often rent.
2 It's a thing made of wood or plastic which people use to clean the floor.
3 It's the thing in a car which you press to make the car go faster.

- Repeat the definitions, and then get SS to vote by a show of hands as to which they think is the correct one (2).

⚠ If any SS actually know what the word means, ask them not to tell the others.

- Now give each team a card. Tell them they have three words on the card. Each word has a correct definition (ticked) and a false definition. The team has to write one more false definition for each word. Give them at least five minutes to do this.
- When they are ready, each **A** team reads their first word and the three definitions to the **B** team, who have to choose the right one. Then the **B** team reads their first word and definitions. The team that guesses most words right wins.
- If you have time, you could give each team another card (there are enough for each team to have three different cards).

7 A Third conditional game

A group board game

SS revise third conditionals by moving around a board and completing sentences. Copy one sheet per group of 3 or 4.

LANGUAGE	Third conditional: *If I had known it was your birthday, I would have bought you a present.*

- Put SS in groups of 3 or 4 and give each group a copy of the board game. They will also need counters (or pieces of paper) and a coin.
- Explain the rules of the game. SS throw the coin and move one square for heads and two for tails. When they land on a square, they must finish the sentence so that it is grammatically correct and makes sense. Encourage them to use contracted forms. The rest of the group are 'judges', but they should ask the teacher in case of dispute. If the sentence is correct, they can stay on the square they have landed on. If not, they have to go back to where they came from.
- The youngest student in each group starts. If a student lands on the same square as another student has been on previously, he / she must complete the sentence in a different way, e.g. if **A** lands on square 1 and makes the sentence *If it hadn't been subtitled, I wouldn't have understood it*, and then **B** also lands on square 1, he / she can say, e.g. *If it hadn't been subtitled, I wouldn't have gone to see it* or *I would have been very bored*, etc.
- SS play the game in groups. The game finishes when someone reaches the finish square.

Example sentence endings
1 …wouldn't have understood anything.
2 …would have won.
3 …hadn't taken a taxi.
4 …wouldn't have left him.
5 …had taken a map.
6 …had worked harder.

7 ...hadn't been so expensive.
8 ...had told us you were coming.
9 ...would have bought you a present.
10 ...had studied more.
11 ...had loved me.
12 ...hadn't driven so fast.
13 ...would have studied history.
14 ...hadn't had two cups of coffee.
15 ...had phoned earlier.
16 ...would have gone to the zoo.
17 ...hadn't missed the bus.
18 ...had been a bit taller.

7 B The scariest places in London

A pairwork information gap activity

SS role play being tourists and use indirect questions to find out about four 'scary' tourist attractions in London. Copy one sheet per pair and cut into **A** and **B**.

LANGUAGE Indirect questions: *Could you tell me what time the museum closes?*

- Put SS into pairs, ideally face to face and give out the sheets. **Make sure SS can't see each other's sheets.** Go through the instructions.
- First, give SS time to think about their questions, and read their information.

Extra support You could also put all the **A**s in pairs, and all the **B**s in pairs to write their questions.

Sherlock Holmes museum
Could you tell me if the museum opens / is open on Saturdays?
Could you tell me what time it closes?
Could you tell me where it is?
Could you tell me how much an adult's ticket costs / an adult's ticket is?
The Bloody Tower
Could you tell me if the Bloody Tower opens / is open on Sundays?
Could you tell me what time it opens?
Could you tell me what the nearest tube station is?
Could you tell me how much a child's ticket costs / a child's ticket is?
Chamber of Horrors
Could you tell me if the Chamber of Horrors opens / is open on Saturdays?
Could you tell me what time it closes?
Could you tell me what the nearest tube station is?
Could you tell me how much an adult's ticket costsvan adult's ticket is?
The London Dungeon
Could you tell me where the London Dungeon is?
Could you tell me if it opens / is open every day?
Could you tell what time it closes?
Could you tell me how much a child's ticket costs / a child's ticket is?

- **A** plays the role of the tourist first, and asks **B** politely for his / her missing information. Then they swap roles.
- When they have both finished, focus on **c**, and give them a few minutes to decide which place they want to visit. Get feedback to see which place is the most popular.

7 C Phrasal verbs race

A brainstorm activity

SS race to think of answers to questions using phrasal verbs. Copy one sheet per student, or per group of 3 or 4.

LANGUAGE Phrasal verbs (*ask for, break up, check in*, etc.)

- Put SS in pairs or groups of 3 or 4. Give each pair or group a sheet face down.
- Explain that the activity is a race. Each group should have a 'secretary' who writes down the answers. The winner is the pair or group who can find the most correct answers in the time limit. They only have to write one answer to each question unless it specifies more, and if they are stuck with one question, they should move on to the next.
- Set a time limit, e.g. five minutes, and tell SS to start. Give more time if you can see that SS need it.
- When the time limit is up, check answers, encouraging SS to use full sentences, e.g. *When you get to a restaurant the first thing you usually ask for is a table (or a menu).*

Suggested answers (but others are possible)
1 a table, a menu
2 (use a recent example)
3 before you catch a plane, when you arrive at a hotel
4 shoes, a coat (i.e. anything with buttons or laces)
5 by looking on the Internet, phoning the cinema, etc.
6 sugar, bread, potatoes, etc.
7 footballer / actress, etc.
8 Bye.
9 the summer holidays, national holidays, e.g. Christmas
10 (use recent examples)
11 Bill Gates.
12 when they are driving (or talking) too fast
13 a lawyer
14 the lights, the TV, the heating, etc.
15 jogging, tennis, etc.
16 the receipt
17 your seat belt
18 a bank, a cash machine
19 before they play a match or before they train
20 TV, hi-fi, DVD player, etc.

7 Revision

Questions to revise vocabulary and verb forms and tenses

SS ask each other questions about key vocabulary areas using a range of tenses and verb forms from files 1–7. This could either be used as a final 'pre-test' revision or as an oral exam. Copy and cut up one set of cards per pair.

LANGUAGE Grammar and vocabulary of the book

- SS work in pairs. Give each pair a set of cards. Set a time limit, e.g. ten minutes. SS take turns to take a card and talk to their partner about the topic on the card, using the prompts. Encourage SS to ask follow-up questions. Monitor, help, and correct.

Non-cut alternative Make one copy per pair. Give SS a few moments to read through the cards. Then **A** chooses a number for **B** to talk about what's on the card for that number. They continue taking turns to choose a topic for their partner to talk about.

A

a Read your instructions and write your answers in the correct place.

In the star, write your first name and surname.
In circle 1, write the year when you started learning English.
In square 2, write two things you like doing at weekends.
In circle 3, write the number of the month when you were born (e.g. July = 7).
In square 4, write the name of a famous person you admire.
In circle 5, write the name of the last film you saw in the cinema.
In square 6, write the name of the most beautiful city you've ever visited.
In circle 7, write the name of two sports you think are really exciting to watch.
In square 8, write the name of the person you get on with best in your family.
In circle 9, write the name of a famous group or singer you really like (or don't like).
In square 10, write the name of a TV programme you often watch.

b Swap charts with **B**. Ask **B** to explain the information in his /her chart. Ask for more information.

c Explain your answers to **B**.

Why did you write '112'?

Because it's the number of my house.

Which street do you live in?

A

B

a Read your instructions and write your answers in the correct place.

In the star, write your first name and surname.
In circle 1, write the number of brothers and sisters you have.
In square 2, write two things you don't like doing at weekends.
In circle 3, write the number of the house or flat where you live.
In square 4, write the name of a really good friend.
In circle 5, write the name of the place where you spent your last holiday.
In square 6, write the name of a magazine or newspaper you often read.
In circle 7, write the name of a subject you really hate(d) at school.
In square 8, write the name of two kinds of music you really like.
In circle 9, write an animal you have or would like to have as a pet.
In square 10, write the name of a TV personality you really like (or don't like).

b Swap charts with **A**. Explain your answers.

c Ask **A** to explain the information in his / her chart. Ask for more information.

Why did you write 'watching TV and going out with my friends'?

Because they're two things I like doing at weekends.

What kind of programmes do you watch?

B

a Answer the questions in pairs. Complete the **'We think'** column with *morning, midday afternoon, evening* or *night.*

b Now **A** read part 1 of the article on body rhythms, **B** read part 2.

c In pairs, complete the **Expert opinion** column with the exact times. Tell each other why it's the best time of day.

d In pairs say at what time of day you do these things. Who has the 'best' daily routine?

What do you think is the best time of day (for your body) to...?	We think	Expert opinion
1 have a big meal	______	______
2 have a bath	______	______
3 do your maths homework	______	______
4 have an injection	______	______
5 sleep	______	______
6 be creative	______	______
7 phone friends	______	______
8 take vitamins	______	______
9 have a glass of wine	______	______
10 put on face cream	______	______
11 do sport or exercise	______	______
12 eat without putting on weight	______	______

A time for everything

The new science of chronobiology tells us the best time of day to do everything, from writing a poem to taking pills. By following your body's natural daily rhythms, you can get more out of every day.

Part 1

7 a.m.–9 a.m.	Have a good breakfast. The metabolism is at its most active in the morning, and everything you eat at this time gives you energy but doesn't make you put on weight. It's also the best time of day to take vitamins. If you take them in the afternoon or evening, some vitamins can cause indigestion or keep you awake.
9 a.m.–10 a.m.	Go to the doctor's or dentist's. Injections are least painful at this time of day.
10 a.m.–12	Work, study, paint a picture or write a poem. The brain is at its most creative at this time of day.
12–2 p.m.	Eat. This is the best time of the day to have lunch. The digestive system works very efficiently at this time. You should have your big meal of the day now, and not in the evening.
2 p.m.–3 p.m.	Have a siesta. After lunch the body temperature goes down and the brain works more slowly. There are a lot of road accidents at this time of day because drivers fall asleep at the wheel.

Part 2

3 p.m.–5 p.m.	Go to the gym. Physically our body is at its peak now. Most Olympic records are broken at this time of day.
4 p.m.–6 p.m.	Do homework, especially maths. Research shows that children are better at arithmetic at this time of day.
6 p.m.–8 p.m.	Eat and drink (in moderation) and enjoy yourself. Our sense of smell and taste are at their best at this time, so now is the moment for a light but delicious dinner. The liver is also at its most efficient in dealing with alcohol, so it's also the best time of day to have a glass of wine. It is also the time when the skin absorbs cream best, so before dinner is the time to put on face or body cream.
8 p.m.–10 p.m.	Phone your friends. This is the time of day when people most often feel lonely (and it's also cheaper to phone in many parts of the world).
10 p.m.–11 p.m.	Get ready for bed. One of the best ways to make sure you sleep well is to have a hot bath, which will relax your mind and body.
11 p.m.–7 a.m.	Sleep. After 11 o'clock, the metabolism slows down, preparing us for sleep. If we stay awake after midnight, our attention drops dramatically, and this is the time of day when people find it most difficult to concentrate if they are studying or working.

A

a Put the verbs from the list into the story in the past simple, past perfect, or past continuous.

1 come 2 win 3 become 4 notice 5 not sweat 6 investigate 7 see 8 say 9 see 10 take 11 finish 12 cheat

ROSIE RUIZ

ON APRIL 21 1980, 23-year-old Rosie Ruiz 1 _______ first in the Boston Marathon. She 2 _______ the race in the third-fastest time ever recorded for a female runner (two hours, 31 minutes, 56 seconds).

However, the organizers 3 _______ suspicious, because they 4 _______ that when she crossed the finishing line she 5 _______ at all.

When they 6 _______ they found out that none of the course officials 7 _______ her passing checkpoints. Other competitors didn't remember seeing her at all.

Then a few spectators 8 _______ that they 9 _______ Ruiz join the race just for the final kilometre. She had simply sprinted from there to the finish line.

The marathon organizers 10 _______ away Ruiz's medal and gave it to Jacqueline Gareau, who 11 _______ second in the race.

Later they also found out that Ruiz 12 _______ in the New York Marathon, the race she used to qualify for the Boston event, earlier in the same year but in a different way...

b Read the story again and remember it. Tell **B** about Rosie Ruiz.

c Ask **B** *How do you think she cheated in the New York Marathon?* (Answer: She took the underground!)

B

a Put the verbs from the list into the story in the past simple, past perfect, or past continuous.

1 compete 2 wait 3 notice 4 begin 5 win 6 beat 7 say 8 last 9 take 10 take 11 give 12 discover

Ben Johnson

In the Seoul Olympics in 1988, the Canadian runner Ben Johnson was running in the 100 metres final. People called it 'the race of the century' because Johnson 1 _______ against his greatest rival – the American sprinter, Carl Lewis.

When the runners 2 _______ to start the race, some people 3 _______ that Johnson's eyes were yellow.

The race 4 _______ and moments later Johnson was the Olympic champion. His time of 9.72 seconds was a new world record. Johnson was euphoric, because he 5 _______ the gold medal and 6 _______ his American rival, Carl Lewis. After the race, Johnson 7 _______ : 'My name is Benjamin Sinclair Johnson Jnr and this world record will last 50 years, maybe 100 years.'

But he was wrong. His world record 8 _______ only a few hours. That evening, drug tests showed that Johnson 9 _______ steroids before the race.

The Olympic committee 10 _______ away his gold medal and 11 _______ it to Carl Lewis. Johnson was also banned from athletics for two years.

But fifteen years later people 12 _______ some amazing news about Carl Lewis...

b Read the story again and remember it. Tell **A** about Ben Johnson.

c Ask **A** *What do you think people discovered about Carl Lewis?* (Answer: He had also tested positive for drugs in 1988, just before the Seoul Olympics, but the American Olympic committee didn't ban him.)

Where are you going after class?	What are you doing this weekend?	Is anyone in your family getting married soon?	Are you meeting anyone after class?
Are you going out on Friday night?	Where are you having lunch tomorrow?	Are you going away for the weekend soon?	Are you coming to the next English class?
What are you going to do next summer?	Are you going to watch TV tonight? Which programme(s)?	What's the next thing you're going to buy for yourself?	What's the next film you're going to see?
Are you going to use the Internet tonight? Why?	Are you going to cook tonight?	Who do you think is going to get the best marks in the next English exam?	What time are you going to get up tomorrow?
Do you think women's sport will ever be as popular as men's sport?	Do you think people will work more or less in the future?	Do you think you will pass the end-of-year English exam?	Do you think you will ever go and live abroad?
Do you think you will ever speak 'perfect' English?	Do you think you will have the same job all your life?	Do you think you will have more than two children?	Do you think you will live to be more than 80?

A

a Choose what you think is the right answer to each question.

1	What is the approximate population of London?	3,500,000	5,750,000	7,000,000
2	How far is it from New York to Los Angeles?	4,506 km	6,851 km	8,592 km
3	How many countries are there in the United Nations?	124	191	208
4	How far away is the nearest star (not including the sun)? (one light year = about six billion miles)	1.5 light years away	2.75 light years away	4.3 light years away
5	What is $\frac{1}{2}$ divided by $\frac{1}{3}$?	$\frac{1}{4}$	$\frac{1}{5}$	$\frac{1}{6}$
6	How many bones are there in the human body?	206	258	291
7	How far can the fastest snail travel in an hour?	15.2 metres	38.6 metres	48.3 metres
8	How many words does the average woman say a day?	1,400	3,700	6,800

b Tell **B** your answers. He / She will tell you if you are right.

I think the population of London is three million, five hundred thousand.

c Use the information below to correct **B**'s answers.

1 The population of Mexico City is 18,500,000.
2 It is 9,302 km from Moscow to Vladivostok.
3 202 countries took part in the 2004 Athens Olympics.
4 The moon is 384,000 km from the earth.
5 Three quarters of the body is made up of water.
6 19.7% of MPs in the UK are women.
7 A cheetah can run at 100 kph.
8 The average man says 2,400 words a day.

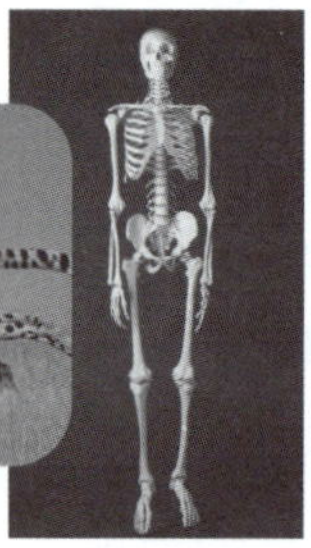

B

a Choose what you think is the right answer to each question.

1	What is the approximate population of Mexico City?	15,500,000	18,500,000	23,000,000
2	How far is it from Moscow to Vladivostok? (route of the trans-Siberian railway)	5,840 km	9,302 km	11,794 km
3	How many countries took part in the 2004 Athens Olympics?	151	202	296
4	How far away is the moon from the earth?	38,400 km	384,000 km	3,840,000 km
5	What proportion of the body is made up of water?	$\frac{3}{4}$	$\frac{1}{2}$	$\frac{1}{3}$
6	What percentage of MPs in the UK are women?	3.5%	19.7%	47.3%
7	At what speed can a cheetah (the fastest mammal) run?	100 kph	150 kph	200 kph
8	How many words does the average man say a day?	1,200	2,400	3,500

b Use the information below to correct **A**'s answers.

1 The population of London is approximately 7,000,000.
2 It is 4,506 km from New York to Los Angeles.
3 There are 191 countries in the United Nations.
4 The nearest star is 4.3 light years from earth.
5 $\frac{1}{2}$ divided by $\frac{1}{3}$ is $\frac{1}{6}$.
6 There are 206 bones in the human body.
7 The fastest land snail can travel 48.3 metres in an hour.
8 The average woman says 6,800 words a day.

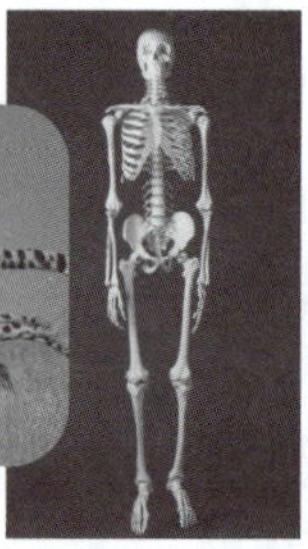

c Tell **A** your answers. He / She will tell you if you are right.

I think the population of Mexico city is twenty-three million.

DRIVING

Do you have a driving licence?
How long / drive?

THIS SCHOOL

Do you like this school?
How long / come here?

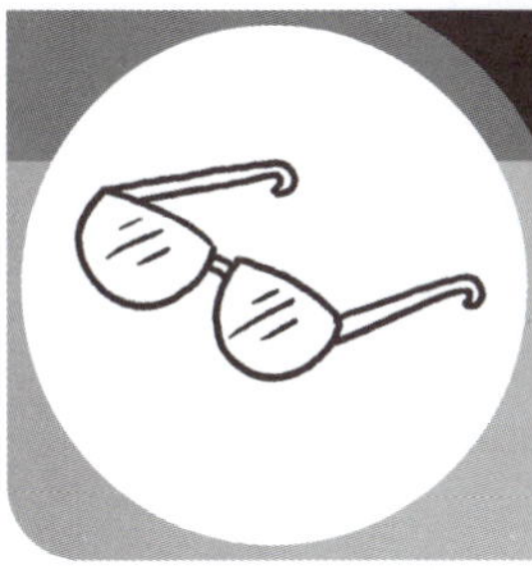

GLASSES

Do you wear glasses or contact lenses?
How long / wear / them?

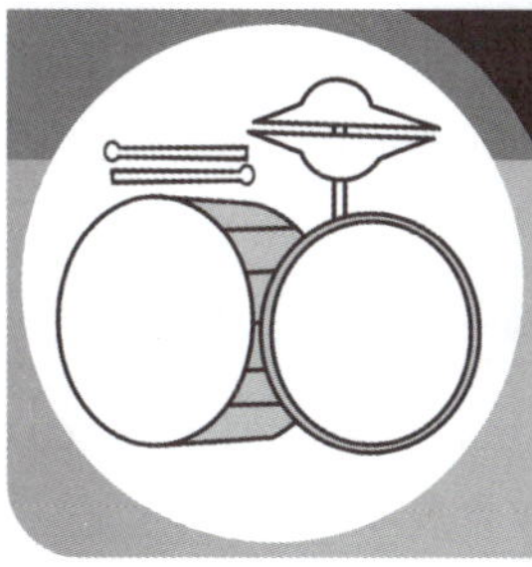

MUSICAL INSTRUMENT

Can you play a musical instrument?
How long / play it?

CLOSE FRIEND

Do you have a close friend?
Male or female?
How long / know him (or her)?

SPORT

Do you play any sport?
How long / play it?

EXERCISE

Do you go to a gym?
How long / go there?

RESTAURANT

Do you have a favourite restaurant?
How long / go there?

HOME

Where do you live?
How long / live there?

BOOKS

What book are you reading at the moment?
How long / read / it?

LANGUAGES

Are you studying another language? Which?
How long / learn it?

CAR

Do you have a car or motorbike?
How long / have it?

A

a Complete the questions with a comparative or superlative.

b Ask **B** your questions. Ask for more information.

LIFESTYLE	
Are you __________ in the morning or in the evening?	ACTIVE
What's __________ thing about your lifestyle?	UNHEALTHY

TRAVELLING	
Which do you use __________, public transport or a car?	OFTEN
What's __________ you've ever travelled?	FAR

ENGLISH	
Apart from English, what do you think is __________ foreign language to learn?	USEFUL
Is your English course __________ this year than last year?	EASY

FREE TIME	
What do you think is __________ thing to do at the weekend?	RELAXING
What's __________ film you've seen recently?	GOOD

YOUR FAMILY	
Who drives __________, your mother or your father?	SAFELY
Who's __________ person in your family?	TALKATIVE

B

a Complete the questions with a comparative or superlative.

b Ask **A** your questions. Ask for more information.

LIFESTYLE	
Are you working or studying __________ than a year ago?	HARD
Do you eat __________ than two years ago?	HEALTHILY

TRAVELLING	
Do you think travelling by yourself is __________ than travelling with a group?	ENJOYABLE
What's __________ holiday you've ever had?	BAD

ENGLISH	
What's __________ thing for you about learning English?	DIFFICULT
Is the level of English in your country __________ than it was ten years ago?	HIGH

FREE TIME	
What kind of music do you listen to __________?	OFTEN
What do you think is __________ way to spend Friday night?	GOOD

YOUR FAMILY	
Who are you __________ to, your mother or your father?	CLOSE
Who's __________ person in your family?	LAZY

a In pairs, read about some strange laws and customs. Four of these are false. Discuss with your partner which ones you think they are.

1 In **China**, when you use chopsticks you shouldn't leave them upright in the bowl. It brings bad luck.

2 In **Sweden**, if you drink and drive, you have to go to prison for six months.

3 In **Argentina**, when you get on a train you should shake hands with all the other people in the carriage.

4 In **France**, you are not allowed to call a pig 'Napoleon.'

5 In **Scotland**, boys have to wear a kilt to school.

6 In **Brazil**, you should never make the 'OK' sign with your thumb. It is very rude.

7 In **Germany**, every office must have a view of the sky.

8 In the **Middle East**, you shouldn't admire anything in your hosts' home. They will feel that they have to give it to you.

9 In **Singapore**, you mustn't eat chewing-gum. It's against the law.

10 In **India**, you shouldn't thank your hosts at the end of a meal. It is an insult.

11 In **Japan**, women mustn't wear trousers to work.

12 In the **UK**, parents don't have to send their children to school. They can teach them at home if they prefer.

13 In **Russia**, men should take off their gloves to shake somebody's hand.

14 In **Iceland**, you mustn't take dogs into the city centre.

15 In **Thailand**, you shouldn't touch a person's head (even of a child). The head is sacred.

16 In **Australia**, women mustn't sit on the top floor of a bus, only downstairs.

17 In **Samoa**, it is against the law for a man to forget his wife's birthday.

18 In **Switzerland**, you aren't allowed to clean your car or cut the grass on a Sunday.

19 In the **USA**, you shouldn't tip taxi drivers. It is considered an insult.

20 In **Italy**, if you give flowers you should give them in odd numbers, e.g. 1, 3, 5, 7, or 9. It is bad luck to give, for example, two flowers.

b Which of these customs and laws would you like to have in your country? Choose your top three.

A

Describe your picture to **B**. Find ten differences. Mark the differences on your picture.

B

Describe your picture to **A**. Find ten differences. Mark the differences on your picture.

Where? **Why not?**

Whose?

What? **Where?**

Why?

Why not? **Who…with?**

Find someone who…	Student's name	More information
1 would like to be able to travel more.		
2 won't be able to come to the next class.		
3 could swim before they were four years old.		
4 has been able to speak English outside class this week.		
5 can't park in very small spaces.		
6 would like to be able to speak another language.		
7 can make good cakes.		
8 hasn't been able to do all the homework this week.		
9 can't ski (but would like to be able to).		
10 needs to be able to speak English in their job (or job they'd like to do).		

As soon as I know anything …	We can't go out …	Hannah will be really angry …
You'll feel better …	I'll never finish this today …	Write that down …
He would like to retire …	I'm not going to start the class …	I'll go to the bank …
Jack won't leave home …	I can't buy the food …	We won't get a cheap flight …
If you make a noise …	Unless we run …	Turn off all the lights and lock the door …
We won't catch the 6 o'clock train …	You can go home …	When I leave school …
… unless we book early.	… if you take an aspirin.	… until I know how many people are coming to lunch.
… as soon as you finish the exercises.	… when he's 55.	… before you forget it.
… I'll call you.	… until everyone stops talking.	… before you go to bed.
… unless we get a taxi to the station.	… I want to go to university.	… you'll wake the baby up.
… as soon as it opens.	… until it stops raining.	… when she finds out.
… unless you help me.	… we won't catch the bus.	… until he gets a job.

Talk to a partner. Say why.

I'd prefer to live in the city centre. If I lived in a village, I'd have to drive to work every day…

If you had to choose…

would you prefer to live in a small village or in the centre of a capital city?

would you prefer to have as neighbours a couple with five children or a couple with five dogs?

would you prefer to live in a fourth floor flat without a lift or in a ground floor flat with a restaurant next door?

would you prefer to have an enormous house with a tiny garden or a tiny house with an enormous garden?

would you prefer to have a house with a gym or a house with a games room?

would you prefer to have central heating or open fires?

would you prefer to live in a beautiful house in an ugly area or an ugly house in a beautiful area?

would you prefer to have a holiday house on the beach or in the mountains?

A

a Write something in each circle. If it has (T) at the end, you must write something true. If it has (L), you must lie, i.e. invent something.

b Tell **B** about one of your circles. **B** will then ask you questions, and decide if you're telling the truth or lying.

c Now listen to **B** tell you about one of his / her circles. Ask questions to see if it is the truth or a lie. If it's a lie, get **B** to tell you what the true answer is!

A game you used to play a lot when you were a child (T)

A food you didn't use to like when you were a child (T)

A relative you used to visit a lot when you were a child (T)

A TV series you used to love when you were a child (L)

Something naughty you used to do when you were a child (L)

B

a Write something in each circle. If it has (T) at the end, you must write something true. If it has (L), you must lie, i.e. invent something.

b Listen to **A** tell you about one of his / her circles. Ask questions to see if it is the truth or a lie. If it's a lie, get **A** to tell you what the true answer is!

c Now tell **A** about one of your circles, and answer his / her questions.

A pop group or singer you used to really like when you were a child (L)

Something you used to be frightened of when you were a child (L)

A teacher you used to hate when you were a child (L)

A toy you used to love when you were a child (T)

A sport or physical activity you used to do when you were a child (T)

A

a Make questions with *How much* and *How many* to ask **B**. Ask for more information.

free time / have?

water / drink a day?

British or American people / know?

novels / read a month?

pairs of trainers / have?

exercise / do?

close friends / have?

chocolate / eat a week?

clothes / have that you never wear?

DVDs / have?

songs / download a week?

hours a week / spend studying?

b Answer **B**'s questions with an expression from the list. Give more details.

a lot / lots too much / many not much / many a few / very few
a little / very little none not enough

B

a Make questions with *How much* and *How many* to ask **A**. Ask for more information.

time / spend on yourself?

photos / have on your mobile?

coffee or tea / drink a day?

hours / usually sleep?

days a week / go out?

hours a day / spend watching TV?

TV / watch a day?

fast food / eat a week?

hot baths / have a week?

kilometres / walk a day?

time / spend on the Internet?

pairs of jeans / have?

b Answer **A**'s questions with an expression from the list. Give more details.

a lot / lots too much / many not much / many a few / very few
a little / very little none not enough

American people are more friendly than British people.

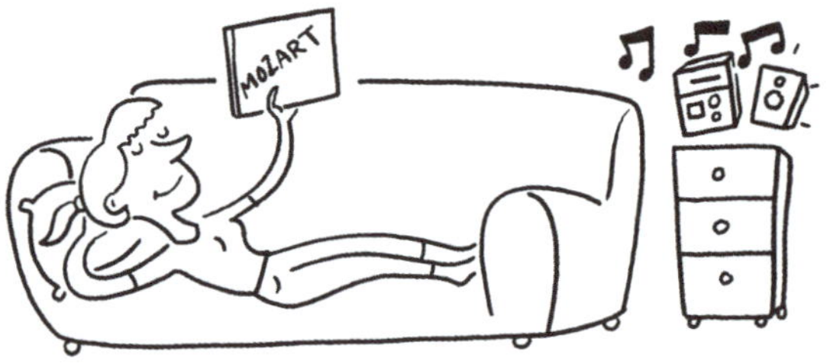

Classical music is the most relaxing kind of music.

Dogs make the best pets.

Friday is the best day of the week for going out.

Food that tastes good is usually bad for you.

Girls are better at learning languages than boys.

Italian food is the most popular in the world.

Money doesn't make you happy.

Most men today help a lot with the housework.

People who have red cars usually drive fast and aggressively.

Sports players are good role models for young people.

Women have a much better sense of style than men.

A

a Complete for your partner with a verb (phrase) in the gerund or infinitive.

I think...

When you go on holiday you love ____________.

When you were young your parents didn't use to let you ____________.

A job in the house you don't mind doing is ____________.

You would like to learn ____________.

You're not very good at ____________.

When you're on your own you enjoy ____________.

When you leave the house in the morning you never forget ____________.

When you were younger you wanted ____________.

This evening you'd like ____________.

When you're with your friends you spend a lot of time ____________.

b Read your first sentence to **B**. He / She will tell you if it's true or not.

B

a Complete for your partner with a verb (phrase) in the gerund or infinitive.

I think...

On Sunday mornings you really like ____________.

You're really good at ____________.

In class you enjoy ____________.

When you were a child your parents used to make you ____________.

This weekend you're planning ____________.

You want to give up ____________.

In the future you hope ____________.

Something that makes you feel good is ____________.

On Saturdays you hate ____________.

You are learning English to ____________.

b Tell **A** if his / her sentence about you is true or not. Then read **A** your first sentence.

1 What's your favourite TV programme?	**2** What kind of computer do you have?	**3** Have you ever changed a wheel on a car?	**4** Are you an optimist or a pessimist?
5 Where will you be at 8 o'clock tomorrow morning?	**6** How often do you wear a hat?	**7** How long have you been learning English?	**8** What time did you wake up today?
9 How much water do you drink a day?	**10** Have you ever worked in a bar or restaurant?	**11** Are you going out tonight?	**12** What's your favourite fruit?
13 How did you come to class?	**14** Would you like to be famous?	**15** Do you have a pet?	**16** Would you prefer to live in the town or in the country?
17 Do you support a football team?	**18** Are you afraid of any animals or insects?	**19** Can you play chess?	**20** What languages can you speak?

FILMS

1 What do these films have in common?

Pride and Prejudice *Bridget Jones' Diary* *Charlie and the Chocolate Factory*

a They are all set in the 19th century.
b They are all based on books.
c They all won an Oscar for best actress.

2 Which Oscar did all these films win?

Spiderman *The Lord of the Rings* *The Matrix*

a best film b best soundtrack
c best special effects

3 In which film (shot in Ireland) did an Australian actor play the part of a Scottish soldier?

a *Braveheart* b *Gladiator*
c *Master and Commander*

PEOPLE

1 Who played the part of James Bond in *Goldeneye*?

a Sean Connery
b Roger Moore
c Pierce Brosnan

2 Which actor was nominated seven times for an Oscar but never won one?

a Richard Burton b Humphrey Bogart
c Cary Grant

3 What do these three films have in common?

Reservoir Dogs *Pulp Fiction* *Kill Bill*

a They all star John Travolta.
b They were all directed by the same person.
c They were all set in New York.

PLACES

1 Match the films to the cities where they were set.

a *Lost in Translation* b *Notting Hill*
c *Amélie*

Paris ☐ Tokyo ☐ London ☐

2 *The Good, the Bad and the Ugly* is called a 'spaghetti western'. Why?

a Because most of the actors were Italian.
b Because it was shot in Italy.
c Because it was made by an Italian studio.

3 What is the boarding school called in the Harry Potter books?

a Hogwarts
b Hogarths
c Howards

FAMOUS LINES

Match the films and these famous lines.

1 'This is my neighbourhood, this is my street. My name is Lester Burnham. I'm 42 years old.'
2 'I'll never let go. I'll never let go, Jack.'
3 'My Momma always said life was like a box a chocolates.'
4 'I'll have what she's having.'
5 'May the force be with you.'

a *Star Wars*
b *Titanic*
c *When Harry met Sally*
d *Forrest Gump*
e *American Beauty*

MUSIC

1 Which 2001 musical starred Nicole Kidman and Ewan McGregor?

a *Chicago*
b *Moulin Rouge*
c *Cabaret*

2 Who composed the soundtrack for *Star Wars*?

a John Williams
b Ennio Morricone
c Howard Shore

3 Which famous musical is based on the true story of the Von Trapp family?

a *West Side Story*
b *The Sound of Music*
c *Phantom of the Opera*

FILM TITLES

Correct these film titles.

1 *Close Encounters of the Fourth Kind*
2 *The Chronicles of Narnia: The Lion, the Witch and the Armchair*
3 *Dead Footballers' Society*
4 *Elephant Dundee*
5 *Four Weddings and Two Funerals*
6 *The Godmother*
7 *A Hundred and Three Dalmatians*
8 *Kill Jill*
9 *Mission Improbable*
10 *Silence of the Cows*

CARD 1

a teetotaller /tiː'təʊtələ/
1 a person who never drinks alcohol ✓
2 the card where you write your score in golf
3 ______

a nightingale /'naɪtɪŋgeɪl/
1 a small lamp which children have on during the night
2 ______
3 a bird which sings at night ✓

a pushchair /'pʊʃtʃeə/
1 a thing you put a small child in when you take it for a walk ✓
2 a thing which people have to push when they are learning to walk again after an operation
3 ______

CARD 4

a busybody /'bɪziˌbɒdi/
1 a person who works in show business
2 a person who is too interested in other people's lives ✓
3 ______

a lullaby /'lʌləbaɪ/
1 a song which you sing to a baby to make it sleep ✓
2 ______
3 a small animal like a kangaroo

a cellar /'selə/
1 the thing you use to charge your mobile
2 ______
3 a room under a house, where people keep things like wine

CARD 2

a midwife /'mɪdwaɪf/
1 a woman who lives with a man but is not married
2 ______
3 a person that helps a woman when she has a baby ✓

a saucepan /'sɔːspən/
1 a thing made of metal which you use for cooking, for example, rice ✓
2 ______
3 a kind of tree which has very long branches

a conservatory /kən'sɜːvətri/
1 a cupboard in the kitchen where you keep food
2 a room with a glass roof and walls attached to a house ✓
3 ______

CARD 5

an undertaker /'ʌndəteɪkə/
1 a person who works for the London underground
2 a person who organizes funerals ✓
3 ______

a jigsaw /'dʒɪgsɔː/
1 ______
2 a dance which is very popular in Ireland
3 a game which has pieces you put together to make a picture ✓

a greenhouse /'griːnhaʊs/
1 a house which uses solar energy
2 a small building made of glass where people keep plants ✓
3 ______

CARD 3

a widower /'wɪdəʊə/
1 a person who watches a TV programme
2 ______
3 a man whose wife has died ✓

a lighthouse /'laɪthaʊs/
1 a small building in a garden where people keep gardening equipment
2 ______
3 a tall building with a light on the top which tells ships when there is danger ✓

an off-licence /'ɒfˌlaɪsəns/
1 ______
2 a shop where you can buy alcohol ✓
3 a place where you go to get a new driving licence

CARD 6

a publican /'pʌblɪkən/
1 a person that owns or manages a pub ✓
2 a thing that you stand on when you speak in public
3 ______

a grasshopper /'grɑːshɒpə/
1 a machine that you use for cutting the grass
2 an insect which can jump very high ✓
3 ______

a jetty /'dʒeti/
1 a place where boats land ✓
2 a kind of dessert that's made with gelatine /'dʒelətiːn/
3 ______

START

1. The film was in Chinese. If it hadn't been subtitled, I …
2. If our best player hadn't missed the penalty, we …
3. I got up late. I would have missed my flight if I …
4. If he had treated his wife better, she …
5. We wouldn't have got lost in London if we …
6. She wouldn't have lost her job if she …
7. The jacket was beautiful. I would have bought it if it …
8. We would have picked you up at the airport if you …
9. If I had known it was your birthday, I …
10. You would have done better in the exam if you …
11. I would have married Sally if she …
12. He wouldn't have crashed his car if he …
13. If I had been able to go to university, I …
14. You would have slept better if you …
15. We would have got a table at the restaurant if we …
16. If the weather hadn't been so bad yesterday, we …
17. I would have been here on time if I …
18. He would have been a great basketball player if he …

FINISH

A

a You are a tourist in London. You would like to visit the Sherlock Holmes Museum and the Bloody Tower. **B** works for tourist information. Ask **B** politely for the following information, using *Could you tell me...?*

Sherlock Holmes Museum
open on Saturdays? ______
what time / close? ______
where? ______
adult's ticket? £ ______

The Bloody Tower
open on Sundays? ______
what time / open? ______
what / nearest tube station? ______
child's ticket? £ ______

b Now you work for tourist information in London. Use the information below to answer **B**'s questions.

If you like murder mysteries and horror stories...
you must visit these places in London

The Chamber of Horrors

This is part of the world-famous Madame Tussaud's museum. Here you can see waxworks of many infamous murderers, including Vlad the Impaler, Jean-Paul Marat, Dr Crippen, and many more.

Address	Madame Tussaud's Marylebone Road (near Baker Street tube station) London
Opening hours	Weekdays 9.30 to 17.30 Weekends 9.00 to 18.00
Admission	Adult £23.99 Child (under 16) £19.99

The London Dungeon

This attraction recreates many of history's most horrific events. Explore the streets of Victorian London that were home to the serial killer Jack the Ripper, relive the Great Fire of London, and take a boat down the River Thames to the infamous Traitors' Gate at the Tower of London.

Address	London Dungeon 28–34 Tooley Street, London SE1 2SZ
Opening hours	Every day 9.30 a.m. to 5.30 p.m.
Admission	Adult £15.50 Child (5 to 15) £10.95

c Compare your information with **B**. You can visit just one of these places. Try to agree which one and why.

B

a You work for tourist information in London. Use the information below to answer **A**'s questions.

If you like murder mysteries and horror stories...
you must visit these places in London

The Sherlock Holmes Museum

Visit the house where Sherlock Holmes lived and where he solved many of his most famous cases!

Address	221b Baker Street, London
Opening hours	Open every day (except Christmas Day) from 9.30 a.m. to 6 p.m.
Admission	Adult £6 Child (under 16) £4

The Bloody Tower

The most famous tower in the Tower of London. This is where the Little Princes were murdered in 1483 by King Richard III and where Anne Boleyn (Henry VIII's second wife) was imprisoned before her execution. If you are lucky, you may see her ghost!

Address	Tower of London London EC3N 4AB (near Tower Hill tube station)
Opening hours	Tuesday–Saturday 9.00–18.00 Sunday, Monday 10.00–18.00
Admission	Adult £14.50 Child (under 16) £9.50

b Now you are a tourist in London. You would like to visit the Chamber of Horrors and the London Dungeon. Ask **A** politely for the following information, using *Could you tell me...?*

Chamber of Horrors
open on Saturdays? ______
what time / close? ______
what / nearest tube station? ______
adult's ticket? £ ______

The London Dungeon
where? ______
open every day? ______
what time / close? ______
child's ticket? £ ______

c Compare your information with **A**. You can visit just one of these places. Try to agree which one and why.

1 What's the first thing you usually **ask for** when you get to a restaurant?

2 Can you name a celebrity couple who have recently **broken up**?

3 Can you think of two places where you have to **check in**?

4 Can you think of two things you can **do up**?

5 How can you **find out** what's on at the cinema?

6 Can you name three things you should **give up** if you're on a diet?

7 What are two typical things young children want to be when they **grow up**?

8 What do people usually say to each other when they **hang up**?

9 Can you name two times of year that people normally **look forward to**?

10 Can you name two books that have recently been **made into** films?

11 Can you name a person who has **set up** a famous successful company?

12 When do you normally tell somebody to **slow down**?

13 What's the name of the person who **sorts out** legal problems?

14 Can you name three things you should **switch off** before you go to bed?

15 Can you name two activities you could **take up** if you wanted to get fitter?

16 What's the thing you need to have when you **take** something **back** to a shop?

17 What do you need to **do up** when a plane **takes off**?

18 Can you name two places where you can **take out** money?

19 When is it important for sportspeople to **warm up**?

20 Can you name three things you can **turn on** with a remote control?

1 The cinema

Think of a film (but don't say the name). Describe it for a partner to guess.

- Where is it set?
- Is it based on a book?
- Who was it directed by?
- Who's in it?
- What's it about?

2 Your education

Tell your partner about your primary school.

- What school did you use to go to?
- Did you use to wear a uniform?
- What subjects did you use to like?
- What subjects weren't you good at?
- What weren't you allowed to do?
- What did the teachers make you do?

3 Your family

Describe a member of your family.

- What does he / she look like? (Describe him / her.)
- What's he / she like? (Give two positive and two negative characteristics.)
- How are you similar / different?

4 Sport

Tell your partner about:

- a sport you really like watching / doing
- a sport you hate watching / doing
- a sport you used to do and why you stopped
- the sporting event / match you most remember

5 Your home

Tell your partner:

- where you live
- how long you've lived there
- who you live with
- if you get on well
- what you argue about

6 Your diet

Talk for a minute about your diet.

- Is your diet healthy or unhealthy? Why?
- Do you eat too much / not enough of anything?
- Are you trying to cut down on anything at the moment?
- What do you usually eat when you eat out?

7 Work

Think of a friend or family member who has a job. Tell your partner about the good and bad side of his / her job. Talk about:

- salary
- working hours
- the kind of contract
- holidays
- stress

8 Transport

Talk to your partner about the kinds of public transport in your town.

- Which do you think is the best? Why?
- How do you get to work or school?
- How long does it take you?

9 Experiences

Tell your partner about a time when you …

■ felt very frightened …
or ■ felt very embarrassed …
or ■ felt very excited …
or ■ felt very stressed or nervous …
or ■ got very angry.

10 Preferences

Tell your partner which you prefer and why:

- holidays abroad / in your country
- travelling by car / by plane
- eating at home / in a restaurant
- living in a big town / small village
- shopping in large supermarkets / small shops

1 Describing game

A card game

SS define words / phrases for other SS to guess. Copy and cut up one set of cards per pair or small group.

VOCABULARY Food, sport, adjectives of personality

- Put SS in pairs or small groups. Give each group a set of cards face down or in an envelope.
- Demonstrate the activity. Choose another word or words (not one of the ones on the cards) from one of the three Vocabulary Banks and describe it to the class until someone says the word, e.g. *It's an adjective. It can describe food you keep in the freezer.* **Highlight that SS are not allowed to use the word on the card in their definition.**
- SS play the game, taking turns to take a card and describe the word / phrase. The person who is describing mustn't let his / her partner see what's on the card. Tell SS to wait until the person has finished his / her description before trying to guess the word.

Extra idea You could get SS to play this in groups as a competitive game. The person who correctly guesses the word first keeps the card. The player with the most cards at the end is the winner.

Non-cut alternative Put SS in pairs. Copy one sheet per pair and cut it down the middle. SS take turns to describe the words to their partner until he / she guesses the word.

2 Split crossword

An information gap activity

SS define words / phrases to help their partner complete a crossword. Copy one sheet per pair and cut into **A** and **B**.

VOCABULARY Money, transport, extreme adjectives (*furious*, etc.)

- Put SS in pairs, ideally face to face, and give out the sheets. **Make sure SS can't see each other's sheets.** Explain that **A** and **B** have the same crossword but with different words missing. They have to describe / define words to each other to complete their crosswords.
- Give SS a minute to read their instructions. If SS don't know what a word means, they can look it up in Vocabulary Banks **Money** and **Transport and travel** and the vocabulary exercise on extreme adjectives in Lesson **2B** (*furious*, *starving*, etc.). Make sure SS understand the difference between *across* and *down*.
- SS take turns to ask each other for their missing words (e.g. *What's 1 across?*). Their partner must define / describe the word until the other student is able to write it in his / her crossword. SS should help each other with clues if necessary.
- When SS have finished, they should compare their crosswords to make sure they have the same words and have spelt them correctly.

3 Pictionary

A group card game

SS draw pictures of words on cards for other SS to guess. Copy and cut up one set of cards per group.

VOCABULARY Telephoning, physical description, *-ed* / *-ing* adjectives

- Put SS in small groups. Give each group a set of cards face down or in an envelope.
- Demonstrate the activity by picking a card and trying to draw the word / phrase from the card on the board until someone guesses the word / phrase you are trying to draw. **Highlight that they are not allowed to say anything, but they can indicate by gesture whether the guesses are good or not.**
- SS play the game, taking turns to pick a card and trying to draw the word / phrase. The person who is describing mustn't let anyone see what's on the card. SS can make guesses while the person is drawing. The person who correctly guesses the word first keeps the card. The player with the most cards at the end is the winner.

Non-cut alternative Put SS in pairs. Copy one sheet per pair and cut it in two horizontally. SS take turns to draw their words for their partner until he/she guesses the word.

4 What's the difference?

A team game

SS have to explain the difference between two words / phrases. Copy and cut up one set of cards.

VOCABULARY Education, houses, friendship

- Divide the class into two teams (or more if you have a lot of students) and explain the activity. You give a card to each team and they have a minute to decide what the difference is between the two words or phrases. **Write the two words / phrases up on the board**. A spokesperson from the team tries to explain the difference to the rest of the class. If the explanation is correct, they get a point. If it isn't correct, the other team can try to win an extra point by explaining it correctly before having their own turn. Then give each team another card.
- Write up the teams' points on the board and add them up to see which team wins.

A **nursery school** is for very small children, e.g. 0–4 years.
A **primary school** is for young children, e.g. 4–11 years.
A **pupil** is someone who studies in a primary / secondary school.
A **student** studies at e.g. a university, college, or evening class.
A **teacher** teaches in any school apart from university.
A **professor** teachers in a university. He / She is usually a head of department.

A **fireplace** is the place in the house where you light the fire.
A **chimney** is a hole in the roof out of which the smoke leaves the house.
A **coffee table** is small and usually found in the living room.
A **bedside table** is the small table next to your bed.
You open and close the **door** to leave / enter your house.
A **gate** is a door in an exterior wall, for example around a garden.
An **apartment** is the American word for a **flat**.
A **sink** is where you wash the dishes in a kitchen.
A **washbasin** is where you wash your hands in the bathroom.
A **town** is a place with many streets and buildings, houses, shops, factories, etc.
A **village** is much smaller than a town and is in the country. Sometimes it is only a few houses.
You **meet** someone when you see and talk to them (for the first time).
You **know someone** when you have already met them.
A **state school** is run by the government and is usually free.
You have to pay to go to a **private school**.
Marks (for an exam) are usually out of 10 or 100.
Grades are usually A, B, C, etc.
To **revise** means to study for an exam, i.e. look again and try to remember what you have studied previously.
To **learn** means to get knowledge of something.
A **detached house** is a house on its own.
A **terraced house** is joined to several others.
A **terrace** is an area next to a house where you can sit and eat, etc. A **balcony** is a kind of platform built onto the outside of the house with a wall or rail around it.
A **dishwasher** is for washing plates, cups, etc.
A **washing machine** is for washing clothes.
The **ceiling** is the top part of a room, opposite the floor.
The **roof** is the part of a house on the outside, which covers the top.
The **country** is the land outside towns and cities where there are trees and plants, etc.
The **suburbs** is the area around a city (i.e. not the centre) where people live.
A **friend** is someone you know and like.
A **colleague** is someone you work with (not necessarily a friend).
You **keep in touch** when you see, phone or write to a friend regularly.
You **lose touch** when you do not see, phone or write to a friend, perhaps because you have lost their email address or phone number.

Non-cut alternative Put SS in pairs. Copy one sheet per pair and cut it down the middle. Set a time limit, e.g. 10 minutes, and SS take turns to ask each other, '*What's the difference between…?*, choosing words at random. SS decide if the explanation is correct. Finally, check answers with the whole class.

5 Pick a card

A pairwork (or group) card game

SS ask each other questions on cards to test their memory of common words and phrases. Copy and cut up one set of cards per pair or group.

VOCABULARY Work, prepositions, word building

- Put SS in pairs or small groups and give each pair / group a set of cards face down or in an envelope.
- Demonstrate the activity by picking a card and asking the question to the group, e.g. *What's the missing preposition? 'I'm applying ___ a job.'* (make the noise 'beep' to show that there is a missing preposition.) Highlight that the answer to each question is written in capital letters on the card.
- SS play the game, taking turns to pick up a card and ask the question to his / her partner or members of the group.

Extra idea You could divide the class into two teams and pick cards yourself and ask the questions. Keep a record of the score on the board.

Non-cut alternative Put SS in pairs. Copy one sheet per pair and cut it down the middle. SS take it in turns to ask each other the questions.

6 Alphabet race

A pairwork vocabulary race

SS read a series of clues and write the words. Copy one sheet per student or pair of students.

VOCABULARY Shopping, professions, cinema

- Put SS in pairs and give out the sheets. Set a time limit. Tell SS that they have to write as many words as they can within the time limit. Each word begins with a different letter of the alphabet. The pair who complete all the words correctly first are the winners.

Audience, **B**argain, **C**omedy, **D**epartment store, **E**xtras, **F**an, **G**uarantee, **H**ero, **I**nventor, **J**ust, **K**ind, **L**ibrary, **M**anager, **N**ewsagent's, **O**nline, **P**lot, **Q**ueue, **R**eceipt, **S**ales, **T**hriller, **U**p, **V**iolinist, **W**estern.

7 Split crossword

An information gap activity

See instructions for **File 2 Split crossword**. The words here come from Vocabulary Bank **Phrasal verbs** and from lessons **7A** and **7B**.

VOCABULARY phrasal verbs, compound nouns, television

Revision

A group card game

See instructions for **File 1 Describing game.**

VOCABULARY Revision from Files 1–7

prawns

a peach

a menu

sausages

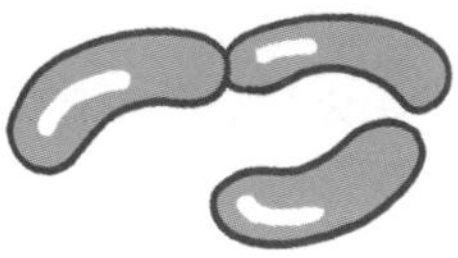

a spoon

a dessert

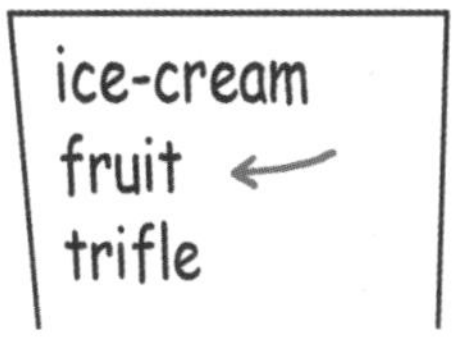

a starter

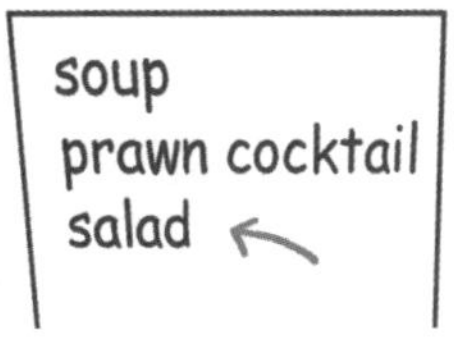

strawberries

a coach

a referee

(to) do aerobics

(to) get injured

spectators

a stadium

a team

(to) draw

aggressive

untidy

bossy

lazy

ambitious

competitive

unsociable

talkative

A

a Look at your crossword and make sure you know the meaning of all the words you have.

b Now ask **B** to define a word for you. Ask e.g. *What's 1 across? What's 2 down?* Write the word in.

c Now **B** will ask you to define a word.

B

a Look at your crossword and make sure you know the meaning of all the words you have.

b **A** will ask you to define a word.

c Now ask **A** to define a word for you. Ask e.g. *What's 1 down? What's 5 across?* Write the word in.

text message	**beard**	**shoulder-length hair**
depressed	**overweight**	**ponytail**
frightening	**handsome**	**moustache**
boring	**fringe**	**ring tone**
dial	**straight hair**	**well-built**
bald	**excited**	**medium height**

a nursery school	a primary school	a private school	a state school
a pupil	a student	marks	grades
a professor	a teacher	revise	learn
a chimney	a fireplace	a detached house	a terraced house
a coffee table	a bedside table	a balcony	a terrace
a door	a gate	a dishwasher	a washing machine
a flat	an apartment	the roof	the ceiling
a sink	a washbasin	the suburbs	the country
a town	a village	a colleague	a friend
meet someone	know someone	keep in touch	lose touch

What's the missing preposition?

I'm applying ___ a job.
FOR

What's the missing preposition?

I work ___ a sales assistant.
AS

What's the missing preposition?

He's not very good ___ cooking.
AT

What are the missing prepositions?

Don't talk ___ me ___ football.
TO, ABOUT

What's the opposite of a full-time job?

A PART-TIME JOB

What's another way of saying 'lose your job'?

get ___________
SACKED

What's another way of saying 'I work for myself'?

I'M SELF-EMPLOYED.

What's the noun from 'qualify'?

QUALIFICATION

What's the noun from 'mad'?

MADNESS

What's the noun from 'survive'?

SURVIVAL

What's the missing preposition?

I don't agree ___ you.
WITH

What's the missing preposition?

He's ___ charge of 50 employees.
IN

What are the missing prepositions?

I'm ___ my third year ___ university.
IN, AT

What's the opposite of a permanent job?

A TEMPORARY JOB

What's the opposite of 'lend to'?

BORROW FROM

What's another way of saying 'make something smaller'?

REDUCE

What's the word for the money you get from your job?

YOUR SALARY

What's the noun from 'govern'?

GOVERNMENT

What's the noun from 'relax'?

RELAXATION

What's the noun from 'decide'?

DECISION

A
the people who watch a film in a cinema or theatre
____

B
something that you buy at a very good price
____

C
a film which makes you laugh
____

D
a big shop usually on several floors where you can buy all kinds of things (two words)
____

E
people who appear in a film, e.g. in crowd scenes, but who don't talk
____

F
somebody who really likes a sports team or film star, etc.
____

G
a written promise that a shop will repair something you buy
____

H
a brave person who people admire
____

I
a person who invents things
____

J
'Can I help you?'
'No thanks.
I'm ______ looking.'

K
What ______ of films do you like?

L
a place where you can borrow books
____

M
a person who is in charge of a shop, restaurant or business, etc.
____

N
the shop where you can buy papers and magazines
____

O
Many people today shop ______ (i.e. use the Internet).

P
the story of a film
____

Q
to stand in line when you are waiting for something
____

R
a piece of paper they give you when you buy something
____

S
a time when shops sell thing cheaper
____

T
a film with a very exciting story, e.g. Hitchcock's *Psycho*
____

U
Bill Gates set ______ a foundation to help children all over the world.

V
a person who plays the violin
____

W
a film about cowboys
____

A

a Look at your crossword and make sure you know the meaning of all the words you have.

b Now ask **B** to define a word for you. Ask e.g. *What's 7 across? What's 3 down?* Write the word in.

c Now **B** will ask you to define a word.

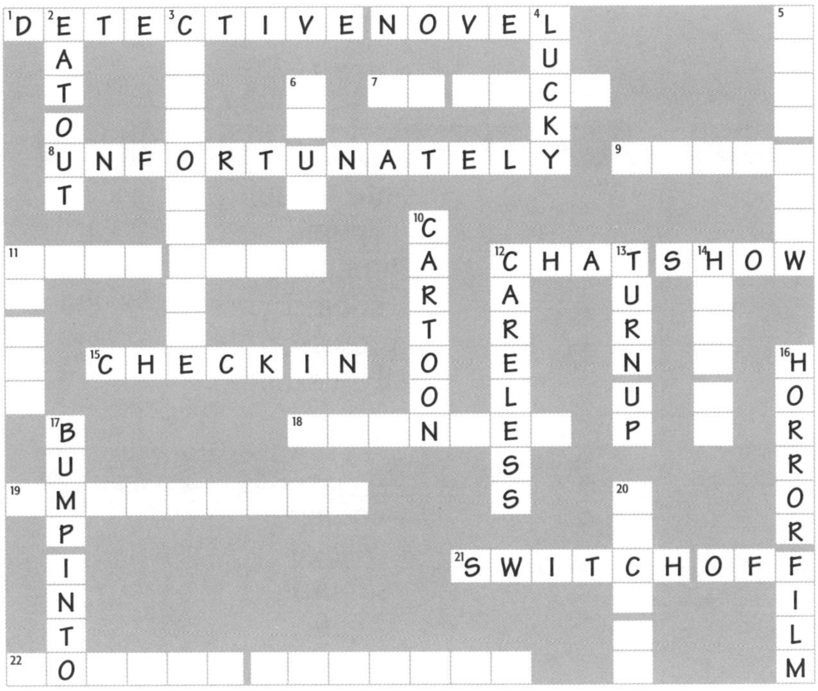

B

a Look at your crossword and make sure you know the meaning of all the words you have.

b **A** will ask you to define a word.

c Now ask **A** to define a word for you. Ask e.g. *What's 1 across? What's 2 down?* Write the word in.

Describing people
in his mid-twenties
bald
beard
overweight
grey hair
fringe

Personality
selfish
bossy
moody
impatient
spoilt
shy

Cinema
horror film
soundtrack
dubbed
cast
sequel
plot

Education
state school
pupil
timetable
subject
professor
fail an exam

Food and restaurants
seafood
spicy
bill
spoon
boiled
napkin

Houses
cottage
village
suburbs
gate
roof
dishwasher

Shopping
complain
discount
customer
butcher's
refund
queue

Sport
referee
coach
tennis court
beat
draw
warm up

Travel and transport
flight
railway station
luggage
lorry
seat belt
traffic jam

Phrasal verbs
check in
turn down (e.g. the TV)
call back
give up
throw away
take off

Money
waste (money)
inherit
loan
note
tax
borrow

Work
unemployed
qualifications
retire
contract
salary
temporary job

1 C We are family 1.12 CD1 Track 13

Correcting words

LANGUAGE Mixed vocabulary

- Give each student a sheet and focus on **a**. Go through the words in **bold** and explain that SS have to listen and decide if these words are right (what the singer sings) or wrong (different). The first time they listen, SS just have to put a tick or a cross in column **A**. They shouldn't try to correct the words at this stage.
- Check answers (i.e. if the words are right or wrong), but don't tell SS what the right words are.
- Now focus on **b**. Play the song again and this time SS have to try to correct the wrong words.
- Let SS compare with a partner and then check answers, going through the song line by line.

1 ✗ together	10 ✓
2 ✓	11 ✗ future
3 ✓	12 ✓
4 ✗ tell	13 ✗ depressed
5 ✗ people	14 ✓
6 ✗ close	15 ✗ things
7 ✓	16 ✗ wrong
8 ✗ love	17 ✓
9 ✗ fun	

- If there's time, get SS to read the lyrics in pairs with the glossary. Help with any other vocabulary problems which arise.
- You may want to play the song again for SS to sing along.
- Finally get SS to read the **Song facts**.

3 C You can get it if you really want 3.14 CD1 Track 55

Listening for specific words

LANGUAGE Modal verbs

- Give each student a sheet and focus on **a**. Highlight that the missing words are all verbs, but not necessarily in the infinitive form (for example, one is a past participle).
- Give SS a minute or so to read through the lyrics once before they listen. Tell them not to worry about the meaning of the song at this stage.
- Play the tape/CD once for SS to try and write the missing words. Get SS to compare their answers with a partner and then play the song again for SS to fill all the gaps. Play specific lines again as necessary. Then check answers.

1 must	6 get
2 succeed	7 get
3 must	8 built
4 Win	9 come
5 lose	10 see

- Now get SS, in pairs, to read the lyrics with the glossary and to do task **b**. Check answers. Help with any other vocabulary problems which arise.

1 You can get it if you really want.
2 You've got your mind set on a dream.
3 Rome was not built in a day.
4 Opposition will come your way.
5 The harder the battle....the sweeter the victory.

- You may want to play the song again for the class to sing along.
- Finally, get SS to read the Song facts.

4 B Our house 4.10 CD2 Track 17

Listening for specific words

LANGUAGE General vocabulary

- Give each student a sheet and focus on **a**. Highlight that the clue in brackets will help SS to decide what the missing words are when they listen.
- Give SS a minute or so to read through the lyrics once before they listen. Tell them not to worry about the meaning of the song at this stage.
- Play the tape/CD once for SS to try and write the missing words. Get SS to compare their answers with a partner and then play the song again for SS to fill all the gaps. Play specific lines again as necessary. Then check answers.

1 Sunday	6 Mum
2 tired	7 late
3 downstairs	8 shirt
4 Brother	9 school
5 always	10 happy

- Now get SS, in pairs, to read the lyrics with the glossary and to do task **b**. Check answers. Help with any other vocabulary problems which arise.

1 His memory of his home seems to be very positive. He talks about 'such a happy time' and he describes his family and home life with affection. However, one line of the song says: Something tells you that you've got to move away from it. Perhaps this is how he felt when he was a teenager and wanted to become independent of his family
2 busy ✓ clean ✓ crowded ✓ traditional ✓

- You may want to play the song again for the class to sing along.
- Finally, get SS to read the **Song facts**.

5 B Sk8er Boi 5.12 CD2 Track 39

Listening for articles

LANGUAGE *a* / *an*, *the*, or no article

- Give each student a sheet and focus on **a**. Then play the song once. Get SS to compare answers and then play it again.

EXTRA challenge Get SS to try to fill the gaps before they listen, and then play the song for them to listen and check. Check answers.

1 a	15 a
2 a	16 (-)
3 a	17 (-)
4 (-)	18 the
5 a	19 the
6 a	20 the
7 a	21 the
8 (-)	22 a
9 (-)	23 a
10 (-)	24 the
11 the	25 the
12 the	26 the
13 the	27 the
14 a	28 a

- Now focus on **b**. Get SS to read the lyrics in pairs using the glossary and the pictures to help them. Help with any other vocabulary problems. Get each pair to decide what they think the moral of the song is, and elicit ideas.

Suggested answer
You shouldn't judge people by their appearance / social status. Losers might end up being winners, etc.

- You may want to play the song again for SS to sing along.
- Finally get SS to read the **Song facts**.

6 C Holding out for a hero 6.10 CD3 Track 11

Listening for adjectives

LANGUAGE Adjectives

- Give each student a sheet and focus on **a**. Then play the song once. Get SS to compare answers and then play it again. Check answers.

1 good	6 fresh
2 white	7 sure
3 Late	8 soon
4 strong	9 larger
5 fast	10 wildest

- Now focus on **b**. Get SS to read the lyrics in pairs, using the glossary and the pictures to help them. Help with any other vocabulary problems and get them to match the highlighted weather words to the definitions. Check answers.

1 storm 2 wind 3 thunder 4 lightning 5 flood

- You may want to play the song again for SS to sing along.
- Finally get SS to read the **Song facts**.

7 A Ironic 7.5 CD3 Track 22

Reading and understanding a song

LANGUAGE General vocabulary and grammar

- Give each student a sheet and focus on task **a**. Highlight that they should just write the number in each box. Give SS a few minutes to read the song and try to guess the missing phrase. Then get them to compare their answers with a partner.
- Focus on task **b**. Play the tape/CD for SS to check their answers. Then check answers with the whole class.

1 B	6 C
2 J	7 H
3 G	8 E
4 A	9 I
5 F	10 D

- If there's time, get SS to read the lyrics in pairs with the glossary. Help with any other vocabulary problems which arise.

EXTRA challenge Get SS to cover the lyrics and try to remember as many examples of bad luck from the song as they can.

- You may want to play the song again for the class to sing along.
- Finally, get SS to read the **Song facts**.

a Listen to the song. Are the words in bold right or wrong? Put a tick (✓) or a cross (✗) in column **A**.

b Listen again and correct the wrong words in column **B**.

We are family

		A	B
Everyone can see we're **friends**	1	____	________
As we **walk** on by	2	____	________
And we flock just like **birds** of a feather	3	____	________
I won't **say** no lie	4	____	________
All of the **women** around us they say,	5	____	________
'Can they be that **friendly**?'	6	____	________
Just let me state for the **record**	7	____	________
We're giving **money** in a family dose	8	____	________

We are family
I got all my sisters with me
We are family
Get up everybody, sing

We are family, etc.

Living life is **great** and we've just begun	9	____	________
To get our share of this **world's** delights	10	____	________
High hopes we have for the **summer**	11	____	________
And our goal's in **sight**	12	____	________
No, we don't get **sad**	13	____	________
Here's what we call our **golden** rule:	14	____	________
Have faith in you and the **work** you do	15	____	________
You won't go **down**, oh-no	16	____	________
This is our family **jewel**	17	____	________

We are family, etc.

Glossary

I got (informal) = I've got
flock like birds of a feather = stay together, like birds of the same species
state for the record = say so that everybody knows it
dose = the amount of a medicine you have to take
delights = nice things
our goal = what we are trying to do
jewel = a valuable stone, e.g. a diamond

Song facts

The song was originally recorded in 1979 by Sister Sledge, four sisters whose surname was Sledge. The writers of the song (Bernard Edwards and Nile Rodgers) got the idea for the song from seeing how well the four sisters got on with each other.

We are family was a worldwide hit and became an anthem for women's groups, sports teams, and political parties.

a Listen to the song and complete the missing verbs.

You can get it if you really want

You can get it if you really want,
You can get it if you really want,
You can get it if you really want,
But you [1]m__________ try, try and try,
Try and try,
You'll [2] s__________ at last.

Persecution you [3] m__________ bear
[4] W__________ or [5] l__________, you've got to [6]g__________ your share
Got your mind set on a dream
You can [7] g__________ it, though hard it seems
Now

You can get it if you really want, etc.

Rome was not [8] b__________ in a day,
Opposition will [9] c__________ your way
But the harder the battle you [10] s__________,
Is the sweeter the victory
Now

You can get it if you really want, etc.

b Read the lyrics with the glossary and find a phrase which means:

1 You will get what you want in the end.
2 You have a clear idea what you want to do or get.
3 It takes a long time to do something well.
4 There will be difficulties.
5 If something is very difficult to do, you'll enjoy it more when you've done it.

Glossary

persecution = making someone suffer for what they believe
your share = the part that belongs to you
got your mind = you have your mind
set on = fixed on
opposition = people or things that are against you

Song facts

You can get it if you really want was written and first recorded by Jimmy Cliff, and was also a number 2 hit in the UK charts hit for Desmond Dekker, another Jamaican singer. It later appeared on the soundtrack to the 1973 film *The harder they come*, which starred Jimmy Cliff and which introduced reggae music and Jamaican culture to an international audience.

a Listen to the song and write the missing words 1–10. Use the clues (in brackets) to help you.

Our house

Father wears his 1 ________ best *(a day of the week)*
Mother's 2 ________ she needs a rest *(adjective)*
The kids are playing up 3 ________ *(part of the house)*
Sister's sighing in her sleep
4 ________'s got a date to keep *(member of the family)*
He can't hang around

Our house, in the middle of our street
Our house, in the middle of our...

Our house it has a crowd
There's 5 ________ something happening *(adverb of frequency)*
And it's usually quite loud
Our 6 ________ she's so house-proud *(member of the family, colloquial)*
Nothing ever slows her down and a mess is not allowed

Our house, in the middle of our street, etc.
(Something tells you that you've got to move away from it)

Father gets up 7 ________ for work *(adverb of time)*
Mother has to iron his 8 ________ *(something you wear)*
Then she sends the kids to 9 ________ *(a place)*
Sees them off with a small kiss
She's the one they're going to miss In lots of ways

Our house, in the middle of our street, etc.

I remember way back then when everything was true
and when
We would have such a very good time
such a fine time
Such a 10 ________ *(adjective)* time
And I remember how we'd play, simply waste the day away
Then we'd say nothing would come between us two dreamers

Repeat first verse (Father wears his ..., etc.)

Our house, in the middle of our street, etc.

Glossary

Sunday best = best clothes
playing up = behaving badly
sighing = making a sad sound
has got a date = has a meeting (with a girl)
hang around = stay here for long
house-proud = a person who likes to keep her house clean and tidy
you've got to = you have to

b Read the song with the glossary and answer the questions.

1 Do you think the singer's memory of his home is positive or negative?

2 Which of these adjectives would you use to describe his house? Tick the boxes.

busy ☐ quiet ☐ clean ☐ untidy ☐ crowded ☐ traditional ☐

Song facts

Our house was the British group Madness's biggest international hit. Twenty years later, the musical *Our House*, based on Madness's songs, opened in London's West End and won the 2003 Olivier Award for 'Best New Musical'.

a Listen and complete the song with *a*, *the* or –.

b What do you think the moral of the song is?

Sk8er Boi

He was [1]_____ boy, she was [2]_____ girl
Can I make it any more obvious?
He was [3]_____ punk, she did [4]_____ ballet
What more can I say?
He wanted her, she'd never tell
Secretly she wanted him as well
But all of her friends just stuck up their nose
They had [5]_____ problem with his baggy clothes.

He was [6]_____ skater boy
She said 'See you later boy'
He wasn't good enough for her
She had [7]_____ pretty face
But her head was up in [8]_____ space
She needed to come back down to [9]_____ earth.

Five years from now, she sits at [10]_____ home
Feeding [11]_____ baby, she's all alone
She turns on TV. Guess who she sees?
Skater boy rocking up MTV.
She calls up her friends, they already know
And they've all got tickets to see his show
She tags along, but stands in [12]_____ crowd
Looks up at [13]_____ man that she turned down.

He was [14]_____ skater boy
She said, 'See you later boy'
He wasn't good enough for her
Now he's [15]_____ superstar
Slamming on his guitar
Does your pretty face see what he's worth? (Repeat)

Sorry girl but you missed out
Well tough luck, that boy's [16]_____ mine now
We are more than just [17]_____ good friends
This is how [18]_____ story ends.
Too bad that you couldn't see,
See [19]_____ man that boy could be
There is more than meets [20]_____ eye
I see [21]_____ soul that is inside.

He's just [22]_____ boy , and I'm just [23]_____ girl
Can I make it any more obvious?
We are in love, haven't you heard
How we rock each other's world?

I'm with [24]_____ skater boy, I said see ya later boy
I'll be back stage after [25]_____ show,
I'll be at [26]_____ studio
singing [27]_____ song we wrote
about [28]_____ girl you used to know. (Repeat)

Glossary
stuck up their nose = thought they were superior
baggy = very loose, not tight
rocking up = playing loud music
tags along = goes with her friends
she turned down = she said 'no' (to him)
slamming on his guitar = playing his guitar loudly
missed out = lost your opportunity
tough luck = bad luck
rock each other's world = make each other happy
back stage = the place behind where the musicians play

Song facts
Sk8er Boi was originally recorded by Avril Lavigne in 2002. Some people say that the song is autobiographical (she was the skater boy!). The song was a worldwide hit.

a Listen to the song and fill the gaps with the missing adjectives (one of them is a comparative and one is a superlative).

b Read the lyrics with the glossary. Match the highlighted words to their definitions.

1 ______________ very bad weather with heavy rain, etc.
2 ______________ air that is moving fast
3 ______________ the loud noise that you hear during a storm
4 ______________ a bright flash of light that appears in the sky during a storm
5 ______________ a large amount of water (from a river, the sea, or heavy rain)

Holding out for a hero

Where have all the ¹ g_________ men gone
and where are all the Gods?
Where's the streetwise Hercules
to fight the rising odds?
Isn't there a ² w_________ knight upon a fiery steed?
³ L_________ at night I toss and I turn and I dream of what I need.

I need a hero
I'm holding out for a hero till the end of the night.
He's got to be ⁴ s_________ and he's got to be ⁵ f_________
and he's got to be ⁶ f_________ from the fight.
I need a hero
I'm holding out for a hero till the morning light.
He's got to be ⁷ s_________ and it's got to be ⁸ s_________
And he's got to be ⁹ l_________ than life
(⁹)L_________ than life.

Somewhere after midnight
In my ¹⁰ w_________ fantasy
Somewhere just beyond my reach
There's someone reaching back for me.
Racing on the thunder and rising with the heat
It's gonna to take a Superman to sweep me off my feet.

I need a hero, etc.

Up where the mountains meet the heavens above
Out where the lightning splits the sea
I could swear there is someone somewhere watching me.
Through the wind and the chill and the rain
and the storm and the flood
I can feel his approach like a fire in the blood.

I need a hero, etc.

Glossary

streetwise = a person who can look after himself
rising odds = the opposition, people who are against us
fiery steed = a wild horse
toss and turn = move, in bed
I'm holding out for = I'm waiting for
beyond my reach = too far away for me to touch
reaching back for me = trying to take my hand
it's gonna take a Superman = he'll have to be a Superman
to sweep me off my feet = for me to fall in love with him
chill = cold
his approach = he's coming nearer

Song facts

Holding out for a hero was written for Bonnie Tyler in 1982 by Jim Steinman and Dean Pitchford. Steinman also wrote all of Meat Loaf's hits as well as *Total eclipse of the heart* for Tyler. A version by Jennifer Saunders was the theme song to the 2004 film *Shrek 2*.

Ironic

An old man turned ninety-eight
He [1] ______________ and died the next day
It's a black fly in your Chardonnay
It's a death row pardon [2] ______________
And isn't it ironic...don't you think?

It's like rain on your [3] ______________
It's a free ride when you've [4] ______________
It's the good advice that you just didn't take
And who would've thought...? It figures

Mr Play-It-Safe was afraid to fly
He [5] ______________ and kissed his kids goodbye
He waited his whole damn life to take that flight
And as the plane [6] ______________ he thought
'Well isn't this nice...'
And isn't it ironic...don't you think?

It's like rain, etc.

Well, life has a funny way of sneaking up on you when
You think everything's okay and everything's going right
And life has a funny way of helping you out when
You think everything's gone wrong and everything blows up
In your face

A [7] ______________ when you're already late
A [8] ______________ on your cigarette break
It's like ten thousand spoons when all you need is [9] ________
It's meeting the man of my dreams
And then meeting [10] ______________
Isn't it ironic...don't you think?
A little too ironic... yeah, I really do think.

It's like rain, etc.

Well, life has a funny way of sneaking up on you
And life has a funny funny way of helping you out, helping you out.

a Read the song and try to match gaps 1–10 with a phrase A–J.

- A already paid ☐
- B won the lottery ☐
- C crashed down ☐
- D his beautiful wife ☐
- E no-smoking sign ☐
- F packed his suitcase ☐
- G wedding day ☐
- H traffic jam ☐
- I a knife ☐
- J two minutes too late ☐

b Listen and check your answers.

Glossary

ironic = strange or amusing because it's the opposite of what you expected

Chardonnay = a kind of white wine

death row = the cells in a prison for prisoners waiting to be executed

It figures. = It makes sense.

sneaking up on you = surprising you

blows up = explodes

Song facts

Ironic was written and first recorded by the Canadian singer Alanis Morissette in 1995. It was her third single and her first top ten hit. It was nominated for a Grammy in the category 'Record of the Year' and in 1996 won the MTV Award for 'Best Female Video'.

QUICKTESTS

Instructions

There are seven photocopiable Quicktests, one for each File 1–7. These test the Grammar, Vocabulary and Pronunciation from the A, B, and C lessons.

There is one mark for each answer so SS will get a total mark out of 50 for each test.

Each test should take between 20 and 30 minutes.

Answers

1 Quicktest

GRAMMAR

a 1 b 2 c 3 b 4 b 5 a 6 a 7 a 8 c 9 a 10 c

b 11 were 12 Shall 13 doesn't 14 won't 15 are 16 will / 'll 17 going 18 will / 'll 19 didn't 20 had

VOCABULARY

a 1 spicy 2 knife 3 pepper 4 prawns 5 raw 6 course 7 takeaway

b 8 spectators 9 coach 10 track 11 fans 12 slope 13 warm up 14 score

c 15 quiet 16 shy 17 dishonest 18 clever / intelligent 19 lazy 20 impatient

PRONUNCIATIONB

a 1 cook 2 grilled 3 spoilt 4 honest 5 charming

b 6 dessert 7 jealous 8 unselfish 9 spectator 10 grandmother

2 Quicktest

GRAMMAR

a 1 b 2 c 3 c 4 b 5 a 6 a 7 c 8 c 9 a 10 c

b 11 hasn't 12 as 13 been 14 ever 15 for 16 yet 17 did 18 most 19 since 20 just / already

VOCABULARY

a 1 filthy 2 furious 3 delicious 4 starving 5 enormous

b 6 cost 7 worth 8 lent 9 mortgage 10 take out

c 11 for 12 from 13 in 14 for 15 back

d 16 speed 17 jam 18 fine 19 transport 20 boarding

PRONUNCIATION

a 1 cost 2 travel 3 gate 4 paid 5 lorry

b 6 motorway 7 underground 8 afford 9 exhausted 10 inherit

3 Quicktest

GRAMMAR

a 1 b 2 b 3 c 4 b 5 a 6 c 7 b 8 a 9 a 10 b

b 11 do 12 was 13 be 14 had 15 being 16 mustn't / shouldn't 17 to 18 been 19 don't 20 can't

VOCABULARY

a 1 well built 2 fringe 3 shoulder-length 4 ugly 5 overweight 6 bald 7 attractive 8 mid-seventies

b 9 hung 10 ring 11 dial 12 call / ring 13 leave 14 engaged

c 15 interested 16 frightening 17 frustrated 18 embarrassing 19 disappointing 20 bored

PRONUNCIATION

a 1 beard 2 bald 3 dial 4 height 5 brown

b 6 attractive 7 moustache 8 interesting 9 frustrating 10 depressed

4 Quicktest

GRAMMAR

a 1 c 2 b 3 a 4 c 5 c 6 c 7 b 8 b 9 a 10 c

b 11 didn't 12 doesn't 13 if 14 as 15 passes 16 would 17 won't 18 to 19 use 20 didn't

VOCABULARY

a 1 literature 2 revise 3 discipline 4 graduate 5 boarding 6 pupils 7 behave 8 cheat

b 9 met 10 got 11 common 12 argue 13 touch

c 14 block of flats 15 chimney 16 suburbs 17 sink 18 detached 19 steps 20 path

PRONUNCIATION

a 1 lose 2 pupil 3 area 4 boarding 5 village

b 6 behave 7 cottage 8 residential 9 professor 10 argue

5 Quicktest

GRAMMAR

a 1 a 2 c 3 b 4 b 5 a 6 c 7 b 8 c 9 a 10 c

b 11 few 12 an 13 take 14 much 15 an 16 lot 17 enough 18 getting 19 go 20 to

VOCABULARY

a 1 similarity 2 government 3 possibility 4 reaction 5 survival 6 organization 7 happiness 8 relaxation

b 9 part-time 10 permanent 11 training course 12 retire 13 apply 14 resigned

c 15 for 16 with 17 at 18 of 19 for 20 about

PRONUNCIATION

a 1 thanks 2 laugh 3 full 4 although 5 until

b 6 experience 7 qualifications 8 contract 9 temporary 10 resign

6 Quicktest

GRAMMAR

a 1 c 2 a 3 c 4 c 5 a 6 b 7 c 8 a 9 c 10 b

b 11 whose 12 told 13 where 14 be 15 not 16 by 17 which 18 who 19 if / whether 20 been

VOCABULARY

a 1 baker's 2 till 3 customer 4 cast 5 plot 6 photographer 7 guitarist

b 8 special 9 fiction 10 store 11 window 12 agent's 13 shopping

c 14 complained 15 try 16 queue 17 based 18 shot / filmed 19 sells 20 dubbed

PRONUNCIATION

a 1 careful 2 script 3 pay 4 special 5 bargain

b 6 inventor 7 politician 8 discount 9 sequel 10 refund

7 Quicktest

GRAMMAR

a 1 c 2 a 3 b 4 a 5 c 6 b 7 c 8 a 9 c 10 b

b 11 didn't 12 'd / had 13 on 14 doesn't 15 'd / would 16 is 17 hadn't 18 are 19 for 20 off

VOCABULARY

a 1 patiently 2 carelessly 3 unfortunate 4 luckily 5 comfortable

b 6 police station 7 department store 8 horror film 9 cycle lane 10 swimming pool

c 11 satellite 12 adverts / advertising 13 series 14 reality 15 channels

d 16 set / start 17 forward 18 up 19 down 20 away

PRONUNCIATION

a 1 chemist's 2 warm 3 find 4 fortune 5 after

b 6 mystery 7 advert 8 comedy 9 unfortunately 10 machine

End-of-course test

Instructions

The End-of-course test is a test of all of the Grammar, Vocabulary, and Pronunciation from the A, B, and C lessons. It also includes Reading, Listening, and Writing.

Grammar

25 marks one mark for each answer

Vocabulary

25 marks one mark for each answer

Pronunciation

10 marks one mark for each answer

Reading

10 marks one mark for each answer

Listening

10 marks one mark for each answer (tapescript *p.215*)

Writing

10 marks We suggest you allocate 6 marks for grammar, vocabulary, and spelling, and 4 marks for content, presentation, and layout.

Speaking

10 marks Either give a mark for their speaking during the course, or use Communicative activity *Revision* on *p.194* as an oral test. Give SS a mark out of 10.

Answers

GRAMMAR

a 1 c 2 a 3 c 4 c 5 a 6 b 7 b 8 c 9 a 10 a 11 c 12 c 13 a 14 c 15 b

b 16 for 17 as 18 must 19 enough 20 many 21 unless / until 22 was 23 who 24 'd / had 25 wasn't

VOCABULARY

a 1 charge 2 selfish 3 referee 4 rush hour 5 luggage 6 subject 7 village 8 receipt 9 set 10 break

b 11 land 12 sell 13 lend 14 dishonest 15 straight 16 fail 17 full-time 18 tiny 19 lose touch

c 20 flight 21 government 22 unfortunately 23 disappointing 24 violinist(s) 25 choice

PRONUNCIATION

a 1 aggressive 2 weight 3 hour 4 coach 5 although

b 6 discipline 7 unemployed 8 complain 9 independent 10 strawberries

READING

1 F 2 T 3 F 4 DS 5 T 6 F 7 F 8 T 9 DS 10 T

LISTENING

a 1 c 2 b 3 b 4 c 5 a

b 6 F 7 T 8 T 9 F 10 F

Listening A CD3 Track 44

1

A Hello, welcome to London. I'm Jack Lawson, Managing Director, and this is my personal assistant Ellen.
B Hello.
C Pleased to meet you. Martin James.
A Did you have a good flight from Switzerland?
C Yes, fine, thank you. But actually, I flew in from Pisa – we have an office there as well as in Geneva.
A You must be very busy this week.
C Yes, I'm taking the overnight flight to Tokyo for a conference and then I'm going on to Hong Kong for a few days.

2

A We were thinking of going out to dinner tonight. Would you like to come?
B Sorry, I can't, I'm broke. I lent my brother some money yesterday and he can't pay me back until he gets paid next week.
A Oh well. How about the end of next week then?
B Yes, that would be great!

3

A Good morning, Sunny Bay Holiday Homes. How can I help you?
B Yes, hello. I'm interested in renting a holiday home for two weeks in September.
A That should be fine. Could you tell me exactly what you're looking for?
B We'd like a four-bedroom house within walking distance of the beach. Oh, and a sea view would be nice!
A OK, we do have a house available, just five minutes from the beach, but unfortunately it only has two doubles and a twin.
B Actually, that would be fine. My brothers won't mind sharing the twin room.

4

A Angela, do you think you could do a bit of overtime this week?
B When?
A Well, Sally is off this week – and Mark has just phoned to say he's not well, so he's not going to be in either. I know you don't usually work on Thursday afternoons, but we're going to be very short staffed, so I wondered if…
B Well, I suppose I could. But if I come in on Thursday, could I have next Friday afternoon off? Instead of the extra money?
A Yes, I think we can probably arrange that. Thanks, Angela.

5

A Have you seen this?
B No, what?
A Michael Foster, that guy you used to work with, he's been arrested! He was caught stealing from the company he was working for!
B You're joking!
A No, I'm not. Read it yourself.
B Wow! It's him. Amazing! He was lazy and he never used to do much work, but I can't believe he would be dishonest.
A Oh I can. It doesn't surprise me at all. He just wanted to have a good time, you know, expensive restaurants and cars and things like that, and he couldn't do that on the salary he was getting.

Listening B CD3 Track 45

J = Journalist, I = Ian

J So Ian, could you tell us a bit about yourself?
I Well, I'm originally from Scotland, but I moved to New Zealand three and a half years ago. Now I own a backpacker's hostel in the North Island.
J Why did you decide to go abroad?
I After graduating from university, I had planned to get a temporary job to save money for travelling. I worked in website design, it was very well paid and I guess I just got comfortable. After a few years, I suddenly thought, why should I spend all day every day looking at a computer screen? I resigned the next day, rented out my flat and bought a round-the-world plane ticket.
J What made you decide to stay in New Zealand?
I I'd travelled in South America, Africa, India, South East Asia, and Australia. They were all fantastic! But when I got to New Zealand, it just felt like home. I loved the outdoor lifestyle. The sunshine, the beaches. It's safe to swim in the sea – no sharks or anything. I go surfing every day.
J When did you have your business idea?
I It was getting near to the end of my year off. I couldn't believe I'd have to go back to my office job in the UK. Then a friend of mine here called Lucas suggested we try to set up a hostel. Now we're business partners – the dream became a reality!
J Could you describe the hostel?
I Sure. We found a great location near the beach, bought the land, then built the hostel. We were both backpackers so when we designed it we thought carefully about what we need when we travel. The hostel has great facilities, a big kitchen, games room and plenty of outdoor spaces for relaxing. We rent out sports equipment and we have a local wildlife expert who does guided walks. The guests love it. The only problem is that most of them feel so at home here they don't want to leave! The hostel is for travellers so we have to limit anyone's stay to fourteen days.
J Do you have any regrets about moving to New Zealand?
I None at all. It is difficult sometimes with my family being so far away, but my parents are going to live here when they retire, and my brother visits every year. I don't earn as much money as I did, but I don't need it. I feel alive and happy. I'm not watching the office clock, waiting for the weekend!

GRAMMAR

a Circle a, b, or c.

Example: My parents _____ in China.
a are born (b) were born c was born

1 I _____ dinner when the phone rang.
a cooking b was cooking c cooked

2 When I arrived at Paul's house, he _____ already eaten.
a has b was c had

3 Today most people _____ on junk food.
a cut down b are cutting down c is cutting down

4 It's hot in here! _____ open the window?
a Will I b Shall I c Do I

5 He _____ swimming on Tuesdays.
a always goes b is always going c goes always

6 **A** Is there anything on TV tonight?
B I don't know. _____ in the paper.
a I'll look b I'm going to look c I look

7 I turned off the TV and then I _____ to bed.
a went b had gone c was going

8 My brother _____ a job at the moment.
a isn't having b don't have c doesn't have

9 The referee stopped the match because someone _____ a bottle on the pitch.
a had thrown b was throwing b had threw

10 We _____ the cinema on Saturday. Would you like to come?
a will go to b go to c are going to

b Complete the sentences with **one** word. Contractions (e.g. *don't*) count as one word.

Example: She's waiting *for* the bus.

11 What ________ you doing when I phoned you this morning?
12 **A** ________ we order some salad?
B Good idea.
13 She ________ eat meat or fish. She's a strict vegetarian.
14 James ________ arrive on time. He's always late.
15 Where ________ you going on holiday this year?
16 **A** I'm going to be late!
B Don't worry. I ________ give you a lift to the station.
17 It's ________ to be a fantastic party.
18 I predict that you ________ marry someone rich and famous!
19 My parents ________ have much money when they were first married.
20 When we got to the hall, the concert ________ already started.

[ ] 20

VOCABULARY

a Complete the food words.

Example: We had sausages and **b***eans* for dinner last night.
1 This curry is really **sp**________. It has lots of chillies in it.
2 Use that sharp **k**________ to cut the bread.
3 Could you pass me the salt and **p**________, please?
4 I love seafood, especially **pr**________.
5 Food that isn't cooked is **r**________.
6 What are you having for your main **c**________?
7 I don't want to cook tonight. Let's get a **ta**________ from the Chinese restaurant.

b Write the word for the definition.

Example: a person who makes sure players obey the rules *referee*
8 the people who watch a sport in a stadium ________
9 a person who trains a team ________
10 athletes run on this ________
11 the people who support a particular team ________
12 you ski down this ________
13 players do this just before a match ________
14 kick or throw a ball into the net ________ (a goal, a basket, etc.)

c Write the opposite adjectives.

Example: generous *mean*
15 talkative ________
16 self-confident ________
17 honest ________
18 stupid ________
19 hard-working ________
20 patient ________

[ ] 20

PRONUNCIATION

a Underline the word with a different sound.

Example: /æ/ van tram <u>lane</u> rank
1 /uː/ sp**oo**n m**oo**dy c**oo**k f**oo**d
2 /aɪ/ fr**i**ed gr**i**lled sp**i**cy w**i**ne
3 /əʊ/ c**oa**ch sp**oi**lt fr**o**zen sl**o**pe
4 /h/ **h**onest **h**amburger **h**ome-made **h**ard-working
5 /ʃ/ ambi**ti**ous so**ci**able fre**sh** **ch**arming

b Under<u>line</u> the stressed syllable.

Example: ex<u>ci</u>ting
6 dessert
7 jealous
8 unselfish
9 spectator
10 grandmother

[ ] 10

Total [ ] 50

GRAMMAR

a Circle a, b, or c.

Example: My parents _____ in China.
a are born (b) were born c was born

1 She _____ had a bank account for five years now.
a had b has c have

2 His latest film isn't _____ the last one I saw.
a as good than b better c as good as

3 **A** How long _____ for me?
B For half an hour!
a are you waiting b do you wait
c have you been waiting

4 I've been playing football _____ I was six years old.
a when b since c for

5 **A** When _____ on holiday to Thailand?
B Two years ago.
a did you go b have you gone c you went

6 Let's eat in this restaurant. It's _____ than the other one.
a less expensive b more cheaper c as expensive

7 **A** Can I speak to Peter, please?
B Sorry, he _____ out.
a has just been b just has been c has just gone

8 You look tired. What _____?
a you have been doing b have you doing
c have you been doing

9 Have you _____? There's blue paint in your hair!
a been painting b painting c painted

10 He was ____ teacher I've ever had.
a the worse b worst c the worst

b Complete the sentences with **one** word. Contractions (e.g. *don't)* count as one word.

Example: She's waiting *for* the bus.

11 He ________ saved enough money yet. He needs another 500 euros.
12 The journey didn't take as long ________ we thought.
13 How long have they ________ going out together?
14 Have you ________ been to South America?
15 We've been living in this house ________ four years now.
16 I haven't finished my exams ________. I've got two more next week.
17 How much money ________ you earn last month?
18 I love Venice. It's the ________ beautiful city I've been to.
19 I haven't seen you ________ last summer. How are you?
20 A Would you like a cup of coffee?
B No, thanks. I've ________ had one.

☐ 20

VOCABULARY

a Write synonyms for the adjectives.

Example: very small *tiny*
1 very dirty ________
2 very angry ________
3 very tasty ________
4 very hungry ________
5 very big ________

b Complete the money words.

Example: Could I **b***orrow* £10 until tomorrow, please?
6 I bought this book yesterday. It **c**________ £20.
7 This ring isn't **w**________ a lot of money, but I love it!
8 Here's the money you **l**________ me last week – thank you.
9 My parents have just finished paying the **mo**________ on their house.
10 Is there a cash machine near here? I need to **t**________ **o**________ some money.

c Write the missing prepositions.

Example: The train went *through* the tunnel.
11 I'll pay ________ this by credit card.
12 My brother borrowed £10 ________ me last month.
13 I paid for dinner ________ cash.
14 The hotel charged me £25 ________ a two-minute phone call.
15 Chris still hasn't paid me ________ the money I lent him!

d Complete the compound nouns.

Example: Please go to the **check-in** *desk*.
16 Slow down! The ________ **limit** here is 40 kph.
17 We arrived late because there was a terrible **traffic** ________.
18 I had to pay a £50 **parking** ________!
19 I never use **public** ________. I always go by car.
20 Before we got on the plane we had to show our ________ **cards**.

☐ 20

PRONUNCIATION

a Underline the word with a different sound.

Example: /æ/ van tram <u>lane</u> rank
1 /əʊ/ **loan** cost **owe** **coach**
2 /eɪ/ save waste pay travel
3 /dʒ/ **charge** **jam** **gate** carria**ge**
4 /aɪ/ paid **aisle** tiny **flight**
5 /ɜː/ **worth** lorry **works** **earn**

b Underline the stressed syllable.

Example: <u>sal</u>ary
6 motorway
7 underground
8 afford
9 exhausted
10 inherit

☐ 10

Total ☐ 50

GRAMMAR

a Circle a, b, or c.

Example: My parents _____ in China.
a are born (b) were born c was born

1 Why _____ work last weekend?
a must you b did you have to c had you to

2 Hurry up! We _____ be late.
a should b mustn't c don't have to

3 I have a problem. What _____ do?
a should I to b I should c should I

4 My sister _____ play the violin very well when she was young.
a can b could c is able to

5 Will you _____ pick me up at the airport tonight?
a be able to b can c be able

6 I've never _____ to dance *salsa* very well.
a could b be able c been able

7 You _____ pay to go in museums in Britain. They're free.
a shouldn't b don't have to c mustn't

8 She _____ be out. She said she would be at home all evening.
a can't b might not c mustn't

9 **A** What kind of food is this?
B I'm not sure. It _____ be Thai or perhaps Indonesian.
a might b must c can

10 I haven't got the keys so you _____ them. I know we brought them.
a might have b must have c can't have

b Complete the sentences with **one** word. Contractions (e.g. *don't*) count as one word.

Example: She's waiting *for* the bus.
11 What time ________ we have to leave?
12 I ________ able to read when I was four.
13 Hello, you must ________ Sarah, the new receptionist.
14 I couldn't find a taxi so I ________ to walk.
15 I hate not ________ able to say what I want in English.
16 You ________ touch that! It's dangerous.
17 We're not allowed ________ eat in the office.
18 I've never ________ able to ice-skate well, but I keep practising.
19 You ________ have to eat it if you don't like it.
20 They ________ be French. They're speaking German.

20

VOCABULARY

a Complete the describing words.

Example: He's got short c*urly* hair.
1 He's tall and **well b**________.
2 I must cut my **f**________. It's getting in my eyes!
3 She's got brown **sh**________**-length** hair.
4 I look so **u**________ in this photo! I'm going to throw it away.
5 She was a bit **ov**________ so the doctor told her to take more exercise.
6 He doesn't have any hair. He's completely **b**________.
7 She's very **at**________. She won a beauty contest last year.
8 He's quite old now. I think he's in his **m**________ **-seventies**.

b Complete with phone words.

9 He didn't answer the phone so I ________ up.
10 Do you like my new ________ tone? It's from my favourite song.
11 Can you _____ the number for me? I can't find my glasses.
12 Can I ________ you back in ten minutes? I'm in a meeting.
13 Please ________ a message after the beep.
14 The line's been ________ for ages. He must be talking to his mother!

c Complete the adjectives with *-ing* or *-ed*.

Example: This book is very **bor***ing*.
15 Are you **interest**____ in modern art?
16 What's the most **frighten**____ film you've seen?
17 I feel **frustrat**____ if I can't do something.
18 It's so **embarrass**____ when you fall over in public!
19 That was a **disappoint**____ film. I didn't like it at all.
20 When was the last time you felt **bor**____?

20

PRONUNCIATION

a Underline the word with a different sound.

Example: /ə/ attractive about <u>ages</u> afraid
1 /ɜː/ curly her early beard
2 /eɪ/ bald engaged wavy grey
3 /ɪ/ pretty built dial fringe
4 /eɪ/ eight straight weight height
5 /əʊ/ tone shoulder brown mobile

b Underline the stressed syllable.

Example: over<u>weight</u>
6 attractive
7 moustache
8 interesting
9 frustrating
10 depressed

10

Total 50

GRAMMAR

a Circle a, b, or c.

Example: My parents _____ in China.
a are born (b) were born c was born

1 You _____ feel better if you took more exercise.
a will b could c would

2 Could you phone Alan before you _____ to lunch?
a will go b go c went

3 If we _____ a lot of money, we'd buy a house in France.
a had b have c has

4 I _____ play squash on Saturdays, but this weekend I'm going away.
a use to b used to c usually

5 _____ it's really cold, we'll have lunch outside tomorrow.
a When b If c Unless

6 I won't speak to her unless she _____.
a apologize b will apologize c apologizes

7 They're staying in a rented flat _____ they find a house to buy.
a before b until c when

8 If I _____ you, I would look for a better-paid job.
a was b were c would be

9 When we were children, we _____ spend all our money on sweets.
a used to b usually c use to

10 If we don't get to the concert early, we _____ get good seats.
a don't b wouldn't c won't

b Complete the sentences with **one** word. Contractions (e.g. *don't*) count as one word.

Example: She's waiting *for* the bus.

11 I ________ use to like spinach when I was a child but now I love it.
12 If the bus ________ come soon, we're going to be late.
13 What will we do ________ we can't find their house?
14 We'll have dinner as soon ________ we get home.
15 He'll be really pleased if he ________ the exam.
16 What ________ you do if you won the lottery?
17 The test ________ start until everybody is quiet.
18 I used ________ get nervous when I took exams at school.
19 Where did you ________ to live when you were a student?
20 I wouldn't say it if I ________ think it was true.

20

VOCABULARY

a Complete the education words.

Example: I did a degree at **un***iversity*.

1 We're reading Shakespeare in English **li**________ this term.
2 I **re**________ a lot before exams so I can get good marks.
3 Was **di**________ very strict at your school?
4 I'm a university **g**________. I have a degree in international law.
5 I wouldn't like to go to a **b**________ school. I like living at home.
6 There are 30 **p**________ in my class at school.
7 Did you always **b**________ well in school, or were you sometimes bad?
8 I'm completely honest. I never **ch**________ in exams.

b Complete with a word related to friendship.

Example: I have a close *friend* called Anna.

9 We ________ for the first time when we were at university together.
10 We ________ on very well right from the beginning.
11 Perhaps that's because we have a lot in ________.
12 We never ________ – we always agree about everything.
13 Although Anna moved to the USA, we still keep in ________.

c Write the house words.

Example: the room where you cook *kitchen*

14 a building with a lot of flats ________
15 smoke comes out of this ________
16 the area outside the central part of a town or city ________
17 where you wash plates and glasses by hand ________
18 a house that is not attached to another house ________
19 you walk up these to get to the front door of a house ________
20 a small road, e.g. from the gate to the door of a house ________

20

PRONUNCIATION

a Underline the word with a different sound.

Example: /eɪ/ take fail behave graduate

1 /s/ promise practise used to lose
2 /ʌ/ result pupil country study
3 /ɑː/ pass armchair garden area
4 /ɜː/ boarding term learn nursery
5 /aɪ/ primary private village revise

b Underline the stressed syllable.

Example: terrace

6 behave
7 cottage
8 residential
9 professor
10 argue

10

Total 50

GRAMMAR

a Circle a, b, or c.

Example: My parents _____ in China.
a are born (b) were born c was born

1 We must work quickly. We don't have _____ time left.
a much b many c a lot

2 I'd like to go to _____ university after I finish secondary school.
a the b a c –

3 It's very hot. Would you mind _____ the window?
a I open b opening c to open

4 _____ is banned in all pubs in Ireland.
a To smoke b Smoking c Smoke

5 The teacher told me to close _____ door and sit down.
a the b – c a

6 She's really good at _____ names.
a remember b to remember c remembering

7 There were _____ people in the supermarket so we didn't go in.
a too much b too many c too

8 That's _____ fantastic dress. Where did you get it?
a the b – c a

9 We don't have _____ to take a taxi. We'll have to walk.
a enough money b money enough c plenty of money

10 ___ children usually like sweets.
a the b a c –

b Complete the sentences with **one** word. Contractions (e.g. *don't*) count as one word.

Example: She's waiting *for* the bus.

11 There are only a ________ parks in this city – two or three.
12 There are three trains ________ hour.
13 Have a good holiday, and don't forget to ________ lots of photos!
14 You spend too ________ time playing those computer games!
15 Doesn't your cousin work as ________ architect?
16 He has a ________ of friends. He's very sociable.
17 I'm not old ________ to vote. I'm only 16.
18 I hate ________ up early in the morning.
19 My parents don't let me ________ out in the evening during the week.
20 I bought a paper ________ find out what's on at the cinema.

[ ] 20

VOCABULARY

a Write the nouns.

Example: attract *attraction*

1 similar ________
2 govern ________
3 possible ________
4 react ________
5 survive ________
6 organize ________
7 happy ________
8 relax ________

b Complete the work words.

Example: You need good **qu***alifications* to get that job.

9 It's a **p**_____**-time** job. I only work three hours a day.
10 My current job is temporary. I'm looking for a **per**________ job.
11 I'm doing a **tr**________ **c**________ to get a management qualification.
12 In the UK most men **r**________ when they are 65.
13 This job in the newspaper looks great. I'm going to **a**________ for it.
14 Jack was unhappy in his job so he **r**________ and found another one.

c Write the missing prepositions.

Example: The train went *through* the tunnel.

15 I'm responsible ________ the advertising department.
16 I'm sorry, I just don't agree ________ you.
17 She's really good ________ maths.
18 I'm afraid ________ flying.
19 Let me pay ________ dinner.
20 Are you worried ________ the interview tomorrow?

[ ] 20

PRONUNCIATION

a Underline the word with a different sound.

Example: /æ/ van tram lane rank

1 /ð/ **th**e wi**th** **th**anks **th**ere
2 /ɔː/ **laugh** b**ough**t c**augh**t th**ough**t
3 /ʌ/ t**ou**gh en**ou**gh f**u**ll m**u**ch
4 /uː/ f**ew** t**oo** thr**ough** alth**ough**
5 /juː/ **u**niversity **u**ntil **u**niform **u**se

b Underline the stressed syllable.

Example: permanent

6 experience
7 qualifications
8 contract (noun)
9 temporary
10 resign

[ ] 10

Total [ ] 50

GRAMMAR

a Circle a, b, or c.

Example: My parents _____ in China.
a are born (b) were born c was born

1 'I've been to a wedding.'
Joe said he _____ to a wedding.
a went b has been c had been

2 My son, _____ lives in Brazil, is a lawyer.
a who b which c whose

3 'When were you born?'
She asked him when _____.
a was he born b you were born c he was born

4 The film _____ in Japan.
a was setted b set c is set

5 That's the button _____ switches off the TV.
a that b who c what

6 'Do you like playing basketball?'
He asked me _____ playing basketball.
a that I like b if I liked c if you liked

7 This cheese has to _____ today.
a be ate b be eated c be eaten

8 The painting, _____ is one of Van Gogh's most famous, was sold for millions of dollars.
a which b who c that

9 The teacher told me _____ talking.
a that I stop b that I stopped c to stop

10 The museum is _____ at the moment so it's closed.
a been painted b being painted c being painting

b Complete the sentences with **one** word.

Example: She's waiting *for* the bus.

11 That's the girl ________ mobile was stolen.
12 She ________ me that she was French.
13 This is the area ________ I grew up.
14 The film will ________ made in Britain.
15 The policeman told me ________ to drive so fast.
16 The best selling book was written ________ an ex-footballer.
17 The film, ________ was directed by George Clooney, was nominated for several Oscars.
18 I met Mrs Evans, ________ used to teach physics at my old school.
19 I asked my sister________ she could lend me a dress for the party.
20 I'm sorry but all the tickets have ________ sold.

[ ] 20

VOCABULARY

a Write words for the definitions.

Example: when you can buy things more cheaply *sales*

1 a shop where you can buy bread ____________
2 where a shop assistant puts the money you give him / her ____________
3 a person who buys things in a shop ____________
4 all the actors in a film ____________
5 the story of a film or book ____________
6 a person who takes photographs ____________
7 a person who plays the guitar ____________

b Complete the compound words.

Example: shop **a**<u>*ssistant*</u>.

8 **s**________ effects
9 science **f**________
10 department **s**________
11 shop **w**________
12 travel **a**________
13 **s**________ centre / mall

c Complete with a verb in the right form.

Example: The film was *directed* by Scorsese.

14 I ____________to the manager because I wasn't happy with my hotel room.
15 Could I ____________ on these jeans, please?
16 We had to ____________ outside for two hours to buy tickets for the concert.
17 The *Lord of the Rings* films are ____________ on the books by J.R.R. Tolkien.
18 *The Beach* was ____________ on location in Thailand.
19 A newsagent's is a shop which ____________ newspapers and magazines.
20 The film was so popular that it was ____________ into seven languages.

[ ] 20

PRONUNCIATION

a <u>Underline</u> the word with a different sound.

Example: /eɪ/ <u>action</u> sales baker's complain

1 /ɑː/ star bargain market careful
2 /s/ receipt script centre audience
3 /aɪ/ buy pay try science
4 /iː/ special sequel refund scene
5 /dʒ/ manager newsagent's bargain change

b Under<u>line</u> the stressed syllable.

Example: di<u>rec</u>tor

6 inventor
7 politician
8 discount (noun)
9 sequel
10 refund (noun)

[ ] 10

Total [ ] 50

GRAMMAR

a Circle a, b, or c.

Example: My parents _____ in China.
a are born (b) were born c was born

1 We would have got here earlier if we _____ got lost.
a didn't b had c hadn't

2 Do you know _____ spicy food?
a if Anna likes b if Anna does like c if likes Anna

3 We had a fantastic time, _____?
a don't we b didn't we c did we

4 If my husband had taken that job, we _____ moved to London.
a would have b had c would

5 I'm _____. Have you seen him?
a look for Adrian b looking Adrian for
c looking for Adrian

6 They've been here before, _____?
a weren't they b haven't they c have they

7 Could you tell me what time _____?
a starts the match b does the match start
c the match starts

8 She wouldn't have eaten the cake if she _____ it had nuts in it.
a 'd known b 'd knew c 've known

9 This jumper doesn't suit me. I'm going to _____.
a take off it b take off c take it off

10 Mary's very difficult. I don't _____ very well.
a get with her on b get on with her
c get her with on

b Complete the sentences with one word. Contractions (e.g. *don't*) count as one word.

Example: She's waiting *for* the bus.

11 You ________ enjoy the film, did you?
12 If I ________ known your number, I would have called you.
13 Put your coat ________ and we'll go for a walk.
14 She likes Jamie, ________ she?
15 If I hadn't missed that train, we ________ never have met!
16 Could you tell me where the bank ________, please?
17 I would have gone to the party if I ________ been ill.
18 You aren't interested in politics, ________ you?
19 Could you ask the waiter ________ the bill?
20 Our plane took ________ late due to bad weather conditions.

[ ] 20

VOCABULARY

a Write the positive [+] or negative [–] adjectives or adverbs.

Example: luck [–] adverb = *unluckily*

1 patience [+] adverb = ________
2 care [–] adverb = ________
3 fortune [–] adjective = ________
4 luck [+] adverb = ________
5 comfort [+] adjective = ________

b Write the compound nouns.

Example: a person who writes novels about criminals
crime writer

6 a place where criminals are taken after they have been arrested ____________ ____________
7 a big shop where you can buy all sorts of things ____________ ____________
8 you feel frightened when you watch this in the cinema ____________ ____________
9 a part of the road where you can ride a bike ____________ ____________
10 a place where you can swim, not the sea ____________ ____________

c Complete the TV words.

Example: I'm watching a fascinating **doc***umentary* about Japanese wildlife.

11 **A** Do you have cable TV?
B No, we have **sa**________ TV.
12 I think **ad**________ for fast food should be banned from children's TV.
13 There's a great **drama s**________ on Channel 6 on Monday nights.
14 I hate **re**________ TV shows. Watching other people doing stupid things is so boring.
15 I enjoy watching music **ch**________ like MTV.

d Complete the phrasal verbs.

16 We'd like to ________ up our own company in the future.
17 I'm really looking ________ to my holiday next month.
18 I'm trying to give ________ eating chocolate. I need to lose weight.
19 Slow ________! You're breaking the speed limit.
20 He was a millionaire but he gave ________ all his money to poor people.

[ ] 20

PRONUNCIATION

a Underline the word with a different sound.

Example: /æ/ van tram lane rank

1 /tʃ/ channel chemist's check chat
2 /ɑː/ drama pass calm warm
3 /ɪ/ find quiz film switch
4 /ʃ/ show patient fortune station
5 /ə/ away after about around

b Underline the stressed syllable.

Example: exciting

6 mystery
7 advert
8 comedy
9 unfortunately
10 machine

[ ] 10

Total [ ] 50

GRAMMAR

a Circle a, b, or c.

Example: My parents _____ in China.
a are born (b) were born c was born

1 **A** Hi, are you free to talk now?
B We _____ dinner. Can I call you back?
a have b having c 're having

2 When they arrived, their friends _____ for them.
a were waiting b was waiting c waited

3 **A** Please remember to send her a card!
B Don't worry. _____.
a I'm not forgetting b I don't forget c I won't forget

4 How long have you _____ karate?
a been do b doing c been doing

5 I think basketball is _____ sport to watch.
a the most exciting b the more exciting
c the excitingest

6 We _____ forget to close all the windows.
a have to b mustn't c don't have to

7 I don't think we _____ to come to the party.
a 'll can b 'll be able c can

8 Let's stay under this tree _____ raining.
a as soon as it stops b until it will stop c until it stops

9 I _____ married if I were you.
a wouldn't get b wouldn't c didn't get

10 This place _____ a cafe – I think it was a baker's.
a didn't use to be b didn't used to be
c didn't used be

11 _____ are often not very good at buying presents.
a The men b A man c Men

12 Has it stopped _____ yet?
a rain b to rain c raining

13 She told the children _____ a noise.
a not to make b that they don't make c to not make

14 The new hospital _____ the Prime Minister next month.
a will open by b will be open by c will be opened by

15 Could you tell me _____, please?
a where is the bank b where the bank is
c where the bank

b Complete the sentences with **one** word. Contractions (e.g. *don't*) count as one word.

Example: She's waiting *for* the bus.

16 I've been living in Lebanon ________ about two years.
17 His garden isn't nearly as big ________ ours.
18 He _____ be very rich. He drives a Rolls Royce.
19 There isn't ________ soup for all of us.
20 There are too ________ people in this class.
21 I can't go to university ________ I pass all my exams.
22 She asked the boy how old he ________.
23 My mother, ________ is 93, can still read without glasses!
24 If I ________ known you were coming for lunch, I would have bought more food.
25 That was a fascinating documentary, ________ it?

☐ 25

VOCABULARY

a Complete the words.

Example: The spectators ran on to the **p***itch*.

1 I'm in **ch**_______ of the marketing department.
2 He's very **s**________. He only thinks of himself.
3 The match ended when the **r**________ blew his whistle.
4 There's a lot of traffic during the **r**________ **h**________.
5 I don't have much **l**________, just one suitcase.
6 My favourite **s**________ at school was maths.
7 He lives in a small **v**________ with only 1,000 inhabitants.
8 When you buy something the shop assistant should give you a **r**________.
9 The film was **s**________ in Italy in the 19th century.
10 My sister wants to **b**________ up with her boyfriend.

b Write the opposite word or phrase.

Example: **win** a match *lose a match*

11 **take off** (from an airport) ________ (at an airport)
12 **buy** a car ________
13 **borrow** money ________
14 **honest** ________
15 **curly** hair ________
16 **pass** an exam ________
17 a **part-time** job ________-________
18 an **enormous** flat ________
19 **keep in touch** with a friend ________ ________

c Complete with one word formed from the **bold** word.

Example: **qualify** What *qualifications* do you need?

20 **fly** The _____________ to Australia lasted 24 hours.
21 **govern** I think the _____________ will change after the election.
22 **fortune** She found the perfect dress, but _____________ it wasn't her size.
23 **disappoint** The film was really _____________. The actors were terrible.
24 **violin** The musicians were fantastic, especially the _____________.
25 **choose** We have to make a very difficult ___________.

☐ 25

PRONUNCIATION

a Underline the word with a different sound.

Example: /æ/ van tram <u>lane</u> rank

1 /dʒ/ exchange generous aggressive jewellery
2 /aɪ/ might buy weight height
3 /ɜː/ learn hour turn journey
4 /ʃ/ ambitious machine sociable coach
5 /ɔː/ although court bought draw

b Underline the stressed syllable.

Example: ex<u>ci</u>ting

6 discipline
7 unemployed
8 complain
9 independent
10 strawberries

☐ 10

READING

Read the newspaper article and circle the right answer, T (True), F (False), or DS (Doesn't say).

Save the planet and get stuff for free!

Freecycle.org was started in 2003 in the USA by 36-year-old Deron Beal. When Beal wanted to give away office supplies he no longer needed, he found that his local charity shop would not take them. He didn't want to just throw away useful items, so he decided to start 'The Freecycle Network' where environmentally-minded groups of people could advertise their unwanted goods online for free.

The idea proved so popular that Freecycle groups are now operating in over fifty countries. It is estimated that this worldwide movement is now responsible for preventing more than 200 tonnes of goods from being thrown away each day.

One of the reasons for the network's popularity is that it is extremely simple to use. Members sign up to an email list on the Freecycle.org website. They then receive lists of items that people in their area would like to give away. Unlike many other online advertising sites, the items are always free. If you find something you want, you simply contact the advertiser. You are then responsible for arranging to pick the item up.

The majority of members sign up because they agree with the environmentally friendly ethics of the network. However, there are some people who do it to make money by selling the items later. The website's voluntary workers say that they don't mind this. The important thing is that the amount of waste being dumped in landfill sites is reduced.

Freecycle is becoming increasingly popular in the UK where there are currently more than 200 groups giving away, on average, around 45,000 items each month. Some local councils now promote Freecycle by handing out leaflets, in the hope that residents put less waste in the bins provided. Others are even considering setting up a similar community advertising programme through their websites.

1	Deron Beal wanted a change of career.	T	F	DS
2	The idea of the website is to help people recycle.	T	F	DS
3	You have to pay to use the Freecycle website.	T	F	DS
4	The biggest Freecycle group is in the USA.	T	F	DS
5	Freecycle has reduced the amount of waste produced.	T	F	DS
6	When you order something from Freecycle, you must exchange an item with the advertiser.	T	F	DS
7	Items which are ordered on the website are sent directly to their new owner.	T	F	DS
8	Not everyone uses the Freecycle site in order to protect the environment.	T	F	DS
9	Residents in the UK separate their rubbish into different coloured bins for recycling.	T	F	DS
10	Some councils in Britain are thinking about starting their own 'Freecycle' networks.	T	F	DS

10

LISTENING

a Listen and circle a, b, or c.

1 Where did Martin fly from?
a Geneva b Tokyo c Pisa

2 Why can't the man afford to go out to dinner?
a He hasn't been paid yet.
b Someone owes him some money.
c He doesn't earn very much.

3 How many bedrooms does the holiday home have?
a Two. b Three. c Four.

4 Why does Angela agree to work extra hours?
a Because one of her colleagues isn't at work.
b Because she needs some extra money.
c Because she will be able to have another afternoon off.

5 Who thinks that Michael is guilty?
a the man b the woman c both of them

b Listen to Ian Robinson talking about why he moved to New Zealand and circle the right answer, T (true) or F (false).

6 Ian's job was badly paid.
T F

7 He stayed in New Zealand because he liked the way of life.
T F

8 Ian's friend had the idea of setting up a hostel.
T F

9 You can stay at the hotel as long as you want.
T F

10 Ian's parents are retired.
T F

10

WRITING

You were on the plane in the article. Write an email to a friend describing the experience.

A flight to nowhere

Passengers on a flight from London to New York spent a long time going nowhere on Monday. Three hours into the flight the plane developed a problem in one of its engines, and the pilot decided to turn round and return to Heathrow, where the flight landed seven hours after taking off. Passengers spent the night in airport hotels before leaving again yesterday morning – this time they reached their destination.

10

SPEAKING 10

Total 100